Lecture Notes
in Business Information Processing   209

Series Editors

Wil van der Aalst
  Eindhoven Technical University, Eindhoven, The Netherlands
John Mylopoulos
  University of Trento, Povo, Italy
Michael Rosemann
  Queensland University of Technology, Brisbane, QLD, Australia
Michael J. Shaw
  University of Illinois, Urbana-Champaign, IL, USA
Clemens Szyperski
  Microsoft Research, Redmond, WA, USA

T0127656

More information about this series at http://www.springer.com/series/7911

Morad Benyoucef · Michael Weiss
Hafedh Mili (Eds.)

E-Technologies

6th International Conference, MCETECH 2015
Montréal, QC, Canada, May 12–15, 2015
Proceedings

 Springer

Editors
Morad Benyoucef
University of Ottawa
Ottawa, Ontario
Canada

Hafedh Mili
Université du Québec à Montréal
Montreal, Québec
Canada

Michael Weiss
Carleton University
Ottawa, Ontario
Canada

ISSN 1865-1348   ISSN 1865-1356   (electronic)
Lecture Notes in Business Information Processing
ISBN 978-3-319-17956-8   ISBN 978-3-319-17957-5   (eBook)
DOI 10.1007/978-3-319-17957-5

Library of Congress Control Number: 2015936470

Springer Cham Heidelberg New York Dordrecht London

Printed on acid-free paper

Springer International Publishing AG Switzerland is part of Springer Science+Business Media
(www.springer.com)

Preface

The Internet pervades many of the activities of modern society and has become the preferred medium for the delivery of information and services. The successful implementation of Internet applications, ranging from online commercial transactions to online education is a multifaceted problem, involving technological, managerial, economic, cognitive, social, ethical, and legal issues.

The sixth edition of the International MCETECH Conference on e-Technologies was held in Montréal, Canada, during May 12–15, 2015. This year's conference featured special tracks on social computing, trust, and the legal issues surrounding the emergence and exploitation of user profiling and big data.

We received a total of 42 submissions on topics ranging from applications of eBusiness, eHealth, eEducation, and eGovernment to methodologies, models, and architectures to their business, social, and legal implications. Of these, 14 papers were accepted directly with minor revisions. Six papers were accepted as conditional papers. The authors of conditional papers were asked to revise their papers and resubmit them for another round of reviews. This resulted in four additional papers accepted for presentation at the conference. The final program contained 18 papers.

We would like to thank all the authors who submitted papers, the members of the Program Committee, and the external reviewers. We are grateful to the Steering Committee for the help we received in preparing the conference. We also thank the local organizers who were key in making this year's MCETECH conference another successful event. In particular, our thanks go to Anis Boubaker for the local arrangements.

May 2015

Morad Benyoucef
Michael Weiss
Hafedh Mili

Organization

The 6th International MCETECH Conference on e-Technologies (MCETECH 2015) received support from the following sponsors: Expedia Canada, Université du Québec à Montréal (UQÀM), and the Research Laboratory on e-Commerce Technologies (LATECE).

Conference Chair

Hafedh Mili   Université du Québec à Montréal, Canada

Steering Committee Chair

Hafedh Mili   Université du Québec à Montréal, Canada

Program Committee Co-chairs

Morad Benyoucef   University of Ottawa, Canada
Michael Weiss   Carleton University, Canada

Program Committee

Silvia Abrahão   Universitat Politècnica de València, Spain
Esma Aimeur   Université de Montréal, Canada
Daniel Amyot   University of Ottawa, Canada
Gilbert Babin   HEC Montréal, Canada
Tony Bailetti   Carleton University, Canada
Ygal Bendavid   Université du Québec à Montréal, Canada
Morad Benyoucef   University of Ottawa, Canada
Jean Bezivin   Université de Nantes, France
Ilia Bider   Stockholm University, Sweden
Andrea Burattin   University of Padua, Italy
Yasmine Charif   Xerox, USA
Vincent Gautrais   Université de Montréal, Canada
Patrizia Grifoni   National Research Council - IRPPS, Italy
Peter Kropf   Université de Neuchâtel, Switzerland
Lamia Labed   Tunis University, Tunisia
Luigi Logrippo   Université du Québec en Outaouais, Canada

Yannis Manolopoulos	Aristotle University of Thessaloniki, Greece
John D. McGregor	Clemson University, USA
Hamid Mcheick	Université du Québec à Chicoutimi, Canada
Jan Mendling	Vienna University of Economics and Business, Austria
Hafedh Mili	Université du Québec à Montréal, Canada
Naouel Moha	Université du Québec à Montréal, Canada
Adrian Mos	Xerox, France
Gunter Mussbacher	McGill University, Canada
Oscar Pastor	Universitat Politècnica de València, Spain
Monalessa Perini Barcellos	Federal University of Espírito Santo (UFES), Brazil
Liam Peyton	University of Ottawa, Canada
Andrés Quiroz	Xerox, USA
Stefanie Rinderle-Ma	University of Vienna, Austria
Missaoui Rokia	Université du Québec en Outaouais, Canada
Colette Rolland	Pantheon-Sorbonne (Paris 1) University, France
Salah Sadou	Université de Bretagne-Sud, France
Carlo Simon	Provadis Hochschule, Germany
Pnina Soffer	University of Haifa, Israel
Stoyan Tanev	University of Southern Denmark, Denmark
Thomas Tran	University of Ottawa, Canada
Ofir Turel	California State University, USA
Michael Weiss	Carleton University, Canada
Christian Zirpins	Karlsruhe Institute of Technology, Germany

Workshops and Tutorial Chair

Anis Boubaker   Université du Québec à Montréal, Canada

Industrial Activities Committee Chair

Abderrahmane Leshob   Université du Québec à Rimouski, Canada

Local Arrangements Committee Chair

Anis Boubaker   Université du Québec à Montréal, Canada

Registrations Chair

Anis Boubaker   Université du Québec à Montréal, Canada

Contents

eHealth

ebusiness, eEducation and eLogistics

Process Adaptation

Ontology-Driven Process Specialization

Abderrahmane Leshob[1,2]($\boxtimes$), Hafedh Mili[2], and Anis Boubaker[2]

[1] University of Quebec at Rimouski, Rimouski, Canada
[2] University of Quebec at Montreal, Montreal, Canada
`leshob.abderrahmane@uqam.ca`

Abstract. Business process design is an important activity for the planning and analysis of information systems that support the organization's business processes. Our goal is to help business analysts produce detailed models of the business processes that best reflect the needs of their organizations. To this end, we propose to, a) leverage the best practices in terms of a catalog of generic business processes, and b) provide analysts with tools to customize those processes by generating, on-demand, new process variants around automatically identified process variation points. We use business patterns from the Resource Event Agent ontology to identify variation points, and to codify the model transformations inherent in the generation of the process variants. We developed a prototype, showing the computational feasibility of the approach. Early feedback from a case study with three *Business Process Management* (BPM) experts validated the relevance of the variation points, and the correctness of corresponding transformations, within the context of key *Enterprise Resource Planning* (ERP) processes. In this paper, we summarize the approach and report of the results of a larger experiment, gaining insights into the strengths and weaknesses of our approach, and suggesting avenues for improvement.

1 Introduction

Business process modeling is an important activity for organizational design and for the planning and analysis of information systems that support the organization's business processes. This work aims at helping business analysts develop precise business process specifications without having to become process designers specialists. Our approach consists of developing: 1) a catalog of broadly useful generic business processes that business analysts can use as a starting point for their organization-specific process, and 2) a set of specialization operators that business analysts can apply to a generic process to obtain a process model that accurately reflects their organization's needs.

With regard to the first point, the very existence of ERP systems and frameworks does suggest that. Nonetheless, to ensure that our process catalog has a "good coverage" with a "manageable" set of processes, we need a "good" representation of business processes that abstracts unimportant details and highlights business meaningful process variations.

© Springer International Publishing Switzerland 2015
M. Benyoucef et al. (Eds.): MCETECH 2015, LNBIP 209, pp. 3–19, 2015.
DOI: 10.1007/978-3-319-17957-5_1

With regard to the second point, our representation of the specialization operators should hide the technical details of the underlying model trans∲forma- tions, and focus on the business-level meaning of these specializations. To this end, we adopted the question-based approach to process specialization.

The rest of the paper is organized as follows. Section 2 surveys related work. Section 3 describes our approach for generalizing the specialization's questions. Section 4 presents the REA framework and patterns with a view towards auto- matic process specialization. Section 5 presents the design and implementation core of our approach. Section 7 discusses validation. We conclude in section 8.

2   Related Work

A number of business process cataloging efforts have used questions or options to manage process variability. Carlson's *Business Information Analysis and Inte- gration Technique* (BIAIT [1]) proposed seven questions based on the concept of generic order to identify the major functional building blocks of the information system. This approach is interesting since variation points are meaningful to a business analyst. Unfortunately, it works only at a macroscopic level.

The MIT process handbook [2] organizes processes along *specialization dimensions*, framed as questions. This approach is helpful in navigating the process catalog, however, the questions and the corresponding process variants are process-specific.

Coad, Lefebvre and De Luca's [3] proposed a questionnaire-based frame- work to specialize generic business models, but they focused on model *fragments* instead of entire models. A number of researchers have explored the problem of managing variability within process models (see e.g. [4], [5]). However, these approaches focus on managing *previously codified process variants*, as opposed to *deriving* those variants.

3   An Approach to Question-Based Specializations

In order to be able to reason about the business process, we will use the business process perspectives as proposed by Curtis [6]. Indeed, Curtis argued that a complete representation of a business process requires four distinct views [6]: 1) the *dynamic view*, which provides sequencing and control dependency between the tasks of a process, 2) the *functional view*, which represents the functional dependencies between the process elements. In our work, we replaced this view by the *REA view* (see section 4), 3) the *informational view*, which includes the description of the entities that are produced, consumed or otherwise manipulated by the process, and, 4) the *organizational view*, which describes who performs each task or function, and where in the organization.

In order to apply our specialization approach to processes from different domains, we needed to define generic questions. Our first attempt consisted of generalizing the sets of questions proposed in the literature, including [2,3,7]. Idem for the underlying model transformations. This sounded reasonable on

Fig. 1. REA metamodel

paper/toy examples, but proved unworkable with real life processes taken from the SAP/R3 blueprint [8]. Indeed, the generalized questions and the corresponding generalized model transformations had lost much of the original business semantics, and became meaningless. For a given process, this resulted into many 'question instances' that did not make sense and spurious model transformations.

We realized that we needed *BIAIT-style* questions. By *BIAIT-style* questions, we mean questions that relate to the *essence* of the business processes. Similar to Carlson's concept of *generic order*, as it pertains to an organizations core activities/processes, we needed a *business ontology* that would enable us to see the similarities between, say, a procurement process and a hiring process. We felt that the *Resource-Event Agent* (REA) framework [9] might offer such an ontology. McCarthy views the core processes of an organization as a sequence of *exchanges* or *transformations* of *resources* between *agents* [9]. In this context, it is easy to see how the concept of a *contract*, for example, becomes relevant to various process areas, as a way of *governing* those exchanges.

4   Variants with REA Business Patterns

In this section, we present the concept of an REA pattern. Finally, we show how such a pattern can be the source of, a) a variation point, framed as a generic question, and b) the corresponding model transformation.

4.1   The REA Framework

McCarthy proposed the REA framework as a way of capturing the economic phenomena that needed to be accounted, from an *accounting* perspective [9]. In REA, an enterprise can increase or decrease the value of its resources through either *exchanges* or *conversions* Hruby2006. In an *exchange,* the enterprise receives economic resources from external economic agents, and provides other resources in return. In a *conversion,* an enterprise uses or consumes resources in order to produce new or modified resources.

Fig. 1 shows the basic REA metamodel. *Economic resources* are objects that are scarce, have utility, and are under the control of an enterprise [9]. Economic events are "a class of phenomena which reflect changes in scarce means resulting from production, exchange, consumption, and distribution" [11]. An *economic event* can be either an *increment* or a *decrement* in the value of economic resources. The duality relationship links increment events to decrement events. An *Economic Agent* is an individual or an organization capable of controlling economic resources, and transferring or receiving that control to or from other individuals or organizations [10].

4.2   REA Business Patterns

Work on REA has identified a number of business patterns. Such patterns are the focus of our generic questions and our specialization operators. Hruby identified more than twenty REA business patterns [10]. Geerts and McCarthy proposed several REA patterns as part of the REA ontology [12]. From these, we focused on a dozen patterns. Each such pattern involved one or more *variation points*, framed as *generic questions*, and *transformation rules* that generated the process variants, corresponding to different answers of those questions.

4.3   Running Example

Consider the procurement process of Fig. 2. It starts by filling out a requisition. The purchaser then sends a request for quotation (RFQ) to potential suppliers. After receiving the quotations, the purchaser selects a supplier, creates a purchase order (PO) and sends it back to that supplier. In turn, the supplier fulfills the order and delivers it to the purchaser. Once the product is received, a goods receipt is generated and payment is made.

A question raised by the exchange pattern is whether the exchange is governed by an *agreement*. A 'yes' answer would impact several views of the process. Indeed, we need to represent the Agreement object in the information view. We also need to simplify the dynamic view by removing the steps for supplier selection. This question can be represented by a one-parameter boolean function, verbalized as follows: *Is there an agreement that governs the business process {0}?* Hruby modeled agreements using the REA *contract pattern* [10], which introduces the related notions of *commitment, contract,* and *agreement* (see Fig. 3). A *commitment* is a promise of economic agents to perform an economic event in the future. A *contract* is a collection of related commitments. Terms are

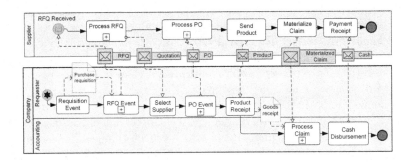

Fig. 2. Generic procurement process

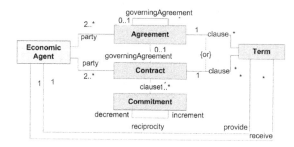

Fig. 3. Contract pattern

potential commitments that are instantiated if certain conditions are met (e.g. commitment not being fulfilled).

5 Business Process Specialization

The initial population of the 4-view generic process catalog relies on the existence of a catalog of REA patterns codified in a way that, 1) identifies the variation points, and 2) operationalizes the transformations corresponding to the different variants. Our main sources for REA patterns have been REA's ontology [12], and Pavel Hruby's twenty two REA patterns [10]. For the purposes of this experiment, we excluded some of the 'trivial patterns', as well as those patterns that dealt exclusively with the data model/the informational view. The end result was a dozen patterns.

To populate our generic process catalog, we explored a number of sources, including the MIT process handbook [2] and SAP R/3 blueprint[13]. To build the four process views (i.e. REA, dynamic, informational and organizational views), we have developed a number of heuristics to support a semi-automated process for generating the views from an annotated BPMN model, discussed in [8].

For process browsing and specialization, we envision a process where a business analyst looking for a particular process starts browsing the process catalog, drilling down progressively, until either they find a process that they can use as is, or they find a process that is close enough, and that they can specialize. To specialize a process, the analyst 'asks' the tool to identify the variation points

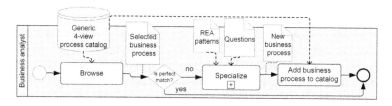

Fig. 4. Overall process of the proposed process specialization approach

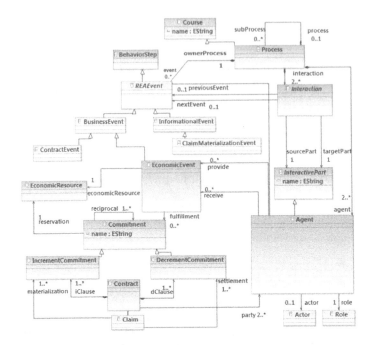

Fig. 5. Excerpts from the implemented 4-view business process metamodel

and present them, along with the various alternatives (answers). The analyst then selects the appropriate answers, and the tool generates a specialized process, resulting from the application of a cascade of transformations. Fig. 4 shows the overall process of the proposed process specialization approach.

6 Preliminary Implementation

6.1 Process Model Representation

Our metamodel is based on the REA business ontology. The REA metamodel does not support the concept of orchestration, since REA is an economic-resource-centred view that focus solely on those resource altering phenomena. Hence, we extended the REA metamodel to cover the informational, organizational and the dynamic views of process models. We implemented our metamodel as an Eclipse plugin with the Eclipse Modeling Framework[TM] (EMF, version 2.7.2), which is an Eclipse-based Java modeling framework that implements a core subset of OMG's Meta Object Facility (MOF). With EMF, the informational view comes out-of-the-box, embodied in the core UML metamodel, with classes such as `EClass`, `EAttribute`, etc. The dynamic view was based on the *Business Process Definition Metamodel* (BPDM, [14]) behavioral model. The organizational view was implemented using the subset of the *Organization Structure Metamodel* (OSM, [15]) used in BPDM. The REA view was implemented with concepts from the REA

```
<!-------------------------------------------------------------->
<!-- The agreement question  (Contract pattern) -->
<!-------------------------------------------------------------->
<question id="q4">
        <name>AGREEMENT_IN_THE_PROCESS</name>
        <description>
                Contract regulates the behavior among organizations and individuals.
                A contract is an entity containing commitments and terms. Agreement
                is a higher level contract that regulates the behavior of individual
                contracts. SLA is an example of agreement.
        </description>
        <core answerType="AnswerType.BOOLEAN" >
                Is there an agreement that governs the business process {0}?
        </core>
        <parameters >
                <parameter>Process</parameter>
        </parameters>
</question>
```

Fig. 6. The representation of generic questions

ontology, including a) core concepts such as `EconomicResource`, the `REAEvent` subhierarchy, and the duality between economic events, and b) specialized concepts coming from various REA patterns, such as `Claim` and `Commitment`. Fig. 5 shows the main classes from the implemented metamodel.

6.2   Implementing Variation Points

Variation points were designed as generic questions, which can be thought of as multi-parameter functions, whose values are taken from an enumeration, and whose parameter types correspond to business process element types. When a 'question' is 'instantiated' for a particular process model fragment, the parameters are bound to specific elements of the fragment, and the function call is presented in a *verbalized* form so as to make sense to the analyst who is then prompted for a value among the enumeration of possible answers.

For example, the question regarding whether a particular exchange were governed by an agreement would be represented by the template *"Is there an agreement that governs the [exchange process] {0}"*, where {0} is a *positional parameter* that will be replaced by an REA exchange process within the value chain. For example, when applied to the procurement process of Fig. 2, this question will be formulated as *"Is there an agreement that governs the process procurement "*. The question model is implemented using an XML schema. Fig. 6 shows the representaion the agreement question.

6.3   Implementing Process Specialization

We implemented our transformations as **if-then** transformation rules that manipulate EMF process models, where the **if** part matches a process model pattern, and the **then** part applies the relevant transformation to process model elements represented as EMF objects. Thus, we looked into open-source hybrid *object-rule* systems, and settled for JBoss Drools version 5.1. We wrote a *single* DROOLS transformation rule, *per* <process model view, answer> combination.

```
1   rule "YES_AGREEMENT_INFORMATIONAL_VIEW"
2   when
3     $q : Question(gQuestion.name==AGREEMENT_IN_THE_PROCESS);
4   then
5     Message m = DynaHandler.getREAContractMessage(process, $q.param(0));
6     Agent agent1 = (Agent) m.getSourcePart();
7     Agent agent2 = (Agent) m.getTargetPart();
8     EClass clazz=InfHandler.addEClass(view,AGREEMENT_CLASS, BpPackage.
          eINSTANCE.getEResource());
9     InfHandler.addEAttribute(clazz, "dateFrom", eINSTANCE.getEDate());
10    ...
11    EReference ref1=InfHandler.addEReference(view,clazz,agent1, agent1.
          toLowerCase(),1,1,null, false);
12    InfHandler.addEReference(view,agent1,clazz,AGREEMENT_CLASS.toLowerCase
          (),1,UNBOUNDED_MULTIPLICITY,ref1, false);
13    ...
14    EReference ref3 = EMFInfViewHandler.addEReference(view, clazz, m.
          getResource(),"contract", 0, UNBOUNDED_MULTIPLICITY, null,false);
15    ...
16    InfHandler.removeElementsByEventType(process,"REAAgentIdentification");
17  end
```

Fig. 7. Transformation rule of informational view for yes answer to agreement question

Hence, the transformation that needs to be applied to the *informational view* in case of a yes answer to the 'is there an agreement that governs the [exchange process] {0}' is represented by a single rule, shown in Fig. 7.

The *when* part binds the variable q to the instance of the specific question that is in the rule engine's working memory (line 3). The *then* part describes the actions. Lines 5 to 7 identify the economic agents. The expression $q.param(0) in line 5 refers to the REA process. Lines 8 to 10 create an Agreement class, and add it to the informational view. Lines 11 to 13 add bidirectional associations between the Agreement class and the classes that represent contract's parties. Lines 14 to 15 add bidirectional associations between the Agreement class and the REA contract class. Finally, line 16 removes the classes that represent objects that are used solely for identifying the exchange partner (i.e. objects related to the business events of type REAAgentIdentification).

7   Validation

We are proposing a methodology for representing and specializing business processes that enables business analysts to find, or derive, a business process that matches their needs. Viewing our work within the context of *method engineering*, we could evaluate the extent to which our approach enables business analysts to produce *better* process models *faster*.

At this stage of the research, we propose to validate: (i) our *representation of business processes,* (ii) our *variation points,* and *(iii)* our *specializations.*

With the exception of the syntactic correctness, the other aspects can only be validated by *human subjects,* who have the expertise to walk through the methodology, and to evaluate the various processes, models, and questions. Of the many

Table 1. Experimental processes

	Business Process	ERP Classification
P1	Procurement	Buy
P2	Sales & Distribution	Sell
P3	Production & Inspection	Make
P4	Maintenance & Customer Service	Service
P5	Hiring	Human Capital Management
P6	Financial Loan	Finance
P7	Insurance	Service
P8	Payroll	Human Capital Management

Table 2. Experimental generic questions

Pattern	Question
Exchange	Q1: Does the process {0} support instantaneous exchange?
	Q2: Does [increment events] {0} precede(s) [decrement events] {1} for the exchange process {2}?
Outsourcing	Q3: Does the organization plan outsourcing the process {0} to a partner?
Contract	Q4: Is there an agreement that governs the process {0}?
Commitment	Q5: Does the process {0} support future obligations?
Claim	Q6: Does the process {0} support a Two-way match strategy for claim processing?
Posting pattern	Q7: Does the organization keep transactions history between partners for the process {0}?

experts we solicited, three generously volunteered to participate. Expert 1 is a business consultant at a major Canadian bank, with an extensive experience with SAP processes. Expert 2 is specialized in business process management (BPM) at a major consulting multinational. Expert 3 is a university professor with an extensive business consulting experience. In addition to the qualitative results obtained from our experts, we conducted a quantitative experiments with twelve graduate students from a business school. All students have a strong experience in aligning business processes in the context of small and large organizations. They have also a very good background in business process modeling with BPMN and information systems design with UML.

7.1 Experimental Data

We studied 22 processes from ERP systems [13,16]. From these processes, we selected 8 processes, one from each ERP process area, shown in Table 1. To validate the applicability of questions and transformations, out of the 12 questions that our study of Hruby patterns identified, we started encoding the ones that were related to the REA patterns that we felt were the most useful. This resulted into encoding seven (7) questions, and the view transformation rules corresponding to the various answers. Table 2 shows the REA patterns, and the corresponding generic questions.

7.2   Validation of Process Representation

Our business process metamodel resulted from a number of iterations. The informational view is handled with EMF's ECore package. The REA metaclasses were added as needed by the new encoded REA patterns. For the dynamic view, the subset of the BPDM metamodel [14] that we implemented proved sufficient.

As expected, the derivation of the REA view from the BPMN view was challenging, for three main reasons. First, there is no one to one mapping between REA concepts and BPMN concepts. Indeed, not all BPMN *data objects* represent *REA resources*, and not all *BPMN activities*, represent *REA economic events*. Second, BPMN models *typically* ignore classes of resources that are nonetheless needed to perform activities, such as *labor* or *equipments*. Finally, the REA patterns rely on the concept of *duality* between resource increment events and decrement events. This was not an issue with exchange-type processes, but was an issue with conversion-type processes where the BPMN models were missing *both* resources *and* dual economic events, which had to be added manually. In total, our 8 processes contained 7 REA exchanges and 4 conversions. We had to complement the initial BPMN models for three of the conversions, to add the missing resources and events.

7.3   Validation of Questions Applicability

A key aspect to our approach is our claim that variation points/questions identified within the context of REA patterns, a) made sense from a business view, and b) were applicable to *many* process areas. To validate this claim, we presented our experts with the 7 questions that we had encoded, and the 8 generic processes that we had modeled, and asked them whether a particular question, as instantiated for a particular process, made sense. If the process contained several REA patterns, then the question was instantiated for each pattern. Experts 1 and 2 volunteered for the exercise, and took 45 minutes to produce Table 3. A value of 1 meant that the question, as instantiated, made sense for the process at hand. A value of NA (Not Applicable) meant that the question did not apply to this kind of process. A value of Partial was used when the same question was instantiated several times for the same process (REA value chain), and where some instantiations made sense while others did not. A value of 0 meant that the questions did not make sense/should not have been instantiated. A closer inspection revealed that all NA values were due to the fact that exchange-type questions were instantiated for conversion-type processes. This also explains the 'Partial' values, which were used when an exchange-type question was instantiated twice for processes that consisted of a combination of an exchange and a conversion, and the experts felt that the question did not apply to the conversion leg of the process (e.g. Sales & Distribution). With hindsight, we could have filtered the instantiation of exchange-type questions (Q1, Q2, Q4, and Q6) for conversions, which would have yielded 95.08 % of sensical instantiations.

Table 3. Questions applicability

Business Process	Q1	Q2	Q3	Q4	Q5	Q6	Q7
Procurement	1	1	1	1	1	1	1
Sales & Distribution (S&D)	Partial	Partial	1	Partial	1	Partial	1
Production & Inspection	NA	NA	1	NA	1	NA	1
Maintenance & Customer Service	Partial	Partial	1	Partial	1	Partial	1
Hiring	0	1	1	1	1	1	1
Financial Loan	0	1	1	1	1	1	1
Insurance	1	1	1	1	1	1	1
Payroll	0	1	1	1	1	1	1

Fig. 8. REA outsourcing pattern

7.4 Validation of Process Specializations

To validate the process specializations, we needed to: a) validate that the models produced by the corresponding transformations conform to the process meta-model syntax and semantics, and b) validate whether the models produced reflect the *expected business semantics*. Metamodel conformance was validated using EMF's *validation framework* (EMF-VF). EMF-VF provides a capability to parse an EMF model and return true if the model satisfies the constraints of its metamodel, and false otherwise. We were able to ascertain that all the generated models conformed to the metamodel.

With regard to *business semantics* correctness, we had to rely on our experts. They had to answer questions of the type 'given initial process P, and answer A to question Q, is the [generated process] Pqa what you would have expected?'. Thus, we had to generate a number of specialization scenarios using our 8 processes, 7 questions, and the possible answers for each question. Notice that taking all the applicable <process, question> combinations from table 3 (49 out of 52) does not guarantee *complete test coverage* because we wanted to evaluate, among other things, combinations or cascades of elementary specializations that may transform the same elements, i.e. *confluent transformations*. Thus, we relied on Expert 1 to generate what he felt were 'interesting specializations', while ensuring that each question (transformation) was exercised at least once. In the end, Expert 1 generated twenty-five (25) new processes, by executing 78 transformations, with an average of about 3 transformations per process. Those 25 processes were then handed to Experts 2 and 3 for validation.

Experts 2 and 3 confirmed that 19 out of 25 processes (76%) corresponded to what they expected. As for the remaining 6 (24%), which all involved a yes answer to question Q3 (outsourcing), they felt that while the net flow of economic resources was correct for all 6 processes, the resulting models were not

Table 4. Evaluation results of G1 and G3

Group	Participant	Evaluation Phase			Generation& Matching Phase		
		P1q1	P3q3	P2q4	P7q6	P6q7	P5q4
G1	Student 1	1	1*	1	1	1	1
	Student 2	1	1*	NA	1-	1	1
	Student 3	1	1	1	1	1	1
G3	Student 7	1	1*	1	1-	1	1
	Student 8	1	1*	1	1-	1	NA
	Student 9	1	1*	1	NA	1	1

the ones they expected. Specifically, they argued that the obtained models were unnecessarily complex. This is because in REA (see REA outsourcing pattern of Fig. 8), we can only exchange (buy/sell) resources, and not processes.

While the experts provided us with a *qualitative* results, we also conducted a *quantitative* experiments with twelve graduate students from a business school. All participating students have a strong knowledge of BPM methodologies. To validate the correctness of our specializations, we first selected 6 generated processes from our repository and then conducted an experiment in two phases: 1) *process evaluation phase* and 2) *process generation & matching phase*. In the process evaluation phase, the students had to answer the same type of questions we have asked our experts i.e. 'given initial process P, and answer A to question Q, is the generated process Pqa what you would have expected? In the process generation & matching phase, they were asked to provide their own transformations of the base processes by applying a yes answer to selected questions and then, compare the resulting processes to our automatically generated processes. To conduct our experiments, we formed 4 groups (G1, G2, G3 and G4) of 3 students each. We presented to each group a set of processes and asked each participant to proceed individually as follow: participants of G1 and G2 started with the evaluation phase and proceeded thereafter with the generation phase while participants of G3 and G4 proceeded inversely. As shown in tables 4 and 5, we asked the groups to validate our specialization methodology using the same set of processes, questions and answers in different sequences. Thus, each student evaluated 3 processes and generated 3 processes. The participants took 3 hours to complete the experimentation. Tables 4 and 5 illustrate the evaluation results of groups (G1, G3) and (G2, G4) respectively. The notation **Piqj** denotes the specialized process obtained/to obtain by transforming the process Pi after applying a yes answer to the question Qj (see table 2).

The meaning of the value 1 depends on the experimentation phase. In the evaluation phase, the value of 1 meant that the process generated by our approach is what the student expected. In the generation phase, it meant that both our process and the process generated by the student are identical. The value of 1* meant that the student found the generated process correct but more complex than what he/she expected. The value of 1+ indicated that the student's generated process highlighted correctly, but differently, the outsourcing concept. The value of 1- indicated that the student kept the *informational event* (see

Table 5. Evaluation results of G2 and G4

Group	Participant	Evaluation Phase			Generation & Matching Phase		
		P7q6	P6q7	P5q4	P1q1	P3q3	P2q4
	Student 4	1	1	1	1	1+	1
G2	Student 5	1-	1	1	1	1+	1
	Student 6	1-	1	1	1	1+	1
	Student 10	NA	1	1	1	1+	1
G4	Student 11	1	1	1	1	NA	NA
	Student 12	NA	1	1	1	1+	1

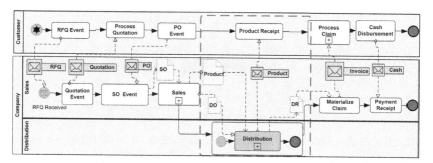

Fig. 9. Generic Sales & Distribution process

[17]) of the invoice value calculation without sending it to the partner while our transformation rule removed the whole *business event* (see [17]) which (1) calculate the invoice value and (2) send it to the partner. Finally, a value of NA (Not Applicable) meant that the student did not evaluate the resulting process or did not generate a complete and a valid process. Thus, the NA values were discarded from our results.

With regard to the value of 1*, all students, except student 3, who evaluated the generated process after a yes answer to the outsourcing question confirmed the results obtained by expert 2 and expert 3. They argued that the generated models were unnecessarily complex. This is because in REA, we can only exchange economic resources. Thus, to outsource a process, we consider its 'performance on our behalf' as a *service*, that we *purchase* (*exchange*), and then *consume* (*conversion*) (see the outsourcing business pattern in Fig. 8). For example, to outsource the *distribution* part of Sales & Distribution process (Fig. 9), our tool generated the model shown in Fig. 10 where *SO, PO, DO, SPO, DS* and *DR* stand for *Sale Order, Purchase Order, Distribution Order, Service Purchase Order, Distribution Service* and *Distribution Receipt*, respectively. Expert 2, expert 3 and all students that generated new processes after outsourcing a part of a process (value of 1+ in Table 5) proposed a simplified, but REA-invalid, process similar to the process in Fig. 11.

Finally, regarding the 1- values, both processes are *semantically equivalent* as the invoice calculation (i.e. informational event) does not affect the business process behavior (see [18]). Fig. 12 illustrates the result of the evaluation

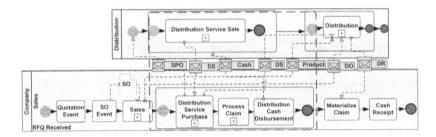

Fig. 10. B2B collaboration after outsourcing the Distribution in S&D process

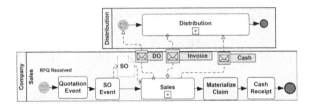

Fig. 11. B2B collaboration after outsourcing the Distribution in S&D process according to experts 2 and 3

phase. Among the 36 evaluations, students confirmed that 72.22 % of the evaluated processes are exactly to what they expected, while 5.56% are different but semantically equivalent. As for the remaining evalutions (13.89%), which all involved a yes answer to the outsourcing question, students felt that while the net flow of economic resources was correct for all processes, the resulting models were not the ones they expected.

7.5   Threats to Validity

This section presents the threats to the validity of the performed experiments.

Threats to External Validity. The external threat comes from the limited set of generic questions (7 questions) which are obtained from REA patterns. To date, we have identified 16 questions but automated transformation rules for 7 of them. To mitigate this concern, a set of 30 variation points were analyzed from the industry and literature, including the specialization patterns from e3-value business ontology [19] and process re-engineering domain [20]. The experimental questions were selected from question-based specialization approaches that were studied in previous work on business process adaptation area to facilitate comparison with previous results.

Threats to Construct Validity. Construct validity refers to the validity that observations or measurement tools actually represent or measure the construct being investigated. In this paper, one possible threat to construct validity arises

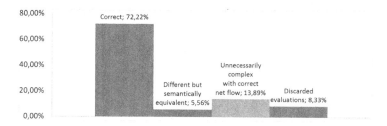

Fig. 12. Correctness of the transformations in the process evaluation phase

from the evaluation method used to prove semantic equivalence of source and resulting business process models. There are several general approaches like ([21, 22]) that can be used to evaluate semantic equivalence between models. Therefore, conclusions obtained from our correctness evaluation might not be representative of other evaluation methods. A mature and widely used technique (semantic consistency) is used to mitigate this concern. Indeed, our experts used the semantic consistency approach based on a set of business constraints to evaluate the semantic correctness of the resulting process models.

8   Conclusion

Business process modeling is an important activity for both organizational design and for the planning and analysis of information systems that support the organization's business processes. The purpose of this work is to assist business analysts in the process of modeling the business processes that best reflect the practice of their organizations. To this end, we proposed to, a) leverage the best practices in terms of a catalog of *generic business processes*, and b) provide business analysts with tools to customize those processes by generating, on-demand, new process variants around automatically identified process variants. Our approach for *automatically* identifying process variants and *automatically generating* user-selected process variants relies on the *projection* of the generic processes along the REA *business ontology* which focuses on *key business abstractions* such as *resource exchanges* and *conversions* that underlie seemingly different business processes.

We developed a prototype of our approach that relies on available standards and open source software. We also conducted experiments with expert analysts and graduated students to validate the *soundness* of the *conceptual ingredients* that underlie our approach. Notwithstanding the small size of our experimental data set, the results support the soundness of the approach. Much remains to be done, both in terms of core functionality, dealing with *confluent* transformations [8], and in terms of *usability* before we can make this into a tool that process analysts will readily use.

References

1. Carlson, W.M.: Business information analysis and integration technique (BIAIT): the new horizon. ACM SIGMIS Database **10**(4), 3–9 (1979)
2. Malone, T.W., Crowston, K., Herman, G.: Organizing Business Knowledge: The MIT Process Handbook. MIT Press (2003)
3. Coad, P., De Luca, J., Lefebvre, E.: Java Modeling In Color With UML: Enterprise Components and Process. Prentice Hall PTR (1999)
4. Hallerbach, A., Bauer, T., Reichert, M.: Capturing variability in business process models: the Provop approach. Journal of Software Maintenance and Evolution: Research and Practice **22**(6–7), 519–546 (2010)
5. Schnieders, A., Puhlmann, F.: Variability mechanisms in E-business process families. In: Proceedings of the 9th International Conference on Business Information Systems (BIS 2006), pp. 583–601 (2006)
6. Curtis, B., Kellner, M.I., Over, J.: Process modeling. Commun. ACM **35**, 75–90 (1992)
7. Wohed, P.: Conceptual patterns - A consolidation of coad's and wohed's approaches. In: Bouzeghoub, M., Kedad, Z., Métais, E. (eds.) NLDB 2000. LNCS, vol. 1959, pp. 340–351. Springer, Heidelberg (2001)
8. Leshob, A.: Representating, classifying and specializing business processes. PhD thesis, UQAM, Montreal (2013)
9. McCarthy, W.E.: The REA accounting model: A generalized framework for accounting systems in a shared data environment. Accounting Review **57**(3), 554–578 (1982)
10. Hruby, P.: Model-Driven Design Using Business Patterns. Springer, Heidelberg (2006)
11. Yu, S.C.: The Structure of Accounting Theory. The University Press of Florida (1976)
12. Geerts, G., McCarthy, W.: The ontological foundation of REA enterprise information systems. Annual Meeting of the American Accounting Association, pp. 1–34, March 2000
13. Curran, T.A., Keller, G., Ladd, A.: SAP R/3 Business Blueprint: Understanding the Business Process Reference Model. Prentice Hall (1998)
14. OMG, Business Process Definition MetaModel (BPDM) (2008)
15. OMG, Organization Structure Metamodel (OSM) (2006)
16. Murray, M.: Discover Logistics with SAP ERP. SAP PRESS (2009)
17. David, J.S.: Three events that define an REA methodology for systems analysis, design, and implementation. In: Proceedings of the Annual Meeting of the American Accounting Association, Dallas, TX (1997)
18. van der Aalst, W.M.P., de Medeiros, A.K.A., Weijters, A.J.M.M.: Process equivalence: comparing two process models based on observed behavior. In: Dustdar, S., Fiadeiro, J.L., Sheth, A.P. (eds.) BPM 2006. LNCS, vol. 4102, pp. 129–144. Springer, Heidelberg (2006)
19. Gordijn, J., Akkermans, H.: Designing and Evaluating E-Business Models. IEEE Intelligent Systems **16**, 11–17 (2001)

20. Reijers, H.A., Dumas, M., van der Aalst, W.M.P., ter Hofstede, A.H.M.: Process design and redesign. In: Process-Aware Information Systems: Bridging People and Software through Process Technology, pp. 207–234. John Wiley & Sons, New Jersey (2005)
21. Engels, G., Heckel, R., Küster, J.M., Groenewegen, L.: Consistency-preserving model evolution through transformations. In: Jézéquel, J.-M., Hussmann, H., Cook, S. (eds.) UML 2002. LNCS, vol. 2460, pp. 212–227. Springer, Heidelberg (2002)
22. Varró, D., Pataricza, A.: Automated formal verification of model tranformations. In: Critical Systems Development in UML, no. Otka 038027, pp. 63–78. Technische Universität München (2003)

Towards Automating Business Process Compensation Scoping Logic

Anis Boubaker[1]([✉]), Hafedh Mili[1],
Abderrahmane Leshob[1], and Yasmine Charif[2]

[1] University of Quebec at Montreal, Montreal, Canada
anis@boubaker.ca
[2] Xerox Webster Research Center, New York, USA

Abstract. Business process compensation is an error recovery strategy aiming at semantically reversing the effects of an interrupted business process execution and restoring it to a valid state. Studies have shown that modeling error handling in general, and compensation in particular, represents the bulk of process design efforts. To that end, we proposed in a previous work an approach to model semi-automatically compensation processes based on a business analysis within the REA framework, restoring it to its initial state. However, we argue that it is neither practical nor desirable to cancel the whole process in some situations. Instead, the process should be reversed to an intermediate state from which it could resume its execution. This work aims at solving this compensation scoping problem by inferring the possible "rollback points". Our approach relies on a resource flow analysis within the context of an OCL-based behavioral specification of business process activities. In this paper, we present our slicing algorithm and lay our ground ideas on how we could identify possible candidates as process' rollback activities.

1 Introduction

A typical e-business transaction takes hours or days to complete, involves a number of partners, and comprises many failure points. With such transactions, strict atomicity is not practical, and we need a way of reversing the effects of those activities that have been committed prior to failure: that is compensation. For a given business process, identifying the various failure points, and designing the appropriate compensation processes represents the bulk of process design effort. Yet, business analysts have little or no guidance, as for a given failure point, there appears to be a variety of ways to compensate for it. We recognize that compensation is a business issue, and argue that it can be explained within the context of the REA ontology [19], in terms of things such as the type of activity, the type of resource, and organizational policies [6]. We propose a three-step process compensation design approach that 1) starts by abstracting a business process to focus on those activities that create/modify value (see e.g. [4]), 2)

© Springer International Publishing Switzerland 2015
M. Benyoucef et al. (Eds.): MCETECH 2015, LNBIP 209, pp. 20–36, 2015.
DOI: 10.1007/978-3-319-17957-5_2

compensates for those activities, individually, based on values of the compensation parameters [6], and 3) composes those elementary activity compensations into failure-specific compensation processes. This paper lies within the scope of this third step (composition).

Compensating a business process by restoring it to its initial state may be neither practical, nor desirable in many circumstances. Consider for example, in a selling-and-delivery process, an error occurring when we realize that the order has been shipped to a wrong address. We may compensate the process by returning it to its initial state - i.e. getting back the parcel, canceling the order all together and asking the customer to replace his order. This will leave the system in a correct state but do not make much business sense. Therefore, a critical aspect of the composition of failure-specific compensation processes is the identification of an activity within the original process - the *rollback point* - that, a) is likely to have caused the (subsequent) failure, and/or b) offers alternative courses of action that offer the possibility of the process succeeding.

This paper's contributions are twofold. First, we propose an algorithm to perform business process slicing relying on a resource flow analysis within the context of an Object Constraint Language (OCL) behavioral specification of business process activities [20]. In order to specify business process activities, we extended the BPMN metamodel by introducing OCL constraints on model flow nodes. In addition to compensation scoping problem, our slicing methodology could be used in various other problems as model verification and debugging. Although slicing is a common technique used in process mining, few authors have considered it for business process analysis. Best and Rakow proposed an algorithm to slice business processes modeled as PetriNets against criterion expressed in temporal logic [3]. Rabbi *et al.* offered a similar approach based on the program syntax tree of a proprietary modeling notation called *CWML* [21]. Although these are robust approaches, their formalism (L/CTL) hinders their usability by a non-technical analyst. Awad *et al.* used a technique similar to slicing to do model verification against queries expressed in BPMN-Q language and using a set of reduction rules [1]. However, their approach only checks against structural rules (e.g. enforcing the order of activities) and does not consider process behavior at the activity level.

Our second contribution is the proposal of a framework and a methodology based on our model slicing algorithm and an optimization approach to extract error-specific rollback point *candidates*. Our final objective is to offer a support tool to analysts and business process modelers to assist them in selecting the more appropriate rollback point from a list of candidates ranked according to their business strategies. Golani and Gal proposed a comparable approach but targeted towards runtime backtracking [15]. Apart from methodological differences, they consider a rollback point being necessarily a decision gateway while we make no such assumption.

The remainder of this paper is organized as follows. First, we set the stage by giving a high level overview of our approach in Sec.2, and present an illustrative running example in Sec.3. Then, we present the details of our business process slicing algorithm in Sec.5 that will be based on an extended BPMN metamodel we describe in Sec.4. The proposed strategies to identify rollback points will then be presented in Sec.6. Finally, we conclude in Sec.7 by discussing our approach, stating its limits and giving an overview of related future work.

2   Approach Overview

The objective of this work is to propose an approach to identify the flow node (the set thereof) in the business process to which it should be rolled back in case of an error that triggered a compensation event. We define a rollback point as:

Definition 1. *A rollback point* rb, *for a given error and interruption point, is an activity in the business process that has the ability to change its initial output s.t. by restoring the business process to its state before rb was executed and re-executing the process from rb will void the error either by (1) following the same path to the interruption point; or (2) taking an alternate valid path to the interruption point.*

This rollback point could be any activity upstream of the activity where the error occurred. In order to reduce our problem, we will reason on a subset of business process' flow nodes by focusing only on those that are related to the observed error. We obtain such a subset of the business process by slicing the model relatively to the observed error. The slice of a business process model M guarantees us that if a rollback point rb exits for a given error, rb is also part of its slice. We describe our slicing algorithm in Section 5.

However, in order to be able to slice the business process model, we need a way to express the observed error as well as to relate it to business process flow nodes. The actual specifications of the BPMN language do not provide a mechanism to define the behavioral aspects of business process activities and events. Thus, we extended the BPMN metamodel by introducing constraints over BPMN Flow Nodes expressed in OCL. Constraints are specified manually by the analyst and are related to the informational view (modeled in UML) supporting the business process. The observed error on which will be based our compensation scoping approach is also expressed in OCL.

Finally, from the set of business process activities previously identified in the slice, we will select (1) the ones that represent a valid rollback point and (2) in case many are qualified, rank them according to a set of metrics. Therefore, the result of our approach is a set of business activities from which the business analyst may choose where the process should be rolled back. Given analyst's choice, the compensation scope is defined by the set of executed activities on the path from the rollback point to the interruption point [1].

3   Running Example

In the remainder of this paper, we will use an example of a sales-and-delivery business process of a typical e-retailer in order to illustrate our approach. The

---

[1] What lies within the scope is not all what should be compensated. See [6].

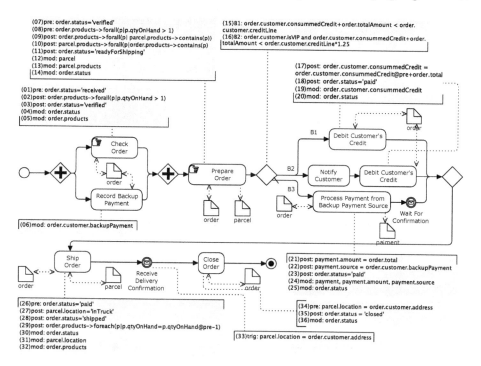

Fig. 1. E-Retailer Sales&Delivery Example

business process starts by receiving an order from a customer along with credit card information that will be used as a backup payment source. Then, two parallel tasks are executed. The first makes sure all the ordered products are actually in stock. Products that are not in stock are removed from the order and the customer is notified. The second verifies the validity of the provided credit card. The order is then made ready for shipping by creating a parcel enclosing the ordered products. Once ready, the payment is proceeded in three different fashions depending on customer's credit line and VIP status. The order amount is charged to his credit line if funds are still available (B1). If the credit line does not suffice but the customer has the VIP status, the company sends him a notification and allows him to exceed the credit line by 25% (B2). Otherwise, the payment is charged to his backup payment source and the business process continues once the company receives a confirmation from his financial institution (B3). The parcel is then sent for delivery and the order is closed as soon as the delivery confirmation is received from the shipping company. This informal description of the process behavior will be formally defined in Section 4 by introducing OCL constraints (see also annotations of activities in Fig. 1).

This dynamic business process view is complemented by the informational view representing the different business objects manipulated by the business

Fig. 2. Informational model supporting the process model in Fig. 1

process and their relationships. We illustrate the informational model as an
UML class diagram in Fig. 2.

4   Extending BPMN with Semantic Constraints

In order to be able to reason about the business process, we need to formally
define its behavior by specifying the effects of each process element on the process' state represented by it's informational model (Fig. 2). We elected to use a
declarative approach relying on the Object Constraint Language formalism [20].

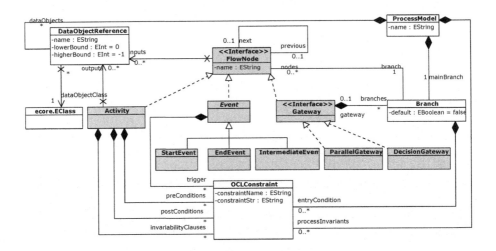

Fig. 3. CBPMN Metamodel

4.1   The CBPMN Metamodel

The BPMN language does not provide any constructs allowing to specify the
behaviors of activities. However, the BPMN specification allows for an extension mechanism that lets tool providers to complement the core elements with
problem specific concepts and attributes.

Our BPMN extension, called CBPMN (for *Constrained BPMN*), is illustrated by the metamodel in Fig. 3. We consider a business process model (*ProcessModel*) as being a succession of *FlowNodes*, each being either an *Activity*, an *Event* or a *Gateway*. These *FlowNodes* are encapsulated within a *Branch* (the *mainBranch* reference of *ProcessModel*). *Gateways* are either *ParallelGateways* or *DecisionGateways* and split a branch into a set of branches being either alternate branches (*DecisionGateway*) or parallel execution branches (*ParallelGateway*). *FlowNodes* might have a sets of *inputs*, each referencing a class from the informational model supporting the business process. Whereas a data input is self explanatory in the case of *Activities*, it has different meanings for *Events* and *Gateways*. For an *Event*, data inputs are the set of objects referenced by the trigger of the event. *DecisionGateway*'s inputs, on the other hand, declare the context on which will be expressed the entry conditions of each of its *Branches*. *Activities* can also declare a set of *outputs* relating to the data objects that will be produced by the *Activity*.

These core concepts presented so far can be related to concepts from BPMN metamodel and are portrayed in Fig. 3 on a grayed background. Our metamodel is in fact an abstraction of the BPMN metamodel, focusing only on high level concepts that needs to be constrained. Therefore, transforming a BPMN model with constraints (either as annotations or through BPMN's extensibility mechanism) into a CBPMN model is a straight forward task - assuming it conforms to the set of validity rules listed in subsection 4.2 - and it is out of the scope of this paper. The main extension we introduced is the concept of *OCLConstraint*. A constraint is an OCL expression declared on activities, events or branches.

Activities have three types of constraints: *preconditions*, *postconditions* and *invariabilityClauses*. A pre-condition is a boolean condition that must be met before the activity could execute. A postcondition is also a boolean condition that evaluates to true if the activity has executed correctly, leaving the system in a valid state. Invariability clauses [17] are a way to cope with the inability to express, in OCL, what an operation is meant to change in the system's state. For example, although OCL lets us verify equalities between object features, it is not possible to specify which side of the equality was assigned (i.e. defined or modified) by an operation. Some authors proposed heuristics to derive invariability clauses from post-conditions by approximating modeler intentions. For example in [7], they consider the order of operands in a binary relation (e.g. ClassA.a=ClassB.b) to infer which of the operands have changed (i.e. ClassA.a). Our approach, inspired by [17], explicitly specify which of the model elements are modified by the related activity. We make a "closed-world" assumption by considering that nothing else changes except those features that have been explicitly specified by invariability clauses.

The other constructs that might hold constraints in our approach are events and branches. A branch's constraint specifies the condition that must hold in order for the branch to be executed. This only concerns branches which are connected to a *DecisionGateway*. A branch might also be declared as the default branch of a gateway, in which case no constraint should be declared. Similarly, events are related to the constraints that must hold for the event to be triggered.

In our e-retailer example in Fig. 1, we annotated each flow node with its set of preconditions (pre), postconditions (post), invariability clauses (mod), event triggers (trig), and branch gateways entry conditions (Bx).

4.2   BPMN Model Validity Criteria

In order to simplify our approach and improve its understandability, we have decided to introduce some limitations over the business process model we use as an input. For each of these restrictions, we explain how it could be alleviated in order not to threaten the generalizability of our approach.

First, we require the business process model to be block structured, as this is enforced by our CBPMN metamodel. Therefore, each splitting gateway must have a corresponding merging gateway. These limitations can be circumvented as some authors propose pattern-based approaches to block-structure a business process (e.g. see [11]).

We also require that each non-gateway flow node must have at most one outgoing control flow link. Therefore, in order to split a branch into multiple branches, a gateway must be used. The number of incoming control flow links to a given flow node is not restricted (as long as the process conforms to the BPMN specifications) in order to accommodate loops. A business process not respecting this restriction car be easily transformed by introducing parallel split and join gateways.

Apart from these syntactic restrictions, we also assume that the business process is semantically sound [27, pp.300-308]. Semantic soundness is a property of business processes that requires that (1) once the business process has started and regardless of which decisions are made, it will reach its end event; (2) when it reaches an end event, the process has completely terminated; and (3) each process activity participates in at least one execution. The latter statement ensures that any activity from the business process could be a potential candidate as a roll back point, whereas the first two statements guarantee that any alternate path will be free of any deadlocks and livelocks. These properties can be systematically checked by transforming the business process model into a WorkflowNet (i.e. a special PetriNet) on which static soundness analysis could be performed (e.g. see [25]).

5   Business Process Slicing

As mentioned in section 2, in order to identify rollback point candidates, we perform a problem reduction by slicing the process model and keeping only the flow nodes that are related to the observed error. After giving a brief overview on slicing theory, we will present our algorithm and describe its implementation.

5.1   Program Slicing - Background Theory

Slicing is a program analysis and reverse engineering technique introduced by Weiser [26] as a program decomposition based on its data flow and control flow graphs. "Starting from a subset of program's behavior, slicing reduces that program to a minimal form which still produces that behavior"[26]. This technique is extensively used in program debugging and generally implemented into development environments. Several other problems make use of slicing for program analysis like compiler optimization, metric computations, quality assurance, fault injections, to cite only a few.

In lay terms, a slicing algorithm aims at extracting the minimal set of program statements that affects a given variable at a given statement. The couple formed by the variable and the statement on which the slicing is performed is called the *slicing criterion*. There are several orthogonal dimensions into which we can classify slicing techniques.

Slicing can be static or dynamic. A static slice only considers the program statements and produces slices being valid for all possible program inputs. Dynamic slices, on the other hand, are concerned with a particular execution of the program with a given set of inputs (that become part of the criterion). Dynamic slicing produces smaller slices (i.e. higher precision) but are not generalizable. From a theoretical perspective, slicing can be reduced into either a data flow analysis problem or into a graph reachability problem. Slicing could also be performed backward or forward, within an intra or inter procedural context. See [24] for a comprehensive survey on slicing techniques.

In the next section we will describe our backward static slicing algorithm for business process models that we approached as a data flow analysis problem.

5.2 BPMN Slicing Algorithm

Our business process slicing algorithm is based on a data flow analysis using the static slicing approach. Given an interruption point flow node and an error observed, expressed as an OCL query, our objective is to extract, from the set of business process flow nodes, the ones that may have caused the error. We perform the slicing relatively to the set of variables that appear in the OCL expressions, both from flow node constraints and the observed error expression.

First, we need to determine the slicing criterion provided as an input to our algorithm. A criterion C is defined as a couple $C = <e, V>$, where e is a business process flow node corresponding to the interruption point and V is the set of variables appearing in the OCL expression of the observed error. From our running example, suppose our business process was interrupted before receiving the delivery confirmation as the customer noticed that one of the products expected in the parcel is missing. The interruption point is the last reached flow node (i.e. Ship Order activity) and the observed error could be expressed as:

Example 1. $order.products \rightarrow exists(p|p.qtyOnHand + 1 > 0$ and
$not(parcel.products \rightarrow exists(p2|p2 = p)$)

Therefore, the slicing criterion in our example would be:
$C = <ShipOrder, <order.products, parcel.products, order.products.qtyOnHand>>$.

The slicing algorithm for a CBPMN process model M with respect to a criterion $C =< e, V >$ is presented in Algorithm 1. Each flow node of the process is mapped with three sets of variables:

- *Slicing variables* (*slicing[]* in Alg.1) which are the variables of interest on which we perform the slicing at each node. This set is initialized to the empty set for all flow nodes;
- *Defined variables* (*defined[]*) are those that change during the execution of an activity. Each activity is assigned the set of variables appearing in its invariability clauses. This set is not relevant for events and gateways; and

---

Algorithm 1. CBPMN process models slicing algorithm

Data: M: CBPMN process model
Data: $C<e, V>$: criterion - e: flow node; V: set of variables
Result: $Slice$: set of the flow nodes from M part of the computed slice
1 Initialize $slicing$, $defined$ and $referenced$ sets for each flow node in M;
2 Set $slicing[e] = V$;
3 **if** $defined[e] \cap slicing[e] \neq \emptyset$ **then**
4   Add e to $Slice$;
5   Set $slicing[e] = slicing[e] - (defined[e] \cap slicingVars[c]) \cup referenced[e]$;
6 set $n = e$;
7 **while** $n^{-1} = n.previous \neq null$ **do**
8   **if** n^{-1} *is a gateway* **then**
9   Set $slicing[n^{-1}] = slicing[n]$;
10   Perform a slicing of each branch of the gateway with the criterion $C_1 = <Last\text{-}node\text{-}in\text{-}branch, slicing[n]>$ and add the result to $Slice$;
11   **if** *at least one of the branch slices is not empty* **then**
12   Add the gateway to $Slice$;
13   Let B be the set of branches with a non empty slice and, for any given branch b, let $b(i)$ be its ith flow node (w.r.t control flow);
14   **if** n^{-1} *is a decision gateway* **then**
15   Set $slicing[n^{-1}] = slicing[n^{-1}] \cup \left(\bigcup_{b \in B} slice[b(1)] \right)$
16   **else**
17   Set $slicing[n^{-1}] = \bigcup_{b \in B} slice[b(1)]$
18   **else**
19   **if** $defined[n^{-1}] \cap slicing[n] \neq \emptyset$ **then**
20   Add n^{-1} to the slice and set $slicing[n^{-1}] = referenced[n^{-1}]$;
21   Set $slicing[n^{-1}] = slicing[n^{-1}] \cup \left(slicing[n] - defined[n^{-1}] \right)$;
22   Set $n = n.previous$;
23 **foreach** *decision gateway G in $Slice$* **do** starting from the closest gateway to e
24   Let V_G be the set of variables from the entry conditions of all G branches having at least one flow node in $Slice$;
25   Slice M with criterion $C_G = < G, V_G >$ and add the results to $Slice$;

– *Referenced variables* (*referenced[]*) are the variables appearing in activities' postconditions, events triggers and branch conditions. For activities, variables in the *defined variable* set are removed from this set.

After the initialization steps (lines 1-2), we determine if the criterion flow node is actually relevant to the slice. Indeed, the criterion flow node is no more than the node at which the business process has stopped. Process interruption may have been triggered by a manual intervention, a process-level event or by an erroneous state created by criterion flow node itself. Therefore, it is included if it defines one of the variables in V (lines 3-5).

Then, we consider the immediate predecessor of the last visited flow node; last visited flow node being the criterion flow node at this stage. We must consider two cases as whether the predecessor is a gateway or not. In case of a gateway (lines 8-17), we have to consider each of the gateway branches as the business process may have taken none, one (decision gateway) or all (parallel gateway) of the paths. For each branch, we perform a recursive call to the slicing algorithm (line 10) on the last node of the branch and criterion variables set to the slicing set of the last visited node (i.e. n). If any of the branches generated a non empty slice, we add the results as well as the gateway to the global slice. If the gateway is parallel (each branch must be taken by the business process), we reset gateway's slicing set to the union of slicing sets of the first nodes of each branch having a non-empty slice. In case it is decision gateway, we also add the slicing set of the last visited flow node to gateway's slicing set in order to account for cases where no branch entry condition is satisfied.

The second case scenario (lines 18-22) happens if the predecessor is not a gateway. The flow node is included in the slice if it defines at least one variable from the slicing set of the last visited flow node. If so, we add it to the slice and add its referenced variables to its slicing set. Then, variables from the slicing of the last visited node are added to predecessor's slicing set, except for those that were defined by the predecessor.

This process is repeated, the predecessor becoming the last seen flow node until we reach the start event. Before and during its execution, the loop maintains two invariants: (1) the slicing set of all visited flow nodes is the set of the variables that directly or transitively affect the value of one of the criterion variables; and (2) the slice set contains the closest flow nodes to the criterion flow node that define/modify the variables from the criterion variables set.

The final step of our algorithm (lines 23-25) considers the *decision* gateways that were included in the slice. A decision gateway being in the slice implies that at least one of it's branches contains at least one flow node that is part of the slice. Therefore, we need to know which flow nodes, upstream of the gateway, may influence the branches' entry conditions. This boils down to slicing the model starting from the gateway on variables appearing in each of relevant branches' entry condition. If multiple gateways are in the slice, we iterate over the gateways from the closest to the farthest to flow node e. The resulting sub-slices are then included in the global slice.

We illustrate in Fig. 4 the resulting slice on the process model from Fig. 1 with the criterion defined in Example 1. Each process flow node in the slice is annotated with the set of *slicing* variables computed through our algorithm.

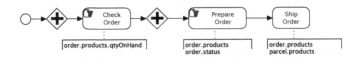

Fig. 4. Slicing result

5.3   Slice Property

Our slicing algorithm ensures us with the following property on the produced slices:

Theorem 1. *Let* M *be a business process model. Let* $C =<F,V>$ *be a slicing criterion on* M *with* F *being the interruption point and* V *the set of variables referenced by the observed error. Let* $RB \subset M$ *be the set of possible rollback points for the observed error. Then* $\forall rb \in RB$, $rb \in slice(M,C)$.

Proof. Suppose $\exists rb \in RB$ s.t. $rb \notin slice(M,C)$. As by the definition of rb (see Def.1), we could recover from the error by re-executing the process starting from rb either:

- By following the original path: in such case, rb is the closest flow node to the interruption point having a postconditions defining a variable that transitively change a variable in the observed error. This contradicts the second loop invariant of our algorithm.

- By taking an alternate path: an alternate path must be connected to a gateway leading to a branch with at least one activity that changes an error variable. In this case, rb would be an activity that may lead us through the alternate path. Step 4.a of the algorithm makes sure the gateway is part of the slice and every flow node that can enable any of the relevant branches will be in the slice (lines 23-25 and loop invariant); which contradicts our hypothesis.∎

5.4   Implementation

To be able to assess the feasibility and the usability of our approach, we implemented a library that takes as an input a process model definition (instance of the CBPMN metamodel), a supporting informational class model, an error flow node from the process definition, and an OCL expression of the observed error. Its output is a set of business process flow nodes that constitute the slice.

Our implementation is based on the Eclipse Modeling Framework [12]. Therefore, our CBPMN metamodel is an instance of the ECore meta[2]model as well as

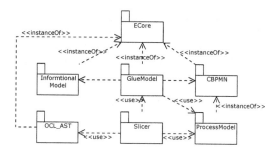

Fig. 5. The architectural view of our prototype

the input informational model. The OCL framework [13] we used is also based on the EMF framework and can parse/interpret OCL expressions for both ECore and UML metamodels. Figure 5 gives an overview of our architecture.

While analyzing the OCL constraints of the process model and the error, we needed to ensure both their syntactic and semantic validity. Syntactic validity means all constraints respect the OCL language specifications [20]. Semantic validity ensures that all informational model features referred to by a constraint are valid and accessible within the context of the constraint. The OCL framework used provides syntactic checking through its parser and semantic checking through its interpreter. However, OCL expressions from CBPMN model cannot be interpreted directly as they must be defined within a context that could be either a class or an operation. Therefore, to ensure semantic validity, we create dynamically an intermediate Ecore model (the glue model in Fig. 5) that connects both the informational model and the process model. The glue model contains a class for each business process flow node that references the input and output objects from the informational model, respecting the cardinalities defined by *DataObjectReferences* (see Fig. 3).

The slicer in our prototype uses an iterator it gets through the dependency injection pattern. We developed a set of iterators to walk-through the business process (forward, backward and simulation mode). This let us perform either backward or forward slicing. Forward slicing will be used in future work.

6   Roll-Back Point Identification

In the previous section, we described our slicing algorithm to extract the set of flow nodes related to the observed error. These flow nodes are the set of *potential* rollback point candidates. However, we argue in the first subsection below that not all candidates should be considered valid rollback points, neither are they the only possible candidates.

In subsection 6.1, we describe the criteria in order to filter those valid candidates from the slice's potential candidates. This will give us a smaller set for the analyst to choose from. Then, we go further on and try to provide the analyst with more guidance by classifying the identified rollback points based on optimizing metrics such as the overhead and the cost. This optimization problem will be described in subsection 6.2. The reader should note that this section establishes our ground ideas which are open for discussion. Although, these ideas have proven to be worth considering through our preliminary validations on a sample of business processes, they are still to be tested on real world case studies and through experiments.

6.1   Filtering Roll-Back Point Candidates

Before describing how we select valid candidates, let's reflect on the circumstances that may cause an erroneous state in the business process. Some authors have proposed taxonomies about causes of exceptions that may happen during a business process execution [10,14,22,23]. For example, Casati *et al.*[22] classify errors as being caused either by a data exception, a temporal exception, an external exception or a process exception [10]. Assuming that the provided business process model specifies correctly process' behavior and that it should realize its objectives under normal circumstances, we will not consider process exceptions. Temporal exceptions happen when part of the business process is constrained with temporal deadlines that have been violated. This kind of exceptions cannot be recovered by a rollback-and-redo kind of handling and are also ruled out. Data exceptions are "raised by modifications to the process relevant data"[10] during the process execution. External exceptions are notified to the process engine by humans or external applications. We further expand on these external exceptions by considering those that are raised due to a process deviation and those which are unrelated to process state. Our example of a customer not receiving all the products she ordered falls in the former, whereas the latter may be an order cancellation by the customer. Similarly to temporal exceptions, we rule out external exceptions not related to a business process malfunction.

From this analysis, we deduce that business process errors that may be corrected by a rollback and re-execute pattern have the commonality of having an activity (or a set thereof) that did not deliver the expected result (i.e. its postconditions). Therefore, under erroneous circumstances, an activity postcondition should not be considered as a contractual bind once the activity is done, but rather as *an expectation* to fulfill its contract. This is due to the fact that an activity result is not usually validated after the activity has been executed (unless there is a verification task). Hence, the set of activities we get from the slice, are the activities we suspect not having met their expectations.

However, some of activities expectations are implicitly validated by downstream activities' preconditions. Indeed, if activity A, with postcondition $p1$, precedes an activity B having $p1$ as one of it's preconditions, we can safely assume that $p1$ is in fact validated and may not be related to the observed error if B has been executed before the interruption. Hence, we can exclude from the set of candidates those activities in the slice having all their postconditions implicitly validated. In our example and the resulting slice in Fig. 4, the activity *Check Order* has its postconditions verified by the *Prepare Order* activity and is therefore ruled out from the set of candidates.

The remaining activities from the slice are those that have a direct or transitive impact on the related error. However re-executing the business process from any of those flow nodes may not produce any change even by knowing the error that has occurred. Indeed, many of business process activities are automated tasks that produce their outputs systematically. Thus, these activities outputs will not change unless their inputs are modified. Therefore, we distinguish between manual and automated tasks.

Manual activities are performed by human agents who are able to change the outcome of the activity knowing the error that occurred. Thus, they are kept in the set of valid candidates. On the other hand, automatic activities are performed according to business rules and algorithms and are not necessarily under the control of the company (e.g. remote web services). Their output is computed systematically from the inputs they receive and thus cannot change their output unless the input is changed. Therefore, we introduce ad-hoc activities as predecessors intended to change the state of the system in order to modify the input of the automated activity.

6.2 Roll-Back Point Ranking

Selecting a rollback point, when many are qualified, is mainly a business decision that should be made by the analyst. Indeed, given the abstraction level from which we consider the business process, there is only a little we know about other dimensions and views involved, like the business strategies, the type of business objects involved, to cite only a few. Furthermore, there is also many ways a business process realizing a given objective could be modeled. In fact, many variability factors exist as the degree of granularity of the modeled tasks, the analyst's experience, corporate modeling guidelines, etc. We conjecture that there is at least as much strategies to choose the best rollback point candidate. Therefore, at this level of abstraction, the best we could achieve is inferring a score we could attribute to each of the candidates. We propose to use a set of metrics (selected by the analyst) to rank candidates against their score and the final decision should be left to analyst's judgement.

Many authors proposed different business process modeling metrics measuring business processes structural aspects. For example, Balasubramanian *et al.* propose a set of metrics to approximate common performance goals [2]. From these metrics, the *branching automation factor* measures the extent to which process flow decisions are determined through definite business rules (rather than human involvement), whereas the *role integration factor* "denotes the extent of integration in the activities carried out by a role within the process" [2]. Gruhn *et al.* also proposed a set of metrics transposed from traditional software engineering into business process modeling as *McCabee complexity* metric and *nesting depth* calculations [16].

Within the context of error handling, we may suggest a set of other relevant metrics. For example, the analyst may favor re-execution paths that minimize the number of redone activities, minimize the number of manual tasks during a redo or favor/avoid the same execution branch.

Also, as we mentioned, this work is the sequel of a previous work where we proposed an approach to model semi-automatically compensation processes based on a business analysis of the process [5,6]. To do so, we relied on the value-chain of the process expressed within the REA ontology [18]. The value-chain view permits us to answer questions such as *why do we perform each activity?* by linking related activities (dualities) within *exchanges* and *conversions* that produce an added-value. We also proposed a pattern based methodology to infer a value-chain from a BPMN business process model [4]. This value-chain view can be leveraged in order to optimize the choice of a rollback point. Indeed, the REA view lets us measure aspects we should want to minimize like the number of completed exchanges/conversions that need to be reversed, the number of external process participants involvement or the lost value.

Finally, we may also consider the error at stake. Some authors have proposed approaches to transform an OCL constraint into a normal conjunctive form (e.g. see [9]). Given such a transformation, an error will have the form *"error =* t_1 *and* t_2 *and... and* t_n*"*. Therefore, recovering from the error boils down to negating any of the terms. Each term having it's own set of referenced variables, we could affect higher scores to activities nearest to the interruption point letting us negate at least one of the conjunction terms.

7   Conclusion

In this paper we presented a novel approach to discover error-specific business process compensation scopes by identifying flow nodes from the business process model qualifying as valid rollback candidates. Our work relies on (1) an extension of the BPMN metamodel to in order to specify OCL-based behavioral specification of business process activities, (2) a slicing algorithm to extract the flow nodes relevant to the observed error, and (3) a set of rules and metrics to filter and rank the flow nodes from the slice. We implemented our slicing algorithm to prove its feasibility and assess its results. We also verified the suitability of the proposed metrics through preliminary validation. A thorougher validation on real case studies and through experiments has still to be done.

There are a couple of limits in our approach that we intend to consider in future works. First, by relying solely on the slice of the business process at a given interruption point and an observed error, we only consider recovering paths that include the interruption point. Although this covers many cases, there are other scenarios that we should cover by taking alternate paths not going through the interruption point but still enable the process to meet it's objectives.

We are also committed to extend our filtering rules to reduce the set of rollback candidates and increase their precision. For example, while ruling out some activities by validating their postconditions implicitly, we only considered syntactic equality between OCL expressions. As there are many ways to express the same condition in OCL, we believe we can perform a stronger inclusion test through a constraint satisfaction problem approach (e.g. see [8]).

Another aspect we should look into is the usability of our approach. Asking a business analyst to write OCL constraints could be a haunting task. We could alleviate this limit by 1) proposing an alternate domain specific language that would be less expressive but easier to comprehend and closer to analyst's domain, and 2) inferring part of the behavioral specifications from other process views like business process objectives and/or capabilities.

References

1. Awad, A., Decker, G., Weske, M.: Efficient compliance checking using BPMN-Q and temporal logic. In: Dumas, M., Reichert, M., Shan, M.-C. (eds.) BPM 2008. LNCS, vol. 5240, pp. 326–341. Springer, Heidelberg (2008)
2. Balasubramanian, S., Gupta, M.: Structural metrics for goal based business process design and evaluation. BPM Journal **11**(6), 680–694 (2005)
3. Best, E., Rakow, A.: A Slicing technique for business processes. In: UNISCON 2008, Klagenfurt, Austria, pp. 45–51 (2008)
4. Boubaker, A., Cherif, D., Leshob, A., Mili, H.: Value-chain discovery from business process models. In: Frank, U., Loucopoulos, P., Pastor, Ó., Petrounias, I. (eds.) PoEM 2014. LNBIP, vol. 197, pp. 26–41. Springer, Heidelberg (2014)
5. Boubaker, A., Mili, H., Charif, Y., Leshob, A.: Methodology and tool for business process compensation design. In: EDOC Workshops, Vancouver, Canada (2013)
6. Boubaker, A., Mili, H., Charif, Y., Leshob, A.: Towards a framework for modeling business compensation processes. In: Nurcan, S., Proper, H.A., Soffer, P., Krogstie, J., Schmidt, R., Halpin, T., Bider, I. (eds.) BPMDS 2013 and EMMSAD 2013. LNBIP, vol. 147, pp. 139–153. Springer, Heidelberg (2013)
7. Cabot, J.: From declarative to imperative UML / OCL operation specifications. In: ER 2007, Auckland, New Zealand, pp. 198–213 (2007)
8. Cabot, J., Clarisó., Riera, D.: UMLtoCSP:tool for the formal verification of UML/OCL models using constraint programming. In: ASE, pp. 547–548 (2007)
9. Cabot, J., Conesa, J.: Automatic integrity constraint evolution due to model subtract operations. In: Wang, S., Tanaka, K., Zhou, S., Ling, T.-W., Guan, J., Yang, D., Grandi, F., Mangina, E.E., Song, I.-Y., Mayr, H.C. (eds.) ER Workshops 2004. LNCS, vol. 3289, pp. 350–362. Springer, Heidelberg (2004)
10. Casati, F., Cugola, G.: Error handling in process support systems. In: Romanovsky, A., Cheraghchi, H.S., Lindskov Knudsen, J., Babu, C.S. (eds.) ECOOP-WS 2000. LNCS, vol. 2022, pp. 251–270. Springer, Heidelberg (2001)
11. Dijkman, R.M., Dumas, M., Ouyang, C.: Semantics and analysis of business process models in BPMN. Info. and Soft. Technology **50**(12), 1281–1294 (2008)
12. Eclipse Foundation. Eclipe Modeling Framework. http://www.eclipse.org/emf/
13. Eclipse Foundation. EclipseOCL v. 5.0.3. http://www.eclipse.org/modeling/mdt/?project=ocl
14. Ge, X., Paige, R.F., McDermid, J.A.: Failures of a business process in enterprise systems. In: Cruz-Cunha, M.M., Varajão, J., Powell, P., Martinho, R. (eds.) CENTERIS 2011, Part I. CCIS, vol. 219, pp. 139–146. Springer, Heidelberg (2011)
15. Golani, M., Gal, A.: Flexible business process management using forward stepping and alternative paths. In: van der Aalst, W.M.P., Benatallah, B., Casati, F., Curbera, F. (eds.) BPM 2005. LNCS, vol. 3649, pp. 48–63. Springer, Heidelberg (2005)
16. Gruhn, V., Laue, R.: Approaches for business process model complexity metrics. In Tech. for Business Information Systems, pp. 13–24. Springer (2007)

17. Kosiuczenko, P.: Specification of invariability in OCL. Software & Systems Modeling **12**(2), 415–434 (2011)
18. McCarthy, W.E.: The REA Accounting Model. The Accounting Review **57**(3), 554–578 (1982)
19. Mili, H., Godin, R., Tremblay, G., Dorfeuille, W.: Towards a methodology for designing compensation processes in long-running business transactions. In: MCETECH 2006, Montreal, pp. 137–148 (2006)
20. OMG. Object Constraint Language (2012). http://www.omg.org/spec/OCL/2.3.1/
21. Rabbi, F., Wang, H., MacCaull, W., Rutle, A.: A Model Slicing Method for Workflow Verification. Elect. Notes in Theoretical CS **295**, 79–93 (2013)
22. Russell, N., van der Aalst, W.M.P., ter Hofstede, A.H.M.: Workflow exception patterns. In: Martinez, F.H., Pohl, K. (eds.) CAiSE 2006. LNCS, vol. 4001, pp. 288–302. Springer, Heidelberg (2006)
23. Thaisongsuwan, T., Senivongse, T.: Applying software fault tolerance patterns to WS-BPEL processes. In: 8th JCCSE Conference, pp. 269–274 (2011)
24. Tip, F.: A Survey of Program Slicing Techniques. Journal of programming languages **3**(3), 121–189 (1995)
25. van der Aalst, W.M.P., Hirnschall, A., Verbeek, H.M.W.E.: An alternative way to analyze workflow graphs. In: Pidduck, A.B., Mylopoulos, J., Woo, C.C., Ozsu, M.T. (eds.) CAiSE 2002. LNCS, vol. 2348, pp. 535–552. Springer, Heidelberg (2002)
26. Weiser, M.: Program Slicing. IEEE Transactions on Software Engineering, SE-10(4) 352–357 (1984)
27. Weske, M.: Business Process Management: Concepts, Languages, Architectures, 2nd edn. Springer (2012)

Specification and Detection of Business Process Antipatterns

Francis Palma[1,2](✉), Naouel Moha[1], and Yann-Gaël Guéhéneuc[2]

[1] Département d'informatique, Université du Québec à Montréal, Montréal, Canada
moha.naouel@uqam.ca
[2] Ptidej Team, DGIGL, École Polytechnique de Montréal, Montréal, Canada
{francis.palma,yann-gael.gueheneuc}@polymtl.ca

Abstract. Structured business processes (SBPs) are now in enterprises the prominent solution to software development problems through orchestrating Web services. By their very nature, SBPs evolve through adding new or modifying existing functionalities. Those changes may deteriorate the process design and introduce *process antipatterns*—poor but recurring solutions that may degrade processes design quality and hinder their maintenance and evolution. However, to date, few solutions exist to detect such antipatterns to facilitate the maintenance and evolution and improve the quality of process design. We propose SODA-BP (Service Oriented Detection for Antipatterns in Business Processes), supported by a framework for specifying and detecting *process antipatterns*. To validate SODA-BP, we specify eight antipatterns and perform their detection on a set of randomly selected 35 SBPs form a corpus of more than 150 collected processes from an open-source search engine. Some of the SBPs were modified by adding, removing, or modifying process elements to introduce noise in them. Results shows that SODA-BP has an average detection precision of more than 75% and recall of 100%.

Keywords: Business process · Antipatterns · Specification · Detection

1 Introduction

BPMN (Business Process Model and Notation) [1] is broadly used by business analysts for modeling workflows using a graphical notation. BPEL4WS (Business Process Execution Language for Web Services) [2] provides an executable form for graphical process models and is now the *de-facto* standard to implement structured business processes (SBPs) on top of Web services technology.

Like any other software artefacts, SBPs may evolve, *i.e.*, changes may take place (1) by modifying the existing tasks and–or adding new tasks or elements (2) by modifying the flow in the processes. This evolution of SBPs may deteriorate their designs over time and introduce poor but recurring solutions to process design problems—*process antipatterns*. Process antipatterns describe common design problems in SBPs that may hinder their maintenance and evolution and result in poor quality of design (QoD) [3].

© Springer International Publishing Switzerland 2015
M. Benyoucef et al. (Eds.): MCETECH 2015, LNBIP 209, pp. 37–52, 2015.
DOI: 10.1007/978-3-319-17957-5_3

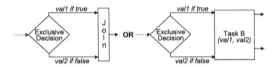

Fig. 1. Deadlock Through Decision-Join Pair

The *Deadlock Through Decision-Join Pair* [3] as shown in Figure 1 using the IBM WebSphere Business Modeling notation[1] is a common process antipattern where a *decision* node may appear before a *join* gateway. This structure leads to a deadlock: the *decision* always triggers a single output while the *join* waits for inputs on all of its branches. Alternatively, as a variant of this antipattern, if a *task* produces two alternative outputs, *i.e.*, behaves like an *exclusive decision*, and the following *task* requires both the outputs as its input, then there is also a *deadlock*. The presence of such antipatterns in SBPs degrades the QoD and may hinder their maintenance and evolution. Therefore, for SBPs, the automatic detection of such antipatterns is an important activity by assessing their design (1) to ease their maintenance and evolution and (2) to improve their QoD.

In the literature, a number of process antipatterns in graphical process models [3–6] have been defined and several approaches have been proposed to analyse and detect those antipatterns [7–13]. To date, however, the detection of antipatterns in structured processes still did not receive much attention. The approaches dedicated to graphical process models from the literature cannot be exploited for SBPs due to several conceptual differences [14]. The transition from graph-oriented BPMN to block-structured BPEL4WS is not isomorphic, prone to semantic ambiguities, differ in representing some *constructs*, and are implemented with two different classes of language.

We introduced an approach in our previous work [14] for detecting process antipatterns in SBPs. We presented seven antipatterns using if-then *inference rules* and performed the detection of two antipatterns on three example processes. In this paper, we provide a complementary approach called SODA-BP (Service Oriented Detection for Antipatterns in Business Processes) supported by an underlying framework, SOFA (Service Oriented Framework for Antipatterns) to specify and detect process antipatterns. We also define a specification language after a thorough domain analysis of process antipatterns from the literature [3–6]. SODA-BP relies on this specification language to specify process antipatterns in terms of metrics, process elements, and–or constructs.

To validate our approach, first, we specify process antipatterns using our defined domain specific language. Then, we implement their detection algorithms following the specified rules, and, finally, we apply those algorithms on several SBPs, which, in turn, return identified antipatterns. Our detection results show the effectiveness of SODA-BP: it can detect eight process antipatterns with an average precision of more than 75% and with a recall of 100% in 35 processes.

---

[1] http://www-03.ibm.com/software/products/en/modeler-advanced

Thus, compared to our previous work [14], the main contributions of this paper are: (1) the definition of a rule-based domain specific language to specify process antipatterns, (2) the definition of ten new business process-specific metrics, (3) the specification of eight process antipatterns from the literature [3–6] using the defined language, (4) the extension of the SOFA framework by adding ten process-specific metrics from its early version [15] to allow the detection of process antipatterns, and, finally, (5) the validation of SODA-BP for eight process antipatterns on a set of 35 BPs randomly-selected form a corpus of more than 150 collected processes from an open-source search engine.

The rest of the paper is organised as follows. Section 2 discuses the motivation. Section 3 briefly describes the contributions from the literature on the specification and detection of process antipatterns. Section 4 presents our approach SODA-BP, while Section 5 presents its validation along with detailed discussions. Finally, Section 6 concludes the paper and sketches future work.

2   Motivation

A typical business-driven development starts with modeling process tasks and later aims at their technical implementations. Thus, models are the central artefact in any development project and are used to map business requirements and information technology (IT).

Modeling phase is the primary step where business analysts visually model business processes, *i.e.*, using BPMN notations [1]. At this step, the models describe the workflow of the processes but do not contain all the information to execute them. In the next step, the execution logic or code to orchestrate predefined services is derived from those design models, *e.g.*, using BPEL4WS [2], which is the standard executable language for interactions among Web services. Antipatterns in a business process can be introduced in the two steps discussed before: (1) due to the Business-IT gap, *i.e.*, when desired user requirements may not properly be achieved by the services during service development step; and (2) due to the IT-IT gap, *i.e.*, during the process implementation step where some technical limitations may hinder the appropriate translation of business models into executable and logically composed services chain in the form of tasks.

From Graph-Based Business Models to Executable Processes: Business analysts mostly rely on BPMN-models to transform user requirements into workflow models trying to reflect users' business goals as well as to guide in-house developers for the technical parts. The BPMN specification [1] provides an informal and partial mapping of such graph-based models to executable concrete processes. Therefore, developers must take caution while writing the structured SBPs because there exist some significant conceptual differences between graphical process models and executable processes. Here, among many, we list some of conceptual differences that may lead to the introduction of antipatterns: (1) The transition from workflow models to executable processes is not isomorphic and prone to semantic ambiguities, which may cause the loss of design considerations; (2) Workflow models and executable processes originate from different sources (*i.e.*, users and business analysts *vs.* technical analysts) and are employed at different stages of the BP management life cycle; (3) Workflow models and executable processes differ in representing some significant *constructs* and *control flows*. For example, block-structured executable processes and graph-oriented models differ in representing *loops, splits, joins, conditions*, and *goto*; and (4) The transformation between artefacts, *i.e.*, from workflow models to executable processes, is mostly performed manually by the architects and developers, which creates higher risk of introducing design anomalies.

Therefore, process antipatterns exist and will likely be introduced and must be detected as early as possible.

3   Related Work

The literature has already a rich catalog of antipatterns defined by the process modeling community [3–6], with some analysis and detection approaches [7–13], most of which deal with graphical models.

For example, Onoda *et al.* [4] described a set of five deadlock antipatterns. Later, Maruta *et al.* [9] proposed detection algorithms for those antipatterns. With a focus on the quality of process modeling, Persson *et al.* [5] and Stirna *et al.* [6] discussed 13 antipatterns with their possible causes and impacts and presented them as common mistakes that the modelers should avoid. Koehler and Vanhatalo [3] also reported 14 antipatterns in IBM WebSphere process models, while Laue and Awad [12] proposed the first visualisation approach of process antipatterns after detecting them in graphical models and argued that visualising the antipatterns can ease their understanding and correction.

Gruhn and Laue [10] employed a heuristic-based approach to detect modeling antipatterns. By translating different elements of graphical models into Prolog facts and rules, the authors detected modeling errors that may hinder the soundness and correctness of the models (*e.g.*, deadlocks). Instead of using Prolog, Trčka *et al.* [11] described eight process antipatterns using temporal logic. Finally, relying on Petri nets, Awad *et al.* [8] performed the detection and correction of data-flow anomalies in graphical process models. Ouyang *et al.* [16], using the Petri nets, mainly focused on the reachability and message-consuming activity analysis.

Based on these previous works, the gaps in the literature can be summarised as follows: (1) the approaches to detect antipatterns were studied mostly for graphical models, while the structured business processes (SBPs) were not considered, *i.e.*, a concrete approach for specifying and detecting process antipatterns in SBPs is lacking and (2) diverse runtime quality aspects, *e.g.*, *availability* or *response time* of involved Web services were not considered, those can be computed by concretely executing the SBPs. We plan to perform such dynamic analysis of SBPs as one of our future works.

Considering the conceptual differences between graph-oriented BPMN and block-structured BPEL4WS representations discussed in [14], the detection approaches discussed above dedicated to graphical process models are not applicable to the structured processes.

4   The SODA-BP Approach

We consequently developed the SODA-BP approach (Service Oriented Detection for Antipatterns in Business Processes) dedicated to structured business processes (SBPs). SODA-BP involves three steps:

Step 1: Specification of Process Antipatterns – In this step, we identify relevant properties of process antipatterns that we use to define a domain-specific language (DSL). We use this DSL to specify process antipatterns based on rules.

Step 2: Generation of Detection Algorithms – This step involves the generation of detection algorithms from the specifications in the former step. In this paper, we performed this step by implementing concretely the algorithms in conformance with the rules specified in Step 1. We plan to automate this step in the future.

Step 3: Detection of Process Antipatterns – In the last step, we apply the implemented detection algorithms from Step 2 on SBPs to detect and report process antipatterns.

The next sections present the first two steps in details. The last step is discussed in Section 5, where we report the validation of SODA-BP.

4.1   Specification of Process Antipatterns

To specify process antipatterns, we carried out a thorough domain analysis of antipatterns for SBPs by investigating their definitions and descriptions from the literature, namely [3–6,11,17]. After the domain analysis, we identified all the quantifiable properties related to each antipattern, which include all static properties related to process design, *e.g.*, presence of *fork*, *merge*, *gateways*, *inputs*, and *outputs*, etc. In general, we can easily identify those static properties from the abstract processes. Those properties play a key role and are sufficient in defining a DSL, which allows engineers to specify antipatterns in the form of rules, using their own experience and expertise.

The DSL provides the engineers with a high-level domain-related abstractions to express various properties of process antipatterns. Indeed, a DSL gives more flexibility than implementing the *ad-hoc* detection algorithms by focusing on *what* to detect and not *how* [18]. Other rule-based declarative languages exist, like the Object Constraint Language (OCL) [19] that describes rules to apply on Unified Modeling Language (UML) models However, these languages do not suit our purpose because we specify process antipatterns with a higher level of abstraction with discrete *domain* expressiveness.

We define the syntax of our DSL using a Backus-Naur Form (BNF) grammar. We apply a rule-based technique for specifying process antipatterns, *i.e.*, each rule card combines a set of rules. Figure 2 presents the grammar of our DSL. A *rule_card* denoted with RULE_CARD includes a name and a rule body (see Figure 2, line 1). The content of the rule card is identified as *content_rule* (line 3), and may enclose a *metric*, a *process_fragment*, or even a reference to another RULE_CARD (lines 3 to 4). A *process_ fragment* is the smallest part of a process model with the arrangement of at least two process elements that modelers place while modeling the processes [20]. A *process_fragment* (see lines 5 to 7) can be a binary

```
 1  rule_card        ::= RULE_CARD rule_cardName {(rule)⁺};
 2  rule             ::= RULE ruleName {content_rule};
 3  content_rule     ::= metric | process_fragment
 4                     | RULE_CARD rule_cardName
 5  process_fragment ::= binary_rel | binary_rel relType element
 6                     | element relType binary_rel | ruleType operator binary_rel
 7                     | element relType binary_rel relType element
 8  ruleType         ::= ruleName | rule_cardName
 9  metric           ::= id_metric comparator num_value
10  id_metric        ::= NICF | NIDF | NII | NIO | NOF | NOM | NUI | NUO | NIU | NIP
11  comparator       ::= < | ≤ | = | ≠ | ≥ | >
12  binary_rel       ::= element relType element | element operator element
13                     | ruleType operator ruleType | element operator ruleType
14                     | ruleType operator element
15  operator         ::= AND | OR | NOT
16  relType          ::= S:PRECEDE | W:PRECEDE | BACKCONN
17  element          ::= PROCESS | FORK | MERGE | JOIN | TASK | S_NODE | X_DECISION | I_DECISION
18  rule_cardName, ruleName ∈ string
19  num_value ∈ double
```

Fig. 2. BNF grammar of the DSL of SODA-BP (we show only BP-specific metrics)

relation (*binary_rel*), *i.e.*, a simple relation between two elements (line 12) or can describe more complex relations by combining different *binary_rel* with other elements through a relation type, (*i.e.*, *relType*). A *binary_rel* may also connect two rules or elements using an *operator* (line 13). The *operator* set includes common logical operators like AND, OR, NOT (line 15). The *metric* can contain an *id_metric* compared with a numeric value (line 9). The *comparator* includes the common mathematical comparators (line 11). The DSL has three typical relation types (*relType*), *e.g.*, a strong or immediate precedence (S:PRECEDE), a weak precedence (W:PRECEDE), and a back connection (BACKCONN) (line 16). In W:PRECEDE, an *element* may not appear right after another *element*. In contrast, for a S:PRECEDE, the precedence is with the immediate *element*. The *element* set includes most common modeling elements from a task (TASK) to different types of decision gateways, such as X_DECISION or I_DECISION (line 17). Other elements are FORK, MERGE, JOIN, the stop node (S_NODE), etc.

Our metric suite (line 10) currently includes 23 static and dynamic metrics. The ten newly defined process-specific static metrics are: number of identical control-flows (NICF), number of identical data-flows (NIDF), number of identical inputs (NII), number of identical outputs (NIO), number of forks (NOF), number of merges (NOM), number of unused inputs (NUI), number of unused outputs (NUO), number of inputs undeclared (NIU), and number of inputs unproduced (NIP). New metrics can be added in the DSL to specify new antipatterns.

Figure 3 shows the rule card for *Deadlock Through Decision-Join Pair* [3] antipattern, introduced in Section 1. When an *exclusive decision* appears before a *join* gateway (or a *task*), as shown in the rule card: X_DECISION S:PRECEDE (JOIN OR TASK), *i.e.*, an *exclusive decision* immediately precedes a *join* (or a *task*). Then, this structure in the process may lead to a deadlock because the *exclusive decision* always triggers a single output, whereas the immediate *join* or *task* in the process requires input on all of its branches. We specify seven other process antipatterns as shown in Figure 5.

```
RULE_CARD Deadlock {
  RULE Deadlock {X_DECISION S:PRECEDE (JOIN OR
  TASK)};
};
```

Fig. 3. The *Deadlock Through Decision-Join Pair* process antipattern

4.2 Generation of Detection Algorithms

The second step involves the implementation of the detection algorithms from the rule cards specified for each process antipattern. For each process antipattern, we implement all the related metrics following its specification and implement the detection algorithm in JAVA, which can directly be applied on any BP. However, in the future, we want to automate this algorithm generation process following a similar technique presented in [15].

4.3 Detection of Process Antipatterns

To ease the detection step, we preprocess the SBPs and generate process structure trees (PSTs). Such parsing of processes also helps their comprehension and allows finding reusable sub-processes and applying rules on process trees [21]. For our purpose, we automatically transform the SBPs into more abstract and simplified PSTs after eliminating inessential process elements and attributes.

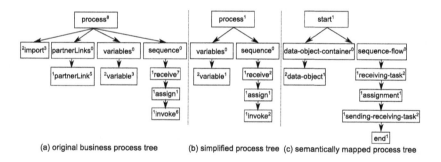

(a) original business process tree   (b) simplified process tree (c) semantically mapped process tree

Fig. 4. An example process structure tee (PST) of a business process (each node is preceded by a integer representing the number of instances of that node and succeeded by another representing number of attributes of a node)

SBPs are complex entities and their sizes cause their structural complexity to grow further. However, every implementation details are not required for our analysis since we are interested in the static analysis of SBPs. In fact, we do not lose any essential process information specific to our rules-based approach, *i.e.*, all the tasks, input/output data, control-flow information, and so on (see Figure 4(b)). Subsequently, we automatically generate a final process tree that is semantically equivalent to the previous tree and are mappable to our language (see Figure 4(c)). Engineers can use the latter version of the process tree for further analysis, *e.g.*, for implementing rules to apply on business processes.

Underlying Framework: The SOFA (Service Oriented Framework for Antipatterns) framework was originally presented elsewhere [15] supported detecting antipatterns in service-based systems. We further extend the framework to support the detection of process antipatterns. SOFA itself is developed using the SCA standards [22] and is composed of several components with distinct functional supports. The SOFA framework includes several components: (1) the *Rule Specification* component for specifying rules, (2) the *Algorithm Generation* component for automatically generating detection algorithms based on specified rules, and (3) the *Detection* component for applying generated detection algorithms on the SBPs.

We added a new `Process Handler` component to SOFA to allow the detection of process antipatterns. The different functionalities performed by the `Process Handler` component are: (1) it parses a given process and filter unnecessary information for generating a PST, (2) it then maps the abstract process model to our rule-based language, and (3) uses the *Detection* component to apply the detection algorithms on the process trees, which reports the detected process antipatterns.

We extended the SOFA framework from its early version by adding ten new business process-specific metrics as described in Section 4.1. Combining those new metrics and different *process elements*, we specify eight business process-specific antipatterns. We list them in Table 1 and show their specifications in Figure 5. The addition of an antipattern requires the implementation of each of its metric if it is not already available following its specification. A metric can be reused for other antipatterns if they share that metric in their specifications.

5 Validation

Through our experiment, we aim to show (1) the generality and extensibility of our DSL and SOFA framework and (2) the accuracy and performance of the detection algorithms in terms of precision and recall.

Assumptions: We define three assumptions to evaluate in our experiment:

A1. Generality: *The DSL allows the specification of different process antipatterns.* This assumption supports the applicability of the SODA-BP, which relies on metric-based rule cards for specifying process antipatterns.

A2. Accuracy: *Antipattern detection algorithms have at least a precision of 75%, and a recall of 100%.* Assuming that the antipatterns have a negative impact on the design, we target a recall of 100% for antipatterns, which ensures that we do not miss any existing antipatterns. The *precision* concerns the detection accuracy of our specified rules and the corresponding detection algorithms. We also measure the *specificity* of our specified rules.

A3. Extensibility: *Our DSL and SOFA framework are extensible by adding new metrics and process antipatterns.* Through this assumption, we show that new antipatterns can be specified by adding new or combining existing metrics, *process elements*, and different operators and comparators, and later, those antipatterns can be detected using the extended SOFA framework.

Table 1. Description of the eight process antipatterns

Cyclic Deadlock through Join-Fork and Join-Decision Pair: A *backward connection* exists from an *exclusive decision* (or a *fork*) to a *join*. The *join* waits for inputs on all of its branches. However, one of its *incoming branches* can only receive the input after the *join* has been executed in the first cycle, because its input is initiated from an *exclusive decision*, later in the process. This *cyclic dependency* between the *join* and the *decision* (or *fork*), where the *join* must be executed before the *decision* (or *fork*) may cause a *cyclic deadlock* [3].

Cyclic Lack of Synchronisation through Merge-Fork Pair: Occurs in the cyclic structures when *backward connections* appear in *branches* that are executed in *parallel*, which are *not synchronised* by a *join* before the backward connection is added to the process. In such case, each of the backward connections results from the same *fork* and ends in a *merge* located earlier in the process. This antipattern may result in an infinite iterations of the process [3].

Dangling Inputs and Outputs: The *inputs* and *outputs* of an *activity* or gateway remain *unconnected* or *unused*. Dangling outputs are *produced* by a *task* or *sub-process*, but *never used* anywhere in the process. In contrast, dangling inputs might cause *deadlocks* if the data input of– a *gateway* or an *activity* is never provided, which is required by the process [3].

Deadlock Through Decision-Join Pair: The *decision* node appears *before* a *join* gateway. This structure leads to a *deadlock*: the *decision* triggers a single output, while the *join* waits for inputs on all of its branches, but only one input is supplied. Alternatively, if a task produces two alternative outputs, *i.e.*, behaves like an *exclusive decision*, and the following task requires both the outputs as its input, then there is also a *deadlock* [3].

Lack of Synchronisation through Fork-Merge Pair: The *fork-merge* pair appears. The *fork* triggers *output* on all of its **outgoing branches**, while the *merge* always wait for input on only one of its incoming connections. Later in the process, another final *merge* may cause *synchronisation problem* because the latter *merge* requires all the inputs, which are *not available* yet [3].

Missing Data: Certain *data elements* are *required* but were *not created* or have been *deleted*. This may cause *deadlock* for a certain activity, or even for the whole process depending on the execution context and the design of the process [11].

Multiple Connections between Activities: The *redundant control-flow* and–or *data-flow* connections exist between tasks. This antipattern has two variants: (i) *multiple control-flows* between *tasks* that increase the process structural complexity, and (ii) *multiple data-flow connections* of the *same type* from a task [3].

Passing Shared Data along Several Branches: Shared inputs or *outputs* are *duplicated* along several *branches*. Typically, the duplication of outputs or inputs of a task hinders the reusability of a process fragment. The best practice is to use a *fork* for *distributing* single *input* among the *branches* and a *join* for *aggregating* unique outputs into a single flow [3].

Subjects: We specify eight process antipatterns by applying our SODA-BP approach. Table 1 describes those antipatterns collected from the literature [3–6,11,17]. We selected those antipatterns because they were described in the literature as being most common and frequent. In Table 1, we mark the relevant properties related to the specification for each antipattern in bold-italics. We show the specifications and graphical representations of those antipatterns in Figure 5 using the IBM WebSphere notation[1] to ease their understanding.

Objects: Real structured business processes (SBPs) are often not freely available for validation purposes. We used the ohloh.net portal as our source of SBPs because it provides a collection of publicly-available processes. That portal facilitates searching business processes along with their underlying Web services. We performed the experiment on a set of 35 SBPs randomly-selected form a corpus of more than 150 collected processes from ohloh.net. The complete set of analysed SBPs is available online at sofa.uqam.ca/soda-bp/, where we also detail their modifications.

```
RULE_CARD CyclicDeadlock {
  RULE CyclicDeadlock {JOIN:i W:PRECEDE
  (X_DECISION OR FORK) BACKCONN JOIN:i};
};

RULE_CARD CyclicLackOfSynchronisation {
  RULE CyclicLackOfSynchronisation
  {MERGE:i W:PRECEDE (FORK OR I_DECISION)
  BACKCONN MERGE:i};
};

RULE_CARD DanglingInputs {
  RULE DanglingInputs {NUI = 0};
};
RULE_CARD DanglingOutputs {
  RULE DanglingOutputs {NUO = 0};
};

RULE_CARD LackOfSynchronisation {
  RULE LackOfSynchronisation {(MultiForkAndMerge AND
  MergePrecedence) W:PRECEDE MERGE:i};
  RULE MultiForkAndMerge {MultiFork AND MultiMerge};
  RULE MultiFork {NOF ≥ 1};
  RULE MultiMerge {NOM > 2};
  RULE MergePrecedence {FORK W:PRECEDE MERGE:j};
};

RULE_CARD MissingData {
  RULE MissingData {RequiredInputData AND DanglingInput};
  RULE RequiredInputData {UndeclaredData AND UnproducedData};
  RULE UndeclaredData {NIU ≥ 1};
  RULE UnproducedData {NIP ≥ 1};
  RULE DanglingInput {RULE_CARD DanglingInputs};
};

RULE_CARD MultipleConnection {
  RULE MultipleConnection
  {MultiControlFlow OR MultiDataFlow};
  RULE MultiControlFlow {NICF > 1};
  RULE MultiDataFlow {NIDF > 1};
};

RULE_CARD PassingSharedData {
  RULE PassingSharedData {MultiInput OR MultiOutput};
  RULE MultiInput {NII > 1};
  RULE MultiOutput {NIO > 1};
};
```

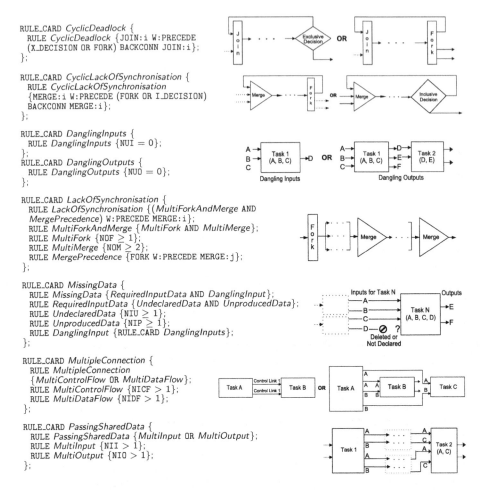

Fig. 5. Rule cards for different process antipatterns.

Process: We specified the rule cards for eight process antipatterns, implemented their detection algorithms, and applied those algorithms on the 35 SBPs to detect any existing antipatterns in two steps. First, we introduced some noise within the selected SBPs by adding, removing, or changing process elements to thoroughly validate the detection. The introduction of noise was performed by two Master students who were not the part of our experiment by adding or removing variables and parallel or sequence of tasks, and so on. However, they made sure such introduction of noise did not affect the stability of the original processes. Then, we performed detection on the set of 35 SBPs.

We performed the validation of the detection results by analysing the process elements manually (1) to validate that those process elements are true positives and (2) to identify false negatives, *i.e.*, occurrences of antipatterns missed in the SBPs. We used the measures of precision and recall to show our detection accuracy. Precision concerns the ratio between the true detected antipatterns and all

Table 2. Details on the eight antipattern detection results for the 35 processes

Antipatterns	Processes	Metrics	Elements Involved	P	R
Cyclic Deadlock	none detected	*N/A*	*N/A*	–	–
Cyclic Lack Of Synchronisation	none detected	*N/A*	*N/A*	–	–
Dangling [.5pt/1pt] *Inputs* [.5pt/1pt]	Loan	NUI=0	"creditRatingInput123"	[3/3]	[3/3]
	purchaseOrder	NUI=0	"shippingRequest1"	100%	100%
	SalesforceFlow	NUI=0	"output1"		
[.5pt/1pt] *Dangling* [.5pt/1pt] *Outputs* [.5pt/1pt]	AbsenceRequest	NUO=0	"createTaskResponse1"		
	FlightBooking	NUO=0	"Output2"	[4/4]	[4/4]
	Loan	NUO=0	"creditRatingOutput123"	100%	100%
	SalesforceFlow	NUO=0	"Output1"		
Deadlock	none detected	*N/A*	*N/A*	–	–
[.5pt/1pt] [.5pt/1pt] [.5pt/1pt] *Lack of* [.5pt/1pt] *Synchronisation* [.5pt/1pt] [.5pt/1pt] [.5pt/1pt]	auction	NOF=2,NOM=2	*MergePrecedence=true*		
	BuyBook	NOF=1,NOM=3	*MergePrecedence=true*		
	LoanFlowPlus	NOF=1,NOM=2	*MergePrecedence=true*		
	nrbc	NOF=4,NOM=7	*MergePrecedence=true*	[8/8]	[8/8]
	Travel	NOF=1,NOM=2	*MergePrecedence=true*	100%	100%
	AbsenceRequest	NOF=1,NOM=3	*MergePrecedence=true*		
	GovernanceBPEL	NOF=1,NOM=3	*MergePrecedence=true*		
	VacationRequest	NOF=1,NOM=2	*MergePrecedence=true*		
[.5pt/1pt] *Missing Data* [.5pt/1pt] [.5pt/1pt] [.5pt/1pt]	ClaimsApproval	NIU=1,NIP=1,NUI=0	"dummyVar"		
	Correlation	NIU=1,NIP=1,NUI=0	"CorrelationProcess-OperationIn"	[5/5]	[5/5]
	Loan	NIU=1,NIP=1,NUI=0	"creditRatingInput123"	100%	100%
	purchaseOrder	NIU=1,NIP=1,NUI=0	"shippingRequest1"		
	SalesforceFlow	NIU=1,NIP=1,NUI=0	"output1"		
Multiple [.5pt/1pt] *Connections*	loan_approval	NICF=2	"receive-to-assess"	[2/2]	[2/2]
	purchaseOrder	NICF=2	"ship-to-invoice" "ship-to-scheduling"	100%	100%
[.5pt/1pt] *Passing* [.5pt/1pt] *Shared Data* [.5pt/1pt] [.5pt/1pt]	BuyBook	NII=2	"BookRequest"		
	LoanFlowPlus	NII=2	"loanApplication"	[3/5]	[3/3]
	Travel	NII=2	"FlightDetails"	60%	100%
	DlLoanService	NII=2	"output"		
	GovernanceBPEL	NII=2	"applicationDeployerPL1"		
Average				93.3%	100%

detected antipatterns. Recall is the ratio between the true detected antipatterns and all existing true antipatterns. Two students performed a thorough and independent analysis after we provided them with the SBPs and a short description of each process antipattern. The manual validation of the processes was a laborious task that demanded 30 minutes to an hour per process depending on the size of the process, for each antipattern.

5.1 Results

Table 2 shows the detailed detection results of the eight process antipatterns. We found six antipatterns, namely *Lack of Synchronisation, Passing Shared Data,* and *Dangling Inputs/Outputs*, and so on, in 16 processes. In Table 2, we report the antipatterns in the first column, followed by the list of processes having these antipatterns in the second. In the third column, we present the metric values and the different process elements involved in the detected antipatterns in column 4. Finally, the last two columns report the precision (P) and recall (R). Detailed detection results are also available online at sofa.uqam.ca/soda-bp/.

5.2   Discussions of the Results

Figure 6(a) graphically shows the detection of the *Lack of Synchronisation* antipattern in the original version of the auction process. The auction process involves two *forks* (NOF=2) and two *merges* (NOM=2), with the first fork receiving values from the users through the provide task simultaneously and storing them into two different variables, *i.e.*, buyerData and sellerData. After the two process threads merge, there is another parallel invocation of answer task again with two different parameters, *i.e.*, sellerAnswerData and buyerAnswerData.

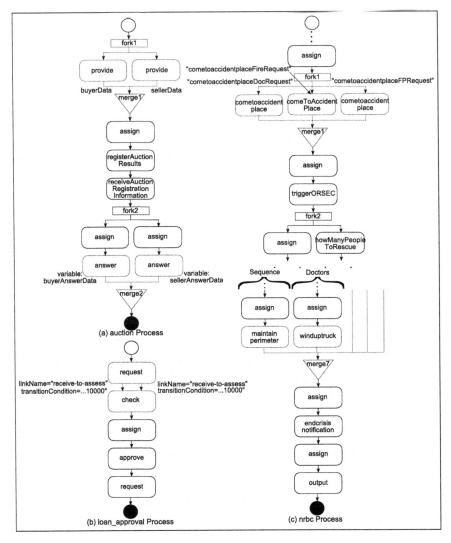

Fig. 6. The detection of *Lack of Synchronisation* in auction process and nrbc process; and the detection of *Multiple Connections* in loan_approval process

A synchronisation problem occurs in the first place where the process may not receive values from the **provide** task at the same time and the *merge* may proceed even with a single response. A good practice to avoid this synchronisation problem is to use a *join* gateway instead, considering the operational difference between the *merge* and *join* gateway.

We detected *Multiple Connections* in the noisy version of loan_approval process (see Figure 6(b) and Table 2) because it contains more than one control-flows (NICF>1). In Figure 6(b), the same "receive-to-assess" control-flow link was defined with the duplicated transition conditions for the **request** receiving task, hence, NICF=2 for "receive-to-assess". Manual validation confirmed this antipattern detection and thus we had a precision and recall of 100%.

The occurrence of *Lack of Synchronisation* was also detected in the original versions of the BuyBook, LoanFlowPlus, and nrbc process. The nrbc process (see Figure 6(c)) has four *forks* (NOF=4) and seven *merges* (NOM=7) within its full process scope. A synchronisation problem may occur in the beginning of the process flow with the invocation of comeToAccidentPlace task simultaneously with three input variables cometoaccidentplaceDocRequest, cometoaccidentplace FireRequest, and cometoaccidentplaceFPRequest. After those three threads *merge*, later in the process, another concurrent execution of two control-flows, *i.e.*, Sequence and Doctors follow a final *merge*. The first *merge*, *i.e.*, merge1, may trigger even without the three invocations of the comeToAccidentPlace task having finished. If that happens, the latter concurrent execution of Sequence and Doctors will not wait and proceed with the consequent execution, which may lead to a lack of synchronisation at the final *merge*, *i.e.*, merge7. The manual analysis confirmed the detection and we thus have a precision and recall of 100% for the *Lack of Synchronisation* antipattern.

The *Dangling Inputs*, *Dangling Outputs*, and *Missing Data* antipatterns were detected in five modified processes. We also detected the *Lack of Synchronisation* antipattern in three other modified SBPs, namely, AbsenceRequest, GovernanceBPEL, and VacationRequest. However, we did not detect any occurrences of three antipatterns within the selected SBPs, namely *Cyclic Deadlock*, *Cyclic Lack of Synchronisation*, and *Deadlock*.

5.3   Discussions of the Assumptions

Following our detection results, we assess all the three assumptions.

A1. Generality: We specified eight process antipatterns (see Table 1) using the rule cards (see Figure 5) from the literature [3–6,11,17]. We defined simpler process antipatterns with few rules, such as *Dangling Inputs and Outputs* and *Passing Shared Data* but also more complex antipatterns with rules combining metrics and *process elements*, such as *Lack of Synchronisation*. Also, we specified rule cards in combination with other rule cards, such as the specification of *Missing Data* antipattern, which includes the *Dangling Inputs* antipattern. Similarly, we can specify other antipatterns defined in the literature. Thus, we can support our first assumption regarding the generality of our DSL.

A2. Accuracy: As shown in Table 2, we obtained an average recall of 100% and an average precision of 93.3% with the set of 35 SBPs. We also have an average specificity, *i.e.*, the proportion of true negatives identified correctly, of 99.02%. Therefore, with an average precision of 93.3%, recall of 100%, and specificity of 99.02%, we positively support our second assumption on the detection accuracy.
A3. Extensibility: We claim that our DSL and SOFA framework are extensible for new antipatterns. In this paper, with ten new process-specific metrics, we specified and detected eight process-specific antipatterns using our framework. In our previous work [15], we specified ten SCA-specific antipatterns using the rule-based language and detected them in SCA systems using SOFA. The designed language is flexible enough for integrating new metrics in the DSL. SOFA also supports the addition of new antipatterns through the implementation of new metrics. With this extensibility feature of our DSL and the SOFA framework we support our third assumption.

5.4   Comparison with the State of the Art Approaches

We compare here SODA-BP with 11 state-of-the-art approaches shown in Table 3. Most of the approaches do not support automatic detection of antipatterns, but the ones that do, focus only on BMPN models and use Petri nets. For example, Maruta *et al.* [9] has an accuracy of 100% with five antipatterns, but the reported results are only for three process models. Gruhn *et al.* [10] and Laue *et al.* [12] have accuracy close to SODA-BP with only six antipatterns after analysing more than 100 models. In contrast, SODA-BP analyses and performs detection for eight antipatterns on 35 processes with the accuracy of more than 90%. Overall, considering the trade-off between the number of BP antipatterns specified and detected and the number of processes analysed, SODA-BP has a good detection accuracy of more than 90%.

Table 3. Comparison of SODA-BP with the state-of-the-art approaches

Contributions	Focus Groups	Perform Automatic Detection?	Number of Patterns / Antipatterns	Accuracy
Awad *et al.* [8]	Data-flow anomalies	×	5	-
Gruhn *et al.* [10]	BPMN soundness properties	✓	6	98.31%
Koehler *et al.* [3]	BPMN modeling errors	×	18	-
Laue *et al.* [12]	BPMN modeling errors	✓	6	95.41%
Lei *et al.* [13]	Data access exceptions in BPEL	×	2	-
Maruta *et al.* [9]	Deadlock patterns in BPs	✓	5	100%
Onoda *et al.* [4]	Deadlock patterns in BPs	×	5	-
Ouyang *et al.* [16]	Reachability analysis	×	3	-
Persson *et al.* [5]	Enterprise modeling practices	×	13	-
Stirna *et al.* [6]	Enterprise modeling practices	×	9	-
Trčka *et al.* [11]	Data-flow errors in models	×	9	-
SODA-BP	Process antipatterns in BPEL4WS	✓	8	93.3%

6   Conclusion and Future Work

Structure business processes (SBPs) are now the prominent means to build enterprise solutions by orchestrating Web services. The presence of process antipatterns in SBPs may hinder maintenance and degrade their quality of design.

Therefore, the detection of antipatterns is important to maintain and improve the process quality.

In this paper, we presented the SODA-BP approach to specify and detect process antipatterns. We specified eight process antipatterns from the literature to support their detection. Then, we applied SODA-BP on a set of 35 SBPs randomly-selected form a corpus of more than 150 collected processes from an open-source search engine, some of which were modified by adding, removing, or modifying process elements to introduce noise within the models. Results show that SODA-BP detects process antipatterns with an average precision of more than 75% and the recall of 100%.

In this paper, we analysed the SBPs statically and currently we are performing dynamic analyses by executing them to collect their runtime properties. We plan also to replicate our evaluation of SODA-BP on real SBPs from our industrial partners. Finally, we intend to focus on the automatic correction of process antipatterns in the future.

Acknowledgments. This work is supported by the NSERC grant, a Canada Research Chair, and a FRQNT grant.

References

1. OMG: (Object Management Group): Business Process Modeling Notation (BPMN) version 1.2. Technical report, January 2009. www.bpmn.org
2. Alves, A., et al.: Web Services Business Process Execution Language Version 2.0. Technical report (2007)
3. Koehler, J., Vanhatalo, J.: Process Anti-Patterns: How to Avoid the Common Traps of Business Process Modeling. IBM WebSphere Developer Technical Journal, February 2007
4. Onoda, S., Ikkai, Y., Kobayashi, T., Komoda, N.: Definition of Deadlock Patterns for Business Processes Workflow Models. IEEE Computer Society (1999)
5. Persson, A., Stirna, J.: How to transfer a knowledge management approach to an organization - A set of patterns and anti-patterns. In: Reimer, U., Karagiannis, D. (eds.) PAKM 2006. LNCS (LNAI), vol. 4333, pp. 243–252. Springer, Heidelberg (2006)
6. Stirna, J., Persson, A.: Anti-patterns as a means of focusing on critical quality aspects in enterprise modeling. In: Halpin, T., Krogstie, J., Nurcan, S., Proper, E., Schmidt, R., Soffer, P., Ukor, R. (eds.) Enterprise, Business-Process and Information Systems Modeling. LNBIP, vol. 29, pp. 407–418. Springer, Heidelberg (2009)
7. Dijkman, R., Dumas, M., nuelos, L.G.B., Käärik, R.: Aligning business process models. In: IEEE International Enterprise Distributed Object Computing Conference, pp. 45–53, September 2009
8. Awad, A., Decker, G., Lohmann, N.: Diagnosing and repairing data anomalies in process models. In: Rinderle-Ma, S., Sadiq, S., Leymann, F. (eds.) BPM 2009. LNBIP, vol. 43, pp. 5–16. Springer, Heidelberg (2010)
9. Maruta, T., Onoda, S., Ikkai, Y., Kobayashi, T., Komoda, N.: A deadlock detection algorithm for business processes workflow models. In: IEEE International Conference on Systems, Man, and Cybernetics, vol. 1, October 1998

10. Gruhn, V., Laue, R.: A Heuristic Method for Detecting Problems in Business Process Models. BPM **16**, 806–821 (2010)
11. Trčka, N., van der Aalst, W.M.P., Sidorova, N.: Data-Flow anti-patterns: discovering Data-Flow errors in workflows. In: van Eck, P., Gordijn, J., Wieringa, R. (eds.) CAiSE 2009. LNCS, vol. 5565, pp. 425–439. Springer, Heidelberg (2009)
12. Laue, R., Awad, A.: Visualization of business process modeling anti patterns. In: Proceedings of the 1st International Workshop on Visual Formalisms for Patterns, vol. 25 (2010)
13. Lei, K., Zhang, P.P., Lang, B.: Data access exception detecting of WS-BPEL process based on workflow nets. In: International Conference on Computational Intelligence and Software Engineering (CiSE), 2010, pp. 1–6 (2010)
14. Palma, F., Moha, N., Guéhéneuc, Y.G.: Detection of process antipatterns: A BPEL perspective. In: Mili, H., Charif, Y., Liu, E., (eds.) Proceedings of the 1st Workshop on Methodologies for Robustness Injectioninto Business Processes, pp. 173–177. IEEE Computer Society, September 2013
15. Moha, N., Palma, F., Nayrolles, M., Conseil, B.J., Guéhéneuc, Y.-G., Baudry, B., Jézéquel, J.-M.: Specification and detection of SOA antipatterns. In: Liu, C., Ludwig, H., Toumani, F., Yu, Q. (eds.) Service Oriented Computing. LNCS, vol. 7636, pp. 1–16. Springer, Heidelberg (2012)
16. Ouyang, C., Verbeek, E., van der Aalst, W.M., Breutel, S., Dumas, M., ter Hofstede, A.H.: WofBPEL: A tool for automated analysis of BPEL processes. In: Benatallah, B., Casati, F., Traverso, P. (eds.) International Conference on Service-Oriented Computing. LNCS, vol. 3826, pp. 484–489. Springer, Berlin Heidelberg (2005)
17. Van Der Aalst, W.M.P., Ter Hofstede, A.H.M., Kiepuszewski, B., Barros, A.P.: Workflow Patterns. Distributed and Parallel Databases **14**(1), 5–51 (2003)
18. Blum, A., Marlet, R.: Architecturing software using a methodology for language development. In: Palamidessi, C., Meinke, K., Glaser, H. (eds.) ALP 1998 and PLILP 1998. LNCS, vol. 1490, pp. 170–194. Springer, Heidelberg (1998)
19. Group, O.M.: Object Constraint Language (OCL), February 2014
20. Ma, Z., Leymann, F.: A lifecycle model for using process fragment in business process modeling. In: Proceedings of Business Process Modeling, Development, and Support (2008)
21. Vanhatalo, J., Vlzer, H., Koehler, J.: The Refined Process Structure Tree. Data & Knowledge Engineering **68**(9), 793–818 (2009). Sixth International Conference on Business Process Management (BPM 2008) Five selected and extended papers
22. OASIS: SCA Service Component Architecture - Assembly Model Specification. Open SOA, Version 1.00, March 2007. www.osoa.org

Coping with Uncertainty in Schema Matching: Bayesian Networks and Agent-Based Modeling Approach

Hicham Assoudi[(✉)] and Hakim Lounis

LATECE, Département d'Informatique, Université du Québec à Montréal,
Montréal, Canada
assoudi.hicham@courrier.uqam.ca, lounis.hakim@uqam.ca

Abstract. Schema matching and mapping are an important tasks for many applications, such as data integration, data warehousing and e-commerce. Many algorithms and approaches were proposed to deal with the problem of automatic schema matching and mapping. In this work, we describe how schema matching problem can be modelled and simulated as agents where each agent learn, reason and act to find the best match in the other schema attributes group. Many differences exist between our approach and the existing practice in schema matching. First and foremost our approach is based on the paradigm Agent-based Modeling and Simulation (ABMS), while, as far as we know, all the current methods do not use ABMS paradigm. Second, the agent's decision-making and reasoning process leverages probabilistic models (Bayesian) for matching prediction and action selection (planning). The results we obtained so far are very encouraging and reinforce our belief that many intrinsic properties of our model, such as simulations, stochasticity and emergence, contribute efficiently to the increase of the matching quality and thus the decrease of the matching uncertainty.

Keywords: Schema matching · Schema mapping · Agent-based modelling and simulation · Bayesian networks · Machine learning

1 Introduction

In a this paper, we propose a new release, based on Bayesian Networks, of our Agent-based Modeling and Simulation approach for the Schema Matching problem called "Schema Matching Agent-based Simulation" (SMAS) [1], [2]. In this new release the agent's decision-making and reasoning process leverages probabilistic models (Bayesian) for matching prediction and action selection (planning). In fact we made the agent's model evolve from the Reflex Agent Model (simple Rule-based) to a Rational Agent Model (using Bayes Networks). Although we have got very good results with the first release, we believe that the new agent's "Rationality" (taking the best decision to achieve the goal) is the way to improve uncertainty management during the process of automatic schema matching.

Please note that the LNCS Editorial assumes that all authors have used the western naming convention, with given names preceding surnames. This determines the structure of the names in the running heads and the author index.

© Springer International Publishing Switzerland 2015
M. Benyoucef et al. (Eds.): MCETECH 2015, LNBIP 209, pp. 53–67, 2015.
DOI: 10.1007/978-3-319-17957-5_4

The rest of the paper is organized as follows. The second section gives a brief literature review, the third section describes and justify the Agent-based Modeling and Simulation approach for Schema Matching problem, the fourth section is devoted to the description of the architecture of SMAS (including the transition from Reflex Agent to Rational Agent), the fifth section introduces the experiments done to validate the approach (a prototype and it's evaluation), and finally the the last section discusses the results and concludes the paper with future work.

2   Related Work

2.1   Schema Matching

Schema matching is to find a pairing of attributes (or groups of attributes) from the source schema and attributes of the target schema such that pairs are likely to be semantically related. In many systems finding such a schema matching is an early step in building a schema mapping. Although these tools comprise a significant step towards fulling the vision of automated schema matching, it has become obvious that the user must accept a degree of imperfection in this process. A prime reason for this is the enormous ambiguity and heterogeneity of data description concepts: It is unrealistic to expect a single mapping engine to identify the correct mapping for any possible concept in a set [3], [4].

Schema matching and mapping concepts are often confused and discussed under the single name "Schema Matching". According to Bohannon et al.[5] the concept of "Schema Matching" is concerned with matching schema attributes, while "Schema Mapping" is concerned with the specification of the matching rules (transformation rules).

Unfortunately, schema matching remains largely a manual and time consuming process [6]. Many algorithms and approaches were proposed to deal with the problem of schema matching and mapping [7]–[11].

According to Gal et al. [3], the process of schema matching is performed in two steps. First, a degree of similarity is computed automatically for all element pairs (degree of similarity is typically defined on a [0; 1] scale, where 0 represents no similarity and 1 represents fully similar elements). As a second step, a single mapping is chosen to be the best mapping. When deciding on a best mapping, a matcher should decide which elements from one schema are to be mapped with elements of another schema.

Below a diagram showing a classification of the major schema matching approaches, according to Rahm et al. [10].

Rahm et al., show that an implementation of Match may use multiple match algorithms or matchers. The combination of individual matchers (based on a single matching criterion), can be achieved either by using multiple matching criteria (e.g.,name and type equality) within an integrated hybrid matcher or by combining multiple match results produced by different match algorithms within a composite matcher.

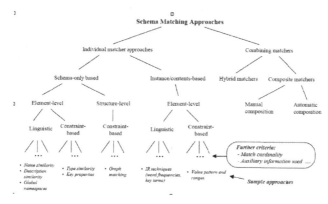

Fig. 1. Classification of schema matching approaches[10]

2.2   Similarity Measures

Text similarity measures play an increasingly important role in text related research and applications. Words can be similar in two ways lexically and semantically. A string metric is a metric that measures similarity or dissimilarity (distance) between two text strings for approximate string matching or comparison. Corpus-Based similarity is a semantic similarity measure that determines the similarity between words according to information gained from large corpora. Knowledge-Based similarity is a semantic similarity measure that determines the degree of similarity between words using information derived from semantic networks [12].

To the best of our knowledge, only a few generalized similarity frameworks exist:

- DKPro Similarity[30] uses implementations of these existing libraries. That way, DKPro Similarity brings together the scattered efforts by offering access to all measures through common interfaces.
- SimMetrics Library The Java library by Chapman et al.[13] exclusively comprises text similarity measures which compute lexical similarity on string sequences and compare texts without any semantic processing. It contains measures such as the Levenshtein [14] or Monge and Elkan [15] distance metrics. In DKPro Similarity, some string-based measures are based on implementations from this library.
- SecondString Toolkit The freely available library by Cohen et al. [16] is similar to SimMetrics, and also implemented in Java. It also contains several well-known text similarity measures on string sequences, and includes many of the measures which are also part of the SimMetrics Library. Some string-based measures in DKPro Similarity are based on the SecondString Toolkit.

2.3   Agent-Based Modelling and Simulation (ABMS)

Agent based modeling and simulation (ABMS) is a new modeling approach that has gained increasing attention over the last decade.

In ABMS, active components or decision makers are conceptualized as agents, being modeled and implemented using agent-related concepts and technologies [17].

Agent-based modelling and simulation (ABMS) is a very natural and flexible way to model todays complex, distributed, interconnected and interacting industrial systems: the self-X principles can be mapped on the explicit notion of autonomous agents, modeling a system as a group of interacting agents maps directly onto the distributed and communicative nature of todays systems[18]–[21].

So what is an agent in the first place. According to Russell et al. (AIMA) [22] "*An agent is anything that can be viewed as perceiving its environment through sensors and acting upon that environment through effectors.*"

Russell et al. group agents into five classes based on their degree of perceived intelligence and capability:

- simple reflex agents
- model-based reflex agents
- goal-based agents
- utility-based agents
- learning agents

2.4   Bayesian Networks

Bayesian networks (BN) are directed acyclic graphs (DAGs) in which the nodes represent variables of interest (e.g., the temperature of a device, the gender of a patient, a feature of an object, the occurrence of an event) and the links represent informational or causal dependencies among the variables. The strength of a dependency is represented by conditional probabilities that are attached to each cluster of parents-child nodes in the network [23].

According to Pearl et al. [23], Bayesian network constitutes a model of the environment rather than, as in many other knowledge representation schemes (e.g., rule-based systems and neural networks), a model of the reasoning process. It simulates, in fact, the mechanisms that operate in the environment, and thus facilitates diverse modes of reasoning, including prediction, abduction and control.

In agent we use BN to reason about actions as basis for planning under uncertainty.

3   Agent-Based Modeling and Simulation for Schema Matching Problem

In a nutshell our idea is to model the Schema Matching process as interactions, within a self-organized environment, between agents called "Schema Attribute Agent". In the rest of the paper we are going to refer to the "Schema Attribute Agent" simply as agent. Each schema attribute is modeled as an agent belonging to one of two groups: source or target schema group. Furthermore, the schema matching process is modeled as the interaction between the two group's agents.

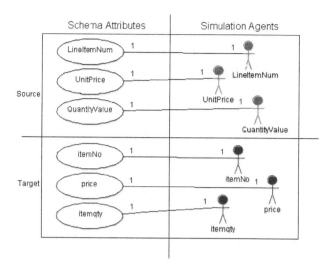

Fig. 2. Representation of Schema Attributes as Simulation Agents

The figure illustrates how the schema source and target attributes could be represented as agents in a simulation environment.

In our model the agents have as a main goals to find the best matching agent within the other group of agents. They execute behaviors based on rules with some randomness (stochasticity).

Macal et al.[24], propose a list of criteria to determine (if one the criteria is met) when is it beneficial to think in terms of agents or when agent-based modeling can offer distinct advantages to conventional simulation approaches.

The table below summarizes the criteria, as proposed by Macal et al, and our justification for our approach of agent based modeling and simulation for schema matching problem.

4   Schema Matching Agent-Based Simulation (SMAS)

4.1   Reflex Agent Model

The first release of our agent model was simple Rule-based. The foundation of the rules governing the agents behaviors is stochasticity (randomness). In fact, a certain degree of randomness is present in each step executed by each agent during the simulation.

Below are the steps executed during each tick of the simulation run:

- Step1 - Calculation of the name similarity: each agent calculates the similarity between its name and all other agent names (in the other group) and identify the best match based on the best name similarity score. For each similarity calculation a similarity measure is selected randomly from a similarity measures list. The score should be grater than a random TREASHOLD (generated random threshold value within interval)

Table 1. Agent-based Modeling criteria

Criteria	Schema matching problem
When there is a natural representation as agents	Yes. A schema attribute is atomic, and thus could be seen as distinct entity with its own specific identity (name, description, type, etc.)
When there are decisions and behaviors that can be defined discretely (with boundaries)	Yes. In schema matching problem, instead of having all the rules centralized within the matching algorithm, we can delegate the responsibility of finding the best match to each schema attribute.
When it is important that agents adapt and change their behaviors	Yes. The schema attribute agent can decide, after trying to find a match, that there is no match possible for him
When it is important that agents learn and engage in dynamic strategic behaviors	Yes. The schema attribute agent can learn patterns that help him to find the best match or decide to stop searching for the best match
When it is important that agents have a dynamic relationship with other agents, and agent relationships form and dissolve	Yes. The ultimate goal for a schema attribute agent is to establish relationship with attributes from the other schema (best matches)
When it is important to model the processes by which agents form emergent organizations, and adaptation and learning are important at the organization level	Yes. The solution of the schema matching is the result of the individual solutions at the schema attributes level
When it is important that agents have a spatial component to their behaviors and interactions	N/A for schema matching problem
When the past is no predictor of the future	Yes. Finding the best match in the past should not predict that it will be always the case in the future (simulation multiple runs)
When scaling-up to arbitrary levels is important in terms of the number of agents, agent interactions and agent states	Yes.
When process structural change needs to be a result of the model, rather than a model input	Yes. The relationships are emerging from agents behaviors.

- Step2 - Calculation of the Comment Similarity: each agent calculates the similarity between its comment and all other agent comments (in the other group) and identify the best match based on the best comment similarity score. Again, for each similarity calculation a similarity measure is selected randomly from a similarity measures list. The score should be grater than a random TREASHOLD (generated random threshold value within interval)
- Step3 - Compare the best matches: If the best match for name and the best match for comment are converging to the same Agent (in the other group) then the agent identify it as the candidate match and update its status from "NO_MATCH" to "CANDIDATE_MATCH". An aggregation calculation is done between name similarity score and comment similarity score of the candidate match. The aggregation function is selected randomly from an aggregation function list (MAX, AVERAGE, WEIGHTED). If the new aggregated score is grater than a random TREASHOLD (generated random threshold value within interval) and is better that the one obtained previously the object CandidateMatchingAttribute is updated with the new scores (name and comment).
- Step4 - Check for Consensus:
  ○ Consensus watching: watch for other agents candidate match update in order to check if a consensus was reached with another agent (both agents are referring to each-other as candidate match). If so then the agent coalition is updated with the name of the other agent and the state is changed to "CONSENSUAL_MATCH"
  ○ Consensus timeout: If after a certain number of ticks (e.g. 250) the agent has not yet reached a consensus with another agent (both are referring to each-other as candidate match) then the agent beliefs about the candidate match are reset to null and the state is changed to "NO_MATCH"
- Step 5 - Ending Simulation: If all agents have reached consensus about their matchings then their status is changed to "STABLE_MATCH" and the simulation is ended.

The main random element influencing the simulation are as follows:
1 Similarity Calculation based on a similarity measures selected randomly from a similarity measures list.
2 Similarity Scores aggregation based on aggregation functions selected randomly from an aggregation function list (MAX, AVERAGE, WEIGHTED).
3 Similarity score validation based on generated random threshold value (within interval)

The simulation ends when each agent has reached a consensus, about its candidate matching, with another agent (both agents are referring to each-other as candidate match).

As opposed to deterministic solutions for schema matching, such as the largely known matching solution COMA++ [25], the nondeterministic and stochastic nature of our agent-based simulation increases the confidence in the quality of the matching results. Despite the fact, that the agent's behaviors are based on randomness (e.g. during the similarity calculation), our model can often produce the right matchings at the end of each simulation run.

4.2   Rational Agent Model (Using Bayes Networks)

Agents execute actions in the environment depending on what they can observe. Each simulation step (tick) can be described as follows:

- The agents perceive the world
- The agents decide on their actions
- The actions are executed

As self-interested and rational agents, they have behaviors, rules and goals (implemented in the agent class) that lead them to a state that maximizeses their utility.

In addition to the lexical similarity calculations (name and comment matchers) implemented in our first model "the reflex agent", below the new calculations (matchers) implemented in the rational agent release. The new calculations are performed during "Sensing the environment" phase executed during each tick of the simulation run:

- Calculation of the Name and Comment Semantic Similarity: each agent calculates the semantic similarity (using Explicit Semantic Analysis) between its name/comment and all other agent names/comments (in the other group) and identify the best match based on the best name/comment similarity score. Explicit Semantic Analysis (ESA) [26]is a method which computes similarity based on word occurrences in a given document collection.
- Calculation of the BayesNet Prediction for the best match: use Weka Classifier to predict the best match among the all other agents (in the other group).

4.2.1 BayesNet Prediction

Along with the different similarity calculations (lexical, semantic), SMAS performs a machine learning classification using BayesNet classifier (Weka) in order to predict the best match.

The training data to build the classifier was generated from multiple runs of multiple simulation for multiple schema matching scenarios for which the expert mapping was provided.

Below the different features selected and used to train and test the classifier BayesNet. For each agent in the other group an instance is generated.

4.2.2 Planning Under Uncertainty

Sometimes during the simulation, the agent should choose between conflicting actions (e.g. exploit or explore, wait or reset, commit or abort, etc.). With uncertainty, the agent typically cannot guarantee to satisfy its goals. We modeled the flowing Bayesian Decision Network (DN also called also Influence Diagram) to help the agent to choose the most rational action given the different calculations performed by the agent during the sensing phase.

Table 2. BayesNet model features

#	Feature Name	Feature Description
0	OtherAgentName	Other agent name (optional. Excluded from the weka dataset)
1	matchResetCount	Count of the agent reset it's belief from candidate match to the initial state
2	lexSimTotCalcCount	Count lexical similarity calculations
3	lexNameSimAboveThresholdCount	Count lexical name similarity calculations above the threshold
4	lexNameSimBelowThresholdCount	Count lexical name similarity calculations below the threshold
5	lexCommentSimAboveThresholdCount	Count lexical comment similarity calculations above the threshold
6	lexCommentSimBelowThresholdCount	Count lexical comment similarity calculations below the threshold
7	lexNameCommentSimConvergenceCount	Count of lexical name and comment similarity convergence (referring to the same match)
8	lexNameSimScoreBestCount	Count of lexical name best score
9	lexCommentSimScoreBestCount	Count of lexical comment best score
10	SemNameCommentSimScore	Semantic name and comment similarity score
11	SemNameCommentSimScoreBest	Semantic name and comment similarity true or false
12	inboundReferralCount	Count of referrals from other agents (candidate match for others)
13	outboundReferralCount	Count of referrals to other agents (others as candidate match)
14	matchExpert	Class attribute (label provided by the expert)

In this sequential decision problem, there are two decisions to be made. First, the agent must decide whether to continue the exploration (perform other similarity calculation hoping to find a better match), exploit (set it self as having a candidate match) or abort (leave the simulation). The information that will be available when it makes this decision is mainly the result of the similarity calculations and BayesNet prediction. Second, the agent must decide whether or not to wait (wait for consensus), reset (reset from candidate match status to initial status), exploit (commit to a consensus match) or abort (leave the simulation).

In the example above the DN gives the action "Exploit" for the first decision (commit to candidate match) given the similarity calculation and prediction variables. For the second decision, the DN makes the recommendation for the action "Wait" given the fact that the simulation just started and there is no referral from other agents to this agent.

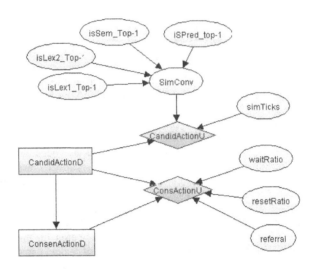

Fig. 3. SMAS Bayes Decision Network (Influence Diagram)

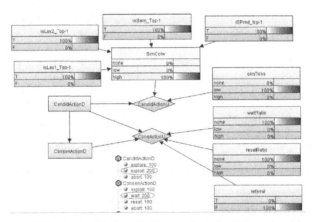

Fig. 4. Compiled SMAS Bayes Decision Network

Below the agent internal logic algorithm.

```
Agent program
  while agent Running repeat
    sense();
    reason();
    act();
  end while
end;

sense ()
  perform Similarity calculations(lexical, semantic, ML
prediction between the agent and the other agents in
the opposite group);
```

```
perform other calculations(simulation execution time
(simTicks), Agent wait time (waitRatio), Agent Reset
count (resetRatio), Other Agent Referral (referal));
end;

reason()
  load the Bayesian Decision Network;
  query the node SimConv to get the agent in the other
group with the Best Sim Convergence Score;
  query the decision nodes (candidate match decision
and consensus match decision) to get the best action
for the the agent in the other group with the Best
SimConvergence Score;
end;

act()
  execute the best action (from the Decision Network);
end;
```

4.3 SMAS Architecture

The main component of SMAS architecture is the model itself developed in Repast framework. High-level steps for producing Schema Matching scenario are as follow:

- The source and target schema are imported to the simulation model
- The model is executed in batch mode for n runs (e.g. 10 runs)
- The multi-run output is then passed to R for statistical analysis
- The final Schema Matching result output is produced

The main class of our model is the agent class. It contains the agent's beliefs, goals and behaviors. Along with the agent class, we find other important classes such as the class that stores the similarity measures (the class SimMeasure) and the class that stores the similarity scores (the class SimScore). Another important class is the Candidate-MatchingAttribute class which holds the information about the best matching for an agent). The class SimMeasure stores a list of the Similarity measures belonging to the similarity measures framework DKPro (DKPro measures implement the interface TextSimilarityMeasure). The class diagram below describes the main SMAS classes.

5   Experiment

5.1 Motivating Example

As Motivating Example to illustrate our approach, suppose we have two simple schemas for which we need to perform an automatic matching. The source, target schemas and the expected matching, provided by the human expert, as describe in the table below.

Table 3. Expected Schema matchings.

Source Name	Attr. Source Desc.	Attr. Target Name	Attr. Target Desc.	Attr.
LineItemNum	item number	itemNo	the item identifier number	
UnitPrice	unit price	price	the item unit price	
QuantityValue	item quantity	itemqty	the item quantity	

As a benchmark to compare our approach to other approaches, we used the well known automatic matching tool COMA (coma 3.0 ce) to perform an automatic matching for the schemas described above. The results obtained, from COAM, clearly demonstrate that the user involvement is necessary because the results were incomplete. The two first expected matching ("LineItemNum<->itemNo" and "Unit-Price<->price" and) were successfully resolved by COMA, on the contrary it fails to resolve the third expected matching "QuantityValue<->itemqty" (missing from the results). Notice that the results obtained with the other COMA workflows resolved only one expected matching "UnitPrice<->price" out of the three expected matchings.

Another observation is that repeating the experiment, with the same input, does not lead to a different or better results. One could argue that this observation is obvious, and thus not worth mentioning, but for us it is very important to highlight this characteristic because it is one of the key differences between COMA like tools and our stochastic agent-based approach (SMAS).

5.2   SMAS Prototype

We developed a prototype for SMAS and performed preliminary tests for which the results1 obtained were encouraging and confirmed our initial intuition about the fact that ABMS can be an efficient and a well suited paradigm for resolving the schema matching problem.

The SMAS simulation model was implemented in Java using the open source ABMS framework Repast Simphony (2.1) [28], [29], the open source framework for Text Similarity DKPro Similarity (2.1.0) [30], the open souce R language (R 3.1.0) [29] was used for For statistical data analysis, the open source Machine Learning tool Weka for BayesNet Classifier [31] and the open-source tool for Bayesian Network UnBBayes [32]–[34].

Below a screenshot of the display panel after the end of the simulation.

The decision each agent takes for selecting a best matching agent is based on random selection of three major elements: Similarity measure, aggregation function and threshold along with the use of Bayesian classifier for prediction and Bayesian Decision Network for action selection. In other words, two agents in a matching calculate and decide about their candidate matching agent in two different ways and yet reached a consensus about the fact that they are the best matching for each others.

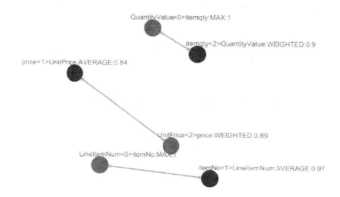

Fig. 5. End of the Simulation screenshot

The results obtained, clearly demonstrate that SMAS successful resolved all the expected matchings ("LineItemNum<->itemNo", "UnitPrice<->price" and "QuantityValue<->itemqty") as opposed to the benchmark obtained from COMA where only two expected matching were found.

6   Discussion and Conclusion

In this work, we described how schema matching problem can be modeled and simulated as agents where each agent acts, learn or evolve in response to interactions in its local environment. The self-regulation of the whole system (schema matching process), in turn, becomes a product of local adaptations and interactions between the Attribute Agents.

As far as we know there is no previous literature describing a solution approaching the Schema Matching and Mapping problem under the angle of Agent-Based Modelling and Simulation.

Many differences exist between our proposed approach and the existing practice in schema matching. First and foremost our approach is based on the paradigm ABMS, while, as far as we know, all the current methods do not use ABMS paradigm.

Even though, the experiments we conducted so far are still preliminary, nevertheless the results we obtained are very encouraging and reinforced our initial idea about the fact that modelling schema matching as agent-based simulation could be not only a novel way for resolving the problem but also can contribute to the goal of coping with uncertainty inherent to the automatic matching process. We believe that many intrinsic properties of our model, derived from ABMS paradigm, contribute efficiently to the increase of the matching quality and thus the decrease of the matching uncertainty. In fact, we can summarize those intrinsic properties as follows:

- Emergence: The emergence of the macro solution (schema matching) from local behaviors, rules and interactions between agents (micro solutions). The sum of the whole is greater than the sum of the individual parts.
- Cooperation: The cooperation of source and target schema attributes

(represented as agents) to reach a consensus about their best matching.

- Stochasticity (randomness): The randomness on which the model is based enables the ability to perform multiple simulations and the statistically analyze their outcome (statistical analysis)

The current release resolve only 1:1 matching, in the next releases of SMAS we are planning to improve our model in order to tackle the problem of Complex Mappings (Complex mappings map a set of attributes in the source to a set of attributes in the target [35]).

References

1. Hicham Assoudi, H.L.: Towards a Self-Organized Agent-Based Simulation Model for Schema Matching. Int. Sci. Index Knowl. Innov. Sci. **2** (2014)
2. Assoudi, H., Lounis, H.: Agent-based Stochastic Simulation of Schema Matching
3. Gal, A.: Managing uncertainty in schema matching with Top-K schema mappings. In: Spaccapietra, S., Aberer, K., Cudré-Mauroux, P. (eds.) Journal on Data Semantics VI. LNCS, vol. 4090, pp. 90–114. Springer, Heidelberg (2006)
4. Gal, A.: Uncertain schema matching. Synth. Lect. Data Manag. **3**(1), 1–97 (2011)
5. Bohannon, P., Elnahrawy, E., Fan, W., Flaster, M.: Putting Context Into Schema Matching, pp. 307–318
6. Gal, A.: Evaluating Matching Algorithms: The Monotonicity Principle (2003)
7. Doan, A., Domingos, P., Halevy, A.: Reconciling Schemas of Disparate Data Sources: A Machine-Learning Approach, pp. 509–520.
8. McCann, R., AlShebli, B., Le, Q., Nguyen, H., Vu, L., Doan, A.: Mapping maintenance for data integration systems. VLDB Endowment (2005)
9. Madhavan, J., Bernstein, P., Rahm, E.: Generic Schema Matching With Cupid, pp. 49–58
10. Rahm, E., Bernsteinm, P.A.: A survey of approaches to automatic schema matching. VLDB J. **10**(4), 334–350 (2001)
11. Nottelmann, H., Straccia, U.: Information retrieval and machine learning for probabilistic schema matching. Inf. Process. Manag. **43**(3), 552–576 (2007)
12. Gomaa, W.H., Fahmy, A.A.: A Survey of text similarity approaches. Int. J. Comput. Appl. **68**(13), 13–18 (2007)
13. Chapman, S.: SimMetrics-open source Similarity Measure Library, URL Httpnazou Fiit Stuba Skhomedocumentationconcomconcom Doc Visit, 2007 (2005)
14. Levenshtein, V.I.: Binary codes capable of correcting deletions, insertions and reversals. In: Soviet Physics Doklady, vol. 10, p. 707 (1966)
15. Monge, A.E., Elkan, C.P.: Efficient domain-independent detection of approximately duplicate database records. Dep. Comput. Sci. Eng., p. 92093–0114 (1997)
16. Cohen, W.W., Ravikumar, P., Fienberg, S.: Secondstring: An open source java toolkit of approximate string-matching techniques. Proj. Web Page Httpsecondstring Sourceforge Net (2003)
17. Klügl, F., Bazzan, A.L.: Agent-based modeling and simulation. AI Mag. **33**(3), 29 (2012)
18. De Wolf, T., Holvoet, T.: Towards autonomic computing: agent-based modelling, dynamical systems analysis, and decentralised control. In: IEEE International Conference on Industrial Informatics. INDIN 2003. Proceedings, pp. 470–479 (2003)
19. Macal, C.M., North, M.J.: Agent-based modeling and simulation. In: Winter Simulation Conference, pp. 86–98 (2009)

20. North, M.J., Macal, C.M.: Managing business complexity: discovering strategic solutions with agent-based modeling and simulation. Oxford University Press (2007)
21. Macal, C.M., North, M.J.: Tutorial on agent-based modelling and simulation. J. Simul. **4**(3), 151–162 (2010)
22. Russell, S.J., Norvig, P., Candy, J.F., Malik, J.M., Edwards, D.D.: Artificial Intelligence: A Modern Approach. Prentice hall (2010)
23. Pearl, J.: Bayesian networks. Dep. Stat. UCLA (2011)
24. Macal, C.M., North, M.J.: Agent-based modeling and simulation: ABMS examples. In: Proceedings of the 40th Conference on Winter Simulation, pp. 101–112 (2008)
25. Massmann, S., Raunich, S., Aumüller, D., Arnold, P., Rahm, E.: Evolution of the coma match system. Ontol. Matching, 49 (2011)
26. Gabrilovich, E., Markovitch, S.: Computing semantic relatedness using wikipedia-based explicit semantic analysis. In: IJCAI, vol. 7, pp. 1606–1611 (2007)
27. Aumueller, D., Do, H.-H., Massmann, S., Rahm, E.: Schema and ontology matching with COMA++. In: Proceedings of the 2005 ACM SIGMOD International Conference on Management of Data, pp. 906–908 (2005)
28. North, M.J., Tatara, E., Collier, N.T., Ozik, J.: Visual agent-based model development with repast simphony. Tech. rep., Argonne National Laboratory (2007)
29. North, M.J.: R and Repast Simphony (2010)
30. Bär, D., Zesch, T., Gurevych, I.: DKPro similarity: An open source framework for text similarity. In: Proceedings of the 51st Annual Meeting of the Association for Computational Linguistics: System Demonstrations, pp. 121–126 (2013)
31. Bouckaert, R.R., Frank, E., Hall, M.A., Holmes, G., Pfahringer, B., Reutemann, P., Witten, I.H.: WEKA—Experiences with a Java Open-Source Project. J. Mach. Learn. Res. **9999**, 2533–2541 (2010)
32. Matsumoto, S., Carvalho, R.N., Ladeira, M., da Costa, P.C.G., Santos, L.L., Silva, D., Onishi, M., Machado, E., Cai, K.: UnBBayes: a java framework for probabilistic models in AI. Java Acad. Res. IConcept Press Httpunbbayes Sourceforge Net (2011)
33. Carvalho, R., Laskey, K.B., Costa, P., Ladeira, M., Santos, L., Matsumoto, S.: UnBBayes: modeling uncertainty for plausible reasoning in the semantic web. In: Semantic Web Gang Wu Ed INTECH, pp. 1–28 (2010)
34. Carvalho, R., Laskey, K., Costa, P., Ladeira, M., Santos, L., Matsumoto, S.: UnBBayes: modeling uncertainty for plausible reasoning in the semantic web. In: Wu, G. (Ed.), Semantic Web. InTech. ISBN: 978-953-7619-54-1 (2010)
35. Bellahsene, Z., Bonifati, A., Rahm, E.: Schema Matching and Mapping, vol. 20. Springer (2011)

Legal Issues

Geolocation Hazards in Geosocial Networks

Zakaria Sahnoune(✉), Cheu Yien Yep, and Esma Aïmeur

Département d'Informatique et de Recherche Opérationnelle (DIRO),
Université de Montréal, Montréal, Canada
{sahnounz,yepcheuy,aimeur}@iro.umontreal.ca

Abstract. A GeoSocial Network (GSN) is an online social network enhanced with built-in location services; it can associate user data and content with location coordinates. This content-location link is getting stronger, due to the swift development of fully location-based social networks, and to the fast expansion of the mobile technologies market. As the location information thus gathered generates a huge amount of publicly-available location data, one can perform location-based social discovery with millions of users around the planet. This may sound disturbing to some, since location information has always been considered private, or at least known only to friends or family.

Hence, this raises a serious privacy threat. Is being tracked in real time, in most cases by strangers, or having location history disclosed to almost everyone, considered as a privacy invasion that needs to be addressed before all control is lost?

In this paper, we look at issues related to GSN applications and explore several questions, such as "How much are we at risk?" and "Are existing location privacy-protection techniques adopted by GSNs sufficient to protect us efficiently?"

Keywords: Geosocial networks · Privacy · Impact assessment · Mobile location.

1 Introduction

The development and popularization of the Internet in the world has led to a revolution in global communication. There is no doubt today that the analysis, presentation and communication of geographic information via the Internet is one of the main channels required by users, who are increasingly demanding interactive queries in which a map is the fundamental part of the interaction.

Moreover, the frenetic evolution of new technologies, more specifically mobile technology, has managed to contribute to what we know as social networking. People connected by relationships such as friendship, family or common interests are now connected by geography. This means that now, more than ever, the world is interconnected and we live in a global village of information but with strong local components. In other words, geolocation is becoming one of the hottest trends in social networking.

Nowadays, nearly every social network has incorporated a location-based service that allows users to enjoy connecting with friends at nearby locations in real-time and

© Springer International Publishing Switzerland 2015
M. Benyoucef et al. (Eds.): MCETECH 2015, LNBIP 209, pp. 71–88, 2015.
DOI: 10.1007/978-3-319-17957-5_5

businesses to take the opportunity to tie their locations to their online marketing. These are referred to as *"Location-Based Social Networks"* (LBSNs). For instance, *Google Latitude* (retired in August 2013) worked using a *Google* account (the same used for *Gmail, Blogger* or *YouTube*) and a smartphone to not only know the user's location very accurately but to share it with his network of friends, in the same way as photos are shared on *Facebook*. *Google Latitude* itself worked like a mini-social network of *Google*, totally independent of other social Internet giants like *Google Reader, Buzz* and *Gmail*.

Foursquare is another very popular GSN, almost identical to *Google Latitude*: it can locate a user's current position, share his location and allow him to "Check-In" at many places and cities. It even uses Google Maps services. Some particular features of *Foursquare* are the "badges" and "mayors", i.e. as the users run the application, they can gain some status and may even become "mayor" of a place by attending frequently. Another feature is that they can see how many people share their same location. For example, if a user is at Starbucks, he could know how many people using *Foursquare* are there at the same time. The same feature is available on *Yelp*, another online community service that offers reviews of restaurants, bars and stores in the user's vicinity.

Others GSNs, such as *AroundTheWay*, *GyPSii* and *iPling*, allow individuals to access and upload their location information and obtain not only other users' addresses and telephone numbers, but also the instructions on how to reach them. Services like *Skout, WhosHere, OkCupid* and *Girls Around Me* use individuals' smartphone locations to identify potential mates nearby. The idea of this network is to find nearby people and to get in touch via chat, messages, adding them as favourites or sending them virtual gifts. One can also check out their pictures and profiles, and the GSN will reveal how far away they are located.

These features seem attractive and they have become widely used by smartphone users, but as users provide more information about their location, serious privacy implications are beginning to surface. For instance, "checking in" on Foursquare is seen as a fun way to tell people where you are. But, as this information is often made public, it can also be used to inform people of when you are not at home (perfect time for a robbery!) or identify places you are likely to visit.

The first privacy implications of GSNs were demonstrated in 2010 by the website *"Please Rob Me"*[1], which linked peoples' physical locations through geolocation services with data about their residence from other publicly available data. Even though the intention of this website is not, and never has been, to have people burgled, when people were "checked in" at other places, malicious individuals could find out and take advantage through this website. Another example, in March 2012, occurred with the mobile application *"Girls around me"*, which uses *Foursquare* data to tell users where they can find girls nearby. *Foursquare* banned this site from using its data because this application displayed a map using cross-platform social discovery by gathering data of where women using *Foursquare* were checking in and whatever details they had left public on *Facebook*. In other words, anyone with the application could see information about them without their consent.

---

[1] http://pleaserobme.com/

Many people may not be aware of how much information they are publicly broadcasting. And many are not aware of some of these services that organize and display this data in such a visual and location-centric way. People have been largely sceptical of check-in services. But increasingly we see users getting more comfortable with sharing all kinds of information and broadcasting their location through these GSNs. This may prompt some people to rethink how much they want to share through various GSNs and pay constant attention to privacy in order to ensure that they still feel in control about how much they are sharing.

Furthermore, studies have shown that more than a half of survey respondents who used geolocation services were worried about their privacy[2]. Additionally, other studies proved that only four spatiotemporal coordinates are sufficient to uniquely identify 95% of the individuals [1]. Moreover, to have a clear idea of how location data could be sensitive, researchers demonstrated that, by using inference attacks on user location traces, it is possible to discover their Points Of Interests (POIs) such as where they live, where they work, their usual itineraries, their habits, interests, activities, relationships, etc. [2]. These research studies have clearly illustrated that the privacy of GSNs is a serious concern for most smart device users.

The purpose of this paper is to demonstrate the potential danger of exposing our location in some GSNs applications by sharing it with others, and how this could leak sensitive information such as real identities, home and work locations. The paper is organized as follows: Section 2 defines and classifies currently deployed GSN applications. Section 3 focuses on the nature of collected information on GSNs and the techniques used to do so. Section 4 describes some social discovery leaks. Section 5 explains the location-privacy impact of these GSN applications and how they affect the population. Section 6 examines some legal issues about the protection of user privacy in GSNs. Finally, Section 7 presents some discussions and draws conclusions.

2 Geosocial Networks

In this section, we discuss basic GSN concepts, and propose a suitable classification scheme accordingly.

2.1 Location-Based Services

Location-Based Services (LBS) are services that exploit knowledge about where a user is located based on geographical coordinates. In other words, LBS applications take advantage of available technologies to accurately locate a device, and use this location information to provide a value-added service.

Although LBS present a fairly new science domain, there are several similar definitions found in the literature:

---

[2] http://www.webroot.com/ca/en/company/press-room/releases/social-networks-mobile-security

"LBS are information services accessible with mobile devices through the mobile network and utilizing the ability to make use of the location of the mobile device." [3]

"LBS are IT services for providing information that has been created, compiled, selected, or filtered taking into consideration the current locations of the users or those of other persons or mobile objects." [4]

"LBS is an information or entertainment service, accessible with mobile devices through the mobile network and utilizing the ability to make use of the geographical position of the mobile device." [5]

LBS refer to any application that uses device location as a primary source to deliver context-sensitive services. Therefore it covers a wide range of applications. Nowadays, most of the mobile devices (mainly smartphones or tablets) are equipped with a Global Positioning System (GPS) and a data connection in order for people to access multiple real-time geographic services, ranging from obtaining directions to a particular place up to getting in touch with friends or meeting new people with similar tastes or interests.

To better understand what GSNs are, a precise definition is given by Zheng, who defines GSNs as "a network that does not only mean adding a location to an existing social network so that people in the social structure can share location-embedded information, but also consists of the new social structure made up of individuals connected by the interdependency derived from their locations in the physical world as well as their location-tagged media content, such as photos, video, and texts." [6]

In other words, GSNs allow their users to build a location-enhanced profile, in which their data and activities are combined with their location. Because all data is associated with specific position coordinates, this leads to more accurate social discovery than by using the data usually found in a simple search request on a traditional online social media.

2.2   Classification of GSNs

There are many GSN sites throughout the web. Each one serves a different purpose and may be categorized according to its targeted users or the kind of content it publishes. In order to understand this new social reality; one must learn more about the different types of GSNs operating on the web.

There are several possible classifications of GSNs; scholars usually classify them according to their study's context. For instance, based on the studies and the growing popularity of GSN, Zheng defined three major ways to group them [7]:

Geotagged-media-based: services that enable users to add location labels and comments on media content such as text, photos, videos or others. Examples include *Flickr*, *Panoramio* and *Geo-twitter*.

Point-location-driven: services that encourage people to share their current location by checking in into the places they visit and adding "tips" to venues. *Foursquare* is an example of this type.

Trajectory-centric: services that provide not only a point location but also the detailed path navigated by users by connecting the locations of several points. Users receive not only basic information (such as distance, duration and velocity) for a trajectory, but also information on user experiences (such as tips, tags and photos). Examples include *Bikely* and *SportsDo*.

Other classification approaches are based on the type of GSN application. For example, Lopez divides GSNs into six categories [8]:

Safety Services: low usage services designed to provide end-user assistance in case of an emergency. For example: *FlagMii.*

Information Services: refer mostly to the digital distribution of information based on device location, time specificity and user behaviour. It includes traffic information, navigation assistance, yellow pages, travel/tourism services, etc. *TripAdvisor* is an example.

Enterprise Services: these services include vehicle tracking, logistic systems, fleet management, workforce management, and people finding. *Shaw Tracking* is an example.

Consumer Portal Services: delivers local news, weather, and traffic information determined by the location of the device. For example, *Google News* and *Google Weather*

Telematics Services: most often used to describe vehicle navigation systems in which drivers and passengers employ GPS technology to obtain directions, track their location and obtain assistance when a vehicle is involved in an accident. For instance, *TomTom* Solutions

Triggered Location Services: are services that are triggered when a consumer or corporate client enters into a predetermined area. Examples: location-sensitive advertising, location-sensitive billing and location-sensitive logistics.

2.3   Classifying GSNs and Location Accuracy

Although the above classifications seem to be accurate and detailed, the fact that no well-defined classification exists yet cannot be neglected. Taking into consideration the existing studies, we have categorized GSN services based on their accuracy in determining the user's location, since gathering an accurate location directly influences the user's location privacy. In other words, the following classification considers, in some manner, the user privacy-in group GSNs.

GSNs that give a location's coordinates

These services provide the exact location of their users. A user of this type of network typically has a closed circle of users, generally known in real life, and upon whom they rely. In fact, there are GSNs focused on informing others about where we are on a continuous basis. However, in the majority of the cases, the target audience consists of family groups or friends and is not open to the general public. For instance:

Foursquare is a GSN for mobile devices. Users "check in" at places by selecting from a list of venues the application locates nearby. Hyper-specific check-ins are encouraged, in which one can check into a certain floor/area of a building, or indicate a specific activity while at a venue.

Google Latitude, Glympse, Life360 and *Find my Friends* are applications that enable users to share where they are with a selected group of family and friends, and to see where these people are in real time. Latitude lets users share their locations in the background, even when the application is closed or the device screen is locked.

Highlight is a mobile application that shows the user information on whoever happens to be around him at a given moment. Highlight uses information from Facebook accounts to determine if other Highlight users in the vicinity should know about each other. It also notifies the user when someone with similar interests is nearby. The application sends a push notification once someone comes into the user's radius.

SayHi is an application that seizes the GPS from the device to show, in real time, where the user's friends are or where new interesting people he could meet are located.

Other applications such as *Banjo, IAm, IAround, Split, Beetaun, Commandro, IMEasy, LifeAware* and *Cloak* also fall under the same category.

GSNs that give a relative location

These services provide information on a geographic radius of their users instead of their exact location coordinates. In other words, they only disclose the relative distance among the mobile users, yet hiding their exact location by limiting the localization accuracy to a certain range or restricting the display coverage to a particular area. For instance:

Tinder is a location-based social discovery application that facilitates communication between mutually interested users. Using Facebook profiles, Tinder analyses user information to create potential matches that are most likely to be compatible based on geographical location, number of mutual friends and common interests. Contact cannot be made unless both individuals 'like' each other and a match is made.

Skout, WhosHere and *Badoo* are other similar social networks. These applications make use of the device's geolocation, which allows users to locate other people within close proximity. This is accomplished through a user interface that displays a grid of representative pictures, arranged from nearest to farthest away. Tapping on a picture will display a brief profile for that user, as well as the option to chat and send pictures.

WeChat is a cross-platform communication service similar to *Whatsapp*, the mobile messaging application recently acquired by *Facebook*, which enables users to send instant text and audio messages. However, WeChat also has social media-style features such as a newsfeed (Facebook), focus on short messages (Twitter), video calling (Skype) and a localization feature that allows users to find out if their contacts are nearby (Foursquare). One can also filter the type of people he would like to see, making the feature even more social.

Momo is an instant messaging mobile application that emphasizes location and interest-based social networks instead of acquaintance-based social circles. It allows users to connect with others in the same location and exchange text messages, audio notes, and photographs over the Internet. The application helps users find like-minded people around them anywhere and anytime.

In addition to the above-mentioned classification, it is important also to distinguish between two different types of GSNs: service location and person location GSNs, which are discussed in the next section.

2.4   Service Location vs. Person Location

While discussing the topic of accuracy of location-based social discovery, one of the most important criteria to be considered is the link between locating a service and locating a person: how service location can invade peoples' privacy.

Service location can be defined as services on which a user requests delivery of information or service. Person location, on the other hand, allows the user to broadcast his location publicly or among his social network.

It is a fact that we share more and more often details about our life on social networks that we have at our disposal. We access them through our smartphones, tablets and computers, sharing photos, videos and messages of all kinds. Similarly, we trust our "virtual friends" (often without really knowing who they are) and we are exposed to a lot of pitfalls in the network, many of which are unknown. Often, we do not have a proper appreciation of their consequences and ramifications in real life.

From simple phishing attacks to the theft of our credentials or banking details to cyberbullying or grooming, social networks are true reflections of the dangers that can be found in the real world. It is therefore advisable to take certain measures and adopt safety habits as means of prevention.

Sometimes we become a cybercriminal's target because of the quantity (or quality) of contacts that our virtual account has. It is amazing how even the black market for digital goods has evolved, trading nowadays more for a stolen Twitter account than for a stolen credit card number. We must always remember that the use of social networks, despite appearances, is not free: we are paying with our information, which lets us determine the amount we want to contribute.

According to a report conducted by Kaspersky's Lab and B2B International concerning the behaviour of the modern Internet user, only a small number of participants understand the risks associated with active use of social networks[3]. People are often careless with what information they share while using social media networks. Survey statistics show that 78% of the respondents believe that they are not of any interest to cybercriminals or are unsure about this issue. However, cybercriminals are always lurking and often look through social networks searching for information inadvertently left by the user. This topic is discussed in detail further in the paper.

3   Geosocial Networks and Mobile Applications

Due to the fact that GSNs deal directly with user locations, the best way to collect such data is to provide a mobile implementation. The proliferation of the smartphone market as evidenced by the fact that in 2014, 76.6% of Quebec adults aged between 18 and 44 own a smartphone[4]; together with the ease of accessing location services on them, provide the major motivation.

3.1   Information Collected

Most GSN mobile applications collect data from user devices using phone built-in location services; others use network information to do it. In all cases, GSNs gather accurate location information of their users; the question is how this data will be exposed.

---

[3] http://media.kaspersky.com/en/Kaspersky_Lab_Consumer_Security_Risks_Survey_2014_ENG.pdf

[4] http://www.cefrio.qc.ca/blogue/numerique-par-generation/plus-75-des-18-44-ans-disposent-dun-telephone-intelligent/

Collecting data using built-in location services

In order to allow applications to locate a mobile device, all modern smartphones have built-in location services, which can be accessed through the operating system's (OS) Application Programming Interface (API). The access to location data is granted either by a simple one-line declaration in the manifest file before using the API, such as in Android devices; or just by using it, since location APIs are considered to be publicly available, such as in the case of iOS devices.

Actually, the location service, or even specific permission for location access, can be disabled on any modern smartphone. However, since GSN applications are location-based applications, they will not work without enabling location; most of them will require it to be enabled before starting. In other words, despite the permissions and the ability to disable location, using GSNs is equivalent to giving your location, and agreeing to all the consequences.

The accuracy of the location data can be either coarse or fine; it is up to the application developer to select the desired level of accuracy. Figure 1 shows how an application obtains user location data in the case of an Android device.

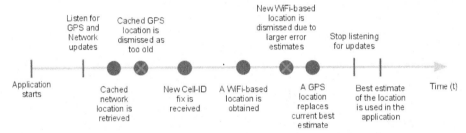

Fig. 1. Updating and listening to location data on a mobile device[5]

As we can see on the illustrated timeline in Figure 1, mobile applications can get very accurate location coordinates by using GPS, Wi-Fi and Cell-ID. The location stored in cache is used for tracking; hence, a complete history of user location could be gathered by any GSN mobile application.

Collecting data using network information

Some GSNs collect user location data using their network information, more specifically their IP addresses. Using this technique to get location data is not very accurate: it yields only the user's city in most cases. Nonetheless, IP address information can be used in many malicious ways like denial-of-service attacks or others.

This technique is used to only filter country-based content on GSNs. Therefore, we focus on data collection using built-in location services for the rest of this paper.

4   Geosocial Networks and Privacy Disclosure

Once the user location data are gathered and stored on a GSN, the problem is to determine the access radius. In other words, who can see it? And how can one see this

---

[5] http://developer.android.com/guide/topics/location/strategies.html

data? Henceforth, we discuss the nature of the information sought, and try to illustrate this on two GSN mobile applications.

4.1   Information Sought

We now analyse the nature of data available on GSNs. First, note that the overwhelming majority of GSNs collect their users' data through other popular social network APIs. They easily connect location data to an already existing user information profile. Similarly, GSNs keep the location data up to date, together with user retrieved content. Although this had been a complicated task in the past, it became much simpler due to the proliferation of mobile GSN implementations.

In the remaining of this section, we focus on two GSN mobile applications, one for each type, which differ with respect to the accuracy of location information [Section 2.3]. Our selection of these two applications is primarily related to the fact that they all possess GSN functionalities on the one hand, and they are trending on mobile platforms, and attracting more users each day on the other.

The first application is *Highlight*, with an estimated 25K daily active users in early 2013[6], a number that is, no doubt, much bigger now. Highlight uses a precise location strategy. The application uses a combination of cell tower signals, nearby Wi-Fi hotspots, GPS and (optionally) Bluetooth to determine user locations in the background[7].

Our second choice is the application called *WhosHere*, another trending GSN, but this time with a relative location strategy. Table 1 shows a high-level comparison between the two applications.

Table 1. A High-level Comparison Between *Highlight* and *WhosHere*

Property	Highlight	WhosHere
Number of registered users	unknown	≈ 8M
Location strategy	Precise coordinates	Relative location
Account requirement	Yes	No, but creating an account gives additional features
Cross-platform discovery	Yes	No
Follow users	Yes	Yes, by friendship requests
Private Conversations	Yes	Yes
Adjustable location	No	Yes
Managed content's audience	No	Yes

---

[6] http://www.businessinsider.com/where-is-it-now-highlight-the-most-talked-about-app-of-last-spring-2013-3

[7] http://devblog.highlig.ht/

As shown in Table 1, the main differences between the two applications are:

- The location strategy used, which presents a key property in any location-based mobile application.
- The account requirement to discover other users' profiles. As we can see in both of them, one can retrieve the location and content of others easily with an account registration. However, *WhosHere* provides additional features to registered users.
- Cross-platform discovery, which is not available on *WhosHere*.
- The ability to follow other users, by using request approvals on *WhosHere*.
- Private conversations supported.
- The adjustment of the current location, which lets users modify their location, a paid feature on *WhosHere*.
- The management of content audience, the other paid feature available only on *WhosHere*.

More precisely, both applications reveal user private information, except that the second one gets paid to protect it.

The next part of this section discusses the ability to retrieve some valuable information just by performing social discovery on the two GSNs.

Fig. 2. Highlight location map

4.2   Scenario of Data Retrieval

We conducted a simple social discovery on 30 randomly chosen profiles from each of the applications mentioned above, in order to prove that anyone can retrieve sensitive user information by following a few simple steps.

One common vulnerability in these GSNs is the ability to create fake accounts. Indeed, there is no way to detect accounts with fake identity and attackers can create as many accounts as they wish, since the only way to verify them is their email addresses.

Highlight Application Case:

We began by installing the Android version of the *Highlight* application, which allows new users to login using *Facebook* or *LinkedIn* accounts, in order to reduce registration with fake accounts. Once done, we noticed that the main interface contains other users' briefs, with a photo, relative location information and the number of common interests.

At this step, and after signing in with a *Facebook* account, the application was able to collect a huge set of user's data from *Facebook*, including all his photos, his entire friend list, and all friends' information that he can access.

The next step was to discover the revealed data; we were stunned by what we could find out about a completely unknown person. The user's profile page contains photos retrieved from *Facebook* or *LinkedIn,* a brief history of his last locations, links to his other social networks accounts, and a button to follow him. *Highlight* keeps collecting and sharing the user location without his explicit consent.

Next, we viewed the location history. The locations revealed on *Highlight* were not just relative as we expected by viewing the main interface. Indeed, we found we could locate the user on a map with very accurate coordinates. Figure 2 presents the map shown by *Highlight* when trying to check a user's location, which clearly shows the precise location of the random user presented on a Google map.

The next profile component we looked at were the links to other social networks, in the case of our random user; the available links on his profile were *Facebook*, *Twitter* and *LinkedIn* links.

In addition, a "recent posts" section loaded content from other users' profiles, which made the cross-platform discovery process even easier.

In conclusion, a truly alarming privacy invasion has been identified, as we were able to view the name, the photos, the exact location, and all publicly available data on the linked social networks of a complete stranger.

In fact, we had the feeling that we were dealing with a data aggregator, where all sensitive information is collected in one place.

Our next application is *WhosHere*, another popular GSN, which offers mobile implementation for Android phones and iOS together with the web interface.

WhosHere Application Case:

Like the *Highlight* case, we began by installing the application; once we ran it, we discovered that we were able to see user photos and relative locations without the need to sign in.

Next, we logged in with a *Facebook* account; we noticed that *WhosHere* collects only some basic data from *Facebook*, mostly publicly available content such as the birthdates and the friends' list. We also noticed that only the public profile is required to run the application, and that access to other data can be denied using the Facebook application settings.

The other trump card for *WhosHere* is that the user can control the visibility of his data, except for the location of course: he can select which content will be visible to others.

Although, *WhosHere* seemed to be more "private" compared to *Highlight*, the fact that the user can adjust his location negates this benefit. WhosHere allows the user, in our case the attacker, to select an exact location in order to discover information around that neighbourhood. According to works on space partition attacks [9], we can define the exact location of the target by changing our location and some geometric calculations. This feature is a part of the premium version of *WhosHere*, which becomes available only if purchased.

Table 2 shows the number of users whose personal information we could success-fully obtain from their profiles. We can clearly notice that such data presents a real privacy invasion, since it can be used to accurately identify persons.

Table 2. The Amount of Gathered Data in Highlight and WhosHere Application

Information	Numbers of users	
	Highlight	**WhosHere**
Full name	30	30
Home/Work addresses	28	0
Photos	30	18
Location	30	26
Contacts list	26	0

As we can see in Table 2, we were able to collect sensitive information from the 30 randomly chosen profiles on each GSN.

The privacy offered by *WhosHere* seems better than that of *Highlight*. However, in both applications, attackers can still locate their targets accurately. In other words, even when using relative location strategies in order to protect user privacy, their location information is still exposed to attackers.

We would like to add also, that the risk of privacy invasion can be reduced by using wise privacy settings in GSN applications. Although, most GSNs offer possibilities to limit audience or restrict public sharing; users are still using the default settings, which are in most cases of an opt-out nature.

In the next section, we discuss the impact of disclosing such data on GSNs users.

5   Location Privacy Impact Assessments

We focus in this section on the impact of location data disclosure on individuals, and the possible consequences.

5.1   Privacy Impact on Individuals

The use of new technologies is already part of our daily lives and as a result of this, new products and services are offered every day. People use their mobile device equipped with Internet access as a tool to download multiple applications with social networks representing the most requested downloads. The problem with these appli-cations is that they were created with a specific purpose and a clear economic goal. It is rare, when designing and building a product or service that one thinks of how, once completed, it will affect or protect its users' privacy. Among the existing risks to the users' privacy, we identify: the invasion of their private life, communication of their data to third parties when this is not needed, improper anonymization, the gathering of data kept longer than is strictly necessary for the purpose for which it is collected, and the loss of reputation for companies.

In the literature, scholars from many fields have begun to investigate the impact of GSNs, trying to understand how these sites affect our identity, privacy, social capital, youth culture and education. For instance, according to some studies [10], users do not think or are not aware of the risks of sharing their information online. For them, the decision of sharing something online is "made at the moment". Similarly, a study conducted by Acquisti et al.[8] found that "people's ideas about privacy are malleable depending on the context of interaction". Their research suggest that people are more willing to divulge sensitive personal information on a social network website than on other sites. They also observed that people disclose information when they see others doing it. This trend, in their opinion, may explain why so many people are ready to provide personal information online [11].

A study entitled Young Canadians in a Wired World, conducted by *MediaSmarts* in 2013[9], reveals that 68% of young people wrongly believe that if a website has a privacy policy, it will not share their personal information with others. Similarly, 39% of them think that companies are not interested in what they do online.

Other studies were able to recognize that some users uninstalled their apps after they became aware that some apps were accessing their location, but most users might prefer to disable the location access permission, which is impossible [12].

Another study showed that users grant access to applications for which location information is critical for them to function, but deny access when it is less clear what benefits sharing of location information can bring to them [13].

Other researchers demonstrated that people disclose their personal location depending on: who is requesting it, why the requester wants to know the location, and which details would be the most useful to the requester. Other factors are: the relationship with the applicant (they are more willing to share information with family and friends), the place where the user is located, the activity that is taking place, and whether they feel depressed, happy or sad [14].

Similarly, other scholars investigated user concerns when using applications that access location data. They found that users are initially concerned about their privacy, but their level of concern diminishes when they use geolocation services. Indeed, users find these services less intimidating after they begin using them [15].

Finally, according to a Pew Research study published in June 2013, most GSN users do not have a completely public profile, and they try to not share sensitive information.

As with any technology, geolocation can be a double-edged sword. Henceforth, we discuss several examples of its positive effects, but also how it could endanger our lives.

---

[8] http://www.ted.com/talks/alessandro_acquisti_why_privacy_matters
[9] http://mediasmarts.ca/ycww/life-online

5.2   Positive Effects

Some capabilities of social networks help in law enforcement and provide protection against unwarranted surveillance of individual activities, or serve to improve medical research, by identifying the exact location of an injured mountaineer in the middle of a hardly accessible geographic point, or helping to locate stolen vehicles.

An example occurred in 2012, when Higinio O. Ochoa, a 30-year-old Galveston programmer and a member of "CabinCr3w", an offshoot of the hacking collective Anonymous, hacked into official websites. He released the names, home addresses, home telephone numbers and mobile phone numbers of several police officers, while leaving a taunting message along with a photo of his girlfriend's barely-clad breasts. Thanks to the position tagging on this photo, FBI agents were able to identify the exact location where his girlfriend lived and later arrested him[10].

Geolocation and the ability to assign coordinate information to exploit it from a computer is used in many different domains. As an example of success in institutional communication, consider *Harvard University*. This was the first American university to use *Foursquare* to help students explore their campus and surrounding places of interest. In 2010, they announced a new location-based mobile social networking application with which students can create and update reviews and rating guides of stores, restaurants, businesses and other venues on campus; they can also earn points and acquire *Foursquare* "badges" for their reviews[11].

In the case of the 'anti-social network' trend, an application for Apple's iPhone, called "Cloak", was launched to help people avoid unwanted friends nearby, using data from other GSNs (Instagram and Foursquare) to pinpoint the location of contacts based on their latest check-ins and photographs. Users can track their friends and acquaintances in order to steer clear of those they do not want to encounter[12].

5.3   Negative Consequences

While online disclosures can have positive results, negative consequences that facilitate criminal acts are also a possible outcome of GSNs and information sharing.

Information from GPS and geolocation tags, in combination with other personal information, can be used by criminals to identify an individual's present or predicted future location, thus facilitating the ability to cause harm to others and their property. This ranges from burglary and theft to stalking, kidnapping and domestic violence.

Cybercriminals, ex-lovers and/or jealous friends are the main perpetrators of computer crimes that threaten the integrity, morality, self-esteem and safety of persons. The lack of caution when posting photos, comments and stories, along with their physical location, can become the best tools for kidnapping, robbery, rape, dismissal from work, divorce, and so on.

---

[10] http://www.smh.com.au/technology/technology-news/hacking-cases-body-of-evidence-20120411-1wsbh.html

[11] https://foursquare.com/harvard

[12] http://www.bbc.com/news/technology-25554192

A survey conducted by "Credit Sesame" in 2011, revealed that 78% of ex-burglars had used *Facebook*, *Twitter*, *Grupo* and *Foursquare* to track people locations for robbery, and 74% of criminals had used *Google Maps* and *Street View* to review and locate an empty residence prior to committing robbery in it[13].

Nowadays, location information is among the most sensitive and highly valued data being collected. It contains the historical record of the individual whereabouts and can be used to reconstruct their movements across space and time.

From our point of view, one of the major problems is that we simply do not know how people perceive the risks of using GSNs. Further research is necessary in order to understand the relationship between the behaviour of people concerning personal information disclosure on GSNs and their perception of the associated risks. In the next section, we discuss the main legal issues around GSN privacy.

6   Legal Issues

As mentioned earlier in this paper, sharing our location can reveal far more than just a latitude and longitude; it implies also the disclosure of personal and intimate aspects of our life, information that is rightfully considered private.

In the current technological era, where online social life is taking a great portion of our time, it is more important than ever to protect our online identity. Under this reality, people are starting to worry about location privacy and wonder about what kind of information is stored, where it is stored, how securely it is stored and, most importantly, what is the purpose for the information collected? Furthermore, they wonder if we are legally protected and if we can trust that our sensitive location information will remain private.

Unfortunately, the laws and legal protection are not keeping pace with the current technological advancements.

During the past years, personal privacy policymakers and lawmakers have proposed and approved significant new regulations with the intent to protect users. However, location privacy has not received equal attention in the legal system due to the novelty of this concept.

These issues affect all governments. In The United States, the *Cable Act* (47 USC § 551) and the *Electronic Communications Privacy Act* (ECPA) (47 USC § 551) prohibit operators and telecommunication providers from disclosing a customer's location information to a third party without their consent, and restrict the use of a tracking device to monitor an individual's movement without a warrant from federal agencies. However, these acts do not provide any standards on the collection and use of location information.

According to Kar *et al.*, although the United States legislation differs from state to state, there does not currently exist any codified or coherent case law that protects personal privacy, especially location privacy [16].

---

[13] http://smallbusiness.yahoo.com/advisor/being-too-social-crime-200544050.html

Nonetheless, a draft of the *Online Communications and Geolocation Protection Act* was presented in March 2013, with the highest impact thus far. The reasons lie in its good definition of measures and safeguards, rightly referring to the protection of all kinds of information, especially location. It includes not only GPS data, but also log data, traceability of people and goods, and geolocation technology.

The rule that inspired this new legislation is that location data may only be disclosed by legal requirement or court order. Among the new measures proposed, carriers have to publicly publish an annual "transparency report" in which they report their location information requirements and what kind of information they reveal[14].

In May 2013, the *Office of the Privacy Commissioner of Canada* released a position paper calling for substantial changes to the *Personal Information Protection and Electronic Documents Act (PIPEDA)*. It argued that PIPEDA is currently insufficient to meet the challenges posed by the advent of technology that allows organizations to collect, use, and disclose an unprecedented amount of data that includes personal information[15].

Similarly, on the other side of the Atlantic, efforts have been made to legally protect user privacy. For instance, the Spanish Data Protection Agency (AEPD) introduced its privacy guidelines designed to identify and avoid privacy risks[16]. "The AEPD's guidance on data protection impact assessments" (PIAs) encourages privacy by design – *i.e.*, building privacy protections into products or services and maintaining them throughout their life. The guide strongly recommends PIAs for companies that employ "particularly invasive technologies," such as geolocation, data mining, biometrics, genetic techniques, video surveillance, etc. The guide also suggests measures that companies can take to avoid or mitigate risks. The aim is, first, to achieve a more active protection of the fundamental right of data privacy law, and second, to reinforce preventive policies between organizations to avoid costly redesign of the systems once they have been developed as well as prevent potential damage to their reputation and image.

While the gap between new technologies and the legal system is recognized, the privacy policies of companies that provide geolocation services play an important role in the market.

Other research [17] considers that the goal of all laws is to provide people with a set of rights, so that they can have control over the collection, use and disclosure of their own personal information and decide how to manage their privacy. In other words, an individual can determine by himself how to weigh the costs and benefits of sharing his information with the companies. These rights consist basically of rights to notice, access and consent regarding the collection, use and disclosure of personal data. This is known as "privacy self-management".

It also states that several cognitive problems exist that prevent people from having full control over their data. These can be summarized as follows: (1) people do not read privacy policies; (2) if they read them, they do not understand their content; (3) if

---

[14] http://beta.congress.gov/bill/113th-congress/house-bill/983/text

[15] http://www.priv.gc.ca/parl/2013/pipeda_r_201305_e.asp

[16] http://www.passwordprotectedlaw.com/tag/privacy-impact-assessment/

they read and understand them, they usually lack the knowledge and expertise needed to make an informed decision; and (4) if they read, understand and can make an informed choice, their decision could be influenced by several difficulties that may arise in the decision-making process.

Similar studies [18] affirm that the existence of a privacy policy only protects company interests and not the consumer. They argue that the privacy protection of GSN users is often inadequate or uncertain.

In our opinion, legal reform is needed in order to match today's new online and mobile world and provide proper safeguards for individual privacy rights. Until then, the responsibility of ensuring privacy protection falls primarily upon the shoulders of the designers of GSNs, who should take the necessary measures to eliminate user privacy concerns and thus motivate them to use privacy self-management applications.

7   Conclusion

The fact that GSNs invade our lives swiftly cannot be ignored as their ease of use attracts more users each day. This leads to a serious form of privacy invasion when our location information becomes easily accessible. Indeed, building profiles from the publicly available content of a user has become an easy task [19], which is certainly enhanced when location history is also available.

We have seen through this paper the location strategies used on GSNs, and the weakness of using relative location as a privacy protection technique. We have assessed the location privacy impacts on individuals, and discussed some positive and negative aspects. Finally, we reviewed the main legal texts about privacy and GSNs.

We have conducted simple discovery tests on two trending mobile GSN applications and found that the results were nearly similar. In fact, any user can be tracked using GSNs. Our future work will focus on an in-depth analysis of the attacks that can be performed on GSN applications; we believe that the existing GSN location strategies need to be improved.

In conclusion, it is a nice feature that the GSNs offer, but should it cost us our privacy? In fact, the use of GSNs comes with increased threats that our personal information will be disclosed.

References

1. De Montjoye, Y.A., Hidalgo, C.A., Verleysen, M., Blondel, V.D.: Unique in the crowd. In: The Privacy Bounds of Human Mobility. Scientific Reports, 3 (2013)
2. Gambs, S., Killijian, M.O., Del Prado Cortez, M.N.: Show me how you move and i will tell you who you are. In: Proceedings of the 3rd ACM SIGSPATIAL International Workshop on Security and Privacy in GIS and LBS, pp. 34–41 (2010)
3. Steiniger, S., Neun, M., Edwardes, A.: Foundations of location based services. Lecture Notes on LBS 1, 272 (2006)
4. Küpper, A.: Front Matter. John Wiley & Sons, Ltd. (2005)

5. Roebuck, K.: Location-Based Services (LBS): High-impact Strategies-What You Need to Know: Definitions, Adoptions, Impact, Benefits. Vendors, Emereo Pty Limited (2011)
6. Zheng, Y.: Tutorial on location-based social networks. In: Proceedings of the 21st International Conference on World Wide Web, WWW, vol. 12 (2012)
7. Zheng, Y.: Location-based social networks users. In: Computing With Spatial Trajectories, pp. 243–276. Springer, New York (2011)
8. Lopez, X.: The future of GIS: real-time, mission critical, location services. In: Proceedings of Cambridge Conference (2003)
9. Li, M., Zhu, H., Gao, Z., Cheny, S., Reny, K., Yu, L., Hu, S.: All Your Location are Belong to Us: Breaking Mobile Social Networks for Automated User Location Tracking. arXiv:1310.2547 [cs.SI] (2013)
10. Das, B., Sahoo, J.S.: Social Networking Sites – A Critical Analysis of Its Impact on Personal and Social Life. International Journal of Business and Social Science 2(14), 222–228 (2011)
11. Gross, R., Acquisti, A.: Information revelation and privacy.in online social networks. In: Proceedings of the 2005 ACM Workshop on Privacy in the Electronic Society, pp. 71–80 (2005)
12. Fu, H., Yang, Y., Shingte, N., Lindqvist, J., Gruteser, M.: A field study of run-time location access disclosures on Android smartphones. In: Proc. USEC 2014 (2014)
13. Fisher, D., Dorner, L., Wagner, D.: Location privacy: user behavior in the field. In: Proceedings of the 2nd ACM Workshop on Security and Privacy in Smartphones and Mobile Devices (SPSM 2012), pp. 51–56. ACM (2012)
14. Consolvo, S., Smith, I.E., Matthews, T., LaMarca, T., Tabert, J., Powledge, P.: Location disclosure to social relations: why, when, & what people want to share. In: Proceedings of the SIGCHI Conference on Human Factors in Computing Systems (CHI 2005), pp. 81–90. ACM (2005)
15. Barkus, L.: Privacy in location-based services, concern vs. coolness. In: Proceedings of the 2004 Workshop on Location System Privacy and Control (2004)
16. Kar, B., Crowsey, R.C., Zale, J.J.: The Myth of Location Privacy in the United States: Surveyed Attitude versus Current Practices. The Professional Geographer 65(1), 47–64 (2013)
17. Solove, D.J.: Privacy Self-Management and the Consent Paradox. Harvard Law Review 126 (2013)
18. Ozer, N., Conley, C., O'Connell, D.H., Gubins, T.R., Ginsburg, E.: Location-Based Services: Time For a Privacy Check-In. ACLU of Northern California (2010)
19. Aïmeur, E., Brassard, G., Molins, P.: Reconstructing profiles from information disseminated on the internet. In: Privacy, Security, Risk and Trust (PASSAT), 2012 International Conference on Social Computing (SocialCom), pp. 875–883. IEEE (2012)

Information Technology Artifacts in the Regulatory Compliance of Business Processes: A Meta-Analysis

Okhaide Akhigbe[1](✉), Daniel Amyot[1], and Gregory Richards[2]

[1] School of Computer Science and Electrical Engineering,
University of Ottawa, Ottawa, Canada
okhaide@uottawa.ca, damyot@eecs.uottawa.ca
[2] Telfer School of Management, University of Ottawa, Ottawa, Canada
richards@telfer.uottawa.ca

Abstract. To address recent calls for better regulatory compliance of business processes (electronic or not), this study synthesizes research findings of nine peer-reviewed systematic literature reviews and state-of-the-art studies on business process compliance to examine Information Technology artifacts used in the compliance of business processes to laws and regulations. Results from the 342 unique studies covered by these reviews demonstrate that eight types of Information Technology artifacts are used in the *design*, *execution* and *after-execution* lifecycle phases of regulatory compliance to perform compliance *modeling*, *checking*, *analysis* and *enactment* tasks. The results also demonstrate with statistical evidence that compliance enactment (which involves putting mechanisms in place to address changes in the compliance representations, business processes or regulatory requirements) has received the least attention. This is a worrisome situation given the dynamic environment in which businesses operate. We argue that the findings in this work are relevant toward understanding the current state of the domain, providing insights on what phases and tasks need improvement.

Keywords: Business process compliance · IT artifacts · Meta-analysis · Regulatory compliance · Requirements · Systematic reviews

1   Introduction

The introduction of Information Systems (IS) to better facilitate different functions in organizations served as the foundation for research on the compliance of business process with laws and regulations. The rationale is that if IS can help to improve operational functions in organizations, it can also help to facilitate compliance behaviors, which are important elements in the success of organizations. Recent events in the financial sector, the advent of social media along with continued concerns for privacy, have created a strong impetus for organizations to carefully consider ways of monitoring and tracking adherence of their business processes (electronic or not) with laws and regulations. Governments have the responsibility and authority to create or prescribe laws over a country, region, province or state. Regulations are based on laws and are usually more detailed and procedural to facilitate interpretation. Both

© Springer International Publishing Switzerland 2015
M. Benyoucef et al. (Eds.): MCETECH 2015, LNBIP 209, pp. 89–104, 2015.
DOI: 10.1007/978-3-319-17957-5_6

laws and regulations affect the activities of individuals and corporate entities. An understanding of business processes enables corporate entities to know how well they are meeting their objectives. Some of these processes in turn are subjected to laws and regulations enacted by governments to ensure, among other concerns, safety and security as well as protection of individuals and their information, or of society in general.

Individuals within corporate entities therefore are obligated to comply with relevant laws and regulations. The act and process of ensuring adherence to these laws and regulations is often referred to as *regulatory compliance*. Regulatory compliance management involves discovering, extracting and representing different requirements from laws and regulations that affect a business process. It also involves analyzing, checking and enforcing compliance [7].

Information Systems have been used in regulatory compliance both by *regulators*, i.e., governments and their departments and agencies, as well as by the *regulated parties*. Early uses of IS in regulatory compliance leveraged the technology to help clarify laws and regulations. Over time, the use of IS became much more sophisticated and decision-focused, allowing for differentiation between requirements that were feasible and those that were not. Recently, mainly due to continued need for accountability and traceability and new laws and regulations (such as Sarbanes-Oxley or Basel III in the financial sector, HIPAA in the health sector and the new Bill C-13 to address cyber bullying in Canada), the use of IS in regulatory compliance now addresses the need for analysis and for the mapping of interrelationships [23].

Given this state of affairs, the need to evaluate the application of IS to this domain is apparent. To explore and evaluate the current situation related to regulatory compliance of business processes, this study employs a *meta-analysis* of existing reviews and state-of-the-art studies that have been done on regulatory compliance to identify Information Technology artifacts types, compliance tasks that create and use them and the lifecycle phases where they occur. The rest of this study is organized as follows. Section 2 explores Information Technology artifacts types in regulatory compliance, and tasks that create or use them. Section 3 discusses the systematic literature review process applied and the results obtained. Section 4 contains a meta-analysis to highlight the different Information Technology artifacts and research approaches where they are employed. Section 5 addresses threats to the validity of this study while Section 6 provides conclusions and recommendations.

2   Information Technology Artifacts and Regulatory Compliance

Artifacts generally are objects or phenomena designed to meet certain desired goals [30]. In the regulatory compliance domain, interrelationships exist between legal artifacts, business artifacts and Information Technology artifacts. The use of the latter is based on the notion of the creation of innovative artifacts to solve real-world problems as argued by the design science research paradigm [15].

Activities in regulatory compliance aim to meet desired goals such as identifying respective legal requirements from laws and regulations, checking and enforcing business process compliance, and reporting on the state of compliance or addressing any change in the process or identified requirements. These goals can be contextualized in such a way as to enable the application of Information Technology artifacts. In recent times, the seminal work on design science research by Hevner and Chatterjee [15] provides a generally acceptable working definition of Information Technology artifacts. Eight categories were defined for *constructs*: vocabulary and symbols, *models*: abstractions and representations, *methods*: algorithms and practices, and *instantiations*: implemented and prototype systems (Table 1).

Table 1. Artifact topology (adapted from Offermann et al. [21])

Artifact Type	Use	Structure	Hevner & Chatterjee [15]
System design	Description	Structure or behavior-related description of a system, commonly using some formalism (e.g., UML) and possibly text.	Instantiations, Model
Method	Support	Definition of activities to create or interact with a system.	Method
Language / Notation	Support	A (generally formalized) system to formulate statements that represents parts of reality.	Construct, Model
Algorithm	Description	Executable description of system behaviour.	Method
Guideline	Support	Suggestion regarding behaviour in a particular situation (if in situation X do Y).	Construct
Requirements	Description	Statement about Systems (a system of type X shall have some property Y [because of Z])	Construct
Pattern	Support	Definition of reusable elements of design with its benefits and application context	Instantiations, Model
Metric	Support	A mathematical model that is able to measure aspects of systems or methods	Model, Method

These categories are structured along the artifact typology described by Offermann et al. [21] consisting of eight different artifact types. These artifact types are argued to "faithfully mirror what practitioners in Information Technology and Information Systems would recognize as key types of artifacts" [17]. Table 1 shows the artifact topology adopted for this study and our postulated matching to the working definition of Information Technology artifacts by Hevner and Chatterjee [15].

The activities involved in regulatory compliance *create* and *use* different types of Information Technology artifacts in any of the three lifecycle phases of regulatory compliance: *design*, *execution* and *after-execution*. These lifecycle phases represent the different stages in ensuring compliance of a business process with a law or regulation and are synonymous with the three phases of compliance checking [6,8]. The design phase covers activities involved in the discovery, extraction and formalization of relevant compliance requirements. The execution phase covers activities such as checking, monitoring, measuring, analyzing and reporting the compliance of the business process with legal/regulatory requirements. Finally, activities in the after-execution phase address change management issues such as i) needs for adaptation due to changes in the characteristics of the identified requirements or ii) needs for evolution as a result of the introduction of new requirements (or their modification).

These activities, as suggested by the Software & Systems Process Engineering Meta-model (SPEM 2.0) [22], represent the basic units of work within regulatory compliance and are described as *tasks*. In the application to the lifecycle phases of regulatory compliance, a task *"provides complete step-by-step explanations of doing all the work that needs to be done to achieve"* the respective desired goal [22]. In particular, these phases indicate when Information Technology artifacts are created or used by tasks towards addressing functions or problems of regulatory compliance. These tasks have been described in the literature as compliance programs [5] or more detailed compliance dimensions [7].

In this work therefore, compliance *modeling* tasks address sourcing and elicitation towards discovery and formalization of requirements from relevant laws and regulations while compliance *checking* tasks ensure that the formalized representations created are valid and meet the relevant compliance requirements. Compliance *analysis* tasks involve getting insights on the state of compliance with measurements, reporting and traceability, and finally compliance *enactment* tasks include mechanisms to dynamically react to violation occurrences to re-establish compliance.

3   Systematic Literature Review

Two foremost definitions show how systematic literature reviews are used today [16]:

i.   as a process: *"systematic reviews provide a systematic, transparent means for gathering, synthesizing, and appraising the findings of studies on a particular topic or question. They aim to minimize the bias associated with single studies and non systematic reviews"* [28], and

ii. as a product: *"a systematic review is a research article that identifies relevant studies, appraises their quality and summaries their results using scientific methodology"* [18].

This work utilizes systematic review both as a process and a product. As a process, it reviews literature on the usage and creation of Information Technology artifacts in regulatory compliance. As a product, it comprises the referenced reviews from studies obtained during the review process and utilized in the meta-analysis stage described in section 4. The objective of our review is a systematic selection of existing reviews, surveys and state-of-the-art studies that address the creation and use of Information Technology artifacts in the discovery, extraction and representation of legal requirements, the creation of law compliant business processes, the checking and enforcement of the business processes against laws and regulations, the measurement of compliance of business process with laws or regulations, and the management of changes in the compliance processes and in laws and regulations. The research method used here is in line with Kitchenham and Charters [19]. It consists of three stages: "planning", "conducting the review" and "reporting the results".

3.1   Planning Stage

To identify the compliance tasks that create or use Information Technology artifacts, we determined research questions, engines to search from, keywords and queries, and finally inclusion and exclusion criteria to select or exclude relevant studies. Based on the objective of the systematic literature review, we defined four research questions. The first two questions are addressed in this section and the last two in the meta-analysis described in section 4. The research questions are:

1. What are the phases in the lifecycle of regulatory compliance?
2. What compliance tasks create or use Information Technology artifacts?
3. What are the types of the Information Technology artifacts created or used in regulatory compliance?
4. What are the research approaches that define the usage or creation of Information Technology artifacts within the domain of regulatory compliance?

We identified academic search engines where we could obtain relevant studies. This selection was based on academic knowledge and experience of the authors and was verified by a Librarian at the University of Ottawa. At this stage, seven engines were chosen: ACM Digital Library (ACM), Business Source Complete (BSC), IEEE Xplore (IEEE), ProQuest, Scopus, Web of Science (WOS) and Google Scholar (GS). Next we identified keywords that capture the essence of our objective as articulated by the research questions. These keywords were assembled in a search query:

("Business process compliance" OR "Regulatory compliance" OR "Legal compliance") AND ("Systematic review" OR "Systematic survey" OR "Literature review" OR "Literature survey" OR "State-of-the-art")

We then defined two exclusion/inclusion criteria to enable the selection of appropriate studies for review. For the first level, studies from searches that did not fit the purpose of the search query (e.g., they just included the keywords without discussing them) or that were not written in English were excluded from the selection. For the second level, we checked each selected study for two inclusion criteria: (C1) it addressed the compliance of business processes with laws and regulations with an Information Technology artifact, and (C2) it had an accessible list of all reviewed studies. These surveyed studies could either be explicitly mentioned as a list, referenced in the paper, or made available as a web link. Finally, the studies that met these exclusion/inclusion criteria were further categorized based on stages in the lifecycle and compliance tasks. These stages are the *design, execution* and the *after-execution* phases while the tasks are compliance *modeling, checking, analysis* and *enactment*.

3.2   Conducting the Review Stage

In this stage, to get the primary studies of interest, the search query was applied to the seven selected search engines. Since each engine is unique, where necessary, the searches were adapted to suit the database options and constraints such as selecting all available databases for searches done on ProQuest and Business Source Complete. All searches did not restrict the studies obtained to any time frame.

We found a total of 364 possible unique papers, most coming from Scopus and Google Scholar. From the result obtained, we did a quick scan through of title and abstract to ensure the studies met the criterion in the first level of exclusion/inclusion. In the end, 10 studies were selected and we reviewed all their referenced studies to see if our search query missed any that met our purpose. A Google search was also done on each author for any relevant work done before and after the studies we selected from them. The 10 studies selected from the search and four additional studies obtained from references and searches on the authors are shown in Table 2. This table indicates for each study: its title and publication year, whether it was returned by an engine or by a reference/author search, and the inclusion criteria results (C1 and C2).

Table 2. Summary of selected studies and satisfaction of the second-level inclusion criteria

Studies	Title	Year	Source	C1	C2
1 [23]	Addressing legal requirements in requirements engineering	2007	Reference	Y	Y
2 [5]	State-of-the-art in the field of compliance languages	2008	Reference	Y	Y
3 [6]	Business process compliance checking: current state and future challenges	2008	Scopus GS	Y	Y
4 [29]	Compliance in e-government service engineering: state-of-the-art	2010	Scopus WOS	Y	Y
5 [27]	A systematic review of compliance measurement based on goals and indicators	2011	Scopus WOS, GS	Y	Y
6 [10]	A systematic review of goal-oriented requirements management frameworks for business process compliance	2011	IEEE Scopus	Y	Y
7 [7]	Business process regulatory compliance management solution frameworks: a comparative evaluation	2012	ACM	Y	Y
8 [3]	Generalizability and applicability of model-based business process compliance-checking approaches — a state-of-the-art analysis and research roadmap	2012	BSC ProQuest GS	Y	Y
9 [15]	State-of-the-art of business process compliance approaches: a survey	2014	Scopus GS	Y	Y
10 [1]	A study of compliance management in information systems research	2009	Scopus	Y	N
11 [4]	Regulatory compliance in information systems research – literature analysis and research agenda	2009	Scopus WOS	N	Y
12 [20]	A framework for the systematic comparison and evaluation of compliance monitoring approaches	2013	Scopus GS	Y	N
13 [24]	The challenge of empirical research on business compliance in regulatory capitalism	2009	Reference	N	Y
14 [2]	Information systems research: aligning to industry challenges in management of regulatory compliance	2010	Reference	Y	N

While getting a professional/industrial, non-academic viewpoint on Information Technology artifacts created and used by compliance tasks is very valuable, it remains difficult to obtain such studies. In this stage, we attempted searching on two of the major search engines on the web, namely Microsoft Bing and Google, for studies. Apart from the searches producing numerous irrelevant results, a scan through the relevant search results (mostly yearly "state of the art" regulatory compliance reports from international consulting firms) reveals that these professional surveys, reviews and executive summaries do not mention the kinds of artifacts types of interest here. They rather focus on cost and implications of regulatory compliance (e.g., see Price-waterhouseCoopers' 2014 report [26]). Hence, the results obtained from the professional/industrial, non-academic searches were not included in the study.

The studies that were excluded from this work are: 10) Abdullah et al. [1], as it did not provide the studies reviewed; 11) Cleven and Winter [4] for a focus on the different layers and interrelationships affected by regulatory compliance in an enterprise instead of Information Technology artifacts; Ly et al. [20] for their mixed use of a systematic literature review and case studies inconsistent with our meta-analysis approach, 13) Parker and Nielsen [24] for its focus on compliance of businesses rather than business processes, 14) Abdulla et al. [2] for its use of answers from professionals rather than surveys. The focus of was on the different layers and interrelationships affected by regulatory compliance in an enterprise and as such it was excluded since it did not address Information Technology artifacts.

3.3   Reporting the Results Stage

The nine studies (numbered 1 to 9 in Table 2) that met our exclusion/inclusion criteria were categorized with respect to how they answered the first two research questions. That is how they addressed the phases in the lifecycle of regulatory compliance and compliance tasks that use or create Information Technology artifacts. Studies 1 and 4 had referenced studies with compliance *modeling* and *checking* tasks that created or used Information Technology artifacts in the *design* and *execution* phases of regulatory compliance. For Studies 2 and 3, the compliance *modeling, checking* and *analysis* tasks created or used Information Technology artifacts also in the *design* and *execution* phases as observed in their referenced articles. Finally, Studies 5 to 9 had referenced articles with compliance *modeling, checking, analysis* and *enactment* tasks that created or used Information Technology artifacts in the *design, execution* and *after-execution* phases of the lifecycle of regulatory compliance.

4   Meta-Analysis

A meta-analysis is a statistical technique employed by researchers while carrying out research synthesis. Originally invented and defined by Glass as "*the statistical analysis of a large collection of analysis results from individual studies for the purpose of integrating the findings*" [13], the meta-analysis approach is taken advantage of here for the rigor it brings when analyzing the product of the systematic literature review done in section 3.3, namely the nine selected studies. This section analyzes these nine studies to answer the remaining two research questions (#3 and #4) described in section 3.1. In answering these questions, this meta-analysis highlights the different types of Information Technology artifacts observed from the referenced studies, the compliance tasks that characterize their creation and usage, as well as the type of research approach employed in their use.

4.1   Descriptive Analysis

The nine studies selected in this systematic literature review collectively identified over 2,366 studies of interest (including some duplicates) in answering the different research questions asked or in addressing the motivations of each respective study. From this collection, a total of 457 referenced studies (e.g., the combination of the *selected* studies from all nine surveys following their own inclusion/exclusion criteria, including duplicates) were included in the meta-analysis. These studies were then assessed individually to identify Information Technology artifacts corresponding to the eight types described in section 2, the compliance tasks that create or use them, as well as their research approach.

To identify the artifact types, the artifact topology described in section 2 was used. For the compliance tasks, studies were also searched for the following key words, which capture the essence of their respective compliance tasks:

- Modeling: *discovery, elicitation, sourcing, representation* and *specification.*
- Checking: *verification, enforcement, monitoring, validation, audit,* and *detection.*
- Analysis: *reporting, explanation, traceability, modularity* and *measurement.*
- Enactment: *adaptation, evolution, violation response, recovery* and *resolution.*

Since most authors indicated whether their work is exploratory research or a proto-type, or a solution implemented in a real-life scenario or test case, this information was used to identify the research approach used. We further observed that all studies that involved a real-life implementation mentioned it explicitly. As such, for studies that did not indicate any approach, we inferred one based on the description of compliance tasks in the study.

Table 3. Studies, artifact types, tasks and research approaches

Study	Artifact Types									Tasks				Research Approaches	
	SD	M	L/N	A	G	R	P	Mr	N	CM	CC	CA	CE	Ex/Pr	Sc/TC
1	9	21	10	6	21	7	12	1	5	32	19	1	0	22	11
2	57	65	39	10	48	38	7	3	10	84	84	25	5	78	10
3	15	14	10	2	13	8	1	0	1	19	20	4	2	17	4
4	9	15	1	0	14	0	3	1	0	15	14	7	0	6	9
5	18	30	4	5	29	3	8	8	1	30	30	22	7	18	13
6	48	63	11	4	58	5	10	9	13	68	67	32	4	43	28
7	18	25	18	2	21	7	9	0	0	28	30	6	6	23	8
8	2	31	29	10	28	7	7	0	0	39	46	15	7	41	7
9	51	69	26	16	51	18	11	2	7	67	76	37	7	61	16
Total	247	333	148	55	283	93	68	24	37	382	386	149	38	309	106
	1251								37	955				415	

Legend
SD = System Design, M = Method, L/N = Language/Notation, A = Algorithm, G = Guideline, R= Requirements,
P= Pattern, Mr = Metrics, N = No Information Technology artifact mentioned.
CM = Compliance Modeling, CC = Compliance Checking, CA = Compliance Analysis, CE = Compliance Enactment
Ex/Pr = Exploratory Research/Prototype, SC/TC = Real-life Scenario/Test case
NOTE: Results are exclusive of 3 studies identified as part of the main study, 1 study that could not be found and 1 study not written in English. Duplicates are however counted in the totals.

Of the 457 studies reviewed (**available online at http://bit.ly/1BUK182**), 73 studies were duplicates, three studies were part of the original nine studies selected from the systematic literature review stage, one study was not written in English, and one study could not be found. We also identified 37 studies that did not mention any Information Technology artifact. In total, 309 studies were identified to employ an exploratory research approach or prototypes, both towards enhancing the knowledge on regulatory compliance. In addition, 106 studies included real-life scenarios or test cases. We observed also that a total of 1251 Information Technology artifacts in different combinations were created or used by 955 tasks, as illustrated in Table 3. These results include duplicates, whereas the next section focuses on the 342 *unique* studies.

4.2   Artifact Types

Of the 342 unique referenced studies reviewed that indicate the creation or use of an Information Technology artifact, there were in total 1026 Information Technology artifact type occurrences identified.

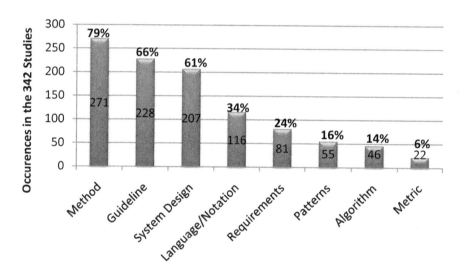

Fig. 1. Information Technology artifact types in regulatory compliance

We observe in Fig. 1 that "Methods" and "Guidelines" appear to be the most frequently created or used Information Technology artifacts types, occurring in 79% and 67% of the referenced studies respectively. "Metrics" and "Algorithm" are the least-often created or used, occurring in 6% and 14% of the studies.

Further observation from the correlation results in Table 4, produced using the Minitab statistical software (http://www.minitab.com/), reveals strong significant correlations between "Guidelines" and "Methods" at r(342) = 0.647, p < 0.001 and between "Requirements" and "Language/Notation" at r(342) = 0.647, p < 0.001. These correlations suggest a link with the frequent use of methodologies in the regulatory compliance of business processes. While methods indicate activities carried out in creating or interacting with business processes and regulations, guidelines provide generalized suggestions on how to practically go about using methods.

Table 4. Correlation statistics for Information Technology artifact types

	M	G	SD	L/N	R	P	A
G	0.647 0.000						
SD	0.073 0.176	0.140 0.010					
L/N	-0.440 0.000	-0.607 0.000	-0.217 0.000				
R	-0.393 0.000	-0.627 0.000	-0.249 0.000	0.647 0.000			
P	-0.129 0.017	-0.045 0.407	-0.249 0.000	-0.045 0.411	-0.057 0.296		
A	-0.031 0.572	-0.085 0.117	-0.137 0.011	-0.138 0.011	-0.018 0.740	-0.033 0.548	
Mr	0.017 0.759	0.034 0.534	0.017 0.759	-0.087 0.108	-0.090 0.097	-0.017 0.748	0.036 0.503
Legend M = Method, G = Guideline, SD = System Design, L/N = Language/Notation, R= Requirements, P = Pattern, A = Algorithm, Mr = Metrics **Note:** the top number is the *Pearson's correlation* whereas the bottom number is the *p-value*							

In the studies, reviewed methods and guidelines were often represented together as *methodologies*, e.g., see Ghanavati et al. [11] and Young and Antón [31]. We also observed a significant use of languages/notations with requirements since the former constitute formalized structure to formulate statements about a system and the latter provides assertions about required behaviours and functions of the system, as seen in Governatori et al. [14] and Giblin et al. [12]. Interestingly, Table 4 also suggests two fairly strong negative correlations: when guidelines are present, requirements ($r(342)$ = -0.627, $p < 0.001$) and languages/notations ($r(342)$ = -0.607, $p < 0.001$) tend *not* to be present.

4.3   Tasks that Use or Create Information Technology Artifacts

For tasks that create or use different Information Technology artifacts in regulatory compliance, 315 studies identified *modeling* tasks, 316 studies *checking* tasks, 121 studies *analysis* tasks, and 30 *enactment* tasks. These counts are decomposed on a per-period basis in Fig. 2. We observe that compliance *modeling* and *checking* tasks account for 80% of tasks in the 342 referenced studies reviewed. These tasks involve activities of discovery and representation of requirements business processes comply with from relevant laws and regulations. They also involve activities that ensure these representations are correct. Compliance *analysis* tasks, which involve activities for providing insights on the state of compliance, and compliance *enactment* tasks, which involve activities that address changes in the compliances representations, business processes or requirements from laws and regulations, were identified in just 16% and 4% of the reviewed studies, respectively.

The reason for this elaborate coverage in the literature of compliance *modeling* and *checking* tasks could be a result of continued advancements in technology. In this respect, much effort has been invested towards utilizing the most current technologies as they emerge, in the discovery and representation of relevant requirements in laws and regulations as well as ensuring these representations are in line with the respective requirements. This implies that little effort, often initiated as afterthoughts, has been devoted towards gaining insights about the state of compliance of business processes or to exploring relationships between Information Technology artifacts and other artifacts involved in the lifecycle of regulatory compliance as the business, laws and regulations evolve. This is further demonstrated in Fig. 2, where we observe that in spite of rapid advances in technology since year 2001, compliance *modeling* and *checking* tasks have still received the most attention. Inasmuch as we also observe a decrease in attention to compliance *modeling* and an increase in attention to compliance *analysis*, compliance *enactment* still receives little attention.

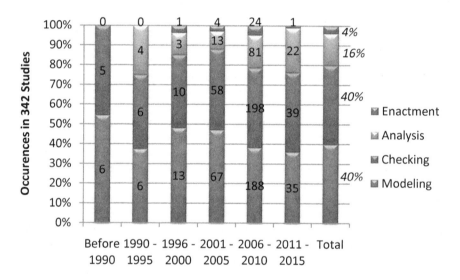

Fig. 2. State of regulatory compliance tasks over time, despite technological advances

This further suggests that compliance with laws and regulation by business processes is currently viewed as basically identifying relevant requirements from laws and regulations and ensuring that business processes comply with them, without much attention to compliance *enactment*. This is an unfortunate position that prevents further advances in technology. This also prevents the opportunity to achieve business-IT alignment through the use and creation of Information Technology artifacts for activities such as anticipation, adaptation and management of change to business processes as and when they occur.

4.4   Research Approach

Of the 342 studies finally selected, 82 studies indicated that the research approach involved the creation or use of Information Technology artifact in compliance *modeling, checking, analysis or enactment* tasks for real-life regulatory compliance scenarios, while 260 studies indicated that they were for prototypes or exploratory research geared towards improving knowledge on regulatory compliance. This result suggests that much research is still ongoing on improving the knowledge on regulatory compliance than they are towards solutions addressing the different concerns faced by professionals in the industry with regards to compliance.

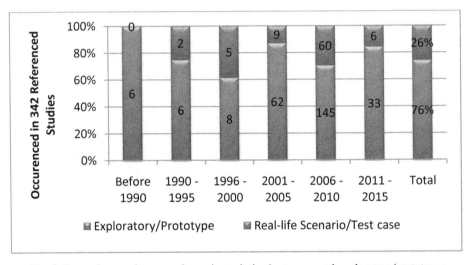

Fig. 3. State of research approaches using solution/test cases and exploratory/prototypes

As observed in Fig. 3, before 1990, research done in regulatory compliance that involved compliance tasks that used or created Information Technology artifacts was solely exploratory in nature. While over time the majority of research was still exploratory or involving the creation of prototypes, there was a steady increase in research that involved a real-life regulatory compliance scenario in the same period until 2006 to 2010, where we observe a sharp increase. Since 2011 however, for every six papers published on regulatory compliance that is a prototype or exploratory research one in nature, just one publication involves a real-life regulatory compliance scenario or test case.

Interestingly, Abdullah et al. [1] had argued in 2009 that research in regulatory compliance has "predominantly focused on exploratory studies, rather than proposition of solutions that can assists organizations in their compliance management regimens". Five years later, the statistical evidence still suggests that not much has been done towards proposing solutions within the domain of regulatory compliance.

5   Threats to Validity

It is anticipated for any research to be limited by influences, often called threats to validity, which may affect the ability to obtain, interpret and conclude from data about the hypothesis outlined in the research [25]. In this paper, we did a validity analysis to identify possible threats and ways of addressing them [9].

Construct validity refers to how well the studied parameters and their outcomes are relevant to the research questions addressed [9]. In order to ensure that we obtained the appropriate studies to address the research questions, we selected many (seven) search engines with a fairly open query, with validation by a Librarian at the University of Ottawa. Bias however might have been introduced in the identification of compliance tasks that create or use Information Technology artifacts. To mitigate this, in addition to using keywords and synonyms that capture the essence of these compliance tasks, we also checked how the *referenced* studies were described in the main selected study from the systematic literature review. We however observed that some literature reviews on regulatory compliance are reported with insufficient raw data, e.g., when the list of articles reviewed is not accessible. These reviews were excluded, but they might have discussed topics that could have influenced our results.

Internal validity refers to research that identifies statistical significant relationships where one checks the certainty that the treatment introduced is related to the actual outcome observed [9]. The statistical analysis employed in this study is in line with the fundamental nature of meta-analysis in integrating research findings of individual studies using statistical means [13]. The research questions outlined in section 3.1 enabled us to obtain appropriate studies and their references, which were used in the meta-analysis in section 4. We are aware that our approach in this study might not have identified all relevant studies in regulatory compliance. The attempt to only analyze studies identified through existing literature reviews and state-of-the-art studies availed us of many appropriate studies, with no time limitations of when the studies were done. However, through the manual inspection of these papers, we might have been biased since we did the data collection and selection ourselves. We also did the categorizations of studies for the Information Technology artifact types, compliance tasks and lifecycle phases of regulatory compliance. This could be mitigated better in the future by involving more people to handle each aspect specifically, with a resolution process for when individual assessments do not match.

External validity refers to the ability of generalizing research findings obtained to other domain under different settings [9]. Although generalization over time is supported here given that our selection of studies was not limited along that dimension, the results cannot be easily generalized to domains outside the scope of this study, for example business compliance or compliance outside the Information Systems area (e.g., e-commerce applications or software compliance in general).

6   Conclusions and Recommendation

In this study, to give insight on the current state of research on regulatory compliance in light of dynamic business environments and changing laws and regulation, we employed a meta-analysis to highlight the different types of Information Technology artifacts used or created in the different phases of regulatory compliance applied to business processes. This approach shows maturity levels within the different phases of the lifecycle of regulatory compliance, compliance tasks that characterize the usage or creation of the Information Technology artifacts, and research approaches where theses artifacts are used.

The results of the systematic literature review and meta-analysis indicate that:

1. "Methods" and "Guidelines" are the most common Information Technology artifacts types while "Algorithms" and "Metrics" are the least frequently used in regulatory compliance. They respectively appear in 79%, 67%, 14% and 6% of the reviewed referenced studies.
2. There are strong positive correlations between "Guidelines" and "Methods" ($r = 0.647$, $p<0.001$), and between "Requirements" and "Languages/Notations" ($r = 0.647$, $p<0.001$).
3. Regulatory compliance is currently viewed as basically identifying relevant requirements in laws and regulations and ensuring business processes (electronic or not) comply with them. This is evidenced by 80% of the referenced studies reviewed focusing on compliance *modeling* and *checking* tasks.
4. Compliance *analysis* tasks and especially compliance *enactment* tasks have been neglected, as they are mentioned in only 16% and 4% of the referenced studies reviewed, respectively.
5. Since 2000, compliance *modeling* tasks have received decreasing attention whereas compliance *analysis* tasks have received increasing attention, but attention to compliance *enactment* is still not picking up.

The results from the meta-analysis also indicate that there are three times as many regulatory compliance papers that include prototypes and exploratory research than those (more mature ones) that have involved real-life regulatory compliance scenarios or test cases. Interestingly, only 16% of the papers in the past 4 years have involved a real-life scenario/test, so this situation is not improving. We also observed from this study that many ambiguities exist in the terminology currently in use in regulatory compliance. These ambiguities apply not only in reference to Information Technology artifacts but also to legal and business process concepts. While future research should address unifying or defining generic terms acceptable to researchers and professionals, in this work, our use of the artifact typology posited by Offermann et al. [21] to identify Information Technology artifacts together with our mapping to the working definition by Hevner and Chatterjee [15] (Table 1) provide a direction towards an approach to reduce and eliminate ambiguities in the domain of regulatory compliance of business processes, and likely other domains.

Finally, while a meta-analysis was utilized to identify Information Technology artifacts types, tasks that create or use them and research approaches where they are used, we are aware that it could be suggested that a meta-analysis in the domain of regulatory compliance is premature. From the results obtained however, we argue that this meta-analysis provides some useful statistical insights with which to view, explore and evaluate the current state of this domain. We can also identify research directions that have been investigated. In particular, future work should put more emphasis on:

i) metrics, algorithms, and patterns artifact types, ii) compliance *enactment* tasks, and iii) real-life regulatory compliance scenario.

Future systematic literature reviews and meta-analyses in this domain should also attempt to mitigate the remaining threats identified in the previous section.

Acknowledgements. This work was supported in part by NSERC (Discovery program) and by the University of Ottawa. We also thank Mish Boutet for library resources and Prof. Rocci Luppicini for early feedback and guidance on this work.

References

1. Abdullah, S., Hikmi, S., Indulska, M., Sadiq, S.: A Study of Compliance Management in In-formation Systems Research. In: 17th ECIS, paper 5. AISeL (2009)
2. Abdullah, N.S., Sadiq, S.W., Indulska, M.: Information Systems Research: Aligning to Industry Challenges in Management of Regulatory Compliance. In: PACIS 2010, paper 36. AISeL (2010)
3. Becker, J., Delfmann, P., Eggert, M., Schwittay, S.: Generalizability and Applicability of Model-Based Business Process Compliance-Checking Approaches – A State-of-the-Art Analysis and Research Roadmap. BuR – Business Research Journal 5(2), 221–247 (2012)
4. Cleven, A., Winter, R.: Regulatory Compliance in Information Systems Research – Literature Analysis and Research Agenda. In: Halpin, T., Krogstie, J., Nurcan, S., Proper, E., Schmidt, R., Soffer, P., Ukor, R. (eds.) Enterprise, Business-Process and Information Systems Modeling. LNBIP, vol. 29, pp. 174–186. Springer, Heidelberg (2009)
5. COMPAS FP7 Project Consortium D2.1.: State-of-the-Art in the Field of Compliance Languages (2008)
6. El Kharbili, M., de Medeiros, A.K.A., Stein, S., van der Aalst, W.M.P.: Business Process Compliance Checking: Current State and Future Challenges. In: MobIS 2008. LNI, vol. 141, pp. 107–113. GI (2008)
7. El Kharbili, M.: Business Process Regulatory Compliance Management Solution Frameworks: A Comparative Evaluation. In: APCCM 2012. CRPIT, vol. 130, pp. 23–32. ACS (2012)
8. Fellman M., Zasada A.: State-of-the-Art of Business Process Compliance Approaches: A Survey. In: Proceedings of the 22nd European Conference on Information Systems (ECIS), http://ecis2014.eu/E-poster/files/0939-file1.pdf (2014)
9. Feldt, R., Magazinius, A.: Validity Threats in Empirical Software Engineering Research- An Initial Survey. In: Proceedings of the 22nd International Conference on Software Engineering and Knowledge Engineering, pp. 374-379 (2010)
10. Ghanavati, S., Amyot, D., Peyton, L.: A Systematic Review of Goal-oriented Requirements Management Frameworks for Business Process Compliance. In: 4th Int. Work. on Requirements Engineering and Law, RELAW, pp. 25–34. IEEE Computer Society (2011)
11. Ghanavati, S., Amyot, D., Peyton, L.: A Requirements Management Framework for Privacy Compliance. In: 10th Workshop on Requirements Engineering (WER), pp. 149–159 (2007)
12. Giblin, C., Liu, A.Y., Müller, S., Pfitzmann, B., Zhou, X.: Regulations expressed as logical models (REALM). In: Proc. 18th Legal Knowledge and Information Systems (JURIX). Frontiers Artificial Intelligence Appl., vol. 134, pp. 37–48. IOS Press, Amsterdam (2005)

13. Glass, G.V.: Primary, Secondary, and Meta-Analysis of Research. Educational Researcher 5(10), 3–8 (1976)
14. Governatori, G., Rotolo, A., Sartor, G.: Temporalised normative positions in defeasible logic. In: Gardner, A. (ed.) Proc. 10th International Conference on Artificial Intelligence and Law, pp. 25–34. ACM Press, New York (2005)
15. Hevner, A., Chatterjee, S.: Design Science Research in Information Systems. In: Design Research in Information Systems, Volume 22 of Integrated Series in Information Systems, Chapter 2, pp. 9–22. Springer US, Boston, MA (2010)
16. Jesson, J., Matheson, L., Lacey, F.M.: Doing Your Literature Review: Traditional and Systematic Techniques. SAGE Publications Ltd (2011)
17. Johannesson, P., Perjons, E.: Knowledge Types and Forms. Springer International Publishing (2014)
18. Khan, K., Kunz, R., Kleijnen, J., Antes, G.: Systematic Reviews to Support Evidence-Based Medicine. CRC Press (2011)
19. Kitchenham, B., Charters, S.: Guidelines for Performing Systematic Literature Reviews in Software Engineering, Version 2.3. Tech. rep., Keele Univ. and Univ. of Durham (2007)
20. Ly, L.T., Maggi, F.M., Montali, M., Rinderle-Ma, S., van der Aalst, W.M.: A Framework for the Systematic Comparison and Evaluation of Compliance Monitoring Approaches. In: 17th Enterprise Distributed Object Computing Conference (EDOC), pp. 7–16. IEEE (2013)
21. Offermann, P., Blom, S., Schönherr, M., Bub, U.: Artifact Types in Information Systems Design Science – A Literature Review. In: Winter, R., Zhao, J., Aier, S. (eds.) DESRIST 2010. LNCS, vol. 6105, pp. 77–92. Springer, Heidelberg (2010)
22. OMG: Software Process Engineering Meta-model (SPEM) Specification. Version 2. Object Management Group, Technical Report ptc/2008-04-01 (2008)
23. Otto, P.N., Antón, A.I.: Addressing Legal Requirements in Requirements Engineering. In: 15th IEEE International Requirements Engineering Conf., pp. 5–14. IEEE CS (2007)
24. Parker, C., Nielsen, V.: The Challenge of Empirical Research on Business Compliance in Regulatory Capitalism. Annual Review of Law and Social Science 5, 45–70 (2009)
25. Perry, D., Porter, A., Votta, L.: Empirical Studies of Software Engineering: A Roadmap, Future of Software Engineering, pp. 345–355. ACM (2000)
26. PricewaterhouseCoppers: Building on the Past, Seeking the Future. PWC Report. Retrieved November 10, 2014, from http://www.pwc.com.au/industry/asset-management/assets/Risk-Compliance-Benchmarking-Aug14.pdf (2014)
27. Shamsaei, A., Amyot, D., Pourshahid, A.: A Systematic Review of Compliance Measurement Based on Goals and Indicators. In: Salinesi, C., Pastor, O. (eds.) CAiSE Workshops 2011. LNBIP, vol. 83, pp. 228–237. Springer, Heidelberg (2011)
28. Sweet, M., Moynihan, R.: Improving Population Health: The Uses of Systematic Reviews Milbank Memorial Fund, pp. 1–84. Retrieved November 22, 2014, from http://wwwmilbank.org/uploads/documents/0712populationhealth/0712populationhealth.html (2007)
29. Turki, S., Bjekovic-Obradovic, M.: Compliance in e-Government Service Engineering: State-of-the-Art. In: Morin, J.-H., Ralyté, J., Snene, M. (eds.) IESS 2010. LNBIP, vol. 53, pp. 270–275. Springer, Heidelberg (2010)
30. Vaishnavi, V., Kuechler, W.: Design Science Research in Information Systems. http://www.desrist.org/design-research-in-information-systems (2004)
31. Young, J.D., Antón, A.I.: A Method for Identifying Software Requirements Based on Policy Commitments. In: IEEE Int. Conf. Req. Eng., pp. 47–56 (2010)

Information Flow-Based Security Levels Assessment for Access Control Systems

Sofiene Boulares$^{(\boxtimes)}$, Kamel Adi, and Luigi Logrippo

Département d'Informatique et d'Ingénierie, Université du Québec en Outaouais,
Gatineau, QC, Canada
{bous42,kamel.adi,luigi.logrippo}@uqo.ca

Abstract. Access control systems are designed to allow or deny access to data according to organizational policies. In many organizations, the access rights of subjects to data objects are determined in consideration of clearance levels of subjects and classification levels of objects. In most formally-defined traditional access control systems, levels are predetermined and policies are rigid. However, in practice organizations need to use flexible methods where the levels are determined dynamically by information flow criteria. In this paper, we develop a method that is both formal and flexible to determine entities' security levels on the basis of access history, which characterizes the data that subjects can know or objects can contain. Our approach is motivated with a number of different examples, showing that the method meets real-life organizational requirements.

Keywords: Information security · Access control · Information flow · Access history · Clearance · Classification

1 Introduction

Organizations are dependent upon information to do business and information requires protection for confidentiality, integrity and availability. For this reason, data objects (files, databases, etc.) are typically marked with classification levels e.g. unclassified, restricted, confidential, secret and top secret, to protect personal privacy or competitive secrets. The choice of objects classifications is often based on impact assessment and access to information is restricted by security policies to particular trusted subjects (process, machine, etc.). Thus, security clearance is required to access classified information.

Security levels (clearances and classifications), such as levels in Multi-Level Systems (MLS) [1] are often assumed to be exact and correct. In reality, levels are assigned empirically and could result in too restrictive or too permissive policies. If levels were more accurate, they could be used to take better access control decisions. This would help reduce the risks to the information and the organization's ability to conduct its missions.

For example, suppose that an object, initially of low classification level, has been allowed to store more highly classified information, then its classification level should

© Springer International Publishing Switzerland 2015
M. Benyoucef et al. (Eds.): MCETECH 2015, LNBIP 209, pp. 105–121, 2015.
DOI: 10.1007/978-3-319-17957-5_7

increase so that future access control decisions can take into consideration this fact. Situations such as these can occur in many enterprises, and especially in highly dynamic environments such as the Web or the Cloud.

To this end, the main contribution of this paper is to propose a set of precise principles to determine object classifications and subject clearances. Our approach has the potential to address issues related to inference problems (information association and information aggregation).

Information flow is the transfer of information from subjects to objects and vice versa. Some information flows are more important than others, because of their possible consequences. For example, the information flow of a Top secret subject writing on an Unclassified object is more dangerous than the information flow of the same subject writing in a Secret object. In the first case, Top secret information could be leaked to the public, in the second case this information would remain secret. To our knowledge, only two access control models known in the literature today are based on concepts of classification and information flow: the High-water mark [3] which predates the Bell Lapadula model [4] and the Low-water mark [3] which is an extension of the Biba Model [5]. These models, known under the collective names of Multi-Level Security (MLS) models, will be discussed in Section 5.

The access history of subjects to objects and the resulting possible information flow could have an impact on their security levels. We will see that information can be transferred not only directly, but also by association and aggregation. In our access control model, we consider information that can be obtained or inferred from previous accesses and information that could be inferred from these and the data now requested. Information inference could present a security breach if more highly classified information can be inferred from less classified information [2].

To determine when more highly classified information can be inferred from less classified information, we need to determine precisely what a subject can know and what an object can store.

More precisely, there are two important cases of information inference:

- **Information aggregation,** that occurs whenever there is a collection of data items that is classified at a higher level than the levels of individual data items by themselves [2].
  Example. The content of a single medical file is Secret, but the aggregate information concerning all the medical files is Top Secret.
- **Information association,** that occurs whenever two values seen together are classified at a higher level than the classification of either value individually [2].
  Example. The list consisting of the names of all employees and the list containing all employees' social insurance numbers have low confidentiality levels, while a combined list giving employees names with their social insurance numbers has a high confidentiality level.

Thus, information flow is an important element in order to decide security levels of subjects and objects, and it is determined by the history of subjects accessing objects.

In this paper, we present a history and an information flow-based approach to determine subjects and objects security levels. We use many examples as a basis for developing and identifying a set of principles.

The rest of the paper is organized as follows. Section 2 presents a set of basic concepts for our approach. Section 3 describes our subjects and objects confidentiality levels assessment approach. Section 4 shows how to assess subjects and objects integrity levels. In Section 5, we compare our work with related works of the literature. We draw conclusions and outline opportunities for future work in Section 6.

2   Basic Concepts for Our Approach

We assume the existence of the following entities: S a set of subjects, O a set of objects and L a set of security levels. Members of these sets are denoted by lower-case letters s, o, and l with subscripts and primes. According to [2] and [6], confidentiality is related to disclosure of information, while integrity is related to modification of information. In our approach, confidentiality levels of subjects and objects increase when information can flow down to them, and their integrity levels decrease when information can flow up to them. These ideas are behind the properties of the mentioned MLS models.

We adapt the following concepts presented in [6] as follows:

- Two relationships between subjects and objects or between objects respectively: CanKnow and CanStore.
- Two relationships that express previous accesses between subjects and objects: HasRead and HasWritten.

We use the following abbreviations:
CK for CanKnow, CS for CanStore, HR for HasRead and HW for HasWritten.

Table 1 defines two rules: The rule for CK expresses the fact that, if there exists a subject who has read an object, then the subject can know information from that object. The rule for CS deals with storing and expresses the fact that information transfer can occur between objects by effect of subjects reading from and writing in objects. Throughout this paper, we will use the intuitive meaning of these rules in place of their logic formulation.

Table 1. Deductive system

```
1. The inference rule for CK is:
   HR(s,o)→ CK(s,o)(If s has read o, then s can
   know information from o)
2. The inference rule for CS is:
   HR(s,o) ∧ HW(s,o'))→ CS(o',o)(If s has read from
   o and s has written in o',then o' can store
   information from o)
   CS(o,o) is always true.
```

We also define the functions CSS and CKS, as follows:

- For any s, CanKnowSet(s) or CKS(s) is the set of objects o for which CK(s, o) is true: $CKS(s) =_{def} \{o \mid CK(s, o) = true\}$.
- For any o, CanStoreSet(o) or CSS(o) is the set of objects o' for which CS(o, o') is true: $CSS(s) =_{def} \{o' \mid CS(o, o') = true\}$.

The following simple example will introduce the idea of our method. Consider a system with two subjects s_1 and s_2 and two objects o_1 and o_2. Suppose we have the following:

a. $HR(s_1,o_1)$: s_1 has read o_1.
b. $HW(s_1,o_2)$: s_1 has written in o_2.
c. $HR(s_2,o_2)$: s_2 has read o_2.

We can conclude that $CKS(s_1) = \{o_1\}$, $CSS(o_2) = \{o_2, o_1\}$ and $CKS(s_2) = \{o_2, o_1\}$. In other words, subjects can know information by reading them from objects, and objects can store information that is written in them by subjects. Objects can also contain information initially. The effects of the relationships a, b and c, can be shown in figure 1, where subjects are represented by rectangles and objects by circles. A rectangle containing a circle means that the subject can know data from that object. A circle containing a circle means that the object can store data from that object.
Figure 1 (a) shows that s_1 can know data from o_1.
Figure 1 (b) shows that o_2 can store data from o_1.
Figure 1 (c) shows that s_2 can know data from o_1 and o_2.

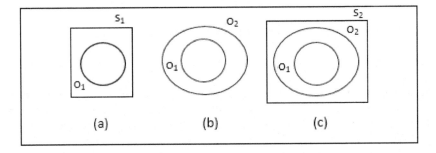

Fig. 1. Effects of a, b and c

3   Access History and Information Flow-Based Confidentiality Levels Assessment

Throughout this section, we present a series of examples for developing the conceptual foundation of our history and information flow-based confidentiality levels assessment approach. We consider that confidentiality levels of subjects and objects have been previously assessed at initial values. They can change as a result of information flow: a Read action creates an information flow from an object to a subject and a Write action creates an information flow from a subject to an object. Subjects can increase their confidentiality levels as they acquire information from higher levels and objects can increase their confidentiality levels as they store information from higher levels. The number of accesses is another factor to be considered when assessing subjects and objects confidentiality levels. We define a total order on L and for each security level in L, we assign a numerical value corresponding to the defined order. For example, if L = {Unclassified, Restricted, Classified, Secret, Top Secret}, then the value Unclassified corresponds to the number 1, Restricted corresponds to the number 2 and so on. To simplify the notation, L will be considered to be understood and so it won't need to be mentioned: in each system, there is only one L which applies to subjects as well as objects. Throughout this paper, the following concepts will be needed to develop our approach:

- sl : S → L formally represents the assignment of security levels to subjects that reflects the trust bestowed upon each of them by the organization that owns the data.
- ol : O → L formally represents the assignment of security levels to objects that reflects the protection needs of the data each of them holds.
- For s ∈ S, CKSL(s) is the multiset of levels of objects o for which CK(s, o) is true, in addition to the level of the subject assigned by the administrator.
  Example. CKSL(s) = {l',l, l'} means that subject s can know data from two different objects belonging to level l' and one object belonging to level l.
- For s ∈ S, $CKSL^+(s)$ is the multiset of levels of objects o for which CK(s, o) is true such that sl(s) ≤ ol(o).
  Example. $CKSL^+(s)$ = {l',l''} means that subject s can know data from two different higher level objects belonging to levels l' and l''. So sl(s) ≤ l' and sl(s) ≤ l''.
- For o ∈ O, CSSL(o) is the multiset of levels of objects o' for which CS(o,o') is true.
  Example. CSSL(o) = {l',l ,l'} means that object o can store two different objects belonging to level l' and one object belonging to level l.
- For o ∈ O, $CSSL^+(o)$ is the multiset of levels of objects o' for which CS(o, o') is true such that ol(o) ≤ ol(o').
  Example. $CSSL^+(o)$ = {l',l''} means that object o can store data from two different higher level objects belonging to levels l' and l''. So ol(o) ≤ l' and ol(o) ≤ l''.

3.1 Access History and Information Flow-Based Subjects Confidentiality Levels Assessment

As mentioned, a main assumption in this paper is that the confidentiality levels of subjects may be assessed by referring to their read access history. We further justify this assumption with relation to a number of intuitively reasonable requirements or principles, as follows:

Principle 1: The confidentiality level of a subject increases as the subject reads objects having confidentiality levels equal to or greater than its own, i.e. as information it can know grows.

Principle 2: The confidentiality level of a subject increases as the subject reads greater *numbers* of objects having confidentiality levels equal to or greater than its own.

Principle 3: For a subject that has no history of reading objects, the confidentiality level is set to a minimum/default value. This can be determined by the system administrator.

Running Example. In this section, we describe a scenario that will be used in the rest of the paper for motivating our approach. Table 2(a) shows the confidentiality levels of the following subjects: Nadia, Claude, Bruno, Carl and Sabrina. Table 2(b) shows the confidentiality levels of the following objects o_1, o_2, o_3, o_4, o_5, o_6, o_7 and o_8.

The objective of our work in this section, is to compare subjects confidentiality levels. Hence, throughout this section, we only cite examples where $sl(s) \leq ol(o)$ for read accesses because subjects confidentiality levels change only when subjects can know higher information at levels equal to or higher than their own.

Table 2. Confidentiality levels

Subject	Confidentiality level
Nadia	2
Claude	2
Bruno	1
Carl	1
Sabrina	1

(a)

Object	Confidentiality level
o_1	4
o_2	4
o_3	3
o_4	2
o_5	1
o_6	1
o_7	1
o_8	1

(b)

We now give examples that motivate our technique.

Example 1. Suppose a case where Bruno has read object o_1 and Carl has read object o_4. We have the following from Table 2: $sl(Bruno) = 1$, $sl(Carl) = 1$, $ol(o_1) = 4$ and $ol(o_4) = 2$. So Bruno and Carl start at the same confidentiality level. If Bruno reads object o_1 and Carl reads o_4, then according to **Principle 1**, Bruno's confidentiality level becomes higher than the confidentiality level of Carl. In the above example, we were able to understand which read access has a more important effect on the subject confidentiality level by simply comparing the levels of objects read. However, as we show below, such a technique is no longer sufficient when objects confidentiality levels are the same.

Example 2. Let us extend Example 1 by considering an additional subject Sabrina and an additional object o_2. The confidentiality levels are given in Table 2 as follows: $sl(Sabrina) = 1$ and $ol(o_2) = 4$.

Suppose that Bruno has read objects o_1 and o_2 while Sabrina has only read o_2. Now, if we were to determine which of these two subjects has a higher confidentiality level, then according to **Principle 2**, we are likely to conclude that Bruno's confidentiality level has become higher than Sabrina's confidentiality level. This is because the number of objects that Bruno has read with a confidentiality level 4 (2 objects) is higher than the number of objects that has been read by Sabrina and having the same confidentiality level (1 object).

Example 3. Let us extend Example 2 by considering an additional object o_3 and an additional subject Nadia. The confidentiality levels are given in Figure 2 as follows: $sl(Nadia) = 2$ and $ol(o_3) = 3$.

Suppose a case where Nadia has read o_1 and o_3 while Carl has read o_2 and o_4. Now, if we were to determine which of these two subjects has a higher confidentiality level, then according to **Principle 1** and **Principle 2** we are likely to conclude that Nadia's confidentiality level has become higher than Carl's confidentiality level.

This is because the two subjects have read o_1 and o_2 which have the same confidentiality levels but Nadia has also read object o_3 having a confidentiality level 3. The latter is higher than the confidentiality level 2 of o_4 which has been read by Carl.

Remark 1 (from Examples 1, 2 and 3)
On the basis of our definitions, assumptions and principles, we propose the following confidentiality level assessment method:

- Always apply **Principle 1**.
- Whenever higher confidentiality levels of objects read by the subject are the same, apply **Principle 2**.

The following definitions will be needed to formalize the principles of Remark 1:

Multisets
Multisets are like sets, but allow multiple occurrences of identical elements. Formally, a multiset is a pair (L, m) where L is the support set and $m : L \rightarrow N$ is the multiplicity function. In the multiset (L, m), the level x appears $m(x)$ times. For example, $\{1,2,1,2, 2,4\}$ is the multiset $(\{1,2,3,4,5\}, m)$ where m is the function such that $m(1) = 2$, $m(2) = 3$, $m(3) = 0$, $m(4) = 1$ and $m(5) = 0$.

Multisets Order
We deal with finite multisets whose support set is a set of natural numbers. We suppose the usual ordering relationship of natural numbers. We define two relations: $>_{mul}$ and $=_{mul}$ on multisets in the following way: we write the multisets as ordered sequences and then we compare them according to the usual lexicographical order [7].

Example. To compare the multisets $\{4,4,5,1\}$ and $\{4,3,2,3,1,5\}$, we compare the ordered sequences $(5,4,4,1)$ and $(5,4,3,3,2,1)$. Since $(5,4,4,1)$ is lexicographically greater than $(5,4,3,3,2,1)$, it follows that $\{4,4,5,1\} >_{mul} \{4,3,2,3,1,5\}$. In the same way, we can see that $\{3,3,4,0\} =_{mul} \{3,4,0,3\}$.

It can be seen that we can compare subjects confidentiality levels, in terms of their previous read accesses by adhering to the principles of Remark 1. Essentially, these principles can be formalized as follows:

Table 3. Formal definition of Remark 1

```
1.sl(s) > sl(s') if   CKSL⁺(s) >mul CKSL⁺(s')
2.sl(s) = sl(s') if   CKSL⁺(s) =mul CKSL⁺(s')
```

Based on Remark1, we obtain the following ordering of subjects confidentiality levels in Examples 1, 2 and 3: sl(Bruno) > sl(Nadia) > sl(Carl) > sl(Sabrina). This is because $CKSL^+(Bruno) = \{4,4\} >_{mul} CKSL^+(Nadia) = \{4,3\} >_{mul} CKSL^+(Carl) = \{4,2\} >_{mul} CKSL^+(Sabrina) = \{4\}$.

3.1.1   Consideration of Information Association and Information Aggregation for Subjects Levels Assessment

In the previous section we considered information that can flow from objects to subjects. In this section, we consider information that could be inferred from previous read accesses. This concept is known in the literature as the inference problem [2]. An inference presents a security breach if more highly classified information can be inferred from less classified information [2]. There are two important cases of the inference problem:

- Information aggregation problem, in the context of access control systems, occurs whenever there is a collection of data items that can be known by a subject or can be stored by an object and that is classified at a higher level than the levels of individual data items by themselves.
  Example. The content of a medical file is Secret, but the aggregate information concerning all the medical files is Top Secret. The blueprint of a single piece is Secret, but the blueprint of a whole artifact is Top Secret.
- Information association problem, in the context of access control systems, occurs whenever two or more values that can be known by a subject or can be stored by an object are classified at a higher level than the classification of either value individually.
  Example. The list consisting of the names of all employees is unclassified and the list containing all employees social insurance numbers are secret, while a combined list giving employee names with their social insurance numbers is Top secret.

We define the following functions that their values are determined by system administrators as a result of enterprise policies where PL is the power multiset of L, PO is the power set of O and N is the set of natural numbers:

- Agg : $N \times L \rightarrow L$ formally represents the assignment of confidentiality levels to information that could be inferred after a number of accesses to a set of objects having the same confidentiality level.
  Example. $Agg(3,2) = 4$ means that the confidentiality level of the information that could be inferred from 3 accesses to level 2 is 4.
- Ass : $PO \rightarrow L$ formally represents the assignment of confidentiality levels to information that could be obtained from a set of objects.
  Example. $Ass(\{o, o', o''\}) = 3$ means that the confidentiality level of the information that could be inferred from objects o, o' and o'' is 3.

In order to apply our approach for subject confidentiality level assessment presented in the previous section and to consider at the same time, cases where more highly classified information could be inferred from less classified information, we define the following functions:

- Agg_l : $PL \rightarrow PL$ formally represents the multiset of confidentiality levels that could be inferred as a result of information aggregation.
  Example. $Agg\_l(CKSL(s)) = \{4,4\}$ means that two items of information of confidentiality levels 4 could be inferred from the multiset of levels CKSL(s).
- Ass_l : $PO \rightarrow PL$ formally represents the multiset of confidentiality levels of information inferred as a result of information association.
  Example. $Ass\_l(CKS(s)) = \{4,2\}$ means that CKS(s) contains objects such that, when associated, information of confidentiality levels 4 and 2 could be inferred.
- For $s \in S$, CKSLA(s) is the multiset containing the multiset CKSL(s) and levels of information inferred from CKSL(s) and CKS(s). More formally, $CKSLA(s) = CKSL(s) \cup Agg\_l(CKSL(s)) \cup Ass\_l(CKS(s))$.
- $CKSLA^+(s)$ is the submultiset of CKSLA(s) having values equal to or greater than sl(s). More formally, $CKSLA^+(s) = \{l \in CKSLA(s) \mid l \geq sl(s)\}$.

Example. Let us assume that $Ass(o_4,o_7) = 3$, $Agg(2,1) = 4$, $CKS(Claude) = \{o_6,o_4,o_7\}$, $CKSL(Claude) = \{2,1,4,1\}$ and $sl(Claude) = 2$.
Thus, we have the following:
$Agg\_l(CKSL(Claude)) = \{4\}$, $Ass\_l(CKS(Claude)) = \{3\}$.
$CKSLA(Claude) = \{2,1,4,1,4,3\}$, $CKSLA^+ (Claude) = \{2,4,4,3\}$.

Remark 2
We can compare the confidentiality levels of subject s and subject s', in terms of their previous read accesses and information inferred from these accesses, by comparing $CKSLA^+(s)$ with $CKSLA^+(s')$. This remark can be formalized as follows:

Table 4. Formal definition of Remark 2

```
1.sl(s) > sl(s') if  CKSLA⁺(s) >mul CKSLA⁺(s')
2.sl(s) = sl(s') if  CKSLA⁺(s) =mul CKSLA⁺(s')
```

3.1.2 Subjects Levels Assessment When a Write Access Is Requested

In this section, we present a subject level assessment approach when a write access is requested. We consider the information that could be inferred from information that can be known by a subject and information that can be stored in the requested object. Whenever a subject requests a write access to an object, the history of its accesses is analyzed to determine whether the information that can be stored in the requested object, correlated with information that can be known by the subject, could result in an inference generating higher level information [1]. If the possibility of an inference arises, the subject's confidentiality level used to determine the access decision for the request in question should be recalculated by considering this possibility. We then need to constitute a new set of objects confidentiality levels where the new levels added are higher than the subject's confidentiality level. In order to apply our approach, we define the following functions:

- $sol : S \times O \rightarrow L$ formally represents the assignment of a confidentiality level to a subject when it requests to write in a particular object.
- For $s \in S$ and $o \in O$, $CKSSL(s, o)$ is the multiset of levels of objects o' for which $CS(o, o')$ is true and levels of objects o'' for which $CK(s, o'')$ is true, $o' \neq o''$, in addition to the level assigned by the administrator to the subject s. More formally, $CKSSL(s, o) = \{ol(o') \mid CS(o, o') = true\} \cup \{ol(o'') \mid CK(s, o'') = true\} \cup sl(s) \setminus \{ol(o') \mid CS(o, o') = CK(s, o')\}$. The symbol $\setminus$ denotes set difference.
- For $s \in S$ and $o \in O$, $CKSS(s, o)$ is the set of objects o' for which $CK(s, o')$ is true and the set of objects o'' for which $CS(o, o'')$ is true , $o' \neq o''$. More formally, $CKSS(s, o) = \{o' \mid CS(o, o') = true\} \cup \{o'' \mid CK(s, o'') = true\} \setminus \{o' \mid CS(o, o') = CK(s, o')\}$.

We defined the functions $CKSSL(s, o)$ and $CKSS(s, o)$ to avoid the consideration of cases where the same object can be known by subject s and can be stored by object o. This is to be in accordance with our definitions in section 3 when we consider multiple accesses by the same subject to the same object only once.

- For $s \in S$ and $o \in O$, $CKSSLA(s, o)$ is the multiset of levels in $CKSL(s)$ and the levels of information inferred from $CKSSL(s, o)$ and $CKSS(s, o)$. More formally, $CKSSLA(s, o) = CKSL(s) \cup Agg\_l(CKSSL(s, o)) \cup Ass\_l(CKSS(s, o))$.
- $CKSSLA^+(s, o)$ is the submultiset of $CKSSLA(s, o)$ having values equal to or greater than $sl(s)$. More formally, $CKSSLA^+(s) = \{l \in CKSSLA(s) \mid l \geq sl(s)\}$.

Example. Suppose that Nadia requests to write in o_3.
Let us assume that $sl(Nadia) = 2$, $CKSL(Nadia) = \{2,1,1,1\}$, $CKS(Nadia) = \{o_7, o_6, o_5\}$, $CSSL(o_3) = \{3,1,1,4\}$, $CSS(o_3) = \{o_3, o_7, o_8, o_1\}$, $Agg(4,1) = 4$ and $Ass(o_8, o_6) = 3$.
Thus, we have the following:
$CKSSL(Nadia, o_3) = \{3,1,4,2,1,1,1\}$, $CKSS(Nadia, o_3) = \{o_3, o_8, o_1, o_7, o_6, o_5\}$.

$Agg\_l(CKSSL(Nadia, o_3)) = 4$, $Ass\_l(CKSS(Nadia, o_3)) = 3$.
$CKSSLA(Nadia, o_3) = \{2,1,1,1,3,4\}$, $CKSSLA^+(Nadia, o_3) = \{2,3,4\}$.

Remark 3

We can compare confidentiality levels of subject s and subject s' when they request write access to an object o, in terms of their previous read accesses, information that can be known or inferred from previous accesses or the current one, by comparing $CKSSLA^+(s, o)$ with $CKSSLA^+(s', o)$. This remark can be formalized as follows:

Table 5. Formal definition of remark 3

```
1. sol(s,o)> sol(s',o)if CKSSLA⁺(s,o) >mul CKSSLA⁺(s',o)
2. sol(s,o)= sol(s',o)if CKSSLA⁺(s,o) =mul CKSSLA⁺(s',o)
```

3.2 Access History and Information Flow-Based Objects Confidentiality Levels Assessment

The confidentiality levels of objects may be assessed by referring to information that can be stored in the objects. In this section, we say that object o can be stored in object o' instead of saying that information from object o can be stored in object o'. Our method is designed to satisfy the following requirements:

Principle 4: The confidentiality level of an object increases as the object can store objects having confidentiality levels equal to or higher than its own, i.e. the confidentiality level of objects that it can store increases.

Principle 5: The confidentiality level of an object increases as the object can store greater *number* of objects having confidentiality levels equal to or higher than its own, even if their confidentiality level does not increase.

Principle 6: For objects that have not yet been written by subjects with higher confidentiality levels, the confidentiality level is set to a default value. This can be determined by the system administrator.

Running Example. We describe a scenario for motivating our history based objects level assessment approach. The objective of our work in this section is to order object confidentiality levels. Hence, if CS(o, o') is true, we only cite examples where ol(o') ≥ ol(o) because objects confidentiality levels change only when objects can store information from objects having equal to or higher confidentiality level than their own.

We now give examples that motivate our technique for object confidentiality level assessment that is primarily based on the confidentiality levels of objects that can be stored in objects.

Example 4. Suppose a first case where object o_1 can be stored in object o_5 and a second case where object o_4 can be stored in object o_6. We have the following from Table 2: $ol(o_1) = 4$, $ol(o_4) = 2$, $ol(o_5) = 1$ and $ol(o_6) = 1$.

According to **Principle 4**, the fact that object o_1 can be stored in object o_5 makes o_5's confidentiality level higher than the confidentiality level of object o_6 where object o_4 can be stored. This is simply because the confidentiality level of object o_1 is higher than the confidentiality level of o_4. In the above example, we were able to understand which object has a more important effect on the object's confidentiality level by simply comparing the levels of those two objects that can be stored in each object. However, as we show below, such a technique is no longer sufficient when the confidentiality levels of objects are the same.

Example 5. Let us extend Example 4 by considering the following objects o_2 and o_7. The confidentiality levels are given in Table 2 as follows: $ol(o_7) = 1$ and $ol(o_2) = 4$. Suppose that objects o_1 and o_2 can be stored in o_5 and o_2 can be stored in o_7.

Now, if we were to determine which of these two objects (o_5 and o_7) has a higher confidentiality level, then according to **Principle 5** we are likely to conclude that o_5's confidentiality level is higher than o_7's confidentiality level. This is because the number of objects that can be stored in o_5 with a confidentiality level of 4 (2 objects) is higher than the number of objects with the same confidentiality level that can be stored in o_7.

Example 6. Let us extend Example 5 by considering additional objects o_3 and o_8. The confidentiality levels are given in Table 2 as follows: $ol(o_3) = 3$ and $ol(o_8) = 1$.

Suppose a case where objects o_1 and o_3 can be stored in o_8 and, at the same time, o_4 can be stored in o_6. Now, if we were to determine which of these two objects has a higher confidentiality level, then according to **Principles 4** and **5** we are likely to conclude that o_8's confidentiality level is higher than o_6's confidentiality level. This is because o_8 can store object o_3 having a confidentiality level 3 which is higher than the confidentiality level of o_4 that can be stored in o_6.

Remark 4 (from Examples 4, 5 and 6)
The previous principles and examples suggest the following method for assessing confidentiality levels of objects:

- Always apply **Principle 4**.
- Whenever higher confidentiality levels of objects which can be stored in the object, are the same, apply **Principle 5**.

It can be seen that we can compare objects confidentiality levels, in terms of the objects that can be stored in them by adhering to the principles of Remark 4. Essentially, these principles can be formalized as follows:

Table 6. Formal definition of Remark 4

```
1. ol(o) > ol(o')  if  CSSL⁺(o) >_mul CSSL⁺(o')
2. ol(o) = ol(o')  if  CSSL⁺(o) =_mul CSSL⁺(o')
```

Based on Remark4, we obtain the ordering of objects confidentiality levels in Examples 4, 5 and 6 as follows: $ol(o_5) > ol(o_8) > ol(o_6) > ol(o_7)$. This is because $CSSL^+(o_5) = \{4,4\} >_{mul} CSSL^+(o_8) = \{4,3\} >_{mul} CSSL^+(o_7) = \{4\} >_{mul} CSSL^+(o_6) = \{2\}$.

3.2.1 Consideration of Information Association and Information Aggregation for Objects Levels Assessment

In this section, we consider the inference of information in addition to information obtained from previous accesses. In order to apply our approach for objects confidentiality levels assessment and to consider cases where more highly classified information could be inferred from less classified information, we define the following functions:

- For $o \in O$, CSSLA(o) is the multiset containing the multiset CSSL(o) and levels of information inferred from CSSL(o) and CSS(o). More formally, $CSSLA(o) = CSSL(o) \cup Agg\_l(CSSL(o)) \cup Ass\_l(CSS(o))$.
- $CSSLA^+(o)$ is the submultiset of CSSLA(o) having values equal or greater than ol(o). More formally, $CSSLA^+(o) = \{l \in CSSLA(o) \mid l \geq ol(o)\}$.

Example. Let us assume that $CSS(o_3) = \{o_3,o_6,o_4,o_7\}$, $CSSL(o_3) = \{3,1,2,1\}$, Ass $(o_4, o_7) = 3$, Agg $(2, 1) = 4$ and $ol(o_3) = 3$.
Thus, we have the following:
$Agg\_l(CSSL(o_3)) = \{4\}$, $Ass\_l(CSS(o_3)) = \{3\}$.
$CSSLA(o_3) = \{3,1,2,1,4,3\}$, $CSSLA^+(o_3) = \{3,4,3\}$.

Remark 5

We can compare confidentiality levels of object o and object o' in terms of objects which can be stored in them and information inferred as a result of previous accesses, by comparing $CSSLA^+(o)$ with $CSSLA^+(o')$. This remark can be formalized as follows:

Table 7. Formal definition of remark 5

```
1. ol(o) > ol(o') if  CSSLA⁺(o) >ₘᵤₗ CSSLA⁺(o')
2. ol(o) = ol(o') if  CSSLA⁺(o) =ₘᵤₗ CSSLA⁺(o')
```

3.2.2 Objects Levels Assessment When a Read Access Is Requested

In the previous section, we considered information that could be inferred from information which can be stored in an object. In this section, we consider information that could be inferred from information which can be known by a subject and information which can be stored in the requested object. Whenever a subject requests a read access to an object, the history of its accesses is analyzed to determine whether the information that can be stored in the requested object, correlated with information that can be known by the subject, could result in an inference generating high level information although the information written had a low level. Therefore if an inference arises, the object's confidentiality level to be used to determine the access decision for the request in question, should be recalculated by considering this inferred information. In order to apply our approach, we define the following functions:

- $osl : O \times S \rightarrow L$ formally represents the assignment of a confidentiality level to an object when a subject requests to read it.
- For $o \in O$ and $s \in S$, $CSSSLA(o, s)$ is the multiset of levels in $CSSL(o)$ and levels of information inferred from $CKSSL(s, o)$ and $CKSS(s, o)$. Formally, $CSSSLA(o, s) = CSSL(o) \cup Agg\_l(CKSSL(s, o)) \cup Ass\_l(CKSS(s, o))$.
- $CSSSLA^+(o, s)$ is the submultiset of $CSSSLA(o, s)$ having values equal to or greater than $ol(o)$. More formally, $CSSSLA^+(o, s) = \{1 \in CSSSLA(o, s) \mid 1 \geq ol(o)\}$.

Example. Suppose that Nadia requests to read o_3 and let us assume that $ol(o_3) = 3$, $CKSL(Nadia) = \{2,1,1,1\}$, $CKS(Nadia) = \{o_7,o_6,o_5\}$, $CSSL(o_3) = \{3,1,1,4\}$, $CSS(o_3) = \{o_3,o_7,o_8,o_1\}$, $Agg(4,1) = 4$ and $Ass(o_8,o_6) = 3$.

Thus, we have the following:
$CKSSL(Nadia, o_3) = \{3,1,4,2,1,1,1\}$, $CKSS(Nadia, o_3) = \{o_3,o_8,o_1,o_7,o_6,o_5\}$.
$Agg\_l(CKSSL(Nadia, o_3)) = 4$, $Ass\_l(CKSS(Nadia, o_3)) = 3$.
$CSSSLA(o_3, Nadia) = \{3,1,1,4,3\}$, $CSSSLA^+(o_3, Nadia) = \{3,4,4\}$.

Remark 6

We can compare confidentiality levels of object o and object o' when a subject s requests read access to them, in terms of objects stored in them, information inferred from these objects and information that could be inferred from information known by the subject and information stored in the object, by comparing $CSSSLA^+(o, s)$ with $CSSSLA^+(o', s)$. This remark can be formalized as follows:

Table 8. Formal definition of Remark 6

```
1. osl(o,s) > osl(o',s) if CSSSLA⁺(o,s) >_mul CSSSLA⁺(o',s)
2. osl(o,s) = osl(o',s) if CSSSLA⁺(o,s) =_mul CSSSLA⁺(o',s)
```

4   Access History and Information Flow-Based Integrity Levels Assessment

In the previous sections, we have presented an approach for subjects and objects confidentiality levels assessment. This approach is based on the idea that confidentiality levels of subjects and objects increase when information can flow down to them. In this section we will present a set of principles to assess the integrity levels. Our approach is based on the idea that integrity levels of subjects and objects decrease when information can flow up to them [6]. In other words subjects can decrease their integrity levels as they can know information from lower levels and objects can decrease their integrity levels as they can store information from lower levels. The number of accesses is another factor to be considered when assessing subject and object integrity levels.

Our history and information flow-based subject's integrity level assessment approach is based on the principles that are contextually defined below:

- Always apply **Principle 7** that is, the integrity level of a subject decreases as the subject reads (can know) objects having integrity levels equal to or lower than its own.
- Whenever lower integrity levels of objects read by the subject are the same, apply **Principle 8** that is, the integrity level of a subject decreases as the object can store greater *number* of objects having integrity levels equal to or lower than its own.
- For subjects that has no history of reading objects, apply **Principle 9** that is, the integrity level is set to a maximum / default value. This can be determined by the system administrator.

Our history and information flow-based object's integrity level assessment approach is based on the principles defined below:

- Always apply **Principle 10** that is, the integrity level of an object decreases as the object can store objects having integrity levels equal to or lower than its own.
- Whenever lower integrity levels of objects which can be stored in the object are the same, apply **Principle 11** that is, the integrity level of an object decreases as the object can store greater *number* of objects having integrity levels equal to or lower than its own.
- For objects that have not yet been written by subjects with lower integrity levels, apply **Principle 12** that is the integrity level is set to a maximum / default value. This can be determined by the system administrator.

5   Discussion and Related Work

To the best of our knowledge, the assessment of subjects and objects security levels, by considering information flow, has been presented via two models which were introduced in [3]: the High-water mark which predates the Bell Lapadula model [4] and the Low-water mark which is an extension of the Biba model [5].

Under the High-water mark, when a subject reads an object of higher confidentiality level, the object's confidentiality level is assigned to the subject and when a subject writes in an object of lower confidentiality level, the subject's confidentiality level is assigned to the object. These two properties are similar to **Principle 1** and **Principle 4** presented in this paper. However, in our approach, the highest confidentiality level will not automatically be assigned to subjects and objects. This is because we consider all higher confidentiality levels of objects which can be stored in the object and all higher confidentiality levels of objects which have been read by the subject in addition to the number of accesses.

Under the Low-water mark, when a subject reads an object of lower integrity level, the object's integrity level is assigned to the subject and when a subject writes in an object of higher integrity level, the subject's integrity level is assigned to the object. These two properties are similar to **Principle 7** and **Principle 10** presented in this paper. However, in our approach, the lowest integrity level will not automatically be assigned to subjects and objects. This is because we consider all lower integrity levels of objects which can be stored in the objects and all lower integrity levels of objects which have been read by the subject in addition to the number of accesses. In both cases, our approach is far more sophisticated than these previously known approaches.

6   Conclusion

The main contribution of this paper is a framework that includes a history and information flow-based approach for subjects and objects level assessment. This approach is based on past accesses and considers information which can flow from previous accesses, as well as information that can be inferred from previous accesses (information aggregation and information association). Information that could be inferred from information that can be known by a subject and information that can be stored in an object are also considered. Towards this end, we have presented several examples that justify our approach in intuitive terms. We have also presented a formal definition of our approach.

To the best of our knowledge, our work represents one of the few attempts in the literature to conduct a history and information flow-based approach for entity security levels assessment. We have shown that our approach is a substantial improvement with respect to the previously known approaches of the high and low watermark models. This approach is valuable in Web and Cloud environments where there will be many continuously evolving information flows, since our methods can be invoked dynamically as the information moves between subjects and objects.

As mentioned in Section 1, our ultimate goal is to develop a framework for estimating security levels. This requires us to extend the work reported in this paper by defining mathematical formulas which capture the presented principles.

Acknowledgment. This research was funded in part by grants of the Natural Sciences and Engineering Research Council of Canada.

References

1. Sandhu, R.S., Jajodia, S.: Data and database security and controls. Security and controls handbook of Information Security Management. Auerbach Publishers (1993)
2. Sandhu, R.S.: Lattice-based access control models. Computer 26(11), (1993)

3. Weissmann, C.: Security controls in the ADEPT-50 timesharing system. AFIPS Conference Proceedings FJCC (1969)
4. Bell, D.E., LaPadula, L.J.: Secure Computer Systems: Mathematical Foundations. MITRE Corporation (1973)
5. Biba, K.: Integrity considerations for secure computer systems. Technical Report TR-3153, MITRE Corporation (1977)
6. Logrippo, L.: Logical Method for Reasoning about Access Control and Data Flow Control Models. To appear in the Proc. of the 7th International Symposium on Foundations and Practice of Security (2014)
7. Dershowitz, N., Manna, Z.: Proving termination with multiset orderings. Communications of the ACM 22(8), (1979)

Social Computing

Understanding Consumer Participation on Companies' Brand Microblogs

Kem Z.K. Zhang[1,2(✉)], Morad Benyoucef[1], and Sesia J. Zhao[3]

[1] Telfer School of Management, University of Ottawa, Ottawa, Canada
{zhang,benyoucef}@telfer.uottawa.ca
[2] School of Management, University of Science and Technology of China,
Hefei, China
[3] Management School, Anhui University, Hefei, China
sesia@ahu.edu.cn

Abstract. The purpose of this research is to understand consumer participation on companies' brand microblogs. We propose a research model to explain that such participation may be a positive consequence of consumers' brand attachment process. That is, consumers' perceived self-congruence and partner quality may influence their trust and commitment toward brands. Trust and commitment further affect participation on brand microblogs. We empirically examine our research hypotheses using an online survey. The results show that self-congruence and partner quality positively affect trust and commitment. Trust has significant effects on commitment and participation, while commitment also affects participation. Our findings provide insights on user participation behavior in a social computing context, while practitioners may apply our findings for brand building and to understand consumer participation in similar contexts.

Keywords: Trust · Social computing · Social media · Social commerce · e-Business · Microblog · Participation

1 Introduction

In recent years, microblogging websites such as Twitter have become increasingly popular with consumers, and strategically important to companies. Prior studies show that these websites can be adopted as a promising marketing tool [1, 2]. In practice, a number of companies use these websites to create brand microblogs and then use them to develop relationships with consumers. While creating brand microblogs may be very helpful for these companies to interact with and influence consumers, little research has been conducted to show how positive outcomes may be achieved on such microblogs [3].

In this study, the outcome that we focus on is consumer participation. Participation is defined as the degree to which consumers intend to 1) read messages from brand microblogs, 2) forward these messages, and 3) comment on the messages [4]. Prior research posits that user participation is essential to the survival of online communities

---

Note: A revised and extended paper based on this work is being published in Computers in Human Behavior [9].

M. Benyoucef et al. (Eds.): MCETECH 2015, LNBIP 209, pp. 125–137, 2015.
DOI: 10.1007/978-3-319-17957-5_8

[e.g., 5, 6], and perhaps more so for companies' brand microblogs. Companies can benefit from investigating the determinants of consumer participation because it helps them to understand and influence consumers in this social media setting [7, 8].

The purpose of this study is thus to understand consumer participation on brand microblogs. We develop a research model by proposing that consumer participation may be a positive consequence of their brand attachment process on these microblogs. As Jahn et al. [10] indicated, the brand attachment process addresses the relationships among four factors: self-congruence, partner quality, trust, and commitment. The idea is that a consumer is likely to develop trust and commitment toward a brand, if s/he perceives high self-congruence and partner quality with it. In the context of this study, we further propose that a consumer is likely to participate on a brand microblog if his/her trust and commitment toward the brand are enhanced while following the microblog.

The remainder of this paper is organized as follows. First, we present the theoretical background of this study, after which we develop our research model and hypotheses. Then, we empirically test the model by conducting an online survey. We analyze the collected data using the structural equation modeling method. Finally, we discuss the findings, implications, and limitations of this study.

2   Theoretical Background

2.1   Participation in Online Communities

Even though user participation is an important issue within research on online communities [e.g., 5, 11, 12], scholars often have different understandings of it. For instance, Casaló et al. [13] emphasized participation primarily on whether users actively participate and contribute new information in online communities. On the other hand, some research indicates that lurking behavior is also a component of participation [14] in the sense that lurkers may benefit from finding solutions to problems by browsing in online communities [15]. A recent study by Bateman et al. [4] contended that participation in online communities may include three dimensions: reading messages, posting replies, and moderating community members' discussions. Following this perspective, we can define participation on brand microblogs with three similar dimensions. Since moderating discussions is less likely to occur on brand microblogs, this study considers forwarding messages, which is a more common activity in the context, as a dimension of participation. Recent research does indicate that a company should pay attention to consumers' forwarding behavior on brand microblogs as it increases the odds that the company's messages are shared with consumers' social networks [16]. In short, this study adopts reading, forwarding, and commenting on messages as the three dimensions of participation.

In previous studies, various theoretical perspectives, including the technology acceptance theory [17], motivational theory [18], and commitment theory [4], have been adopted to understand the determinants of participation. However, the inconsistent characterizations of the "participation" concept often led to conflicting findings [e.g., 14, 19]. In addition, there is not sufficient research that examines participation in the context of company-initiated online communities [20, 21]. It has been shown that consumers interact with companies more frequently on company-initiated online communities than they do on consumer-initiated online communities [22]. They do so, for instance, by having frequent and direct interactions with a company on its brand microblog. The company is also expected to engage more intensively in building its brand(s) and interacting with consumers using its microblog(s) [16, 23].

2.2   Brand Attachment Process

The brand attachment process explains consumers' perceptions and feelings toward a brand. Brand attachment is a relationship-based concept that addresses the bond between a consumer and a brand [24, 25]. Prior research indicates that the brand attachment process can be characterized with four factors [10]: self-congruence, partner quality, trust, and commitment. Self-congruence and partner quality represent the degree to which a consumer is attached to a brand, while trust and commitment are the outcomes of that attachment.

Marketing research suggests that consumers' responses may be predicted by the cognitive contrast between their self-concept and the image of a brand [26, 27]. In this case, a high level of self-congruence can be established if consumers find an excellent match between their self-concept and a brand [28]. Consumers are often motivated to establish their self-concept. This is because consumers tend to retain their self-consistency and self-esteem [29]. As Chatman [28] posited, people have the self-consistency need to sustain their favorable self-concept, while they also have the self-esteem need to show themselves as competent and worthwhile. Similar to self-congruence, partner quality is an important factor that influences the consumer-brand relationship [30, 31]. Partner quality may also be referred to as an assessment of a partner relationship [32]. It is defined as the degree to which a consumer perceives that a brand listens to and understands his/her needs [10, 33]. A high level of partner quality suggests that the consumer has faith in the brand [34, 35].

According to the commitment-trust theory [36], trust and commitment are important for developing successful relationships between two parties. Previous research refers to trust as a psychological state where an individual decides to believe others and ignore any vulnerabilities [37]. Trust denotes one's confidence in others' competence and integrity [36]. Meanwhile, commitment emphasizes one's desire to sustain a relationship [38]. The commitment-trust theory also indicates that commitment may be further influenced by trust [39]. Relevant studies suggest that it is important for companies to establish trust and maintain relationship commitment with consumers for the sake of reducing costs and uncertainties [36, 40].

3   Research Model and Hypotheses

To understand consumer participation on companies' brand microblogs, we develop a research model and propose that participation may be a positive outcome of consumers' brand attachment process on brand microblogs. Figure 1 illustrates the research model of this study.

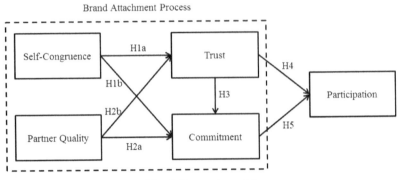

Fig. 1. Research model

3.1   Effects of Self-congruence and Partner Quality

In this research, we expect that a consumer's self-congruence can be developed if s/he compares his/her self-concept with the image of the brand while following the brand's microblog. According to Dunn and Schweitzer [41], a high level of trust is generated if people are able to identify or are closely connected with others. Jahn et al. [10] indicated that self-congruence may affect trust, because if a brand has a close connection with one's self-concept, then it is more likely to be regarded as trustworthy. In a similar vein, it has been shown that a good match between one's self-concept and a brand can influence his/her commitment to keep the relationship with the brand [42]. Based on these considerations, we provide the following two hypotheses:

H1a: Self-congruence will positively affect trust.
H1b: Self-congruence will positively affect commitment.

Partner quality refers to the extent to which a consumer recognizes that the brand cares about him/her. For instance, if a company responds to a consumer's comments on its brand microblog instantly, then the consumer may perceive that the company actually cares about his/her concerns. Prior social psychology research points out that trust is developed if a relationship involves caring and understanding [41]. In addition, caring and understanding can further affect one's desire to keep the consumer-brand relationship [43]. Commitment may be improved if a consumer perceives a high level of partner quality toward a brand [44]. Therefore, we provide the following two hypotheses:

H2a: Partner quality will positively affect trust.
H2b: Partner quality will positively affect commitment.

3.2   Effects of Trust and Commitment

This research employs trust to reflect a consumer's trusting beliefs (e.g., whether a brand is honest) toward a brand when s/he follows a brand microblog. We further propose that trust may have effects on commitment and participation on brand micro-blogs. According to Morgan and Hunt [36], trust can produce a positive influence on commitment. The relationship between trust and commitment is also postulated in long-term exchange theories [45]. In addition, we expect that a consumer's trust toward a brand is likely to affect his/her participation on its microblog. The trustworthiness of information sources has been found to affect people's information processing behavior (e.g., reading a piece of information) [46], as well as the extent to which they believe the received information is helpful [47]. Based on these concerns, we propose two hypotheses to articulate that consumers with a high level of trust are more likely to be committed to a brand. Brand trust is also likely to increase consumers' participation level on brand microblogs:

H3: Trust will positively affect commitment.
H4: Trust will positively affect participation.

Finally, we expect that participation can also be predicted by commitment. We define commitment as an affective factor that captures consumers' desire to sustain a useful relationship with a brand [48]. Prior research contends that if consumers are affectively involved with brands in online communities, then they are likely to have a high level of participation behavior (e.g., lurking and posting behavior) [49]. Following this perspective, we propose that consumers' commitment toward a brand is likely to entice them to sustain a favorable relationship with it through participating on its microblog. The following hypothesis is provided:

H5: Commitment will positively affect participation.

4   Methodology

To empirically test our research model, we conducted an online survey on Weibo (weibo.com), the most popular microblogging website in China. Weibo website has consistently attracted large numbers of online users, and many companies have created successful brand microblogs on its platform. Our focus in this research was specifically on users who had an experience following brand microblogs on Weibo.

We adopted well-validated measures from previous studies to develop our online questionnaire. Only slight modifications of the measures were made to fit the research context. We used a seven-point Likert scale (i.e., from 1=strongly disagree to 7=strongly agree) for the measures. The Appendix shows the measures of constructs, where reflective constructs included self-congruence, partner quality, trust, and commitment, and participation was the formative construct.

Since we conducted the survey in China, we first translated the original English measures to Chinese, and then translated them back from Chinese to English. The two English versions of measures were compared, and all inconsistencies were resolved to ensure the translation quality of the final questionnaire. To reach potential respondents on Weibo, we posted invitation messages with the URL of the questionnaire on many popular brand microblogs. In the questionnaire, we asked each respondent to consider a brand that s/he followed most frequently on Weibo before answering the questions. In around two weeks, we collected 175 usable responses. Table 1 lists the demographic characteristics of the sample. As can be seen in the table, 51.4% of the respondents were males, while most of the respondents were aged between 18 and 30 and had a bachelor degree or above.

Table 1. Demographic characteristics

		Number	Percentage
Gender	Male	90	51.4%
	Female	85	48.6%
Age	18-24	117	66.9%
	25-30	51	29.1%
	31 or above	7	4.0%
Education	Senior high school or below	24	13.7%
	Bachelor	63	36.0%
	Postgraduate or above	88	50.3%
Income (RMB)	Below 1000	77	44.0%
	1000-2000	10	5.7%
	2001-3000	29	16.6%
	3001-4000	29	16.6%
	4001-5000	16	9.1%
	Above 5000	14	8.0%

5   Data Analysis and Results

We adopted Partial Least Squares (PLS) to analyze our research model. PLS is a popular component-based structural equation modeling method in the empirical literature [50]. We followed the two-step procedure by Hair et al. [51], namely the measurement model and structural model, for analyzing the collected data.

5.1   Measurement Model

First, the reflective constructs were assessed to ensure that they had acceptable convergent and discriminant validity. Convergent validity indicates that items of a construct should be highly related as they are under the same conceptual domain. We used composite reliability (CR) and average variance extracted (AVE) to test the convergent validity. It is deemed as suitable if CR values are greater than 0.7, and AVE values are more than 0.5 [52]. Meanwhile, discriminant validity indicates that items of different constructs should have low correlations as they are theoretically different. It is required that the square root of AVE for each construct should be greater than its correlations with others [52]. According to the results in Table 2, the convergent and discriminant validity of the reflective constructs appeared to be sufficient in this study.

Table 2. Convergent and discriminant validity of the reflective constructs

	CR	AVE	Self-Congruence	Partner Quality	Trust	Commitment
Self-Congruence	0.94	0.84	**0.92**			
Partner Quality	0.92	0.78	0.62	**0.89**		
Trust	0.90	0.75	0.57	0.60	**0.87**	
Commitment	0.94	0.84	0.68	0.73	0.62	**0.92**

Note: Diagonal values in bold are square roots of AVEs

Second, we assessed the formative construct, participation, by following suggestions from prior research [e.g., 5] and examining its item weights. Based on the results of Table 3, PA1 and PA2 had significant weights, whereas PA3 had an insignificant weight. Although the weight of PA3 was insignificant, this item was not removed because it was an important dimension (i.e., intention to comment on messages) of participation in this study.

Table 3. Item weights of participation

Item	Weights	t-value	Mean	SD
PA1	0.81	8.44***	4.34	1.29
PA2	0.27	1.98*	3.46	1.41
PA3	0.01	0.09	3.33	1.39

Note: * denotes p<0.05, *** denotes p<0.001.

5.2 Structural Model

Figure 2 illustrates the results of the structural model in this study. We found that self-congruence had positive effects on trust (β=0.33, t=3.89) and commitment (β=0.31, t=4.73). It implied that H1a and H1b were supported. In addition, we found

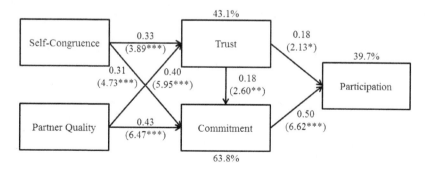

Fig. 2. Structural model

Note: * denotes p<0.05, ** denotes p<0.01, and *** denotes p<0.001.

that partner quality positively influenced trust (β=0.40, t=5.95) and commitment (β=0.43, t=6.47), indicating that H2a and H2b were also supported. Finally, trust positively affected commitment (β=0.18, t=2.60) and participation (β=0.18, t=2.13), while commitment also influenced participation (β=0.50, t=6.62). Hence, H3, H4, and H5 were supported. Overall, 43.1%, 63.8%, and 39.7% of variances were explained in trust, commitment, and participation respectively.

6   Discussion

In this study, we attempt to understand consumer participation on companies' brand microblogs. We propose a research model to explicate that participation may be a positive consequence of consumers' brand attachment process on brand microblogs. We empirically test our model by conducting an online survey. Our findings show that all of the research hypotheses are supported. That is, we find that consumers' perceived self-congruence and partner quality can influence their trust and commitment toward brands, while trust and commitment further positively affect consumers' participation on brand microblogs.

6.1   Theoretical and Practical Implications

We believe that the findings of this study can provide theoretical insights to enrich the extant literature. We provide empirical evidence to show that consumers' participation increases as a positive result of their brand attachment process on companies' brand microblogs. We believe this study to be one of the earliest to try to understand consumer participation behavior on companies' brand microblogs. Prior research has pointed out that participation is an important concern in online communities [e.g., 5, 18, 53]. However, research with a theoretical perspective to understand participation on brand microblogs is rather limited. To address this gap, we review prior research on participation to provide a more comprehensive understanding of it in the current research context. We explain that participation may primarily have three dimensions, namely reading, forwarding, and commenting on messages on brand microblogs.

Our findings show that the brand attachment process perspective provides a viable lens to understand consumer participation on brand microblogs. We believe that this perspective is consistent with prior marketing research about the three stages of brand antecedents and consequences: (1) company actions, (2) what consumers perceive and feel about the brand, and (3) what consumers do about the brand [31]. The brand attachment process addresses the second stage, which helps to explicate consumers' perceptions and feelings on brand microblogs. Meanwhile, consumer participation corresponds to the third stage, showing that participation may be a positive consequence of the brand attachment process. Moreover, this theoretical perspective is consistent with recent research in the information systems literature, which contends that theories of the consumer-brand relationship may help to understand people's responses to brands in social media or social computing contexts [54]. Malhotra et al. [16] further posited that companies' brand microblogs may be more appropriate for building brands than promoting products. Hence, we expect that the findings of this research may also enrich our understanding of brand building and how it affects consumer participation on brand microblogs.

We believe that this research highlights useful implications for practitioners. Klososky [55] stated that "social technology is not a subject for any business to ignore" (p. 41), and we offer direct evidence that companies can benefit from establishing brand microblogs. Consumers are likely to participate (i.e., read, forward, and comment on messages) on such microblogs if companies can facilitate the brand attachment process. More specifically, our findings show that consumers would trust and become committed to a brand if they perceive that their self-concepts have a good match with the brand's image while following that brand's microblog. From this perspective, companies are advised to understand the importance of establishing clear brand images on their brand microblogs. They may take actions to enable consumers to observe "symbols" on the microblogs. For example, managers of brand microblogs can post humanized and well-designed information and pictures. It may further be helpful to use keywords or tags that can demonstrate their brand images on the microblogs. Similar to self-congruence, companies should also understand the significance of developing partner quality on their brand microblogs. For instance, they can show their interest in and understanding of consumers. It would be helpful to value the comments made by consumers and actively provide timely responses on the microblogs. Companies are also urged to consider useful feedback from consumers in order to better fulfill their needs.

6.2   Limitations and Opportunities for Further Research

In addition to the implications of this research, some limitations and opportunities for further investigation remain. First, this study only collects data from a Chinese microblogging site (i.e., Weibo). Thus, the findings may be seen as subjective and bound to the characteristics of our sample. To improve the generalizability, future research is suggested to extend the sample to other microblogging sites (e.g., Twitter). Note that it is possible that the results from other countries may be different from the results in this study. In this case, the role of culture may be taken into account. Further, it will be interesting for future research to consider the influence of user characteristics. For instance, gender differences may exist for some of the factors in the research model. Finally, given that the variances explained in participation are 37.9%, there may be other important factors missing in the research model. Although the focus of this study is not to explore all possible determinants of consumer participation, we encourage future research to extend the research model by incorporating other theoretical perspectives. For instance, prior research [22] indicates that technological characteristics of brand microblogs may be important in influencing participation. In sum, we hope that efforts on these future research opportunities may help to enrich the understanding of consumer participation on brand microblogs.

Acknowledgements. The work described in this study was partially supported by grants from National Natural Science Foundation of China (No. 71201149), Mitacs (No. 310331-110199), and Natural Sciences and Engineering Research Council of Canada (No. 210005-110199-2001).

Appendix: Measures of Constructs

Self-Congruence [56]
1.   I find that the brand is similar to me.
2.   I feel a personal connection to the brand.
3.   I think the brand reflects who I am.

Partner Quality [10]
1.   I feel the brand understands my needs.
2.   I feel the brand shows a continuing interest in me.
3.   I feel as though I really understand the brand.

Trust [57]
1.   I find that the brand is safe.
2.   I believe that this is an honest brand.
3.   I confirm that this is a reliable brand.

Commitment [36]
1.   I find that the relationship that I have with the brand is something I am very committed to.
2.   I believe that the relationship that I have with the brand is something I intend to maintain indefinitely.
3.   I confirm that the relationship that I have with the brand deserves my maximum effort to maintain.

Participation [4]
1.   I will read the messages from the brand microblog.
2.   I will forward the messages from the brand microblog.
3.   I will comment on the messages from the brand microblog.

References

1. Culnan, M.J., McHugh, P.J., Zubillaga, J.I.: How Large U.S. Companies Can Use Twitter and Other Social Media to Gain Business Value. MIS Q. Exec. **9**, 243–260 (2010)
2. Li, Y.-M., Shiu, Y.-L.: A Diffusion Mechanism for Social Advertising Over Microblogs. Decis. Support Syst. **54**, 9–22 (2012)
3. Wang, S., Zhang, K.Z.K., Lee, M.K.O.: Developing Consumers' Brand Loyalty in Companies' Microblogs: The Roles of Social- and Self-Factors. In: Proceedings of the 17th Pacific Asia Conference on Information Systems (2013)
4. Bateman, P.J., Gray, P.H., Butler, B.S.: The Impact of Community Commitment on Participation in Online Communities. Inf. Syst. Res. **22**, 841–854 (2010)
5. Bagozzi, R.P., Dholakia, U.M.: Open Source Software User Communities: A Study of Participation in Linux User Groups. Manag. Sci. **52**, 1099–1115 (2006)
6. Koh, J., Kim, Y.-G., Butler, B., Bock, G.-W.: Encouraging Participation in Virtual Communities. Commun. ACM. **50**, 68–73 (2007)

7. Jansen, B.J., Zhang, M., Sobel, K., Chowdury, A.: Twitter Power: Tweets as Electronic Word of Mouth. J. Am. Soc. Inf. Sci. Technol. **60**, 2169–2188 (2009)
8. Zhang, K.Z.K., Zhao, S.J., Zhang, H., Lee, M.K.O.: An Empirical Research of the Factors Affecting Users to Follow Companies' Microblogs. Int. J. Netw. Virtual Organ. **14**, 129–145 (2014)
9. Zhang, K.Z.K., Benyoucef, M., Zhao, S.J.: Consumer Participation and Gender Differences on Companies' Microblogs: A Brand Attachment Process Perspective. Comput. Hum. Behav. **44**, 357–368 (2015)
10. Jahn, S., Gaus, H., Kiessling, T.: Trust, Commitment, and Older Women: Exploring Brand Attachment Differences in the Elderly Segment. Psychol. Mark. **29**, 445–457 (2012)
11. Fang, Y., Neufeld, D.: Understanding Sustained Participation in Open Source Software Projects. J. Manag. Inf. Syst. **25**, 9–50 (2009)
12. Zhang, C., Hahn, J., De, P.: Continued Participation in Online Innovation Communities: Does Community Response Matter Equally for Everyone? Inf. Syst. Res. **24**, 1112–1130 (2013)
13. Casaló, L.V., Flavián, C., Guinalíu, M.: Antecedents and Consequences of Consumer Participation in On-Line Communities: The Case of the Travel Sector. Int. J. Electron. Commer. **15**, 137–167 (2010)
14. Blanchard, A.L., Markus, M.L.: The Experienced "Sense" of a Virtual Community: Characteristics and Processes. DATA BASE Adv. Inf. Syst. **35**, 64–79 (2004)
15. Madupu, V., Cooley, D.O.: Antecedents and Consequences of Online Brand Community Participation: A Conceptual Framework. J. Internet Commer. **9**, 127–147 (2010)
16. Malhotra, A., Malhotra, C.K., See, A.: How to Get Your Messages Retweeted (2012)
17. Chu, K.-M.: Motives for Participation in Internet Innovation Intermediary Platforms. Inf. Process. Manag. **49**, 945–953 (2013)
18. Sun, Y., Fang, Y., Lim, K.H.: Understanding Sustained Participation in Transactional Virtual Communities. Decis. Support Syst. **53**, 12–22 (2011)
19. Wasko, M.M., Faraj, S.: "It Is What One Does": Why People Participate and Help Others in Electronic Communities of Practice. J. Strateg. Inf. Syst. **9**, 155–173 (2000)
20. Casaló, L.V., Flavián, C., Guinalíu, M.: Determinants of the Intention to Participate in Firm-Hosted Online Travel Communities and Effects on Consumer Behavioral Intentions. Tour. Manag. **31**, 898–911 (2010)
21. Wiertz, C., de Ruyter, K.: Beyond the Call of Duty: Why Customers Contribute to Firm-hosted Commercial Online Communities. Organ. Stud. **28**, 347–376 (2007)
22. Jang, H., Olfman, L., Ko, I., Koh, J., Kim, K.: The Influence of on-Line Brand Community Characteristics on Community Commitment and Brand Loyalty. Int. J. Electron. Commer. **12**, 57–80 (2008)
23. Barwise, P., Meehan, S.: The One Thing You Must Get Right When Building a Brand (2010)
24. Malär, L., Krohmer, H., Hoyer, W.D., Nyffenegger, B.: Emotional Brand Attachment and Brand Personality: The Relative Importance of the Actual and the Ideal Self. J. Mark. **75**, 35–52 (2011)
25. Park, C.W., MacInnis, D.J., Priester, J., Eisingerich, A.B., Iacobucci, D.: Brand Attachment and Brand Attitude Strength: Conceptual and Empirical Differentiation of Two Critical Brand Equity Drivers. J. Mark. **74**, 1–17 (2010)
26. Sirgy, M.J., Grewal, D., Mangleburg, T.: Retail Environment, Self-Congruity, and Retail Patronage: An Integrative Model and a Research Agenda. J. Bus. Res. **49**, 127–138 (2000)
27. Sirgy, M.J.: Using Self-Congruity and Ideal Congruity to Predict Purchase Motivation. J. Bus. Res. **13**, 195–206 (1985)

28. Chatman, J.A.: Improving Interactional Organizational Research: A Model of Person-Organization Fit. Acad. Manage. Rev. **14**, 333–349 (1989)
29. Aaker, J.L.: Dimensions of Brand Personality. J. Mark. Res. **34**, 347–356 (1997)
30. Huber, F., Vollhardt, K., Matthes, I., Vogel, J.: Brand Misconduct: Consequences on Consumer-Brand Relationships. J. Bus. Res. **63**, 1113–1120 (2010)
31. Keller, K.L., Lehmann, D.R.: Brands and Branding: Research Findings and Future Priorities. Mark. Sci. **25**, 740–759 (2006)
32. Fournier, S.: Consumers and Their Brands: Developing Relationship Theory in Consumer Research. J. Consum. Res. **24**, 343–353 (1998)
33. Smit, E., Bronner, F., Tolboom, M.: Brand Relationship Quality and Its Value for Personal Contact. J. Bus. Res. **60**, 627–633 (2007)
34. Kressmann, F., Sirgy, M.J., Herrmann, A., Huber, F., Huber, S., Lee, D.-J.: Direct and Indirect Effects of Self-Image Congruence on Brand Loyalty. J. Bus. Res. **59**, 955–964 (2006)
35. Thorbjørnsen, H., Supphellen, M., Nysveen, H., Egil, P.: Building Brand Relationships Online: A Comparison of Two Interactive Applications. J. Interact. Mark. **16**, 17–34 (2002)
36. Morgan, R.M., Hunt, S.D.: The Commitment-Trust Theory of Relationship Marketing. J. Mark. **58**, 20–38 (1994)
37. Gefen, D., Benbasat, I., Pavlou, P.A.: A Research Agenda for Trust in Online Environments. J. Manag. Inf. Syst. **24**, 275–286 (2008)
38. Sanchez-Franco, M.J., Ramos, A.F.V., Velicia, F.A.M.: The Moderating Effect of Gender on Relationship Quality and Loyalty Toward Internet Service Providers. Inf. Manage. **46**, 196–202 (2009)
39. Li, D.: An Empirical Investigation of Web Site Use Using a Commitment-Based Model. Decis. Sci. **37**, 393–444 (2006)
40. Geyskens, I., Steenkamp, J.-B.E.M., Kumar, N.: A Meta-Analysis of Satisfaction in Marketing Channel Relationships. J. Mark. Res. **36**, 223 (1999)
41. Dunn, J.R., Schweitzer, M.E.: Feeling and Believing: The Influence of Emotion on Trust. J. Pers. Soc. Psychol. **88**, 736–748 (2005)
42. Thomson, M., MacInnis, D.J.: Whan Park, C.: The Ties That Bind: Measuring the Strength of Consumers' Emotional Attachments to Brands. J. Consum. Psychol. **15**, 77–91 (2005)
43. Delgado-Ballester, E., Munuera-Aleman, J.L., Yague-Guillen, M.J.: Development and Validation of a Brand Trust Scale. Int. J. Mark. Res. (2003)
44. Breivik, E., Thorbjørnsen, H.: Consumer Brand Relationships: An Investigation of Two Alternative Models. J. Acad. Mark. Sci. **36**, 443–472 (2008)
45. Perlman, D., Duck, S.: Intimate Relationships: Development, Dynamics, and Deterioration. Sage Publications, Beverly Hills (1987)
46. Petty, R.E., Cacioppo, J.T.: The Elaboration Likelihood Model of Persuasion. Adv. Exp. Soc. Psychol. **19**, 123–205 (1986)
47. Levin, D.Z., Cross, R.: The Strength of Weak Ties You Can Trust: The Mediating Role of Trust in Effective Knowledge Transfer. Manag. Sci. **50**, 1477–1490 (2004)
48. Moorman, C., Zaltman, G., Deshpande, R.: Relationships Between Providers and Users of Market Research: The Dynamics of Trust Within and Between Organizations. J. Mark. Res. **29**, 314–328 (1992)
49. Shang, R.-A., Chen, Y.-C., Liao, H.-J.: The Value of Participation in Virtual Consumer Communities on Brand Loyalty. Internet Res. **16**, 398–418 (2006)
50. Chin, W.W., Marcolin, B.L., Newsted, P.R.: A Partial Least Squares Latent Variable Modeling Approach for Measuring Interaction Effects: Results from a Monte Carlo Simulation Study and an Electronic-Mail Emotion/Adoption Study. Inf. Syst. Res. **14**, 189–217 (2003)

51. Hair, J.F., Anderson, R.E., Tatham, R.L., Black, W.: Multivariate Data Analysis. Prentice Hall, Upper Saddle River, N.J. (1998)
52. Fornell, C., Larcker, D.F.: Structural Equation Models with Unobservable Variables and Measurement Error: Algebra and Statistics. J. Mark. Res. **18**, 382–388 (1981)
53. Zhou, T.: Understanding Online Community User Participation: A Social Influence Perspective. Internet Res. **21**, 67–81 (2011)
54. Pentina, I., Zhang, L., Basmanova, O.: Antecedents and Consequences of Trust in a Social Media Brand: A Cross-Cultural Study of Twitter. Comput. Hum. Behav. **29**, 1546–1555 (2013)
55. Klososky, S.: Social Technology: The Next Frontier. Financ. Exec. **28**, 40–45 (2012)
56. Ha, S., Im, H.: Identifying the Role of Self-Congruence on Shopping Behavior in the Context of U.S. Shopping Malls. Cloth. Text. Res. J. **30**, 87–101 (2012)
57. Sung, Y., Kim, J.: Effects of Brand Personality on Brand Trust and Brand Affect. Psychol. Mark. **27**, 639–661 (2010)

Recommender Engines Under the Influence of Popularity

Guillaume Blot[1]([✉]), Pierre Saurel[1], and Francis Rousseaux[2]

[1] SND FRE 3593, Paris Sorbonne University, Paris 75006, France
guillaume.blot@paris-sorbonne.fr
[2] CRESTIC EA 3804, Reims Champagne-Ardenne University, Reims 51100, France

Abstract. One often thinks that the use of Information Technologies brings an infinity of choices. However, Popularity still influences people in our free, pervasive and connected world. It is a reality: popular items keep power and weak items tend to be forgotten. Several studies demonstrated that this natural phenomenon is accentuated today with recommender engines. In this article we present a comparative study of 8 recommendation techniques. We also present a personal recommendation approach, based on items timeline. We unveil a Popularity Influence index, which evaluates the way recommender engines are influenced by the phenomenon. This experiment is led by a pool of interdisciplinary researchers, either or both epistemologists and computer scientists. It includes diverse examples and references from e-business, cultural studies or participatory democracy along with others. We believe that Popularity belongs to a wide set of fields. Therefore, we chose to run this experiment in an E-learning context, where we observe pieces of knowledge popularity.

1 Background

1.1 Influence of Popularity

We experiment popularity with e-learning resources, but through whole of the article the concept of item has to be understood in a general fashion. For example, items could be: (e-)business products, music artists, political leaders, ideas, facts or even people last names.

Imagine a world where items are freely available and have equal chances to be picked. If people choose items from a fully equal system, the distribution should be a constant curve, where all items received an equal amount of visits.

Several studies have demonstrated this equality to be unrealistic in various segments of our world: for example democratic elections[20], a home video retailer[11], cultural features and family names[33]. Quite the contrary, usual observed distributions fit a *"power law"* shape: few popular items gather a huge majority of attention and the rest remains either marginal or unknown. It is also called the 80-20 rule: 20% is the elite and 80% is the silent majority (of course

© Springer International Publishing Switzerland 2015
M. Benyoucef et al. (Eds.): MCETECH 2015, LNBIP 209, pp. 138–152, 2015.
DOI: 10.1007/978-3-319-17957-5_9

ratio varies, but distributions keep an identical shape). During this article we prefer to quote the term *"power law"*, and call the phenomenon 80-20 rule (also called Pareto distributions or Zipf's law[22]). As a matter of fact, *"Power law"* also describes physical and biological phenomena not handled in this experiment (at least we don't have the knowledge to validate the experiment in these contexts). Besides, the term is commonly used in literature to describe popularity: popular items tend to be more powerful and weak items are apt to disappear.

The phenomenon is regularly observed in the *real world*. But, does emerging IT systems tackle the problem?

Anderson coined the terms: *"long tail"* as the weak 80% and *"head"* as the powerful 20%. In 2006, he argues that the use of Internet brings infinite choices. This fact would help to reshape the curve, and give the opportunity to *"sell less of more"*[3]. Lately, several studies show that the curve still displays the same shape in the digital age. Despite some minor adjustments and some viable niches within the *"long tail"*, many digital environments are still under the influence of the 80-20 rule.

Herring et al. found that a minor set of A-list blogs lead the citation and hyperlink distribution where bloggers tend to cite or/and connect to bloggers with higher or equal reputation[14]. Several studies identified the phenomenon with musicians reputation on Internet, where audience (number of visits, comments, views) and authority (the number of time they have been declared as *"friends"*) have a strong impact[4][29]. Similar behaviors are discovered in *User Generated Content* systems, such as Youtube and Netflix (despite the use of Web 2.0 functionalities)[8]. It is even more clear when systems rank items, like it is the case with search engines[15].

Many researchers speak about an information cascade, even more effective on the Web. More items are pervasive, simpler it is to share them. Information cascade specifically identify this: people trust each other. If one shares an item, most of the time others trust it or share it in turn instead of verify. Observational learning is directly in linked to information cascades[5]. Styles, trends, ideas, facts but even errors and hoaxes emerge this way.

Various phenomena influence popularity. Even though it is always depending on the context, less speculative experiments allow us to make some assertions. Bringing together several studies, Clay Shirky delivers at least three involved factors: (1) intrinsic value of the item, (2) marketing and (3) recommendations [28].

1.2   Our Approach

Although it is not the only cause, we believe that recommendations have a strong impact on people. As a consequence it is a major issue, and it should not operate the same in all contexts: e-business, participative democracy (e-democracy), e-learning, blogs or online newspapers along with others.

Persons, who are friends, colleagues, professionals, teachers or also journalists, recommend items. Computers also make recommendations. Commonly used techniques simply analyze digital traces left by users. Recent studies demonstrated that these trace-based techniques are far more efficient than techniques

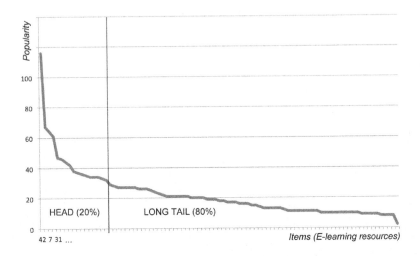

Fig. 1. The distribution of the set of e-learning resources illustrates the 80-20 rule (Our experimental context is an e-learning course with 89 e-learning resources). Resource 42 is the most popular with 116 visits. HEAD is a subset composed with 20% of popular items (17 resources) and LONG TAIL is the less popular subset. 80-20 is an arbitrary repartition; it could be more or less. Actually, 80-20 implies that a minority gathers the majority of popularity.

working with human preset similarities. Nowadays, recommendation tools are everywhere on the web[21].

In this experiment, we compare 7 widespread recommendation techniques, and observe how popularity influences their behaviors (we believe marketing can take the shape of recommendations, but we do not consider these techniques).

Besides, several researchers have analyzed influence of popularity on recommendations. Most of them observed the popularity bias, and proposed algorithms to avoid a payload on popular items[16]. All this enriches traditional methods, sometimes with intricate and complex add-ons. The difficulty here is to keep a balance between speed and accuracy.

Recently, several researchers have identical statements but an opposite approach: they suggest items using the popularity as parameter. Here, they do not see popular bias as an issue but as a solution: novels[25] or tourist attractions[32].

Influence patterns were also observed in recommendation networks. This original approach identifies information cascades through graphs, and use these information as proxy to popularity[18]. The numbers of visits or ranking values do not only express popularity, but here information cascades involvement also does. Therefore, the item can be in the long tail and seen as momently popular.

But, although we noticed in recommendation and prediction literature, that popularity deficiencies is a central question, to our knowledge, no study has already experimented a common measurement of popularity influence on various recommendation methods from the two families: collaborative filtering and link prediction. We find other common measurement, but no measures of popularity: speed[27][9], accuracy[24], recall, precision[26].

Our idea is to observe if all these techniques tend to suggest popular or weak items. In order to do this we unveil a Popularity Influence index PI which gives direct information about the way each technique is influenced by popularity. The index reveals itself to be a rich indicator of the recommendations relevance. It should be used as a metric when one is choosing among recommendation methods.

We picked recommendations techniques from the two main families: link prediction and collaborative filtering. Moreover, we include our Time-graph approach in the experiment, bringing the number of experimented techniques to 8. Like most of recommendation techniques, this approach is based on graph theory, but here we use time as edge metric[6][7].

Moreover, this kind of study is rarely experimented in e-learning context. In the following subsection, we present the dataset: learners digital traces from an e-learning platform. It is the occasion to observe if the 80-20 rule is also present with learning materials. Section 2 deals with existing recommender engines and gives precise information about the 8 experimented techniques. We present results in section 3 (where we unveil the index). This paper is also an occasion to feed the reflection on the use of recommender tools.

1.3   Data Description

The experiment has been led on a Moodle course. Moodle is an open-source LMS (Learning Management System) spread all over the world[1]. GIP-FC, our partner in this experiment, is a french institution expert in e-learning products. They design and maintain several Moodle platforms. They give us access to one of their topic courses called *Biology for health and social development*[2] (table 1).

Table 1. Digital traces left by LMS learners. Moodle records each interaction between a learner and an e-learning resource. The Moodle platform belongs to a french institution called GIP-FC (expert in e-learning). We made the data used anonymous and run the 8 recommendation algorithms.

E-learning course:	
Biology for Health and Social Development	
Items	89 e-learning resources
Users	36 learners
Entries	1950 visits

A topic course is a specific Moodle course format, where all e-learning resources are freely available. Learners can access to any piece of knowledge

---

[1] https://moodle.org/stats/
[2] http://moodle.moodgreta.eu

all over the experiment. E-learning resources can be various: pdf lessons, exercises, audio or also videos. Every time a learner accesses to a resource, a new entry is inserted in the database. An entry goes as a triple: user (learner), item (resource) and a timestamp.

89 e-learing resources have been visited 1950 times by 36 learners. Figure 1 shows that the 80-20 rule is operating over this environment. The data set snapshot has not a huge set of entries, but we did not want to work on large item networks for several reasons. (1) Some algorithms are not adapted to large scale. Working on small set of data allows us to compare more techniques on the same basis. (2) The e-learning course is still in activity, but we had to define a precise moment to run the experiment. It is relevant to choose a moment when the popularity effect hasn't much sharpen the curve yet. (3) The small size of the data set facilitates the quality verification (quality of data set and quality of results).

To make one more comment, the 80-20 ratio is arbitrary. It characterizes one fact: a minority rules the majority. It could be more or less. However, in this experiment, the item where is placed the limit between 80 and 20, gathers 36 visits (17th most visited resource), which is also the exact number of users. Hence, the head is composed of items visited at least once by each user (on average), and long tail gathers all items not visited by all users. It is not a norm, but simply an empirical statement, which gives even more credits to our data quality argument.

2   Recommendation Techniques and Our Method

Different families of recommendation techniques exist. Here, we study link prediction and collaborative filtering. We simulate 8 techniques shown in table 3. In the following 3 subsections, we introduce recommender engines families and more specifically the 8 compared recommendation methods.

In order to have a common basis, our main material for the experiment is the number of visits. It was obvious to us, as it is a relevant, reliable and common measure.

2.1   Collaborative Filtering

Each user is associated with a singular subset of items, which he has visited, liked, ranked, or purchased. The objective of a Collaborative Filtering (CF) algorithm is to understand the utility of specific items to a particular user. Users digital traces are the main information to run CF methods. For example, traces can be a user opinion or a simple visit[12][19].

In this study, we experiment recommendations based only on the CF subgroup *Item-based* filters. *User-based* filters (the other subgroup) would force us to apply some user correlation rules, that we are unable to reproduce with proportional link prediction methods.

Table 2. We compare widespread recommendation techniques. All are based on similarities between items. Each method has its own approach of similarity index. Indices calculations are detailed in this section.

Short	Method	Similarity Index	Technique
COS	Cosine-based	Item-based	Collaborative Filtering
COR	Correlation-based	Item-based	Collaborative Filtering
CN	Common neighbors	Local similarity	Link prediction
PA	Preferential Attachment	Local similarity	Link prediction
RA	Resource Allocation	Local similarity	Link prediction
AA	Adamic/Adar	Local similarity	Link prediction
KA	Katz	Overall similarity	Link prediction
TG	Time graph	Temporal	Experimental

Item-based CF input is a matrix $M = (U, I)$, with a set of n users U and a set of m items I. We use number of visits as coefficients. For example, $a_{(3,5)} = 2$, implies that the item 3 was visited twice by user 5. We compute $sim_{(i,j)}$, the similarity between item i and item j [27].

Cosine-Based Filter. In this case, items are vectors in a m dimensional space. Similarity index is measured with the angle between two vectors.

$$sim_{COS}(i,j) = cos(\overrightarrow{i}, \overrightarrow{j}) = \frac{\overrightarrow{i} \cdot \overrightarrow{j}}{||\overrightarrow{i}|| * ||\overrightarrow{j}||} \tag{1}$$

Correlation-Based Filter. Here, similarity index is based on the Pearson-r correlation corr(i,j). Only co-visited (co-learned) items have impact. $V_{u,i}$ stands for the number of visits of user u on item i. $\overline{V}_i$ is the average number of visits on item i.

$$sim_{COR}(i,j) = corr(i,j) = \frac{\sum_{u \in U}(V_{u,i} - \overline{V}_i)(V_{u,j} - \overline{V}_j)}{\sqrt{\sum_{u \in U}(V_{u,i} - \overline{V}_i)^2}\sqrt{\sum_{u \in U}(V_{u,j} - \overline{V}_j)^2}} \tag{2}$$

2.2 Link Prediction

Link prediction (LP) methods are commonly used to build recommendation tools[9].

Link prediction methods search for future coherent links between items. The first main goal is to predict people future behaviors. Like for CF, LP techniques also search for similarities between items and also have several ways to compute similarity indices. Here, we study 4 methods: the three first work with local similarity index (neighbors only) and the last works with overall paths.

These algorithms generally operate on bipartite networks, which can be quickly adapted to general networks. It is a key fact that helps us to have a common framework between CF and LP methods. The CF matrix is similar to a bipartite adjacency matrix [31].

Network topology is the main information to run link prediction algorithms: G=(I,E). Naturally, the set of vertices is all items: I contains 89 e-learning resources. However, the set of edges E was not as natural to define: it must appear for references between resources. But, we noticed only few explicit links between resources. Hence, we believe that many implicit references exist between pieces of knowledge. Then, we choose to connect together vertices that have been visited in raw. This method is explained in a previous paper[6]. It relies on Connectivism, a recent learning theory which basically says that knowledge can be conceptualized as a knowledge network[10].

The resulting e-learning resource graph is bidirectional, and is either or both weighted or unweight depending on the method. We give details in following subsections.

Common Neighbors (Local Similarity). The method calculates a local similarity index. Here, sim(i,j) implies only neighbors of item i and j. Its name is explicit: the similarity is the intersection of the ith item set of neighbors $\tau(i)$ and the jth item set of neighbors $\tau(j)$:

$$sim_{CN}(i,j) = |\tau(i) \cap \tau(j)| \tag{3}$$

In order to refine our experiment, we run 2 different occurrences of common neighbors algorithm. One on an unweight item graph, and another on a weighted item graph, where edges metric is the number of connections that occurred between the two items. The two results are presented separately in the result section (table 3).

Preferential Attachment (Local Similarity). *"Rich get richer"* is often used as a synonym of Preferential Attachment mechanism. It tends to connect items with a simple operation: the product of items degrees. As a consequence it outputs a small range of items (with the richest in it). But, unlike others it can be launched easily on large-scale networks.

$$sim_{PA}(i,j) = d_i \times d_j \tag{4}$$

Such as for the previous algorithm, here we separate two occurrences of the algorithm: (1) unweighted (2) weighted.

Adamic/Adar (Local Similarity). Based on homepage visits, Adamic & Adar proved that *log* operator brings a more realistic curve to the similarity index[2]. Following the *"strength of weak ties"* heuristic[13], they give more importance to smaller edges and apply a threshold to huge values. Unweighted graph has no importance here, as $log 1 = 0$.

$$sim_{AA}(i,j) = \sum_{z \in \tau(i) \cap \tau(j)} \frac{1}{log(d_z)} \tag{5}$$

Resource Allocation (Local Similarity). This method also follows the "*strength of weak tie*" principle, but do not introduce any customization. As a consequence an infinitely high edge has a negligible contribution to the similarity score. We only run RA on weighted graph, because RA on unweighted graph is equal to CN ($1/1 = 1$).

$$sim_{RA}(i,j) = \sum_{z \in \tau(i) \cap \tau(j)} \frac{1}{d_z} \tag{6}$$

Katz (Overall Similarity). The principle is simple: the more paths between 2 items are, the higher the similarity index gets. In the method demonstrated in 1953, Katz considers all edges (overall similarity) in a very precise way. As a consequence, it is the most complex method (n^3), among the ones we study here[17]. In this paper, we learn that popularity was already an issue 60 years ago.

$$sim_{KA}(i,j) = \sum_{l=1}^{\infty} \beta^l . |path_{i,j}^l| \tag{7}$$

Where $path_{i,j}^l$ is the length of the path between i and j. Here we dissociate weighted and unweighted. β^l coefficient get smaller when paths get longer (β is set between (0,1)). In this experiment, we run the Katz algorithm first with $\beta = 0.25$, then with $\beta = 0.85$.

2.3   Time Graph

Time graph is our experimental method. The graph topology is identical to the one described previously for link prediction methods: items are connected when visited successively. The only difference is that we do not use the number of visits to measure edges. Here, values of ties are the interval of time between two items visits. If a path is used twice, the weight is an average of the two corresponding intervals (similarly for n successive visits).

$$sim_{TG}(i,j,t) = \min(\bigcup |\delta_t - path_{(i,j)}|) \tag{8}$$

δ_t is the difference between the current time and the timestamp t from the triple *(user, item, timestamp)*. Here, the similarity score depends on the moment when the method is called. The method does not return identical value through the time. The idea is that an item a user wants/needs at t, is not necessarily the item the user wants/needs at $t + 1$.

It is interesting to compare this experimental method to existing ones, because here, we lose the number of visits factor. As a consequence the method should be less influenced by popularity. But, we still keep relevant measures with existing ties between items and temporal information. The idea is to get on board both order and what appears as disorder (users singularities). The concept was experimented in various contexts: collections[7], e-learning[6] and Openrendezvous.com, a web-based agenda[3].

2.4   Other Recommender Engines

In litterature we find other general recommender methods (and an infinity of alternatives). We bring no solution here to compare the colossal whole of recommender systems on the same exact basis. There are surely some ways. At least, we bring here a proposal for several methods, from different families (table 2).

Anyway, even if no comparative basis is present, the following approach can be applied independently to any of these engines.

3   Compute Popularity Influence Index

3.1   Experiment Workflow

Data Set Treatment: Recommend Items

(1) First, create the *CF matrix*, the *resource graph* and the *time graph*.
(2) Then, we produce $D = Recommender\ Distribution$ and $PI = Influence$ for each method (and its variants: weighted, unweighted, coefficient modulation). Each time we have 3 inputs: the data set snapshot, the original distribution and the structure produced at phase (1).

For each technique: we launch the corresponding algorithm at each step and gather recommendations. The data set is divided in 1950 entries, then each sequence has 1950 steps. A step is an entry *(user, item, timestamp)*, so the method prototype is **R method(u user, i item, t timestamp)**, where i is the last item visited by u at t.

At each step, the method harvests a set R of n recommendations, with n most similar items. All methods are studied with $n = 1$, $n = 3$ and $n = 5$. When a whole data set is processed, we suggested for each method: 1950 items with $n = 1$, 5850 items with $n = 3$ or 9750 items with $n = 5$.

Recommendations Analysis. At this point, we get two layer of distribution: (1) D_{OH}, an *original distribution* observed from digital traces left by learners(figure 1) and (2) a specific recommendation distribution for each recommender engine (D_{xx}) (figure 2). Our proposal is to compare these two layers:

---

[3] http://www.openrendezvous.com was designed and developed by Blot Guillaume, one of this article authors

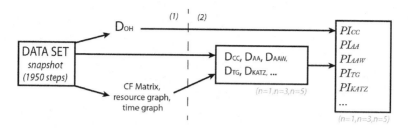

Fig. 2. The full data set snapshot is processed twice. In phase 1 we produce Original Distribution and different structures. In phase 2, we use previous phase productions and outputs recommendation sets R, recommender distribution D (D_{OH} = distribution of Original Head, D_{xx} = distribution of recommender technique xx) and Popularity Influence index PI.

Which resources are recommended the most? Do resources from Original Head (OH) are also present in the Recommendation Heads(RH)? In order to measure this, we unveil the popularity influence index:

$$PI = \frac{\sum_{y \in RH \cap OH} D_y}{\sum_{z \in OH} D_z} \qquad (9)$$

Where OH is the set of items included in the Original Head, and RH is the set of items in the method Recommendation Head. D_i is the distribution of item i in the corresponding set.

PI is included between 0 and 1. The more it is close from 1, the more the method is influenced by popularity (and reciprocally). Table 3 shows all PI.

Table 3. This table presents PI for each method and its variants(number of suggested items n, and graph type if applicable). Bold scores corresponding distributions are displayed in figure3. Last column presents the recommender tendency, where we clearly observe that PI increases or declines when n grows.

	weighted			unweighted (if needed)			
n	1	3	5	1	3	5	
PI_{COS}	**0.53**	**0.51**	**0.42**	-	-	-	↘
PI_{COR}	**0.41**	**0.29**	**0.11**	-	-	-	↘
PI_{CN}	**0.57**	**0.69**	**0.8**	0.52	0.68	0.78	↗
PI_{PA}	**1.00**	**1.00**	**1.00**	1.00	1.00	1.00	→
PI_{RA}	**0.79**	**0.9**	**0.93**	0.52	0.68	0.78	↗
PI_{AA}	**0.52**	**0.68**	**0.78**	-	-	-	↗
$PI_{KA(\beta=0.25)}$	0.66	0.72	0.74	0.51	0.7	0.71	↗
$PI_{KA(\beta=0.85)}$	**0.59**	**0.68**	**0.7**	0.65	0.74	0.72	↗
PI_{TG}	**0.61**	**0.59**	**0.61**	-	-	-	→

Reflection. During all the experiment, the Head is composed with the 20% of most visited items. As we said previously, 20% is arbitrary. Of course, PI index fluctuates depending on the selected Head.

To make one more comment: this experiment measures the overall impact of popularity. Following this workflow, the last visited item is used to suggest the next ones. Then, popular items are more used as sources. That is to say, popular items have more influence on recommendations. If popular items recommend popular items, the model keeps on promoting popularity. If popular items recommend items from the Long tail, we have chances to inverse the model. PI measures this.

3.2   Results

Curves and PI Comments. First of all we noticed a divergence of our experimental Time graph results. As a consequence, we will bring TG observations at the end of this section.

If we consider only CF and LP techniques, PI (table 3) and curves (figures 3) are correlated. The smaller is the PI, the more the curve gets close from a triangle (COS, COR). Coincidentally, large PI tends to shrink the curve against the vertical axis (PA, RA). Then, we choose to display curves at different scales (depending on the highest suggestion): the goal is to see if the curve has a *"power law"* shape. However, comparing closely all charts is still possible with a visual effort.

For example, CN and AA curves share very similar shapes and distributions (most suggested item is 33 which gather 579 and 550 visits). Indeed, we observe a similar PI for all occurrences n=1, n=3 & n=5 (table 3).

Table 4. Here is the detailed distribution of some interesting items. Items number are ordered by original (*ORIG.*) distribution on first line. We can't present the whole 89 items here, but a CSV file is available on the Internet (see footnote). For all methods, we give the number of visits, the position within the distribution and weather it is in Head(H) or Long Tail(LT).

	42		7		54		11		46	
	pos	*vis*	*pos*	*vis*	*pos*	*vis*	*pos*	*vis*	*pos*	*vis*
ORIG	**1H**	**116**	**3H**	**64**	**15 H**	**33**	**45LT**	**18**	**76LT**	**10**
COS	18LT	176	10H	222	78LT	35	70LT	47	65LT	59
COR	27LT	144	6H	232	80LT	28	45LT	344	13H	184
CN	2H	453	73LT	43	7H	278	35LT	91	54LT	60
PA	5H	1832	-	0	-	0	-	0	-	0
AA	5H	382	88LT	0	7H	282	21LT	119	53LT	31
RA	5H	258	-	0	8H	150	-	0	-	0
$KA_{0.25}$	14H	126	79LT	18	8H	373	41LT	54	66LT	38
$KA_{0.85}$	12H	168	81LT	18	10H	275	25LT	80	68LT	30
TG	5H	226	26LT	55	1H	1183	9H	123	89LT	0

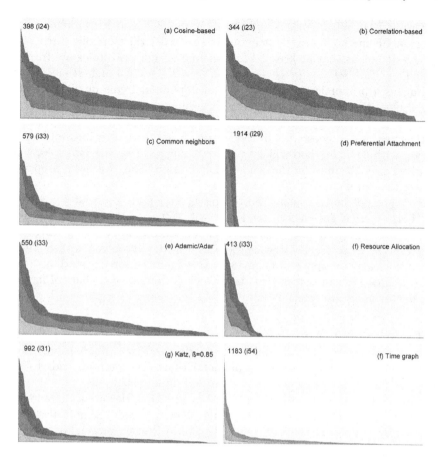

Fig. 3. All distributions are represented by these curves. All scales are not similar. Vertical axis is the number of suggestions and horizontal is items. For each curve we show the most visited items and its number of visits. We display *Time graph* in a different color, in order to remind the experimental characteristic of the method and the diverging behaviors of TG results.

Of course, we remind that we evaluate neither engines accuracy nor engines speed. Our method only measures Popularity Influence. However, we observed that techniques don't return distribution in the same order. For example, COS suggested 222 times item 7, where AA does not suggest item 7 at all (where item 7 is third in the original distribution). This is not an isolated example. It is also illustrated with the most suggested item (the only one displayed on the top left of the charts). We observe here, that only item 33 appears three times at the first position. The rest of most popular recommendations are different. Table 4 gives 5 significant items results. Unfortunately, we couldn't show the whole 89 resources results in the paper, but we made a CSV file available[4].

---

[4] http://www.gblot.com/popularity/recommender_popularity.zip

CF versus LP. What is then remarkable is that CF and LP families behave differently. CF methods are the only ones to go under the symbolic threshold of $PI = 0.5$. It means that at least 50% of the most suggested items are from the original Long Tail. PI_{COR} goes even until 0.11 with a set of 5 suggestions ($n = 5$). This implies a proportion of almost 90% of unpopular items in the suggestion Head. Table 4 first column shows that CF techniques are not influenced by the most popular item: for both COS and COR, item 42 appears in the Long Tail (all other methods suggested it in the Head). We observe a reciprocally similar behavior, with COR method which was able to suggest 184 times item 46, which was visited only 10 times on the original distribution. This testifies a propensity to collect item in niches.

LP PI are not homogeneous. For example, we clearly see that PA and RA follow both a "rich get richer" tendency, with $PI_{PA} = 1$ and $PI_{RA} = 0.93$. However, all have a common behavior: when n is shifting up, LP PI get higher. It means that the more you enlarge suggestions field, the more you gather popular items. It is clearly an opposite behavior that we noticed for CF methods (table 4 last column). We can better visualize this evolution on each chart of figure 3, where lighter areas are small n.

TG Experimental Approach. Experimental TG approach has singular results. It is the only method which is not influenced by n fluctuations. If you keep on gathering a larger set of recommendations, TG method tends to keep on suggest the same proportion of popular and unpopular items.

What is interesting to notice in a second time is that, despite a curve looking like a "power law", PI_{Tg} score is 0.6. Results show that TG is almost always less influenced by popularity than LP methods (even LP using unweighted graphs). One can consult table 4 to illustrate this fact. Even if we see that the method can be influenced either by popularity (item 24) or by unpopularity (item 46), we also observe that the method is able to reach niches (item 11, item 54) and reject popular items (7).

As we said, it is not the moment to study accuracy of the method, but it is something we will surely do in further work.

4   Conclusion and Further Work

Collecting results, we were surprised to see how different the suggested items were, depending on the method. As a matter of fact, Link Prediction techniques are originally made for predictions. It is not a surprise to see a diverging behavior (compared to CF methods). But, if people tend to naturally go toward popular items, it means that LP techniques shall suggest a big amount of popular items. Before we demonstrated it with PI index, it was already proven by the simple fact that these methods are efficient. Then, we commonly use prediction methods to make recommendations. So, why do we recommend items that we know people will visit in the future anyway? It is smart in a highly concurrently universe like e-business, where you have to show that you sale the desired future item. But in other cases it might be better to use a recommender system less influenced by popularity. PI can help to choose.

PI is context dependent (data set, ranking scores, 80-20 cursor dividing Head and Long Tail), and then we encourage others to go through the proposed workflow and share results. Indeed, we are far to end up with popularity. As we said, in this experiment we didn't evaluate suggestions accuracy. But, we wish to examine our experimental TG recommender system in deep focus. TG experiment is divided in two steps. Here, we proved that TG is having an interesting mechanism as it returns an acceptable proportion of popular items. Now, we have to show that TG-based recommendations are accurate. In order to go further, we are developing a Moodle plugin that goes as a recommender.

We will keep working on e-learning use cases, where we still have to tackle popularity. Popularity is rarely studied in this context. We believe that there are plenty of correlations to identify. We also believe that this context is large and open. If we arrive to conjugate pieces of knowledge popularity and timeline, we should reach another level of recommendation techniques.

References

1. Adamic, L., Glance, N.: The political blogosphere and the 2004 U.S election: divided they blog. In: Proceedings of the 3rd International Workshop on Link discovery, pp. 36–43 (2005)
2. Adamic, L., Adar, E.: Friends and Neighbors on the Web. Social Networks. **25**(3), 211–230 (2003)
3. Anderson, C.: The Long Tail: How the Future of Business is Selling Less of More. Hyperion Books, New York (2006)
4. Beuscart, J-S., Couronne, T.: The distribution of online reputation. In: ICWSM Conference, San Jose, USA (2009)
5. Bikhchandani, S., Hirshleifer, D., Welch, I.: Learning from the Behavior of Others: Conformity, Fads, and Informational Cascades. The Journal of Economic Perspectives **12**(3), 151–170 (1998)
6. Blot, G., Rousseaux, F., Saurel, P.: Pattern discovery in e-learning courses: a time based approach. In: CODIT2014 - 2nd International Conference on Control, Decision and Information Technologies, Metz, France (2014)
7. Blot, G., Saurel, P., Rousseaux, F.: Time-weighted Social Network: Predict when an item will meet a collector, I4CS, pp. 115–120, Reims, France (2014)
8. Cha, M., Kwak, H., Rodriguez, P., Ahn, Y-Y., Moon, S.: I tube, you tube, everybody tubes. In: Proceedings of the 7th ACM SIGCOMM Conference on Internet Measurement, New York, USA (2007)
9. Dong, L., Li, Y., Yin, H., Le, H., Rui., M: The Algorithm of Link Prediction on Social Network. Mathematical Problems in Engineering **2013**(125123) (2013)
10. Downes, S.: Connectivism and Connective Knowledge. Self-published on the Internet, National Research Concil, Canada (2012)
11. Elberse, A., Oberholzer-Gee, F.: Superstars and Underdogs: An Examination of the Long Tail Phenomenon in Video Sales, MSI Reports: Working Paper Series 4, pp. 49–72 (2007)
12. Ekstrand, M.-D., Riedl, J.-T., Konstan, J.-A.: Collaborative Filtering Recommender Systems. HumanComputer Interaction **4**(2), 81–173 (2010)

13. Granovetter, M., Hirshleifer, D., Welch, I.: The Strength of Weak Ties. American Journal of Sociology **18**(6), 1360–1380 (1973)

14. Herring, S.G., Kouper, I., Paolillo, J.C., Scheidt, L.A., Tyworth, M., Welsch, P., Wright, E., Yu, N.: Conversations in the blogosphere: An analysis "From the Bottom Up". In: Proceedings of the 38th Annual Hawaii International Conference on System Sciences, Hawaii (2005)

15. Hindman, M., Tsioutsiouliklis, K., Johnson, J.A.: "Googlearchy": how a few heavily-linked sites dominate politics on the web. In: Annual Meeting of the Midwest Political Science Association (2003)

16. Kamishima, T.: Correcting popularity bias by enhancing recommendation neutrality. In: Proceedings of RecSys 2014, Foster City, Silicon Valley, USA (2014)

17. Katz, L.: A new status index derived from sociometric analysis. Psychometrika **18**(1), 39–43 (1953)

18. Leskovec, J., Singh, A., Kleinberg, J.M.: Patterns of influence in a recommendation network. In: Ng, W.-K., Kitsuregawa, M., Li, J., Chang, K. (eds.) PAKDD 2006. LNCS (LNAI), vol. 3918, pp. 380–389. Springer, Heidelberg (2006)

19. Linden, G., Smith, B., York, J.: Amazon.com recommendations: Item-to-Item collaborative filtering, Industry Report. In: IEEE Computer Society (2003)

20. Maulana, A., Situngkir, H.: Power Laws in Elections - SSRN. http://ssrn.com/abstract=1660603 (2010)

21. Mayer-Schonberger, V., Cukier, K.: Big Data: A revolution that will transform how we live, and think (2013)

22. Newman, M-E-J.: Power laws, Pareto distributions and Zipf's law. Contemporary Physics **46** (2005)

23. Newman, M.E.J.: Clustering and Preferential Attachment in Growing Networks. Physical Review Letters E (2001)

24. Meyer, F., Fessant, F., Clerot, F.: Toward a New Protocol to Evaluate Recommender Systems. ACM RecSys, Foster City (2012)

25. Oh, J., Park, S., Yu, H., Song, M.: Novel recommendation based on personal popularity tendency. In: Data Mining (ICDM). IEEE (2011)

26. Olmo, F., Gaudioso, E.: Evaluation of recommender systems: A new approach. Expert Systems with Applications **35**(3), 790–804 (2008)

27. Sarwar, B., Karypis, G., Konstan, J., Riedl, J.: Item-based collaborative filtering recommendation algorithms. In: Proceedings of the 10th International Conference on World Wide Web, New York, USA, pp. 285–295 (2001)

28. Shirky, C.: Power laws, weblogs and inequality. Extreme Democracy: Chapter 3 (2004)

29. Stoica Beck, A.: Analysing the Local Structure of Large Social Networks, Chapter 6: From Online Popularity to Social Linkage, PhD dissertation (2010)

30. Virinchi, S., Mitra, P.: Similarity measures for link prediction using power law degree distribution. In: Lee, M., Hirose, A., Hou, Z.-G., Kil, R.M. (eds.) ICONIP 2013, Part II. LNCS, vol. 8227, pp. 257–264. Springer, Heidelberg (2013)

31. Wasserman, S., Faust, K.: Social Network Analysis: Methods and Applications, pp. 291–345. Cambridge UNiversity Press (1994)

32. Yu, B., Liu, F., Li, T.: Recommendation of Tourist Attractions Based on User Preferences and Attractions Popularity. Journal of Computational Information Systems (2014)

33. Zanette, D., Manrubia, S.: Vertical transmission of culture and the distribution of family names. Physica **295** (2001)

Halo Effect on the Adoption of Mobile Payment: A Schema Theory Perspective

Xiang Gong[1], Kem Z.K. Zhang[1,2(✉)], and Sesia J. Zhao[3]

[1] School of Management, University of Science and Technology of China, Hefei, China
gxustc@mail.ustc.edu.cn, zzkkem@ustc.edu.cn
[2] Telfer School of Management, University of Ottawa, Ottawa, Canada
[3] Management School, Anhui University, Hefei, China
sesia@ahu.edu.cn

Abstract. Whether or how firms can employ the halo effect to facilitate their mobile payment service adoption remains a critical and puzzling issue in e-commerce research. Using the schema theory and the value literature as theoretical lenses, this study investigates the role of halo effect on mobile payment value perceptions and usage intentions. More specifically, we identify two types of mobile payment value: utilitarian and hedonic value. A field survey with 273 responses is conducted to test the research model and hypotheses. Our findings show that the two factors of the web-mobile payment relationship, namely perceived similarity and perceived business tie, can lead to increased value perceptions of mobile payment. Moreover, both utilitarian value and hedonic value are positively associated with mobile payment usage intention. We expect this study can provide valuable insights regarding the significant role of halo effect when consumers make the decision to use mobile payment services. Limitations, theoretical and practical implications are also discussed.

Keywords: Halo effect · Perceived similarity · Perceived business tie · Value perception · Mobile payment adoption · Schema theory

1   Introduction

The convergence of the Internet, wireless technologies, and mobile devices has created an "always-on" society, where mobile services penetrate to every corner of today's life [1]. Attracted by the great market, many providers extend their traditional web services to the mobile context to keep or expand their user population, such as mobile electronic word-of-mouth, mobile game, and mobile payment services. Among them, mobile payment, a critical service supporting mobile business and allowing users to adopt mobile terminals such as mobile phones to conduct payment for bills, goods and services, has received great attention from enterprises [2]. For example, eBay has provided its mobile payment product: PayPal. High-technology companies such as Google and Apple have also released mobile payment services, which allow users to conduct payment through their mobile phones. Undoubtedly, mobile payment services allow web content or service providers to make one step ahead in the war of terminal services.

© Springer International Publishing Switzerland 2015
M. Benyoucef et al. (Eds.): MCETECH 2015, LNBIP 209, pp. 153–165, 2015.
DOI: 10.1007/978-3-319-17957-5_10

For consumers, some benefits of adopting mobile payment services include increased convenience, greater enjoyment over the service process, and time savings [3]. On the other hand, mobile payment services have to be widely used by online customers before their benefits accrue to firms and customers. According to the Internet Data Corporation (IDC) report, only 37.2% of consumers have ever used mobile payment services in the U.S, which is far below the population of consumers (approximately 70%) who reported using traditional web payment services through a biller's site or an online banking site.

Different from those mobile services that are originated in the mobile domain, the mobile payment services are generally transited from web payment services [3]. Thus, potential users of mobile payment services are not just developed from nothing. Existing schemata built by web payment services can be used to facilitate the use of mobile payment services. In the extant literature, the notion of schema is often used to refer to preexisting constellations of beliefs and feelings stored in memory, which further plays a significant role in one's judgments and preferences [4]. Hence, if the existing schemata are congruent with mobile payment services, then people tend to have favorable attitudes toward the mobile payment services, which is known a halo effect [5]. The potential halo effect in this context suggests that mobile payment services may possess a strong relationship with their predecessor, web payment services. Such a relationship can be reflected in the operational consistency [6], functional similarity [7] or business tie between mobile and web service providers [8]. Recent research further posits that the web-mobile relationship may play an important role in consumers' adoption of mobile services [6]. Although the halo effect is likely to take place during web-mobile service transition process, little research has investigated this effect in the mobile payment context. A majority of the existing studies tend to understand users' mobile payment adoption without examining factors related to the web-mobile mobile relationship. For example, based on the technology acceptance model (TAM), prior research shows that mobile payment adoption is primarily explained by perceived usefulness and perceived ease-of-use of mobile payment services [9, 10]. Using the diffusion of innovation theory (DIT), scholars also posit that mobile payment usage is mainly motivated by seeking mobile payment service features, such as relative advantage, compatibility and image [3, 11]. Given these concerns, the purpose of this study is to investigate the halo effect on mobile payment adoption.

We develop a research model and address our research objective by drawing upon the schema theory [4, 17]. Consistent with previous studies [6, 7], we employ two factors that are associated with the web-mobile payment relationship, namely perceived similarity and perceived business tie, to explain the halo effect. We also refer to the literature on value perceptions to understand how the two factors (i.e., the halo effect) play their roles in the process of mobile payment adoption. The value-centric lens has been employed to explain new information technology (IT) usage [12-14]. Consumers' perceived value is their perceptions and attitudes regarding what they can benefit from using ITs [16]. Consumers' value derived from IT adoption would enhance their satisfaction and attitude, which is important in consumers' decision-making. Based on the unique features of mobile payment services (i.e., any-time, any-place, always-on, and personal devices), we identify two mobile payment values: utilitarian value and hedonic value. Utilitarian values are derived from the results of useful, efficient and productive experiences, while hedonic values are the outcomes of fun, pleasurable and enjoyable experiences [17].

The rest of the article is organized as follows. In the next section, previous studies on the schema theory, halo effect, and mobile services value are reviewed. Then, we propose the research model and hypotheses. Next, we empirically analyze the model by conducting an online survey study. Finally, the limitations, theoretical and practical implications of this study are discussed.

2   Theoretical Background

2.1   Schema Theory

A schema may refer to an individual's pattern of beliefs or attitudes. It demonstrates his/her mental structure of thoughts or ideas that act as a framework of integrating old and new knowledge [18]. Louis [18] explicitly argued that "a schema is a cognitive structure that provides situational forecasts on which individuals rely" (p.61). Other terms similar to schema include knowledge structure, conceptual framework, cognitive map, cognitive structure, and mental model [20]. According to the schema theory, people may make judgments through a combination of top-down processes and bottom-up processes. The top-down processes call upon prior knowledge, while the bottom-up processes begin with processing sensory data. If the data are congruent with the person's mental structure, the top-down processes will facilitate data assimilation [12]. The schema theory helps to explain the influence of schemata, as well as the acceptance of new knowledge. Individuals are found to be more likely to accept things that match their schemata, while they may re-interpret inconsistent things as exceptions [21]. The theory further points out that, in general, people construct various schemata with different objects based on their prior knowledge or experience (e.g., knowledge or purchase experience of certain products or services) [12]. Schemata with similar objects allow people to evaluate and respond to new objects based on similar categories [22]. Thus, the schemata accumulated through prior experiences provide a basis for elaborating new information and forming subsequent evaluations [12] .

Given that schemata are effective and play an important role in people's judgments, the schema theory has been recently adopted to explain problems regarding the value perceptions of IT applications. In Xu et al.'s [11] study, they applied this theory to explain the effects of system quality on information quality and services quality. That is, when individuals evaluate information quality and service quality, they tend to access and draw upon their perception of system quality in their mental schema. Dou et al. [22] incorporated the schema theory in studying Internet users' perceptions on the rankings of results in search engine result pages. They found that Internet users have better recall of an unknown brand, which is displayed before well-known brands, in search engine result pages by activating the schema of search engine ranking (i.e. better brands or valuable information tend be listed at top). In a similar vein, Daniel [1] contended that the workers feel more comfortable with business intelligence capabilities embedded within familiar applications than with those from new vendors.

2.2   Halo Effect

Although the concept of halo effect has not reached a consistent understanding in prior research, it generally refers to an individual's cognitive bias such that his/her impression of a certain entity (e.g., a product or brand) can affect his/her evaluation or attitude toward it or similar others [24, 28]. Recent research has shed light on halo effect in the context of brand marketing, where this effect is found to be the antecedent or component of consumers' decision making about new brand extension [26]. For instance, this effect may take place when the popularity of Apple's iPhone has a considerable effect on its following iPad.

On the other hand, halo effect has received relatively little attention in the information systems (IS) literature [11, 23-27]. While recognizing users' choice of a particular IS to is similar to consumers' brand choice [29], Kim [23] described halo effect in organizational contexts such that people may use existing schemata to facilitate the use of new IS functions. Hence, if the new functions are consistent with the existing schemata, then people may establish a favorable attitude toward the IS. Following this line of research, this study refers to halo effect as a cognitive bias where users' existing schemata of web payment services may posit an influence on their feelings or evaluations of the associated mobile payment services. If the existing schemata is positive, then users tend to have favorable attitudes toward the new experience of using mobile payment services. Nevertheless, we also recognize that if the existing schemata are negative, then a reverse halo effect [30] or negative halo effect [31] may take place.

2.3   Mobile Services Value

Consumers' value perceptions are important to understand the potential success of mobile services. Thus, extent research has paid considerable attention to identify key components of value perceptions. Kim and Hwang [32] conceptualized mobile services value as utilitarian value and hedonic value when investigating consumers' adoption of mobile services. Wang et al. [1] found that utilitarian value, hedonic value, and social value are three main motivations for users of mobile electronic word-of-mouth. Venkatesh et al. [14] suggested that utilitarian purpose, hedonic purpose, and monetary purpose play an important role in determining mobile Internet use. In a similar vein, Deng et al. [33] contended that performance value, emotional value, value for money, social value are key sources of perceived value in using mobile short message services. Among these studies, utilitarian value and hedonic value are the most frequently discussed value perceptions of mobile services. Thus, we follow this trend by employing the value-centric lens with utilitarian and hedonic value in the context of mobile payment services.

3   Research Model and Hypotheses

Our conceptual model is shown in Figure 1. Applying the schema theory in mobile payment context, we expect that consumers initially use web payment services to systematically increase value perceptions of mobile payment services. In the model, utilitarian value and hedonic value are regarded as important predictors of users' behavioral intention to use mobile payment services. Further, we argue that perceived similarity and perceived business tie may influence the perceptions of utilitarian and hedonic value of mobile payment services.

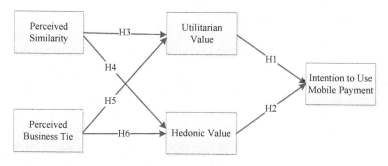

Fig. 1. Research model

3.1   Utilitarian Value, Hedonic Value, and Intention to Use

Consumers' perceived value can be defined as consumers' perceptions of benefits from using IT applications [34]. In the context of mobile payment, we propose that utilitarian value and hedonic value are the two key values in using mobile payment services. Utilitarian value is defined as the degree to which using mobile payment services will provide benefits to consumers in conducting payment conveniently and efficiently. Hedonic value refers to the fun or pleasure derived from using mobile payment services [14]. Mobile payment services enable consumers to access online transactions anytime from anyplace [2]. They satisfy consumers' needs that require prompt transactions [11], as well as reducing waiting time and increasing efficiency [3]. Meanwhile, hedonic motivation has also been found to be an important determinant of mobile payment acceptance. Interface design with aesthetic elements is likely to make the mobile payment service process more enjoyable and consequently stimulate positive feelings of consumers. More importantly, mobile payment services increase consumers' involvement and sense of freedom, which provide consumers with emotional rewards and hedonic experiences [34]. Based on these considerations, we propose the following two hypotheses:

H1: Utilitarian value is positively associated with intention to use mobile payment services.

H2: Hedonic value is positively associated with intention to use mobile payment services.

3.2   Perceived Similarity and Perceived Business Tie

In this study, we expect that the strength of the relationship between a web service and its corresponding mobile service may affect individuals' perceptions about the mobile service [6]. We use perceived similarity and perceived business tie to capture this web-mobile payment relationship. Perceived similarity captures the "internal relationship" between web payment and mobile payment because they share certain same innate features, which make people have similar perceptions about them. Meanwhile, perceived business tie captures the "external relationship" between web payment and mobile payment as they share certain external cues [1].

According to the schema theory, people make judgments through a combination of top-down processes and bottom-up processes [12]. In the transition of web-mobile payment services, bottom-up processes may begin with incoming new information about mobile payment, whereas top-down processes may rely on the schemata built by the adoption of web payment. If mobile payment information does not fit the schemata, people tend to re-interpreting any conflicts to the schemata as exceptions, or simply ignore the information [21]. We therefore expect that knowledge, beliefs, and feelings about web payment services can be store in memory as schemata, which form a basis for shaping subsequent judgments of mobile payment services. If consumers perceive a close relationship between web payment and mobile payment, then they will be more likely to form favorable perceptions toward mobile payment based on schemata built by web payment [7]. As Kim [5] posited that "when the old and new technologies are similar, the schema and script used for the old technology are likely to be evoked for the new technology" (p. 528).

Note that perceptions about a transition relationship may have a dual-effect on the evaluations of a new IT. On one hand, these perceptions may lead to biased evaluations of the new IT because existing schemata built by the prior IT can be negative. For example, some malicious computer programs are designed to cause system dysfunction or privacy breaches [35]. In this respect, people may establish a negative assessment about a similar computer program that has a close relationship with other malicious computer programs. Their perceptions are likely to be biased to fit their existing negative schemata about malicious ITs. On the other hand, perceptions of a relationship can also leads to favorable evaluations of a new IT by fitting the positive schemata of related ITs [7]. Given that web payment has often demonstrated as a successful IT application, the positive schemata built by web payment are likely to help individuals assimilate positive mobile payment information and ignore negative information, especially when consumers perceive high levels of similarity and business tie for the web-mobile payment relationship. In consistent, Sia et al. [36] posited that trustees who share common characteristics and identity with trustors are perceived to be more positive than those who sharing no common characteristics. Sun et al. [6] suggested that the strength of the relationship between the reference object and target object can lead to positive perceptions about the target object if people's trust in the source is high. Based on the schema theory and empirical evidence from prior studies, we posit that consumers' value perceptions of mobile payment are likely to be influenced by their perceptions about similarity and business tie in the web-mobile payment relationship. The following four hypotheses are proposed in for this research:

H3: Perceived similarity is positively associated with utilitarian value of mobile payment services.

H4: Perceived similarity is positively associated with hedonic value of mobile payment services.

H5: Perceived business tie is positively associated with utilitarian value of mobile payment service.

H6: Perceived business tie is positively associated with hedonic value of mobile payment services.

4   Methodology

4.1   Data Collection

An online survey was used to collect data. Since this study examined users' mobile payment adoption by emphasizing the halo effect from web payment services, we targeted at participants should have experience of using web payment services. In total, 273 usable responses were gathered for this study. Table 1 lists the sample's demographic characteristics. Among these respondents, 59.3% were male, whereas 40.7% were females. More than 85% were 30 years or below, while over 70% had a bachelor degree or above. More than 95% had no less than one-year experience of using web payment services.

Table 1. Demographics of sample

Measure	Item	Overall sample count (%)
Gender	Male	162 (59.3%)
	Female	111 (40.7%)
Age	20 or below	16 (5.9%)
	21-30	225(82.4%)
	31-40	22(8.1%)
	41 or above	10 (3.7%)
Education	Below college	29 (10.6%)
	Junior college	49 (17.9%)
	Bachelor or above	195 (71.4%)
Monthly Income	Under 1000	83 (30.4%)
(RMB)	1001-3000	69 (18.4%)
	3001-5000	82 (30.1%)
	5001 or above	39 (14.3%)
Web Payment Experience	>0 and <=1	2 (0.7%)
	>1 and <=3	108 (39.6%)
	>3and <=5	115 (42.1%)
	>5	48 (17.6%)

4.2   Data Measures

We adapted well-validated items of constructs from prior studies [1, 3, 6, 13]. Slight wording modifications were applied to fit the mobile payment context. A seven-point Likert scale was used for the items, from 1=strongly disagree to 7=strongly agree. The items for intention to use mobile payment were adapted from Lu et al. [3]. We used the measures from Wang et al. [1] and Stewart [7] to operationalize perceived similarity and perceived business tie. Further, utilitarian and hedonic value were measured using three items from Venkatesh et al. [14]. The measures of the constructs are listed in Table 2.

Table 2. Constructs and items

Construct	Item	Reference
Perceived Similarity (PS)	PS1: Mobile payment has a lot common with the web payment. PS2: Web payment and mobile payment are similar. PS3: Using web payment and mobile payment can achieve similar functions.	[1, 6]
Perceived Business Tie (PBT)	PBT1: Web payment provider is not connected to mobile payment provider. (Reverse) PBT2: Web payment provider is not likely to recommend an individual to use mobile payment. (Reverse) PBT3: Web payment provider and mobile payment provider have a business relationship with one another.	[7]
Intension to Use Mobile Payment (ITUMP)	ITUMP1: Assuming I have access to the mobile payment, I intend to use it. ITUMP2: Given that I have access to the mobile payment, I predict that I would use it.	[3]
Utilitarian Value (UV)	UV1: I find mobile payment useful in my daily life. UV2: Using mobile payment helps me accomplish payment more quickly. UV3: Using mobile payment increases my payment productivity.	[14]
Hedonic Value (HV)	HV1: Using mobile payment is fun. HV2: Using mobile payment is enjoyable. HV3: Using mobile payment is very entertaining.	[14]

4.3   Data Analysis and Result

We used partial least squares (PLS) for analyzing the collected data. Compared to covariance-based structural equation modeling methods, PLS requires a relatively small sample size, has no restriction on normal distribution, and is more appropriate for exploratory analysis [37]. Thus, PLS is more suitable for the current study. Following the two-step analytical procedures [38], we examine the measurement model and the structural model respectively.

4.4   Testing the Measurement Model

We assessed the measurement model by examining convergent validity and discriminant validity of the constructs. Composite reliability (CR) and average variance extracted (AVE) are the two indicators of convergent validity. It is required that CR values should exceed the 0.7, and AVE values are greater than 0.5. According to Table 3, CR values ranged from 0.93 to 0.98, while AVE values ranged from 0.82 to 0.95. Hence, convergent validity was sufficient in this study. Discriminant validity was assessed by ensuring the square root of AVE for each construct greater than its correlations with other constructs [37]. As shown in Table 3, discriminant validity was also acceptable in this study.

Table 3. Convergent and discriminant validity of the constructs

	CR	AVE	HV	ITUMP	PBT	PS	UV
HV	0.94	0.92	**0.96**				
ITUMP	0.98	0.95	0.63	**0.97**			
PBT	0.94	0.83	0.52	0.64	**0.91**		
PS	0.93	0.82	0.55	0.70	0.74	**0.91**	
UV	0.98	0.93	0.69	0.70	0.60	0.69	**0.96**

Note: Diagonal values in bold are square roots of AVEs

4.5   Testing the Structural Model

We tested the structural model by examining the R^2 of endogenous variables and the significance of path coefficients in the model [37]. The results of the structural model were illustrated in Figure 2. We found that both utilitarian value (β=0.49, t=7.15) and hedonic value (β=0.30, t=4.76) had significant effects on intention to use mobile payment, suggesting that H1 and H2 were supported. The results also showed that perceived similarity positively affected utilitarian value (β=0.57, t=8.22) and hedonic value (β=0.36, t=3.82) of mobile payment services. Thus, H3 and H4 were supported. Similarly, perceived business tie posited significant effects on utilitarian value (β=0.19, t=3.08) and hedonic value (β=0.25, t=2.82), showing that H5 and H6 were also supported. Overall, the variances explained in utilitarian value, hedonic value, and intention to use mobile payment were 50%, 33%, and 53% respectively.

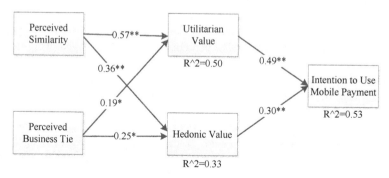

Fig. 2. Structural model (*p<0.01, **p<0.001)

5   Conclusion and Discussion

Motivated by the need to understand the halo effect on mobile payment adoption, this study employs the schema theory and the value-centric lens to investigate how perceived similarity and perceived business tie influence users' intention to use mobile payment. Our results show that utilitarian value and hedonic value can predict the adoption of mobile payment. The results further indicate that perceived similarity and perceived business tie can increase the value perceptions of mobile payment due to the existing schemata built by web payment services. This is an important finding, which suggests that the relationship between web payment and mobile payment plays a significant role on the successful implementation of mobile payment services.

5.1   Limitations and Future Research

Before discussing the implications of the study, we have to address several limitations. First, this study used a convenient sample from an online survey in China to test our hypotheses. To increase the generalizability of the findings, future researchers may consider enlarging the sample size or applying the research model in different regional settings. Second, as stated earlier, the web-mobile payment relationship may have a dual-effect on the adoption of mobile payment services. This study only assumes that people are likely to have established positive schemata about using web payment, thus leading to favorable evaluations of mobile payment. Future studies are then encouraged to consider whether negative schemata are established, which is also known as reverse halo effect [39], in certain circumstances of the mobile payment service context.

5.2   Theoretical and Practical Implications

We expect that this study can enrich our theoretical understanding in the extant literature. We use a value-centric lens to study mobile payment adoption and identify two mobile payment values: utilitarian and hedonic value. We show that utilitarian and hedonic value will significantly affect mobile payment usage intention. More importantly, based on the schema theory, this study investigates the halo effect on the adoption of mobile payment services. We find that perceived similarity and perceived business tie can lead to favorable value perceptions of mobile payment services, thus increasing mobile payment adoption. The halo effect has been identified in the marketing literature, however, to our knowledge, there is limited empirical research to examine its role on the adoption of new ITs during the transition process [12]. To explain this effect, we introduce the schema theory as a core theory for understanding mobile payment adoption. The schema theory posits that existing schemata can be used to facilitate the use of a new IT application. If the existing schemata are congruent with a new situation, then people tend to have favorable attitudes toward the new experience [5]. From this perspective, existing schemata built by web payment may play a significant role on mobile payment usage. Given that most of the existing technology acceptance theories (e.g., TAM and IDT) on mobile payment adoption cannot fully explain this halo effect, this study demonstrates that the schema theory is a valid one to explain it in the mobile payment context. Thus, this study not only makes a significant contribution to the extant IT adoption literature, but also provides theoretical insights and empirical evidence to the halo effect in mobile commerce settings.

This study also provides important practical implications. First, the important role of the halo effect on mobile payment adoption suggests that service providers should take the advantage of existing schemata from web payment services. For example, when designing mobile payment services, service providers should keep in mind to create similar functions or operation interfaces with their web payment services. They may also tag clear labels to show the linkage between the mobile and web payment services to quickly strengthen consumers' value perceptions in the mobile payment services. Second, service providers should also provide convenient, efficient, and user-friendly mobile payment services to satisfy both utilitarian and hedonic needs of mobile payment users, such as designing high quality systems, reducing operation steps, and providing interesting and enjoyable features in mobile payment services.

Acknowledgements. The work described in this study was supported by a grant from National Natural Science Foundation of China (No. 71201149).

References

1. Wang, N., Shen, X.-L., Sun, Y.: Transition of electronic word-of-mouth services from web to mobile context: A trust transfer perspective. Decis. Support Syst. **54**(3), 1394–1403 (2013)
2. Zhou, T.: An empirical examination of continuance intention of mobile payment services. Decis. Support Syst. **54**(2), 1085–1091 (2013)
3. Lu, Y., Yang, S., Chau, P.Y.K., Cao, Y.: Dynamics between the trust transfer process and intention to use mobile payment services: A cross-environment perspective. Inf. Manage. **48**(8), 393–403 (2011)
4. Dou, W., Lim, K.H., Su, C., Zhou, N., Cui, N.: Brand positioning strategy using search engine marketing. MIS Q. **34**(2), 261–279 (2010)
5. Kim, S.S.: The integrative framework of technology use: an extension and test. MIS Q. **33**(3), 513–537 (2009)
6. Sun, Y., Shen, X.-L., Wang, N.: Understanding the role of consistency during web–mobile service transition: Dimensions and boundary conditions. Int. J. Inf. Manag. **34**(4), 465–473 (2014)
7. Stewart, K.J.: Trust transfer on the world wide web. Organ. Sci. **14**(1), 5–17 (2003)
8. Stewart, K.J.: How hypertext links influence consumer perceptions to build and degrade trust online. J. Manag. Inf. Syst. **23**(1), 183–210 (2006)
9. Chandra, S., Srivastava, S.C., Theng, Y.-L.: Evaluating the role of trust in consumer adoption of mobile payment systems: An empirical analysis. Commun. Assoc. Inf. Syst. **27**(29), 561–588 (2010)
10. Liébana-Cabanillas, F., Sánchez-Fernández, J., Muñoz-Leiva, F.: The moderating effect of experience in the adoption of mobile payment tools in Virtual Social Networks: The m-Payment Acceptance Model in Virtual Social Networks (MPAM-VSN). Int. J. Inf. Manag. **34**(2), 151–166 (2014)

11. Yang, S., Lu, Y., Gupta, S., Cao, Y., Zhang, R.: Mobile payment services adoption across time: An empirical study of the effects of behavioral beliefs, social influences, and personal traits. Comput. Hum. Behav. **28**(1), 129–142 (2012)
12. Xu, J.D., Benbasat, I., Cenfetelli, R.T.: Integrating service quality with system and information quality: An empirical test in the e-service context. MIS Q. **37**(3), 777–794 (2013)
13. Brown, S.A., Venkatesh, V.: Model of adoption of technology in households: A baseline model test and extension incorporating household life cycle. MIS Q., pp. 399–426 (2005)
14. Venkatesh, V., Thong, J.Y., Xu, X.: Consumer acceptance and use of information technology: extending the unified theory of acceptance and use of technology. MIS Q. **36**(1), 157–178 (2012)
15. Kim, Y.H., Kim, D.J., Wachter, K.: A study of mobile user engagement (MoEN): Engagement motivations, perceived value, satisfaction, and continued engagement intention. Decis. Support Syst. **56**, 361–370 (2013)
16. Kim, H.-W., Chan, H.C., Gupta, S.: Value-based Adoption of Mobile Internet: An empirical investigation. Decis. Support Syst. **43**(1), 111–126 (2007)
17. Wakefield, R.L., Whitten, D.: Mobile computing: a user study on hedonic/utilitarian mobile device usage. European Journal of Information Systems. Eur. J. Inf. Syst. **15**(3), 292–300 (2006)
18. Brewer, W.F., Nakamura, G.V.: The Nature and Functions of Schemas. Handb. Soc. Cogn., pp. 119–160 (1984)
19. Louis, M.R., Sutton, R.I.: Switching cognitive gears: From habits of mind to active thinking. Human relations. Hum. Relat. **44**(1), 55–76 (1991)
20. Armstrong, D.J., Hardgrave, B.C.: Understanding mindshift learning: the transition to object-oriented development. MIS Q., pp. 453–474 (2007)
21. Nadkarni, S., Narayanan, V.K.: Strategic schemas, strategic flexibility, and firm performance: the moderating role of industry clockspeed. Strateg. Manag. J. **28**(3), 243–270 (2007)
22. Lin, J., Lu, Y., Wang, B., Wei, K.K.: The role of inter-channel trust transfer in establishing mobile commerce trust. Electron. Commer. Res. Appl. **10**(6), 615–625 (2011)
23. Daniel, D.: Four Tips for Better Business Intelligence in 2008 (2008)
24. Parboteeah, D.V., Valacich, J.S., Wells, J.D.: The Influence of Website Characteristics on a Consumer's Urge to Buy Impulsively. Inf. Syst. Res. **20**(1), 60–78 (2009)
25. Ren, Y., Harper, F.M., Drenner, S., Terveen, L.G., Kiesler, S.B., Riedl, J., Kraut, R.E.: Building Member Attachment in Online Communities: Applying Theories of Group Identity and Interpersonal Bonds. MIS Q. **36**(3), 841–864 (2012)
26. Song, P., Zhang, C., Xu, Y., Huang, L.: Brand extension of online technology products: Evidence from search engine to virtual communities and online news. Decis. Support Syst. **49**(1), 91–99 (2010)
27. Li, Y.: The impact of disposition to privacy, website reputation and website familiarity on information privacy concerns. Decis. Support Syst. **57**, 343–354 (2014)
28. Hsieh, M.-H., Pan, S.-L., Setiono, R.: Product-, Corporate-, and Country-Image Dimensions and Purchase Behavior: A Multicountry Analysis. J. Acad. Mark. Sci. **32**(3), 251–270 (2004)
29. Polites, G.L., Karahanna, E.: Shackled to the Status Quo: The Inhibiting Effects of Incumbent System Habit, Switching Costs, and Inertia on New System Acceptance. MIS Q. **36**(1), 21–42 (2012)
30. Sigall, H., Ostrove, N.: Beautiful but dangerous: Effects of offender attractiveness and nature of the crime on juridic judgment. J. Pers. Soc. Psychol. **31**(3), 410 (1975)

31. Montoya, M.M., Massey, A.P., Khatri, V.: Connecting IT Services Operations to Services Marketing Practices. J. Manag. Inf. Syst. **26**(4), 65–85 (2010)
32. Kim, D.J., Hwang, Y.: A study of mobile internet user's service quality perceptions from a user's utilitarian and hedonic value tendency perspectives. Inf. Syst. Front. **14**(2), 409–421 (2012)
33. Deng, Z., Lu, Y., Wei, K.K., Zhang, J.: Understanding customer satisfaction and loyalty: An empirical study of mobile instant messages in China. Int. J. Inf. Manag. **30**(4), 289–300 (2010)
34. Jia, H.M., Wang, Y., Ge, L., Shi, G., Yao, S.: Asymmetric Effects of Regulatory Focus on Expected Desirability and Feasibility of Embracing Self-Service Technologies: JIA, WANG, GE, SHI, AND YAO. Psychol. Mark. **29**(4), 209–225 (2012)
35. Liang, H., Xue, Y.: Avoidance of information technology threats: a theoretical perspective. MIS Q. **33**(1), 71–90 (2009)
36. Sia, C.L., Lim, K.H., Leung, K., Lee, M.K., Huang, W.W., Benbasat, I.: Web strategies to promote internet shopping: is cultural-customization needed? MIS Q. **33**(3), 491–512 (2009)
37. Chin, W.W., Marcolin, B.L., Newsted, P.R.: A partial least squares latent variable modeling approach for measuring interaction effects: Results from a Monte Carlo simulation study and an electronic-mail emotion/adoption study. Inf. Syst. Res. **14**(2), 189–217 (2003)
38. Hair, J.F., Tatham, R.L., Anderson, R.E., Black, W.: Multivariate data analysis, vol. 6. Pearson Prentice Hall Upper Saddle River, NJ (2006)
39. Sigall, H., Ostrove, N.: Beautiful but dangerous: Effects of offender attractiveness and nature of the crime on juridic judgment. J. Pers. Soc. Psychol. **31**(3), 410 (1975)

A Trust Certificate Model for Multi-agent Systems

Basmah Almoaber[✉] and Thomas Tran

School of Electrical Engineering and Computer Science,
University of Ottawa, Ottawa, ON, K1N 6N5 Canada
balmo036@uottawa.ca, ttran@eecs.uottawa.ca

Abstract. Trust plays a vital role in the decision to initiate any interaction. Rational agents may use past experiences and other agents' opinions to decide to trust, but due to the nature of open multi-agent systems, agents can dynamically join and leave the system at any time where agents may find themselves dealing with complete strangers whom neither they nor their friends have encountered before. This situation forces the agents to choose partners randomly, which significantly increases the risk of encountering unreliable agents. In this paper, we address that issue by creating a Trust Certificate model that allows agents to retrieve reputation information and make initial trust evaluations when evidence is unavailable. It also helps agents to avoid the need to make a random partner selection due to the information scarcity. We show how this model enhances the interaction process between agents by evaluating it in the context of a simulated multi-agent system.

Keywords: Trust · Reputation · Trust certificate · Intelligent agents and multi-agent systems

1 Introduction

"Trust is central to all transactions" [2]. The need for trust establishment increases in systems where entities rely on each other in order to achieve their goals. An important version of these systems is open dynamic multi-agent systems. In such systems, agents can freely join and leave the society at any time, which may affect the system's structure. This feature arises the problem of how to choose a partner, especially if we know that agents are self-interested and there is no central authority regulating the selection process. Many researchers address the problem by introducing computational trust models and current state of the art trust models generally consider trust as a function of prior interactions with a potential partner, whether it has been obtained directly or by other agents in the society [6, 12]. However, agents may encounter other agents who have no previous experience with and, at the same time, cannot have an access to other members' evaluations, e.g. when the agent is new to the system or the system itself is newly created. In such cases, agents have no choice but to explore the population and choose partners randomly. This option involves high risk when the agent selects an unreliable partner.

Against this background, we propose a new model Trust Certificate (TC) model that relies on certificates. The TC model allows agents to provide proofs about their

M. Benyoucef et al. (Eds.): MCETECH 2015, LNBIP 209, pp. 166–179, 2015.
DOI: 10.1007/978-3-319-17957-5_11

roles and previous performance to build up the trust in them of their potential partners. It is designed to help new agents integrating into the society as reliable partners.
A certificate is a signed electronic document that contains some claims about the
agent [8]. The main idea is that each agent in the system has a certificate, which
works as a reference providing information about its holder. The information is obtained and stored by the agent itself and is available to other agents who request it to
evaluate the holder's trustworthiness for a potential interaction. The stored information is about the agent's role in the society and its performance in past interactions. In
summary, the contributions of this paper are: First, introducing a new trust model that
enables agents to overcome the absence of trust evidence (direct and reputation).
Second, helping new agents to emerge into the system. Third, providing new agents
with the initial information, which protects them from relying on unreliable partners.
Finally, helping to reduce the risk of choosing partners randomly.

The remainder of this paper is structured as follows. Section 2 presents the related
work. Section 3 presents our proposed approach. Section 4 presents the empirical
evaluation and results. Finally, section 5 concludes with discussion and future work.

2   Related Work

Trust is essential to any interaction within MAS. This explains why many state-of-
the-art trust and reputation models have been introduced. As a common factor, almost
all of the models need some sort of information in order for them to work. The challenge is that the required information is not always available.

Many models have addressed the information scarce problem using different approaches. For example, REGRET model [12] suggests the use of social relationships
in e-commerce systems based on the assumption that agent's behavior can be predicted using the information obtained from the analysis of its social relationships. It
also introduces the use of neighborhood reputation and system reputation to help
newcomers. The problem with REGRET model is that it is not readily available because it does not explain how agents build their sociograms, which display their social
relationships. Also, building such sociograms is based on the agent's knowledge of
the environment, which is not suitable for new agents. It may not be applicable in
environments with random and contradictory agents. Other model [11] introduces the
use of RCertPX, which is a reputation certificate to help evaluating trust in peer-to-
peer systems. However, it does not provide a trust model based on the stored ratings
and it is vulnerable to the cases where a rater and a ratee collude to change the ratings.
In contrast, our approach presents a trust model to calculate the trust value of agents
from ratings stored in the certificate and chooses a suitable partner based on the resulted value. It also incorporates some metrics like rating time, degree of belief and
confidence level in agents, to minimize the collude possibility between agents. FIRE
[5] and [6] presents a robust approach *Certified Reputation* that can decreases the
possibility that the evaluator fails to evaluate the trustworthiness of newly joined
agents, but it does not solve the problem when the provider has no past experience to
share with the consumer. Human organizational behavior has been used by [1] to

solve the problem of cold-start and newcomer cases. The consumer agent classifies its previous experiences with other agents into classes based on their features. Yet, it still needs to gather direct information in order to be built. It does not cover the cases, in which the consumer and the group are new with no direct experience or reputation available to build the stereotype.

On the other hand, our approach is promising to address the problem of newcomers even when they have no previous experience. It introduces tools that enable the consumers to evaluate the trustworthiness and to estimate the future performance of the prospective partners.

3   Proposed Approach

In this paper, we propose the use of certificates to overcome the problem of trust source scarce. The proposed approach can be used as an addition to improve existing trust and reputation models.

3.1   Trust Certificate Overview

In our model, each service provider agent has a trust certificate that consists of three components: ID, role and certified reputation. The first part of the certificate is the ID part, which is used to bind the certificate to its owner. It contains the following elements:

- Owner ID: identifies the owner of the certificate.
- Owner public key[1]: which is used to authenticate the provider identity.

The second part of the certificate is role part, which contains information about the roles that the agent plays in the society. Identifying the provider's role gives the service consumer a way to expect the provider's behavior [10]. In some cases it also gives a predetermined level of trustworthiness about the service provider. The roles can be a membership of a popular organization that provides a quality assurance about its members' services (e.g. authorized dealer) or it can be an endorsement certificate from a trusted agent or organization. An agent can have one or more roles or no role at all. Each role includes: an assigned role indicates the agent's role in the society, an issuer ID and issuer signature to identify who issued the role and prevent any tamper to the role and finally an expiry date to ensure the validity of the role as agents can change their roles from time to time.

The third part of the certificate is certified reputation (CR), in which the provider agent stores the ratings of its past interactions with other agents in a local database to be ready whenever needed by a service consumer prior to an interaction [5]. This type of references helps new agents to attract consumers to interact with them. Each certified reputation contains five components:

---

[1] Each agent has a private key that should be matched with the public key to evaluate the validity of the certificate.

- Rating value: indicates the rater's opinion about the interaction.
- Rater ID: confirms the identity of the rater.
- Rater signature: ensures the validity of the rating.
- Time Stamp: stores the time of the interaction.
- Counter: keeps track of the number of interactions.

Agents can include many ratings in their certificate, but focusing on the recent ones as they carry more weight in trust evaluation.

3.2   Trust Evaluation Using Trust Certificate

Agents in MAS need to establish some level of trust in each other prior to any interaction. Establishing the essential trust requires some sort of information that can be obtained from many different sources. In the proposed TC model, three sources of trust information are integrated in order to estimate the trust value closely: role-based, rate-based and direct experience-based trust. All the trust values are in the form of ratings in the range [-1, 1] where -1, 1 and 0 indicate absolute distrust, absolute trust and neutral, respectively.

Role-Based Trust. The basic idea behind role-based trust is the roles agents are playing in the system provide some information about their capabilities and their future behavior. Agents in the system can have one or more roles. There are a finite number of possible roles in each system, which can be classified into two types:

- First, the roles an agent can have by participating in a known organization or having a membership. The underlying assumption in membership is that agents belonging to a group would behave similarly and memberships can provide a quality assurance about the agent's performance. For example, a seller can obtain permission from a known manufacturer to hold the title 'authorized seller'. So, agents who trust that manufacturer will trust its authorized seller agent. This type of roles is found in the Trust Certificate of the provider.
- Second type of roles is that represents the relationship between agents. It defines the positions of agents in term of their importance to other agents in the system. For instance, authority, seniority, or expert, etc. The agent's owner assigns this type of roles to it at the time of creation.

All agents should authenticate their roles by possessing certificates issued by trusted certificate authority. In our model these certificates are part of the Trust Certificate.

Since trust is a subjective measure, each consumer has its own list of roles with the matching trust values that represent the capacities of the provider, which has the role, in the system and their corresponding confidence level. The confidence level of each role is based on the criteria of that role and the provider who owns it. For example, we tend to trust doctors with more years of experience more than first year doctors despite the fact that both of them have the same role "Doctor". The set of roles is given to the consumer agent at the time of creation and is updated from time to time.

To calculate the role-based trust value for an agent, the evaluator should look up two components from its database for each role played by the agent: the value of the role $v_{ro} \in [-1, 1]$ where -1 means untrusted and 1 means trusted, and the confidence level (degree of belief) on that role $b \in [0, 1]$ where 0 indicates complete uncertainty and 1 for total confidence.

Since each consumer assigns two values (b, v_{ro}) to each role, we want a measure that captures the inter-relation (correlation) between b and v_{ro} values and estimates the future behavior of the provider based on those values. Such measure should reflect the relevance of each role's value because some roles count more strongly than others, in that they are given more weight (b) in the calculation. We can then define the role-based trust value of the provider as the weighted average of all roles based on the degree of belief:

$$T_{RO}(x, y) = \frac{\sum b \cdot v_{ro}}{\sum b} \tag{1}$$

where $T_{RO}(x, y)$ is the role-based trust value that agent x has in agent y based on its roles in the system. In other words, the role-based trust of a provider is calculated as the sum of all its assigned roles weighted by the degree of consumer's belief in each role and divided by the sum of all the beliefs to normalize the value to the range [-1, 1].

Calculating the role-based trust value based on the roles and their individual beliefs only may not be enough. We need to measure the reliability of the provider in terms of how much confidence we should put on the trust value resulted from formula (1) above. Hence, we define the measurement of such confidence in the provider based on the number of roles it has. The greater the number of roles it has, the larger its confidence is. The idea is that, every role has an impact on the provider regardless the role type and agents with multiple roles have more experience than agents with fewer roles.

$$C_{RO} = \min\left(\frac{RO_n - RO_{min}}{RO_{max} - RO_{min}}, 1\right) \tag{2}$$

where C_{RO} is the confidence in the provider y. RO_n is the number of roles the provider has, RO_{min} and RO_{max} are the minimum and maximum number of roles the provider can have, respectively. RO_{min} and RO_{max} are used to normalize C_{RO} into the range of [0, 1] where 0 indicates complete uncertainty and 1 total confidence. The minimum and maximum number of roles are application specific. For example in an agent-based market environment, the roles are perhaps only buyer, seller or advisor whereas in an agent vehicular ad-hoc network, there could be more roles such as authority, seniority, expert and ordinary.

Finally, after calculating the role-based trust value and measuring the confidence level in the provider, the total role-based trust value is calculated as follows:

$$T_{Role}(x, y) = T_{RO}(x, y) \cdot C_{RO} \tag{3}$$

where $T_{Role}(x, y)$ is the total role-based trust value that agent x has in agent y based on y's roles in the system and the confidence level C_{RO}.

Rate-Based Trust. Agents' reputation plays a fundamental role in trust decision process. However, it is not always possible to locate witnesses. That problem raises the need for an effective way to retrieve reputation information and insure its integrity. Rate-based trust is reputation information about the agent's past behavior that is provided by third party agents in the form of ratings. The difference here is that the agent obtains and stores the information in its local database and makes it available whenever needed by other agents for trustworthiness evaluation purposes.

In this type of trust, the consumer checks the previous behavior of the provider by using third party (referees) opinions. The ratings allow the provider to confirm its performance in order to gain the trust of its potential consumer. It starts by the agent asking its partners after every transaction to provide their feedback (ratings) about its performance and then stores it in its local database. So, when a new agent (consumer) is interested in partnership with that agent, the agent can provide its certified references to confirm its past performance and gains the consumer trust. On the other hand, the consumer calculates the rate-based trust from the set of the certified ratings that it received from the potential partner.

Agents may be tempted to alter their ratings to obtain a higher rate. To prevent tampering, each rating is included in a certificate (*certified reputation*) that is digitally signed for verification purposes. If the content of the certificate is tampered, the verification will fail. Another issue is that agents tend to only present the best ratings and hide the bad ones. We can address this issue by considering the time decay effect of ratings using a rating recency function [6]. We use the recency of the ratings, so the effect of old ratings decreases as time goes by, and thus trust values computed based on that old ratings should also be decreased accordingly. That should increase the accuracy of the calculated trust value as agents are forced to share their recent ratings to increase their probability of being selected. The suggested recency function is based on the time difference between current time and the rating time to reflects precisely how old a rating is:

$$t_{r_i} = e^{-\frac{\Delta\tau(r_i)}{\lambda}} \tag{4}$$

where t_{r_i} is recency of the rating r_i, $\Delta\tau(r_i)$ is the time difference between the current time and the time when the rating is recorded, and the parameter λ, called the recency scaling factor, is hand-picked for a particular application depending on the time unit used in order to make the rating recency function adjustable to suit the time granularity in different applications. The exponential function is used in the recency function because its shape over time fits the suggestion that the rating time should affect the trust value evaluation.

To calculate the rate-based trust value we use a similar approach as we use in role-based trust. Since we use recency function as a weight for the ratings, we want a measure that captures the correlation and estimates the future behavior of the provider based on its past behavior. We can then define the rate-based trust value of the provider as weighted average of all rates based on the time decay effect:

$$T_{RA}(x,y) = \frac{\sum t_{r_i} \cdot v_{ra}}{\sum t_{r_i}} \tag{5}$$

where $T_{RA}(x,y)$ is the rate-based trust value that agent x has in agent y based on third party opinion (v_{ra}). In short, the rate-based trust of a provider is calculated as the sum of all its available ratings weighted by the time decay effect, divided by the sum of all the time decay effects to normalize the value to the range [-1, 1].

Now, we define the measurement of confidence in the provider based on the total number of ratings it has. The greater the number of ratings it has, the larger the confidence is. The number of ratings can be seen as a measure of the provider's previous experience based on which we build our confidence. We assume that if the provider has participated in a lot of transactions and gained ratings from different consumers in the past, then it is considered to be an expert that can provide a more reliable service than a provider with less number of transactions.

$$C_{RA=\min} \left(\frac{RA_n - RA_{min}}{RA_{max} - RA_{min}}, 1 \right) \tag{6}$$

where C_{RA} is the confidence in provider y. R_n is the number of ratings the provider has (which is the Counter parameter in the Certified Reputation part of the Trust Certificate), RA_{min} is the minimum number of ratings the provider can have and RA_{max} is the maximum number of ratings. RA_{min} and RA_{max} are used to normalize C_{RA} into the range of [0,1]. The minimum and maximum number of ratings are dependent on the application and the consumers' choice.

Then, the total rate-based trust value is calculated as follows:

$$T_{Rate}(x,y) = T_{RA}(x,y) \cdot C_{RA} \tag{7}$$

where $T_{Rate}(x,y)$ is the total rate-based trust value that agent x has in agent y based on y's previous experience with other agents in the system and x's level of confidence C_{RA}.

Direct Experience-Based Trust. The term direct experience-based trust refers to the trust that is gained through direct observation of agent's behavior. The consumer uses its previous direct interaction with the provider to determine its trustworthiness depending on its satisfaction with the past interactions.

Here we employ the direct experience trust of [13]. Each agent rates its partner after each transaction depending on level of satisfaction and updates its database accordingly. Only the most recent trust values will be stored. Subsequently, the agent can query its database for the ratings to calculate its partners trust value.

At first when x has not interacted with y before, we set $T_{Direct}(x,y) = 0$ as no information about y's behavior is available. Then after the first interaction, the consumer updates its experience with the provider according to the result of the interaction as following:

If the consumer is satisfied with the result, then the trust value increased by

$$T_{Direct}(x,y) \leftarrow \begin{cases} T_{Direct}(x,y) + \alpha(1 - T_{Direct}(x,y)) & \text{if } T_{Direct}(x,y) \geq 0, \\ T_{Direct}(x,y) + \alpha(1 + T_{Direct}(x,y)) & \text{if } T_{Direct}(x,y) < 0, \end{cases} \tag{8}$$

where $0 < \alpha < 1$ is a positive increment factor.

Otherwise, if the consumer is unsatisfied with the result, then the trust value decreased by

$$T_{Direct}(x,y) \leftarrow \begin{cases} T_{Direct}(x,y) + \beta(1 - T_{Direct}(x,y)) & if \ T_{Direct}(x,y) \geq 0, \\ T_{Direct}(x,y) + \beta(1 + T_{Direct}(x,y)) & if \ T_{Direct}(x,y) < 0, \end{cases} \quad (9)$$

where $-1 < \beta < 0$ is a negative decrement factor.

The two factors α and β are used to adjust the trust ratings of providers. The absolute values of α and β are varied depending on the data availability and services' importance. Trust should be difficult to build up, but easy to tear down, so the consumer may set $|\beta| > |\alpha|$ to protect itself from dishonest providers.

Total Trust. Since each trust component uses a separate source of information to produce trust values, we need to combine them to calculate the overall value. There is no guarantee that all the components will be available, so we will use the available sources. If only one source is available, then it is used solely to find the trust value. Otherwise the following formula is used:

$$T_{Total}(x,y) = \sum_{k=0}^{2} w_k T_k(x,y) \quad (10)$$

where $T_{Total}(x,y)$ is the total trust that agent x has in agent y; k is thus one of the Direct experience-based, Role-based or Rate-based trusts; and the weight w_k is set to reflect the importance of each component. These values are set by the user to reflect its belief in every component.

4   Empirical Evaluation

We assess the validity of using the TC model by implementing an agent-based simulator. Our intension is to examine the TC ability to: (1) select reliable service providers; (2) reduce the risk resulting from the lack of information and experiences; and (3) maximize the utility gain of service consumers.

4.1   Description

The simulator is a multi-agent environment that is populated with a set of consumers (who are looking for service providers to interact with and consume the provided service) and providers (who provide services). For the sake of clarity, we assume that providers in the system only offer one type of service. The performance of the providers affects the utility gained by the consumers during the interactions. Each provider can be one of the following types: perfect, average, poor or infrequent. Provider agents of type perfect are always willing to provide good services, while providers of type average perform fairly well but not as exceptionally as the perfect providers do. The infrequent types are used to represent providers who perform based on their own personal motivations or the providers whose performance is affected by external factors. Poor, the last type, represents the providers who cheat all of the time. We consider agents of types perfect and average as good providers, and agents of types poor and infrequent as bad providers.

The agents are situated on a continuous 2-dimensional space field. All agent locations, consumer activity levels (indicating how frequently they use the service), and provider types are assigned randomly as agents are created.

We rely on random generators to set most of the TC model values. To design the role part, we create a set of seven roles. For every role, we assign a different value and degree of belief to reflect the fact that roles are domain-specific. The certified reputation part is set using a random generator to generate the rating as well as the time when they are received. Based on its assigned type, the provider returns a utility gain (UG) value that is randomly selected from the range [-10, 10] as presented in Table 1. The number of roles and ratings for agents is determined randomly between 0 and 5.

In the simulated environment, the consumer selects its partners either using the TC model or randomly. To ensure a fair comparison between the models, the same number of consumers examines each model. The selection process using TC model starts when the consumer contacts the environment to locate interested nearby providers (in our simulation, distance between the agents) and then, evaluates the trustworthiness of these providers. After that, it selects the provider with the highest trust value and uses its service. In return, the consumer gains some utility from that provider based on the provider's performance in that transaction. After the transaction, the consumer rates the provider based on its quality of the service with a trust rating in [-1,1], and stores the rating in its internal database. Finally, the consumer shares the rating it made with the provider and the provider may store that rating as a reference for future interactions.

On the other hand, the agent can choose its partner randomly from the list of interested providers and then evaluate the transaction quality and rate the provider accordingly.

Table 1. Provider agents types

Provider Type	Utility Range
Perfect	[5, 10]
Average	[0, 5]
Poor	[-10, 0]
Infrequent	[-10, 10]

Table 2. Simulation variables

Variable	Symbol	Value
Number of simulation runs	R	10
Number of consumer agents	N_c	500
Range of consumer activity level	a	[0.25,1.00]
Total number of provider agents	N_p	100
Perfect providers	N_{pg}	10
Average providers	N_{pa}	40
Poor providers	N_{pb}	45
Infrequent providers	N_{pi}	5

Table 3. TC model default parameters

Parameters	Symbol	Value
Recencey Scaling Factor	λ	$-(100/\ln(0.5))$
Minimum number of roles	RO_{min}	0
Maximum number of roles	RO_{max}	5
Minimum number of ratings	RA_{min}	0
Maximum number of ratings	RA_{max}	5
Positive increment factor	α	0.1
Negative decrement factor	β	0.2
Role-based coefficient	w_{Role}	0.4
Rate-based coefficient	w_{Rate}	0.4
Direct experience-based coefficient	w_{Direct}	0.2
Satisfactory UG value	satUG	$>= 0$

4.2   Experiments

In each experiment, the simulator executes ten runs. Every run then executes five rounds. At each round, every consumer is given the chance to interact with the system, and the UG that results from any transaction is recorded for analysis and comparison. At the start of the run, consumers change their locations to be able to examine a new set of providers.

The results obtained are presented and examined from two points of view: the average UG over all transactions and the percentage of all transactions in which good providers were selected. Then, the results are presented in graphs. We define good interactions as the interactions where the consumers yield UGs that are greater than or equal to zero.

Typical Environment. In this experiment, we show how consumers behave in a typical environment where approximately half of the providers are good and the other half are bad. The specific set-up used in this environment is in Tables 2 and 3.

Fig. 1(a) shows that the TC model outperforms the Random model in the number of good interactions. Consumers using the TC model choose good providers 100% of the time. On the other hand, in the Random model, the consumers only obtained good interactions 60% of the time.

Considering that the consumers using the TC model select good providers more consistently, they are expected to acquire higher utility than the consumers using the Random model. This is confirmed in Fig. 2(a), where it is noticeable that TC model consumers yield higher UG than Random model consumers, all of the time, by more than 4 UG units. The TC model provides higher utility than the Random model by selecting good providers more often.

In Fig. 2(a), we notice some fluctuates in the average UG values over the number of runs. That is because consumers are changing their locations at the start of each run. The location change means the consumer face a new group of providers to choose from and because providers are situated randomly around the environment, there is no guarantee about their service quality.

Table 4. Providers distribution for dishonest environment

Provider Type	Number
Perfect	5
Average	15
Poor	75
Infrequent	5

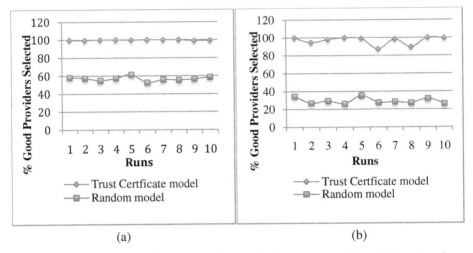

(a)   (b)

Fig. 1. Percentage of good interactions: (a) in typical environment; (b) in dishonest environment

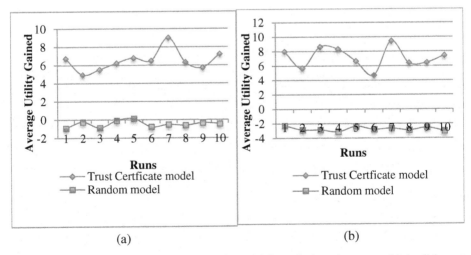

(a)   (b)

Fig. 2. Average utility gain for all transactions: (a) in typical environment; (b) in dishonest environment

Dishonest Environment. Having shown the TC model performance in a typical environment, now we present how the TC model performs in a dishonest environment where the environment is heavily populated with bad providers. We re-ran the same experiment as in the typical environment but with a new provider population distribution, as indicated in Table 4. The remaining variables and parameters are kept the same.

In this experiment, the TC model shows robust results against bad providers (Fig. 1(b)). Consumers in the TC model still chose good providers almost 100% of the time, however the percentage of good interactions in the Random model deteriorated significantly and could not exceed 35%.

In addition, by comparing the average utility gain we notice that the consumers employing the TC model obtain higher UG values than their random counterparts. Which means that the TC model performed better than the Random model, even when the environment is filled with bad providers.

From Fig. 2(b), it can be seen that the increase in bad providers does affect the consumers who choose partners randomly.

As shown in the previous two experiments, the performance of the TC model is not steady. The results are affected because consumers are changing their location after every run, and the nearest providers have different profiles.

Overall, consumers equipped with the TC model outperforms the consumers using the Random model in terms of an increase in the percentage of good providers selected, and a maximization of the average utility gained from the interactions. The results obtained through the previous two experiments demonstrate that the proposed approach of using the TC model solves the problem of the lack of direct history and experience, even in cases where the majority of provider agents in the system are bad.

5   Conclusions and Future Work

In this paper we address the challenge of choosing partners randomly when agents find themselves dealing with complete strangers whom neither they nor their friends have encountered before.

The TC model introduces the idea of equipping every agent in the system with a certificate. The certificate provides information about its holder and work as a reference about its trustworthiness by enabling the agent to collect and store its own reputation information and share it with others. Other agents in the system use the certificate to evaluate the trust value of their potential partners. The trust evaluation process integrates three trust metrics (role-based, rate-based and direct experience-based trust) to closely predict the behavior of the future partner and consequently choose a reliable one.

The work presented in this paper, as well as its contributions, have resulted in a positive solution to the challenge of choosing partners randomly. It also helps in reducing the cost for consumers, in terms of time and resources, since all the information is stored and provided by the providers themselves.

In empirical evaluations, our model performed well compared to the Random model, specifically in enabling consumers to choose reliable providers and maximizing their utility gains. Furthermore, it helps reducing the risk results from the missing information.

In future work, we intend to examine the effectiveness of the application of the TC model compared to other reputation systems. The TC model can be used as an extension to improve existing models, especially in cold-start and newcomer cases.

We also intend to add a reliability measure for the raters and referees who provide the reports of the certificates. In the TC model, we assume that agents report their information trustfully, which is not suitable to the nature of agents. In order to avoid this assumption, we aim to have a reliability measure to evaluate how much confidence should be given to the third-party reporters, and use that measure as a factor in estimating the trust value.

Finally, we plan to conduct more experiments to assess the effects of using the TC model to help new providers building their reputation especially when the consumers become knowledgeable about their environments and already have their acquaintances.

Acknowledgments. Basmah Almober is sponsored by King Khalid University, Abha, Saudi Arabia.

References

1. Burnett, C., Norman, T.J., Sycara, K.: Bootstrapping trust evaluations through stereotypes. In: Proceedings of the 9th International Conference on Autonomous Agents and Multiagent Systems, vol. 1, pp. 241–248 (2010)
2. Dasgupta, P.: Trust as a commodity. Trust: Making and Breaking Cooperative Relations **4**, 49–72 (2000)
3. Hermoso, R., Billhardt, H., Ossowski, S.: Role evolution in open multi-agent systems as an information source for trust. In: Proceedings of the 9th International Conference on Autonomous Agents and Multiagent Systems, vol. 1, pp. 217–224 (2010)
4. Herzberg, A., Mass, Y., Mihaeli, J., Naor, D., Ravid, Y.: Access control meets public key infrastructure, or: assigning roles to strangers. In: Proceedings of Security and Privacy 2000, pp. 2–14 (2000)
5. Huynh, T.D., Jennings, N.R., Shadbolt, N.R.: Certified reputation: how an agent can trust a stranger. In: Proceedings of the Fifth International Joint Conference on Autonomous Agents and Multiagent Systems, vol. 1, pp. 217–1224 (2006)
6. Huynh, T.D., Jennings, N.R., Shadbolt, N.R.: An Integrated Trust and Reputation Model for Open Multi-Agent Systems. Autonomous Agents and Multi-Agent Systems **13**(2), 119–154 (2006)
7. Lu, G., Lu, J., Yao, S., Yip, Y.J.: A Review on Computational Trust Models for Multi-agent Systems. The Open Information Science Journal **2**, 18–25 (2009)
8. Mass, Y., Shehory, O.: Distributed trust in open multi-agent systems. In: Falcone, R., Singh, M., Tan, Y.-H. (eds.) Trust in Cyber-societies. LNCS (LNAI), vol. 2246, pp. 159–173. Springer, Heidelberg (2001)
9. Maximilien, E.M., Singh, M.P.: Reputation and Endorsement for Web Services. ACM SIGecom Exchanges **3**(1), 24–31 (2001)

10. Minhas, U.F., Zhang, J., Tran, T., Cohen, R.: A Multifaceted Approach to Modeling Agent Trust for Effective Communication in the Application of Mobile Ad Hoc Vehicular Networks. IEEE Transactions on Systems, Man, and Cybernetics, Part C: Applications and Reviews **41**(3), 407–420 (2011)
11. Ooi, B.C., Liau, C.Y., Tan, K.-L.: Managing trust in peer-to-peer systems using reputation-based techniques. In: Dong, G., Tang, C., Wang, W. (eds.) WAIM 2003. LNCS, vol. 2762, pp. 2–12. Springer, Heidelberg (2003)
12. Sabater, J., Sierra, C.: Social ReGreT, a Reputation Model Based on Social Relations. ACM SIGecom Exchanges **3**(1), 44–56 (2001)
13. Tran, T.: Protecting Buying Agents in e-Marketplaces by Direct Experience Trust Modelling. Knowledge and Information Systems **22**(1), 65–100 (2010)

eHealth

Efficient Privacy-Preserving Identity Scheme for Electronic Validation of Phase 1 Clinical Trials

Hanna Farah[1], Daniel Amyot[1(✉)], and Khaled El Emam[2]

[1] School of Electrical Engineering and Computer Science,
University of Ottawa, Ottawa, Canada
{hfarah,damyot}@eecs.uottawa.ca
[2] Electronic Health Information Laboratory,
Children's Hospital of Eastern Ontario Research Institute, Ottawa, Canada
kelemam@ehealthinformation.ca

Abstract. New drug studies are essential to advance the pharmaceutical industry's ability to fight diseases. These studies are typically performed in four phases. We are interested in "phase 1" clinical trials where the goal is to evaluate the safety of a new drug. Contract research organizations recruit participants for their studies and need to verify electronically certain criteria without revealing the identity of these participants to other organizations. We outline some potential attacks against current identity representation schemes. Afterwards, we present privacy-preserving techniques to represent the identity of a participant in a scheme where operations can be performed efficiently and accurately. Our methods and scheme can also be applied to other domains to preserve an individual's privacy.

Keywords: Identity · Privacy · Clinical trial · E-health · Cloud computing

1 Introduction

Phase 1 clinical trial protocols are designed to evaluate the effect of a new drug on the human body and determine if it is safe to use. Contract research organizations recruit individuals to consume the new drug and monitor how it affects them. These individuals are not required to have the disease for which the drug is being developed. Therefore, some individuals may be tempted to participate in multiple trials at once for monetary compensation. The participation in multiple trials at once is not allowed because it may affect the integrity of the study performed by the contract research organization: side effects might be caused by one drug or the other, or even the interaction of two drugs. Protocols are required to help protect the identity of the participants while being able to check if a participant is concurrently enrolled in another trial.

It is important to note that privacy breaches can occur at any stage of a protocol. Developing a privacy-preserving scheme should take into consideration the privacy of the data on the storage level (perhaps on a secure cloud platform) and also the privacy of the data when it is manipulated throughout the protocol. Using a reliable encryption scheme

© Springer International Publishing Switzerland 2015
M. Benyoucef et al. (Eds.): MCETECH 2015, LNBIP 209, pp. 183–196, 2015.
DOI: 10.1007/978-3-319-17957-5_12

to protect the data needs to be complemented by a data representation scheme that does not reveal information throughout other means, for example, frequency analysis. In this paper we focus on protecting the privacy of the name of an individual because public resources containing the names of individuals are easy to obtain, for example, phone books. Further research needs to be performed to assess the need of protecting the date of birth field from frequency analysis.

Section 2 describes some of the existing methods for privacy-preserving matching along with their vulnerabilities. Section 3 defines the accuracy metrics that are relevant to phase 1 clinical trials. Using those metrics, we run experiments to determine a cost-effective privacy-preserving scheme to represent identity in section 3.1, a limitation on the length of a name to preserve privacy in section 3.2, and a name representation technique to protect privacy at different stages of a privacy-preserving matching protocol in section 3.3. Section 4 describes the application of our scheme in other domains. In terms of datasets, we use the College of Physicians and Surgeons of Ontario (CPSO) [16] and the Law Society of Upper Canada (LSUC) [17] public datasets to identify the set of attributes that can effectively be used to identify an individual. Different metrics are defined and selected in support of this analysis. In order to reduce bias, we use different datasets, namely parts of the Australian phone book and the North Carolina Voters database [18], in another set of experiments to devise measures to protect privacy.

2   Current Methods and Drawbacks

Bloom filters are gaining an increasing popularity among privacy-preserving methodologies [7,15]. They were initially introduced by Bloom in the 1970s [2]. A Bloom filter consists of an array that contains either 0 or 1 at each position (initially all the positions are initialized to 0). It is used to represent a set of elements efficiently and to determine the membership of an element in the set. To add an element to a Bloom filter, multiple hash functions are used to determine the locations in the Bloom filter that would be assigned a value of 1. To check if an element belongs in the set represented by a Bloom filter, the same hash functions are applied to that element and the locations in the Bloom filter are checked for the value of 1. If the item was already placed in the Bloom filter, all the locations would have been assigned the value of 1. This concept can be used to check similarities between strings: a string can be represented as a set of *bigrams* (consecutive 2-character substrings, for example, *John* is represented as *Jo, oh, hn*) and inserted in a Bloom filter. Two strings that are equal would be assigned a value of 1 in the same positions in two Bloom filters. A string that has only a small difference with another one will have many positions that share the value of 1 and some that do not. To compare the similarity of two Bloom filters, several metrics are available that check the ratio of the common of positions with a value of 1. Bloom filter encodings were thought to offer good privacy measures to encode a string given the use of multiple hash functions on several bigrams.

Kuzu et al. [10] presented the first cryptanalysis attack on Bloom filter encodings and showed that they were able to recover some of the names in a database correctly.

Researchers at the German Record Linkage Center [11] claim that little research on the security of Bloom filters has been published and present an attack that requires less computational effort and less resources than the one presented in [10] to be successful. They also offer techniques to make their attack more difficult to achieve but not infeasible. While the two attacks in [10] and [11] were based on Bloom filters that encode only one field at a time, and some of the previous authors [7] claiming that encoding more than one field in the Bloom filter makes it harder to be decoded, Kroll and Steinmetzer [9] present the first successful automated attack on Bloom filters encoding more than one identifier. In light of these recent attacks that are evolving and becoming less computationally demanding, we do not recommend that Bloom filters be used at the moment where strong privacy guarantees are required. The medical domain requires a strong privacy measure because patient data is of a very sensitive nature and is the subject of many laws.

Hashing is another method used to protect privacy. To protect a name from disclosure, a hash function is a method that takes a text as input and outputs a series of digits that are an alternate representation of that text. The important property of a hash function is that given the digits, it is practically infeasible to discover what the original text is, but the same text will produce the same digits every time we apply the same hash method to it. In the medical sector, if systems stored only the hash digits of a patient instead of their name, it may seem that the patient identity based on their name only is protected but in fact it is not. Statistical attacks can lead to the discovery of the original values. Any form of deterministic encryption (the same text will encrypt to the same value) will suffer against statistical attacks. Some of the protocols that rely on hashing or deterministic encryption are described by Bouzelat et al. [3], Churches and Christen [5], Karakasidis and Verykios [8], Scannapieco et al. [14], and Schnell et al. [15].

Even with the best encryption and guards on the value of a field, we show other techniques in the following to discover the values of that field in a dataset. For an individual record on its own, it is enough to have a strong encryption and limit the length of a field in order to protect its privacy. However, when we are protecting the privacy of a dataset, more factors come into play. Certain fields, for example the last name, do not have the same distribution amongst a population. In the North Carolina voters database, the last name Smith is the most common (1.3%), followed by Williams (0.99%), Johnson (0.89%), Jones (0.88%), Brown (0.74%), and Davis (0.69%). In parts of the Australian phone book, Smith is also the most common last name (0.89%), followed by Williams (0.47%), Jones (0.46%), Brown (0.43%), Taylor (0.39%), and Wilson (0.37%).

If the encryption used to protect the data set did not offer properties to generate multiple encryptions for the same text, it would be very easy for a person looking at the encrypted dataset to immediately notice which fields represent the name Smith because they will be the ones that have the most common encrypted values. We performed several experiments to generate a random data set from the North Carolina database and parts of the Australian phone book. As soon as the data set size passed the 300 person limit, the name Smith immediately started to show the highest frequency in the small random dataset. As we increased the size of the generated dataset, the frequency difference for the most common names in the original dataset was more apparent.

Privacy at the storage level is also not enough to protect a dataset. Even if the dataset was encrypted with an encryption scheme that was able to represent the same fields in different encrypted form. This only means that the encrypted data is protected while it is stored. However, the risk is re-introduced at a later step in the process. The entity performing the decryption knows the status of the match or non-match for a field, even if the cryptosystem did not reveal the original values, the party performing the decryption has to know if there was a match or not. Therefore, there is a risk introduced for the last name, since the frequency of the matching is known, the party performing the decryption can assume a certain value based on the frequency of the matching correlated to the frequency of the name in the original population (with access to that demographic information). An identity scheme that guards against this attack is presented in section 3.3.

3   Privacy-Preserving Identity Scheme

To protect the identity of the participants, protocols rely on encryption mechanisms to maintain the privacy of the data. Encryption schemes can be either symmetrical or asymmetrical. Symmetrical schemes use the same secret key to encrypt and decrypt data while asymmetrical schemes use a private key for decryption and a public key for encryption. Clinical trial sites need to share data while protecting the privacy of their participants so we need an asymmetrical scheme where a central authority holds the private key and distributes the public key to the sites so they can encrypt their data. This scheme offers a privacy benefit: it does not matter if one of the sites is compromised because the knowledge of the public key does not allow the decryption of the data (the authority maintaining the private key is considered to be highly knowledgeable and certified in computer security). However, one disadvantage is that this approach is much slower than symmetrical schemes.

We present a scheme to be used in conjunction with a solid foundation for privacy. This foundation is the exponential ElGamal cryptosystem [6]. This cryptosystem provides important properties to protect against attacks. First of all, it is semantically secure: given an encoded text, it should be infeasible to obtain any information about the original text. Furthermore, the same original text can be encoded to many different encodings based on a random number making it invulnerable to frequency attacks. The two remaining properties we are interested in are the additive homomorphism and the scalar multiplicative homomorphism. Additive homomorphism enables us to perform an addition of two original texts by multiplying their encodings and scalar multiplicative homomorphism enables us to perform a multiplication of the original value by a constant by raising the encoded value to that constant. These operations can be taken advantage of to develop secure protocols that manage encoded data using the ElGamal cryptosystem or other cryptosystems that demonstrate the same properties including the Paillier cryptosystem [12]. The ElGamal cryptosystem offers security guarantee based on the difficulty of computing discrete logarithms. It is used in many industrial applications in real-world scenarios. The computations performed require more computational power than the symmetric cryptosystems, which do not offer the same properties.

In order to make an efficient use of the ElGamal cryptosystem, we need to define which minimalistic combination of fields can be used to identify an individual. The field selection criteria are based on achieving a high level of accuracy. In the following, we will examine which metrics are important in the context of phase 1 clinical trials in order to determine the best combination of fields to identify an individual in this context. We also utilize these metrics in further experiments to protect privacy in sections 3.2 and 3.3.

3.1   Metrics

Quantin et al. performed a quality assessment of an anonymous record linkage procedure [13] (which includes matching a record inside a dataset) where they highlighted the results of the linkage procedure as satisfactory given a sensitivity of 95% and a specificity of 100%. Their quality assessment method included the calculation of the positive predictive value (or precision) and the negative predictive value of the algorithm.

Christen and Goiser studied the quality and complexity measures for data linkage and deduplication [4]. They recommended that the number of true negative matches should not be used because the majority of record pairs will be classified as true negatives. The metrics that use the number of true negatives include accuracy, specificity and negative predictive value. The evaluation metrics that they recommended to use were sensitivity (also known as recall or true positive rate) and precision (also known as positive predictive value).

Weber et al. based their analysis of different record linkage methods and name matching techniques on sensitivity and specificity [19]. Baxter et al. consider accuracy as sensitivity and specificity in their comparison of fast blocking methods for record linkage [1].

There are four variables used to calculate such metrics: the number of true positive matches, the number of false positive matches, the number of true negative matches, and the number of false negative matches. We explain in the following the meaning of each of these variables for phase 1 protocols for detecting concurrent enrolment.

- *True positive* (TP): A true positive value indicates that an individual is participating in a concurrent trial and the validation protocol detected that he is. This parameter is important for phase 1 clinical trials in order to disqualify the individuals that are not eligible for the trial as soon as they are screened. Otherwise, clinical trial sites will incur additional costs and delays to replace that individual if they discover he is not eligible at a later time or risk the integrity and the objectiveness of their study if they do not find out that he was not eligible. The metrics affected by this parameter are sensitivity and positive predictive value (precision).
- *False positive* (FP): A false positive value indicates that an individual is not participating in a concurrent trial but the validation protocol detected that he is. It is desirable to reduce the number of false positive matches because it is hard to recruit individuals for phase 1 clinical trials. However, the true positive parameter is more crucial than this one for our scenario. The metrics affected by this parameter are specificity and positive predictive value.
- *True negative* (TN): A true negative value indicates that an individual is not participating in a concurrent trial and the validation protocol did not detect that he is. This parameter is similar to the "do nothing" option where the operation of the clinical trial is running smoothly. The metrics affected by this parameter are specificity and negative predictive value.

- *False negative* (FN): A false negative value indicates that an individual is participating in a concurrent trial but the validation protocol did not detect that he is. This parameter is an extremely important one for phase 1 clinical trials because the entire purpose of the protocol is to detect such individuals. The metrics affected by this parameter are sensitivity and the negative predictive value.

Table 1 summarizes the importance of the parameters in the use case of phase 1 clinical trial eligibility.

Table 1. Degree of importance of parameters

Parameter	Degree of importance
False negative	Extremely important
True positive	Important
False positive	Desirable
True negative	None

The metrics described in the literature and used in our experiments are presented next. Note that "condition" refers to the condition of an individual participating in more than one clinical trial at a time (or within a specified time period) and "test" indicates the application of a protocol to determine if the condition is satisfied or not.

- *Sensitivity* (S = TP/(TP+FN)): Sensitivity is the most important metric in our evaluation. It measures the true positive percentage given that the condition is positive and some test outcomes are negative. In our scenario, a high sensitivity value ensures that almost all the participants who are enrolled in concurrent clinical trials are properly detected and disqualified.
- *Precision* or *Positive Predictive Value* (PPV = TP/(TP+FP)): Precision measures the percentage of true positives given that the test outcome is positive but sometimes the condition is negative. In our scenario, a high precision value indicates that the protocol disqualifies very few individuals incorrectly.
- *Specificity* (Sp = TN/(TN+FP)): Specificity measures the true negative percentage given that the condition is negative and some test outcomes are positive. In our scenario, a high specificity value indicates that almost all the individuals that are not participating in another trial concurrently are identified as such. This is not a very important measure for our scenario because the focus is on finding the individuals that are participating in other trials at the same time (or within a time period) and disqualifying them.
- *Negative Predictive Value* (NPV = TN/(TN+FN)): The negative predictive value measures the percentage of true negatives given that the test outcome is negative but sometimes the condition is positive. In our scenario, a high NPV indicates that the protocol lets through the biggest number of eligible individuals.

In order to determine the importance of each metric, the following table shows a score calculated using the following method: for each parameter in the metric's formula, the method gets a number of points added to its score. Extremely important parameters are worth 3 points, important parameters are worth 2 points, and desirable parameters are worth 1 point. Table 2 ranks the metrics by order of importance according to their score:

Table 2. Metric scores

Metric	Score
Sensitivity	5
Precision	3
Negative predictive value	3
Specificity	1

Specificity can hence be excluded from further analysis because it is not pertinent to phase 1 clinical trial protocols for identity matching.

3.2   Field Selection for Performance Improvement

Private record linkage protocols typically aim to match records using a wide range of fields including names, addresses, and other demographic information. Our initial datasets were composed of six fields, typically available in healthcare: first name, last name, gender, date of birth, health card number, and postal code. These fields were used to match participant identities.

In order to compare text fields, it is known that approximate comparison techniques perform better than exact matching because they allow for small errors that can be introduced through a typing mistake. The best approximate matching techniques rely on splitting a text into a series of consecutive characters and calculating a similarity index to decide if the entire text is classified as a match or not. The implication of this comparison scheme on private protocols is the added complexity of encrypting every subset of a text instead of the entirety of the text.

In our datasets, we calculate the computational time required to match one record against the dataset. Keep in mind that our datasets do not contain a full address which is sometimes included and used for matching. This means that we are presenting a best case scenario. The text fields being matched are first name, last name, and postal code. In our datasets, including the 1990 US census, the average name length is 7 characters. The postal code is a fixed 6 alphanumeric values in Canada. Therefore the overall text fields produce a total of 23 bigrams to be encrypted on average (typically the fields are padded with a space at the beginning and at the end so a name with length x will be represented by $x+1$ bigrams. In our case, first name + last name + postal code produces $7+1+7+1+6+1=23$ bigrams). The maximum size of a dataset we considered for our clinical trial setup is 20000. If a protocol performed one to one matching, in a worst case scenario, it would have to perform 20000 comparisons. This means that we will have to match $(8*8+8*8+7*7)*20000 = 177*20000=3540000$ bigrams. We developed an optimized code implementing the exponential ElGamal cryptosystem and our experiments showed that on average, a decryption required around one millisecond. The worst case scenario to match a record in that case is roughly one hour on a machine with a single processor. This computation time is unacceptable to check the eligibility of a participant in a trial especially when the participant can be waiting for an answer on the phone or in person. To address this problem, a more powerful machine can be used, one that has multiple processors. Typically, a well-built machine today would have a processor with multiple cores. Record linkage applications are known to be easily parallelizable. Data centers on the other hand have much more powerful machines but they also cost a lot of money. To help reduce computational cost, we tried to minimize the number of bigrams that need to be compared by reducing the number of fields required to identify a participant.

Text fields are a bottleneck for privacy-preserving protocols that aim to provide higher matching accuracy. In the following, we calculate the values of the sensitivity (Fig. 1), negative predictive value (Fig. 2), and precision or positive predictive value (Fig. 3) for the eight different text field combinations for dataset sizes of 1000, 5,000, 10,000, and 20,000 participants in a clinical trial.

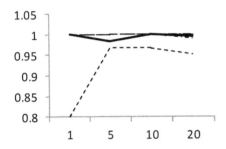

Fig. 1. Sensitivity of the CPSO dataset

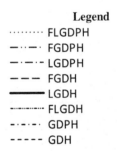

Fig. 2. Negative predictive value of the CPSO dataset

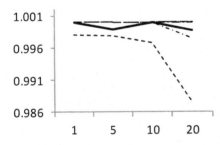

Fig. 3. Precision of the CPSO dataset

Legend

.... FLGDPH
— ·· —· FGDPH
— · — ·· LGDPH
— — — FGDH
——— LGDH
·········· FLGDH
— · — ·· GDPH
— — — — GDH

The horizontal axes of Figs. 1 to 3 show the size of a dataset in thousands. The vertical axes show the metric values.

The displayed values are the averaged results on 15 different sub-datasets of a same size. The legend indicates the selected fields with each letter representing a field that was included in our protocol. 'F' stands for first name, 'L' for last name, 'G' for gender, 'D' for date of birth, 'P' for postal code, and 'H' for health card number. Combinations consisting of only one or two fields are not considered because they lead to very poor results. The datasets we used for this evaluation are based on the lists of doctors from the College of Physicians and Surgeons of Ontario (CPSO) and the list of lawyers from the Law Society of Upper Canada (LSUC). The results for both datasets were comparable. For space limitations, we will only show the results of the CPSO dataset.

We eliminated the GDH combination because it has lower sensitivity and negative predictive value than the other combinations, especially for larger datasets. We also eliminated the FGDH combination because it performed much worse (by at least 34%) in terms of precision than the other metrics for a smaller dataset size.

The remaining combinations perform similarly for the three metrics except for precision, where the LGDH metric performs considerably better especially on smaller dataset sizes, which is typical for phase 1 clinical trials. The difference is meaningful: at least 17% between LGDH and the best one of the remaining metrics for the CPSO dataset.

Our goal was to reduce the number of text fields to the least amount possible with the least sacrifice of accuracy. The experiments above show us that the best field combination with the least amount of text fields and best accuracy is LGDH. We were hence successful in building new datasets that contained only four fields: last name, date of birth, gender, and health card number. The reduction of the text fields by a third allowed our experimental protocol to gain around 64% improvement in terms of performance. Instead of comparing 177 bigrams (first name + last name + postal code) for each record, we only compare 64 bigrams (last name). For larger datasets, the performance improvement is important because it translates into shorter wait times for participants to know whether they are eligible to participate in a trial. We were able to check the eligibility of a potential participant in roughly 40 seconds on a 32-core machine for a dataset size of 20,000 participants, which corresponds to a realistic scenario.

3.3   Bigrams Selection for Privacy

The graphs in Fig. 4 show the name length distribution in the North Carolina voters database and in parts of the Australian phone book (containing around 200,000 names). We notice that the rarest names are the ones towards the end of the curve, where for a name of length 19, there exist fewer than 10 individuals that can be identified without knowing the value of the name.

Given the results reported in Fig. 4, for privacy enhancing reasons, we decided to limit the comparison of names using a maximum of 16 bigrams: beyond that limit, the number of names becomes fewer than 100 and poses a higher risk of identification. We conducted experiments to discover whether the 16 bigram limitation affected the accuracy of our protocol and to find out the best method of choosing these 16 bigrams. The five choices we considered for the latter part were the following: the first 16, the last 16, the most common 16, the least common 16, and finally a random selection of 16 bigrams. The least and most common list of bigrams were compiled from the actual list of names in the database, which provides the most accurate representation compared to compiling them from a list of names extracted from a phone book for example. The results are shown in the following graphs (as the results for the NC dataset and the Australian phone book were similar; we only show the Australian dataset in the graphs). Fig. 5 shows that using 16 bigrams had little effect on the protocol's accuracy and that, in some cases, it improved it. The choice of the 16 bigrams also did not affect the protocol's accuracy in a noticeable way (all of the options explored have overlapping dashed lines in the diagrams). We conclude that it is accurate to limit the number of bigrams that represent a name to only 16.

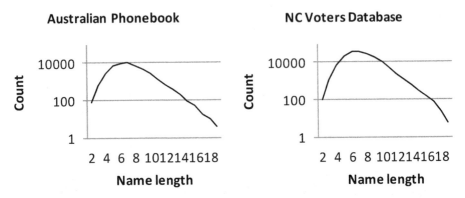

Fig. 4. Name length stats in the Australian phone book and North Carolina datasets

3.4   Name Representation for Privacy

We developed and tested a name representation scheme that offers better privacy and performance in terms of accuracy compared to the popular consecutive bigrams scheme [7,15] (SMITH would be represented as _S, SM, MI, IT, TH, H_). The graphs in Fig. 6, Fig. 7, and Fig. 8 show the average results over 50 independent datasets based on the CPSO and LSUC resources. We notice in particular that the values of the precision are particularly better than the regular bigrams scheme, meaning that protocols using this new scheme will disqualify much less individuals incorrectly and allow contract research organizations to recruit a bigger number of participants as they are striving for.

To represent SMITH with health card number 123456789, our scheme interleaves one character from SMITH with one digit from the health card number. If the health card number is not long enough, we would restart from the beginning. The representation for SMITH would be: *S1, M2, I3, T4, H5*.

This scheme accounts for minor spelling mistakes, for example SMYTH would be represented by the same bigrams except *I3* which would be replaced by *Y3*. The dice coefficient approach to match names has a defined threshold that can account for these mistakes and still declare the two names as a match in most cases. We recommend using the exponential ElGamal cryptosystem, which is fast and provides semantic security. It also allows the use of a random number in each encryption, which will not affect the result of the decryption. Using a different random number each time, our scheme will protect against frequency attacks at the storage level and interleaving the health card numbers with the characters of the last name will allow approximate matching while protecting against frequency attacks at the decryption stage.

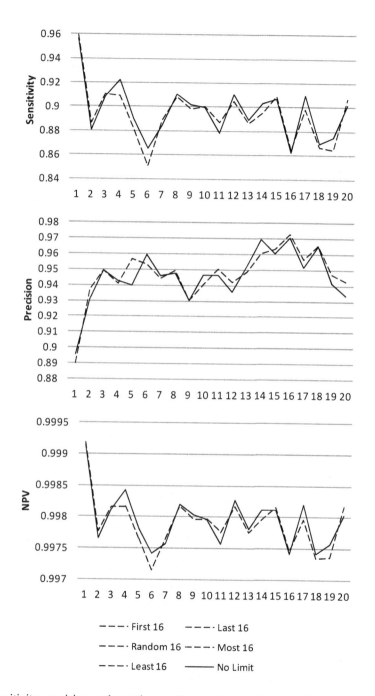

Fig. 5. Sensitivity, precision, and negative predictive value for the Australian phone book dataset for different bigram selection techniques. The horizontal axes show the size of the dataset in thousands whereas the vertical axes show the metric values.

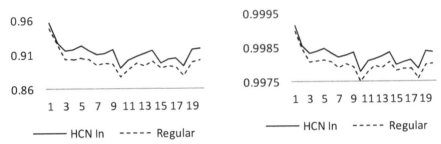

Fig. 6. Comparing the sensitivity of the regular bigrams scheme against our new scheme

Fig. 7. Comparing the NPV of the regular bigrams scheme against our new scheme

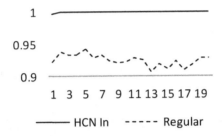

Fig. 8. Comparing the precision of the regular bigrams scheme against our new scheme

4   Application to Other Domains

We presented a scheme that utilizes a person's last name, gender, date of birth, and health card number to encode and detect their identity in a privacy-preserving way. The health card number represents a unique identifier for each person that is coupled with the last name to create a representation of the last name resilient to frequency attacks. The scheme detects the least combination of string fields in order to give a performance boost and lessen computational burden.

The health card number might not be present in domains outside the health care sector. In order for our scheme to be reused in other domains, it is required to have a unique identifier to replace the health card number. A driver's license number could be used to allow privacy-preserving querying of drivers. A passport number could be used for travelers. If the domain has a unique identifier, replacing the health card number in our scheme by that unique identifier will adapt the scheme to the new domain.

Domains can also introduce additional fields to the comparison. These additions will incur additional performance costs. But most importantly, these additions need to be done carefully in order to avoid introducing a field that does not have an even frequency distribution similar to the last name and make the records vulnerable to frequency attacks. If a field with uneven frequency is required, we recommend using a technique similar to the HCN In concept in order to guard against attacks. Users wishing to add extra fields also need to make sure the values of the metrics that are important to their domain are above their acceptable thresholds.

5   Conclusion

We discussed the issue of concurrent enrolment in clinical trials and the need of a solution that respects the privacy of the participants. We explained the meaning and importance of various metrics that are common in the literature to evaluate the accuracy of protocols in the e-health context of phase 1 clinical trials. We highlighted the performance bottleneck for text fields where approximate matching is required and performed an evaluation of the most adequate field selection to identify a participant, leading to a first contribution (namely, the sufficiency of using: last name, date of birth, gender, and health card number). We also showed the importance of protecting the privacy of individuals with lengthy names and defined experimentally a proper limitation of a name representation (16 characters) that does not affect the accuracy of protocols. As third contribution, we defined an appropriate scheme (interleaving characters from the name with the digits of a health card number for the composition of bigrams) that guards against frequency attacks at both the storage and decryption stages of protocols. We believe that these discussions and results can help other researchers build more secure protocols for such trials, especially with information stored in the cloud. We will also develop a full protocol for phase 1 clinical trials in further publications.

Our methods can be adapted to tackle other relevant problems in the pharmaceutical industry including drug prescription monitoring to stop an individual from obtaining the same prescription twice while protecting his privacy. We will also investigate whether such approach can contribute to solving similar issues in more general e-commerce scenarios.

To mitigate the threats to external validity, we used the list of names of doctors and lawyers in Ontario, the North Carolina voters database and parts of the Australian phone book to generate our datasets. However, datasets from other provinces or countries might lead to different results and there might be better combinations not explored here. We are currently extending these evaluations to include additional datasets to reinforce and generalize the current results.

Acknowledgments. This work was supported by Canada's NSERC (Graduate Scholarship) and the Ontario Graduate Scholarship program.

References

1. Baxter, R., Christen, P., Churches, T.: A comparison of fast blocking methods for record linkage. ACM SIGKDD **3**, 25–27 (2003)
2. Bloom, B.H.: Space/time trade-offs in hash coding with allowable errors. Communications of the ACM **13**(7), 422–426 (1970)
3. Bouzelat, H., Quantin, C., Dusserre, L.: Extraction and anonymity protocol of medical file. In: Proc. AMIA Fall Symposium, pp. 323–327. AMIA Inc. (1996)
4. Christen, P., Goiser, K.: Quality and complexity measures for data linkage and deduplication. In: Guillet, F.J., Hamilton, H.J. (eds.) Quality Measures in Data Mining. SCI, vol. 43, pp. 127–151. Springer, Heidelberg (2007)

5. Churches, T., Christen, P.: Some methods for blindfolded record linkage. BMC Medical Informatics and Decision Making 4(9), 17 pages (2004)
6. Cramer, R., Gennaro, R., Schoenmakers, B.: A Secure and Optimally Efficient Multi-authority Election Scheme. In: Fumy, W. (ed.) EUROCRYPT 1997. LNCS, vol. 1233, pp. 103–118. Springer, Heidelberg (1997)
7. Durham, E.A.: A framework for accurate, efficient private record linkage. PhD Thesis, Biomedical Informatics, Vanderbilt University, USA (2012)
8. Karakasidis, A., Verykios, V.S.: Secure blocking+secure matching = Secure record linkage. Journal of Computing Science and Engineering 5(3), 101–106 (2011)
9. Kroll, M., Steinmetzer, S.: Automated Cryptanalysis of Bloom Filter Encryptions of Health Records. arXiv preprint arXiv:1410.6739 (2014)
10. Kuzu, M., Kantarcioglu, M., Durham, E., Malin, B.: A Constraint Satisfaction Cryptanalysis of Bloom Filters in Private Record Linkage. In: Fischer-Hübner, S., Hopper, N. (eds.) PETS 2011. LNCS, vol. 6794, pp. 226–245. Springer, Heidelberg (2011)
11. Niedermeyer, F., Steinmetzer, S., Kroll, M., Schnell, R.: Cryptanalysis of basic Bloom Filters used for Privacy Preserving Record Linkage. German RLC, Working Paper Series, WP-GRLC-2014-04 (2014)
12. Paillier, P.: Public-Key Cryptosystems Based on Composite Degree Residuosity Classes. In: Stern, J. (ed.) EUROCRYPT 1999. LNCS, vol. 1592, pp. 223–238. Springer, Heidelberg (1999)
13. Quantin, C., Bouzelat, H., Allaert, F.A.A., Benhamiche, A.M., Faivre, J., Dusserre, L.: How to ensure data security of an epidemiological follow-up: quality assessment of an anonymous record linkage procedure. International Journal of Medical Informatics 49(1), 117–122 (1998)
14. Scannapieco, M., Figotin, I., Bertino, E., Elmagarmid, A.K.: Privacy preserving schema and data matching. In: Proc. ACM SIGMOD, pp. 653–664. ACM (2007)
15. Schnell, R., Bachteler, T., Reiher, J.: Privacy-preserving record linkage using Bloom filters. BMC Medical Informatics and Decision Making, 9(41), 11 pages (2009)
16. The College of Physicians and Surgeons of Ontario Public Register Website: http://www.cpso.on.ca/Public-Register/Public-Register (accessed December 2014)
17. The Law Society of Upper Canada Directory Website: http://www2.lsuc.on.ca/ LawyerParalegalDirectory (accessed December 2014)
18. Vatsalan, D., Christen, P., O'Keefe, C.M., Verykios, V.S.: An evaluation framework for privacy-preserving record linkage. Journal of Privacy and Confidentiality 6(1), Article 3 (2014)
19. Weber, S.C., Lowe, H., Das, A., Ferris, T.: A simple heuristic for blindfolded record linkage. Journal of the American Medical Informatics Association 19(e1), e157–e161 (2012)

Testing Policy-Based e-Health Monitoring Processes Using TTCN-3

Bernard Stepien[✉], Benjamin Eze, and Liam Peyton

School of Electrical Engineering and Computer Science, University of Ottawa, Canada
{bernard,beze021,lpeyton}@uottawa.ca

Abstract. e-Health processes are data-focused, event-driven, and dynamic. They should be systematically monitored for compliance with legislation, organizational guidelines, and quality of care protocols. Monitoring BPEL-defined online processes in a Service Oriented Architecture (SOA) is complex, especially since healthcare processes often involve the collaboration of different organizations. We extend the traditional SOA framework with policy-based processing of streaming event data using a general publish/subscribe model in a business-to-business (B2B) healthcare network. The testing of such systems is difficult to manage and difficult to implement using general purpose languages because of intensive interleaved behaviors. We propose several TTCN-3 solutions to the interleave problem both at the level of actors behavior and at the level of the end-to-end behavior of the process. Finally, we discuss how TTCN-3 can be used at the design stage to simulate the behavior of actors by an abstract test component behavior emulation in parallel.

Keywords: Event-driven architecture · SOA · Healthcare processes · Policy-based message broker · TTCN-3 · Testing

1 Introduction

e-Health processes are data-driven, and usually depend on a dynamic stream of event data from various processes and devices. Therefore, there is the need to ensure that these processes are systematically monitored to ensure compliance to organizational guidelines, quality of care protocols and government legislation. Palliative and community care that depend on these processes require integration of care processes across all collaborating organization in a business-to-business (B2B) network. Monitoring BPEL-defined online processes in a Service Oriented Architecture (SOA) is complex. In previous work [1], we extended the traditional SOA framework with policy-based processing of streaming event data using a general publish/subscribe model in a business-to-business (B2B) healthcare network. This entailed the use of a policy-based message broker to execute subscription policies expressed in XACML [2], on streaming event messages.

The testing of such systems is difficult to manage and difficult to implement using general purpose languages because of intensive interleaved behaviors. The TTCN-3 central concepts of parallel test component and template can be used to considerably

© Springer International Publishing Switzerland 2015
M. Benyoucef et al. (Eds.): MCETECH 2015, LNBIP 209, pp. 197–211, 2015.
DOI: 10.1007/978-3-319-17957-5_13

reduce test scripting efforts and ensure optimal quality assurance but there are some unique challenges which must be addressed.

In this paper, we examine four challenges in testing policy-based systems and show how they can be addressed in TTCN-3:

- The publish/subscribe approach poses some challenges to TTCN-3 as test suites cannot be specified as simple linear sequences of test events due to the multiple subscriptions that generate highly interleaved behaviors. We propose a subscription-based Parallel Test Component (PTC) model.
- The problem of representing XACML policies which are very verbose. We propose using TTCN-3's abstract data type system to simplify the specification of policies in a test suite.
- We propose two different solutions for the compliance checking problem based on sub-set matching and end to end sequence enforcement.
- We show that for testing, re-usable abstraction of XACML policies via TTCN-3 templates is more efficient than hard coded XACML policies.

TTCN-3 supports design stage testing with abstract representation as well as full implementation. In this paper, we use an abstract representation of a sample SUT.

2   Background

B2B networks comprises of collaborating domains with software systems, application and database processes, mobile devices, and sensors that share data continuously [3] in real-time. The management of the flow of information between collaborating parties in B2B networks is crucial for maintaining effective and efficient collaboration. Service Oriented Architecture (SOA) [4] has emerged the standard framework for systematic and extensible process integration and data sharing. Applications, devices, processes can expose otherwise hidden functionalities as web services allowing external processes to consume or poll such remote interfaces for data. In certain circumstances, though, traditional SOA is limited by its point to point messaging framework which requires unnecessary procedural interaction and data polling, therefore limiting flexible data integration [1] as a result. This is especially true with respect to processes that run within a B2B network as opposed to a single enterprise [5]. The management of process interactions in an enterprise requires either process orchestration or data sharing policies or a combination of both. Process orchestrating standards like Business Process Execution Language (BPEL) [6], allows one to systematically define on-line processes that orchestrate behavior across web services in an SOA. Event-driven architecture (EDA) [7] on the other hand is characterized by its ability to decouple service providers and consumers through messages [8] only. In EDA, data producers and consumers are contextually coupled by the data exchanges and not procedural calls or fixed service interfaces. Publish/subscribe [9] follows the EDA model but allows many clients to subscribe to the same data source, and have event data sent to them as messages, as they become available.

Traditional SOA, process orchestrating systems like BPEL and event-driven systems are challenged to address fully the information management requirements of e-Health monitoring processes. Most prominent of these is lack for support for a common data model for data integration [1] across all collaborating processes in a B2B. A common data model provides a single consistent view to the different types of data from all data producers to the consumers. It simplifies complex data exchanges for designers and developers of both data producers and consumers, thereby creating a consistent view of the data processes in a B2B. This comes at a price with regards to policy and privacy compliance. It is important that such complex data exchanges support robust privacy [10] considerations and enforcement. Privacy Compliance requires services to adhere to privacy legislation, hospital guidelines, and procedures that dictate under what circumstances individuals can view data.

[11] shows how rule-based policies can be used to manage business processes by providing reactive functionalities. By combining publish-subscribe with rule-based policies executed through policy engines, these systems can be made adaptable to a wide range of applications. They can easily adapt to complex service interaction in a B2B, respond to constantly changing business requirements and simplify the enforcement of privacy and policy related compliance requirements. Rule based languages presented in the form of event-condition-action, in XML [12] is a powerful tool for expressing both attribute and role-based access control policies. eXtensible Access Control Markup Language (XACML) [2] is a standardized common security-policy language that "allows the enterprise to manage the enforcement of all the elements of its security policy in all the components of its information systems". It has been applied to compliance, including data sharing, as determined by the message context [13].

Testing event-driven systems using the test specification language TTCN-3 has already been demonstrated in [14][15]; they demonstrate the full specification of test suites of systems already in operation that use the HL7 communication protocol. Our proposal uses policies expressed in XACML to specify routing logic. Our contribution is to show how to specify very verbose XACML policies in a simple way at the TTCN-3 abstract level. Another aspect of this system is its intensive interleaved message flow that makes testing results difficult to analyze. We propose a refinement of the use of TTCN-3 parallel test component (PTC) model found in [14] to represent an actor's subscription and their related message flows that enables a better separation of events using message filtering techniques provided by TTCN-3 tools.

3   Policy-Based Health Care Monitoring Systems

Figure 1 shows an example scenario for policy-based Health Care Monitoring Systems. In this scenario, event-based messages flow between participants in the health care process for managing severe pain in palliative patients. The architecture that supports the scenario is centered on a policy-based message broker [5].

Figure 2 shows the architectural template for our framework which implements the event-driven data integration component shown at the center of the scenario in Figure 1. All data sharing between the participants (physician, nurse, patient, and community care center) in the scenario is accomplished through a publish/subscribe style interaction with a centrally controlled Policy-based Message Broker installed on a server and accessible via SOAP over HTTPs.

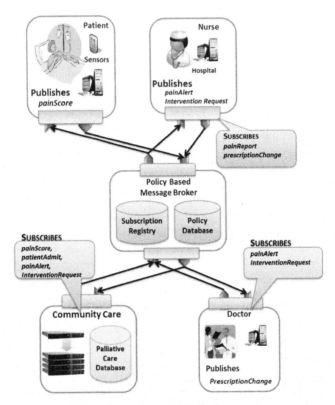

Fig. 1. Palliative Severe Pain Management Scenario

Each participant has a monitoring device, laptop, tablet, desktop, or server computer associated with them on which a Partner Service Component is installed to manage their interaction with the Message Broker. The Partner Service Component can publish a continuous stream of events associated with any of the actors to the Message Broker. At the same time, it also enables each participant to subscribe to a continuous stream of events, generated by other participants that are delivered to the Partner Service Component by the Message Broker. These events are transmitted as messages, with published messages being sent from the associated device to the Partner Service Component *Outbox*, and subscribed messages being delivered from the message broker to an *Inbox* and subsequently forwarded to the associated device.

The Message Broker maintains a registry of the types of events, called Event Topics, and the types of data, called Event Attributes, used to define those topics. This ensures a consistent event data model across the B2B network. A special Partner Service Component in the Figure 1 scenario acts as the Surveillance Portal and is hosted by the Community Care Center. It is special because it automatically subscribes to all events in the B2B network and therefore maintains a streaming data model of all events in the B2B network. It can be used as the streaming event base for compliance monitoring as well as provide comprehensive performance management reporting for all participants.

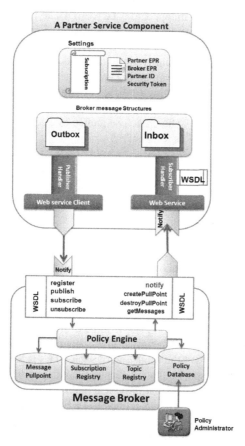

Fig. 2. Policy-Based SOA Publish Subscribe Framework

The Message Broker is also the central policy enforcement point for the B2B network since all sharing of event data through Partner Service Component subscriptions must pass through it. Policies are defined and stored in a Policy Database and enforced by a Policy Engine that control who can publish what events and restrict who is subscribed to receive what data and when. The policies are also used to flexibly customize the format and timing of how event data is delivered for each subscriber. The Message Broker can cache messages in a Message Pullpoint to provide the greatest possible flexibility with respect to timing and format of delivery.

4   Handling Intensive Interleaving of e-Health Alerts in TTCN-3

We now examine some of the challenges faced in testing a policy-based Healthcare monitoring system. In this section we deal with the problem of multiple subscriptions from multiple actors generate highly interleaved behaviors.

In our system, the Message Broker is the System Under Test (SUT). All other actors communicate with the message broker via the Partner Service Components (PSC) residing on the actor's devices that further abstracts the interface of the actors. These actors PSCs can be adequately mapped to TTCN-3 PTCs. The behavior of these actors consists of sequences of events that are the result of subscriptions, and dictate which messages get forwarded to them by the Message Broker. The PTC used to model an actor's behavior is particularly well suited because each actor in our system acts independently. However, since an actor can subscribe to multiple topics, this will result in sequences of events belonging to different subscriptions that come in unpredictable sequences. The most common approach to specify such behaviors is to use the TTCN-3 interleave operator where each sequence of events belonging to a specific subscription can be separated as follows:

```
p.send(subscription_1);
p.send(subscription_2);
  interleave {
      subscription_1_behavior(),
      subscription_2_behavior()
  }
```

However, the execution of the above specification will result in sequences of events that are interleaved and no longer separated, even when using techniques that are provided by some tools like in [24] that can filter events belonging to a selected actor among the set of PTCs. Here the interleave construct is static and implies that all behaviors involved terminate gracefully. We propose a refined architecture that represents each subscription as a PTC with its own behavior that contains only the events related to its specific subscription. In TTCN-3 the modeling of such PTCs is achieved via component typing. In our case, we have specified a subscription handler component type. In TTCN-3, PTCs are implemented as threads that provide a natural interleaving of events belonging to different threads. This is very analogous to OO design where each subscription would also be represented using a class instance. Component types in TTCN-3 are already OO flavored since they allow extensions. This approach of describing interleaved behavior has the advantage to be dynamic, it allows adding actors at any point of time. The results of the execution can now be filtered by selecting these subscription PTCs and display well separated results as shown on Figure 3. Note that additional filtering could split the messages on Figure 3 by individual subscription to allow an even finer inspection of results. The resulting code structure is as follows:

```
var SubscrHandlerType subs_1 := SubscrHandlerType.create("subs_1");
var SubscrHandlerType subs_2 := SubscrHandlerType.create("subs_2");

subs_1.start(subscription_1_behavior());
subs_2.start(subscription_2_behavior());
```

The subscription based PTC approach is particularly efficient because the prime purpose of a test is to verify that all events corresponding to a topic of an actor have occurred. This stream of events can now be specified as strict sequences unless several partners are involved; for example multiple specialists. However, there is another benefit with this architecture. When a failure in the execution occurs due to an unexpected event that was not specified in the test sequence, normally the test will specify to set the verdict to *fail* to avoid blocking. In TTCN-3 the test verdict affects only the execution of the behavior for the component it was started on. This means that other PTCs will continue executing until they reach a verdict of their own (*pass* or *fail*). The above two approaches will display different quantities of results when a failure occurs. The first approach using the TTCN-3 interleave operator will block the entire expression in the scope of the interleave behavior if one of its alternatives fail. For example, in our first approach a failure in *subscription_1_behavior()* will cause the execution to abort whether the execution of *subscription_2_behavior()* has completed or not. The second approach using independent PTCs per subscription will enable *subscription_2_behavior()* to reach the normal end of its execution and thus is not affected by the failure of the *subscription_1_behavior()*, since they each run on a separate component. This is analogous to the early compilers that stopped compiling on the first syntax error. Later, it was quickly discovered that there is an advantage in continuing the compilation process in order to find as many errors as possible on the first pass, therefore reducing the number of iterations required to achieve an error free program.

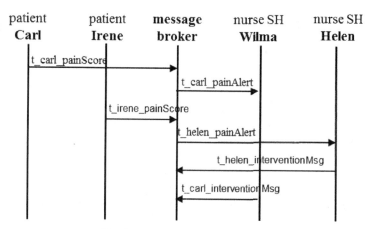

Fig. 3. TTCN-3 PTC architecture

The only drawback of the second approach is that it creates a proliferation of PTCs that complicates the overview of test results provided by some tools in form of MSCs. However, the intensive interleaving of events that is the prime characteristic of event-driven systems makes this overview already difficult and requires some level of filtering by execution tools to make it understandable. Thus, our subscription component approach instead further clarifies the results. However, future work would consist in enhancing the TTCN-3 language in order to differentiate these two different functionalities of PTCs.

5   Specifying XACML Policies for Routing Decision in TTCN-3

The specification of subscriptions using policy languages, such as XACML, is central to our design. Policies in e-Health are increasingly fine-grained and require the capability to represent complex Boolean expressions, which currently only XACML can achieve in the most flexible way, in an Attribute Based Access Control model (ABAC) [16]. Also, XACML provides the capability to structure policies to factor out common logic as shown in [17]. However, XACML is very verbose and specifying complex conditions can be very difficult to achieve by non-technical people or even by people with full knowledge of XML. Non-technical notations like [18][19] can alleviate this problem but it requires a special editor since the notation is only a presentation paradigm and not a language in itself. Thus, the specification of subscriptions in a test suite using TTCN-3 cannot use this notation. Nevertheless, the central concept of separation of concern in TTCN-3 can be adequately used to abstract the XACML specification in a similar fashion as the non-technical notation. A ttcn-3 codec achieves the concrete translation to XML. The language can be abstracted through data typing. Besides the benefits of standardization, TTCN-3 provides semantic checking not present in other solutions such as the metadata approach found in [20]. We have translated the XACML XML schema [21] for targets logic. The advantage of TTCN-3 data types is the full re-usability of templates to compose more complex conditions. This is actually not achievable in XACML itself because it is a strict hierarchical language where no element can be re-used by other branches of a decision tree. For example, the routing policy that specifies that pain alerts from patient Carl should be forwarded to nurse Wilma can be represented by a XACML policy target of which the equivalent Boolean expression show in a non-technical notation [19] as follows:

```
patient matches Carl and resource matches painAlert and
action matches forward and nurse matches Wilma
```

The above representation hides the technical details of complex XACML target anyOf and allOff constructs to the user as shown in [22].

The abstract layer data type to represent the corresponding XACML policy target is very similar to the XACML XML schema [21] as the following excerpt shows where the definition of the data type MatchType has been simplified for the purpose of this example:

```
type record MatchType {
    charstring operator,
    charstring attributeId,
    charstring attributeValue
}
type record of MatchType AllOfType;
type record of AllOfType AnyOfType;
type record of AnyOfType TargetType;
```

The main advantage of using TTCN-3 XACML representation is the re-usability of the concept of template which is used for describing either data to be sent or complex test oracles in a single operation. The above example is represented in TTCN-3 as follows:

```
template TargetType wilmaTarget := {

  {{ carlMatch }},
  {{ painAlertMatch }},
  {{ wilmaMatch }},
  {{ fowardActionMatch }}
}
```

Where for example the template painAlertMatch is defined as follows:

```
template MatchType painAlertMatch := {
 operator := "matches",
   attributeId := "resource",
 attributeValue := "painAlert" }
```

6   Compliance Verification Using TTCN-3

We have designed the compliance verification process as a separate actor that will receive all messages flowing in the system via the message broker. We can use this physical surveillance actor itself for testing and substitute it with a PTC for the purpose of end-to-end testing. Normally it should also be part of the SUT and thus be tested because it raises alarms when compliance violations have been detected. Thus here we take advantage of the existing design of this system where the surveillance component does in deed some implicit testing already but for the purpose of raising alarms in case of non-compliance. The reason for this strategy stems from the fact that the test sequences for the separate actors are necessary but not sufficient. The other actors own component behavior specifications enforce compliance only on the messages that they should receive and not on what they send and especially they do not provide end to end checking for the multiple actors that are involved in one patients case. For example, following pain score messages from a patient's monitoring device, the message broker will generate and send a pain alert to a nurse on messages with pain scores beyond a set threshold. This nurse may discover that the patient needs a new prescription and will send an intervention message back to the message broker. This, in turn, will be relayed to a physician that subscribed to this kind of event for the given patient. He will then send a prescription message to the broker that is once again relayed to the nurse. The role of the compliance verification will be to check the end-to-end flow of messages that belong to various kinds of subscriptions from the actors involved. Here we face the same problem as with interleaved messages, but this time they do not belong to a single actor but to several actors. The subscription criteria can no longer be applied to use the PTC approach that we have used for the actors. We have found two solutions for this end-to-end checking problem:

- Match events subsets against all received messages
- Use PTCs running end-to-end cross-actors behavior sequences

6.1   Subsets Matching Approach

We use templates that contain sets of messages belonging to the handling of a single patient, like the sequence we have described above. This involves checking that, for example, the end-to-end message set for a patient is a subset of the complete set of messages that has occurred during the entire test involving many different actors that in turn made multiple subscriptions. This is a refinement of the technique we have used in [23] where only the entire set of messages that occur in an SOA system was matched. It is performed at the end of the test as a general result evaluation process, and more specifically, at the end of the compliance PTC behavior. This set of messages is composed of heterogeneous data types and requires a TTCN-3 union type. For simplicity, we will assume that we use only one data type. Thus, the verification process requires three steps:

- Define the individual message templates.
- Define sets of related message templates that define a specific patient's case.
- Verify that these sets are subsets of the set of all messages during the test.

For example, the test oracle for the messages for patient Carl could be:

```
template MessageListType t_carlMessages := superset { t_painScoreCarl_1,
        t_painAlertCarlWilma_1, t_interventionRequestWilma,
        t_interventionRequestBob, t_prescriptionBobCarl }
```

Finally, the above t_carlMessages template can be matched against all messages received by the compliance PTC using the TTCN-3 matching mechanism:

```
if( match(allReceivedMessages, t_carlMessages)){setverdict(pass); }
else { setverdict(fail) }
```

Here we can note that the above templates are re-used from the ones needed to define the individual actors behaviors found in their respective PTCs. However, the above approach only checks end-to-end presence of messages but not how they comply with some higher level policies issued, for example, by legislation. In many cases, compliance checking requires complex logic but, in some cases, the use of TTCN-3 matching rules could be sufficient for this purpose. For example, for checking that a prescription has been issued within three hours of an abnormal pain score that exceeds a certain threshold, the template range specification can be appropriate. For that purpose, the compliance template can be derived from the original prescription template using the ttcn-3 *modifies* keyword and by specifying the range for the time as follows:

```
template PrescriptionMsgType t_compliancePrescription modifies
        t_bobCarlPrescription:= { time := { hour := 12..15, 24, 04 }}
```

It is to be noted that the end-to-end technique described here that checks only presence of messages also does not check the sequence in which these messages should occur. However, in E-Health applications, presence is the main concern but it is also a fact that message time stamps implicitly verify sequence. Since TTCN-3 *set of* types are already different from general purpose languages implementations of sets by allowing multiple occurrences of identical elements, a further enhancement of TTCN-3 would also be to enforce the sequence of a subset. In fact, this feature would be more appropriate in the context of the TTCN-3 *record of* types that represents lists of ordered elements.

6.2   PTCs Sequence Behaviors Approach

The second approach is somewhat analogous to the subscription approach used for actors but extended to an end-to-end context. A supervision PTC creates individual PTCs that start behaviors that represent sequences of events from different actors that relate to a specific patient's case only. There will be as many PTCs as patient cases. A supervisor PTC first collects all events from the Message Broker SUT as in the first subset approach. This again results in a set or events list of all events that have occurred among all actors involved in many different patient cases. Now we need to match this set of all events against individual sequences of events pertaining only to specific patient's cases. Again, we can achieve this goal using PTCs that run the individual sequences of events for one patient's case. All we need is the supervisor PTC to go through the list of all events received and send them one by one to such a PTC sequence of events. The PTC sequence will consume only the events it matches and only if they arrive in the sequence specified in its behavior function. The events that do not belong to this sequence must be discarded.

```
function supervisorBehavior(EventList events) runs on ... {
    var integer i;

    for(i:=0; i < sizeof(allEvents); i := i+1) {
        p.send(allEvents[i]);
    }
}
```

This code structure is duplicated for each different patient case and thus could be easily factored out in a function using the all events list and the individual patient case sequence of events function as parameters.

The individual sequence behaviors will need a technique to match only the events relevant to the specified sequence. We achieved this using a ttcn-3 alternative construct in which each expected event is handled in separate alternatives specifications. The first alternative consists of receiving and matching the expected event, while the second is a "catch all receive" whose *body* contains a repeat. The repeat allows us to inspect the next event in the queue and try to match it against the expected event.

Thus, the "catch all receive" will consume all events that do not belong to this specific case's sequence. This implicit loop is of course broken every time an expected event is received and matched. If an expected event is missing from the all events list, this will result in the entire tail of the all events list to be consumed by the "catch all alternative" and will result in a blockage that is resolved using a "timeout alternative" associated to a verdict fail. For example, the code structure for matching the sequence of event e2 followed by e4 is as follows:

```
function sequenceBehavior() runs on PTCType {
    receiveEvent(e2);
    receiveEvent(e4);
    setverdict(pass);
}

function receiveEvent(template EventType event) runs on PTCType {
    alt {
        [] p.receive(event) {}
        [] p.receive { repeat; }
        [] t.timeout { setverdict(fail);}
    }
}
```

7   TTCN-3 as a Modeling Language

It is a well-accepted fact that testing needs to be performed early in the software development cycle. This is usually achieved in the form of unit testing used to test classes and their methods in Object Oriented software (OO). However, it is also well-known that unit testing alone cannot guarantee that a system composed of several components will function flawlessly. This is the domain of integration testing. Logically, integration testing can only be performed once the development of the various components of a system has been fully completed. We have observed that increasingly, Industry has a need to know early in the process how components will work together and be able to immediately test the functioning of a newly developed component in relation to other components of the system. This in addition reduces the time it takes to get the software to the market by having the software development teams work in parallel with test suite development teams. Therefore, test suites addressing integration testing, need to be developed to some degree even before unit testing is started. The TTCN-3 central principle of separation of concerns between an abstract and a concrete layer easily allows test suite development team to focus only on one of the layers during the test suite development lifecycle. In our case, developing an early testing model where the SUT could be replaced by an abstract component would be an interesting proposition. The feasibility of such a strategy depends on the complexity of the logic that such an abstract SUT would need to perform. In our case, the logic is relatively minimal. It merely consists of implementing routing tables and criteria in an abstract way. Also, it is important to note that TTCN-3 PTCs can communicate between each other with potentially minimal coding efforts. PTCs can be connected with a single line of code and, more importantly, any messages sent between them do not require coding and decoding. Thus, TTCN-3 is a good candidate for a modeling language rather than just a test specification language. It has the benefit of being an instant abstract test suite as well where the SUT or parts of it can be restored to their actual concrete representation as they become available. This process somewhat duplicates the modeling process usually achieved using UML but with the important difference that the TTCN-3 abstract test suite is executable and produces a log that can be studied in detail for compliance with requirements. However, there is no longer the need for generating test cases from UML models, as the test suite is developed directly from well understood use cases that illustrate a test purpose. This approach is the result of intensive Industry experience for very complex telecommunication systems. We have used intensively this approach in our project and have executed the resulting test suite using a TTCN-3 tool [24]. This enabled us to discover conceptual flaws early in the process especially after using the TTCN-3 test events filtering techniques that are provided by some of the tools. A complete abstract test suite that includes the abstract SUT for this project has taken one man/day to code and test. The execution of this test suite then provided some tangible information to fuel an unlimited amount of discussions among members of the research team to further refine the intended design.

8   Conclusion

Processes in a B2B are continuously producing and consuming data. Managing this interaction can become complex fairly quickly. In this paper, we have shown how a policy-based publish-subscribe framework can be used to manage these events using declaratively XACML policies to dictate the rules of data sharing. It requires data providers and consumers to interact with a message broker through a special Partner Service Component (PSC) - publishers push data to the message broker while subscribers consume full or subsets of available data based on their subscription policies. A surveillance infrastructure ensures that all events in the framework are captured and archived for compliance with legislation, organizational guidelines, and quality of care protocols and analytics purposes.

We have also shown how the use of the TTCN-3 testing language addresses the three main concerns for testing a publish/subscribe SOA infrastructure for e-Health, namely the intensive interleaving of subscription related events, the specification of subscribers policies using the verbose XACML language and finally the testing of end-to-end specific patient cases events that are even more intensively interleaved among various actors. We identify the message broker as the SUT with publishers and subscribers interacting with it through the PTCs. A special PTC attached to the surveillance infrastructure performs compliance verification based on subset matching and end-to-end sequence enforcement. We are also able to show that XACML can be simplified by the non-technical notations and in a similar way can be mapped to

TTCN-3 through reusable templates which further simplify the test specification process.

Acknowledgements. The authors would like to thank the following TTCN-3 tool providers for providing us the necessary tools to carry out this research as well as NSERC for partially funding this work: Testing Technologies IST GmbH – TTworkbench, Elvior – TestCast T3 and Ericsson – Titan.

References

[1] Eze, B., Kuziemsky, C., Peyton, L., Middleton, G., Mouttham, A.: A Framework for Continuous Compliance Monitoring of eHealth Processes. Journal of Theoretical and Applied Electronic Commerce Research 5(1), 56–70 (2010)

[2] OASIS eXtensible Access Control Markup Language (XACML). http://docs.oasis-open.org/xacml/3.0/xacml-3.0-core-spec-cs-01-en.pdf

[3] Foster, I., Kesselman, C., Nick, J., Tuecke, S.: Grid services for distributed system integration. Computer 35(6), 37–46 (2002)

[4] Huhns, M.N., Singh, M.P.: Service-oriented computing: Key concepts and principles. IEEE Internet Computing 9(1), 75–81 (2005)

[5] Doshi, C., Peyton, L.: Trusted information process in B2B networks. In: Proceedings of the 10th International Conference on Enterprise Information Systems, Barcelona, Spain (2008)

[6] OASIS Standard, Web services business process execution language version 2.0. (April 2007). http://docs.oasis-open.org/wsbpel/2.0/OS/wsbpel-v2.0-OS.html

[7] Niblett, P., Graham, S.: Events and service-oriented architecture: The OASIS web services notification specifications. IBM Systems Journal 44(4) (2005)

[8] Etzion, O., Chandy, M., Ammon, R.V., Schulte, R.: Event-driven architectures and complex event processing. In: IEEE International Conference on Services Computing, Chicago, p. 30 (2006)

[9] Eugster, P.T., Felber, P.A., Guerraoui, R., Kermarrec, A.: The many faces of publish/subscribe. ACM Computing Surveys 35(2), 114–131 (2003)

[10] Peyton, L., Hu, J., Doshi, C., Seguin, P.: Addressing privacy in a federated identity management network for e-health. In: 8th World Congress on the Management of eBusiness, Toronto (2007); Internet Computing 9(1), 75–81 (2005)

[11] Harrocks, I., Angele, J., Decker, S., Kifer, M., Grosof, B., Wagner, G.: What are the rules? IEEE Intelligent Systems 18(5), 76–83 (2003)

[12] Bailey, J., Poulovassilis, A., Wood, P.: An event-condition-action language for XML. In: Proceedings of the 11th International Conference on World Wide Web, Honolulu, Hawaii, USA, pp. 486–495 (2002)

[13] Barth, A., Datta, A., Mitchell, J., Nissenbaum, H.: Privacy and contextual integrity: Framework and applications. In: IEEE Symposium on Security and Privacy, pp. 184–198 (2006)

[14] Vega, D.E., Din, G., Schieferdecker, I.: Application of TTCN-3 Test Language to Testing Information System in e-Health Domain. In: Multimedia and Information Technology (MCIT), pp. 21–24 (2010)

[15] Vega, D.E.: Towards an Automated and Dynamically Adaptable Test System for Testing Healthcare Information Systems. In: 2010 Third International Conference on Software Testing, Verification and Validation (2010)

[16] Hu, V.C., Ferraiolo, D., Kuhn, R., Schnitzer, A., Sandlin, K., Miller, R., Miller, R., Scarfone, K.: Guide to attribute based access control (ABAC) definition and considerations. In: NIST Special Publication 800-162 (January 2014). http://nvlpubs.nist.gov/nistpubs/-specialpublications/NIST.sp.800-162.pdf

[17] Stepien, B., Felty, A., Matwin, S.: Strategies for Reducing Risks of Inconsistencies in Access Control Policies. In: ARES 2010 Proceedings (2010)

[18] Stepien, B., Felty, A., Matwin, S.: A Non-technical User-Oriented Display Notation for XACML Conditions. In: Babin, G., Kropf, P., Weiss, M. (eds.) E-Technologies: Innovation in an Open World. LNBIP, vol. 26, pp. 53–64. Springer, Heidelberg (2009)

[19] Stepien, B., Felty, A., Matwin, S.: A non-technical XACML target editor for dynamic access control systems. In: SECOTS 2014 Proceedings, pp. 150–157

[20] Li, N., Hwang, J., Xie, T.: Multiple Implementation Testing for XACML Implementations. In: ACM 2008 (2008)

[21] OASIS-XACML 3.0 schema. http://docs.oasis-open.org/xacml/3.0/XSD/xacml-core-v3-schema-cd-1.xsd

[22] Stepien, B., Felty, A., Matwin, S.: Challenges of Composing XACML Policies. In: ARES 2014 Proceedings, pp. 234–241 (2014)

[23] Stepien, B., Seguin, P., Peyton, L.: Integration Testing of Composite Applications. In: HICSS 41st Proceedings

[24] Testing Technologies, TTworkbench an eclipse based TTCN-3 IDE. www.testingtech.com

PHEN: Parkinson Helper Emergency Notification System Using Bayesian Belief Network

Hamid Mcheick[1(✉)], Malak Khreiss[2], Hala Sweidan[2], and Iyad Zaarour[2]

[1] Computer Science Department, University of Quebec At Chicoutimi,
555, Boulevard de l'Université, Chicoutimi, Québec G7H-2B1, Canada
Hamid_Mcheick@uqac.ca
[2] Faculty of Sciences (I), Lebanese University, Hadath-Beirut, Beirut, Lebanon
malakkhreis@outlook.com, hala-sweidan@live.com,
i.zaarour@ul.edu.lb

Abstract. Context-aware systems are used to aid users in their daily lives. In the recent years, researchers are exploring how context aware systems can benefit humanity through assist patients, specifically those who suffer incurable diseases, to cope with their illness. In this paper, we direct our work to help people who suffer from Parkinson disease. We propose PHEN, Parkinson Helper Engine Network System, a context-aware system that aims to support Parkinson disease patients on m any levels. We use ontology is for context representation and modeling. Then the ontology based context model is used to learn with Bayesian Belief network (BBN) which is beneficial in handling the uncertainty aspect of context-aware systems.

Keywords: Context-aware applications · Parkinson disease · Health care system · Bayesian belief network · Ubiquitous computing · OWL · Tele-medicine

1   Introduction

Pervasive computing, also known as ubiquitous computing, have made a dramatical evolution in our century. Its main purpose is to create and correlate a strong environment between computing and communication components in order to adapt to the user's context. Context awareness is regarded as the enabling technology for pervasive computing systems.

However, one of the main problems of context aware system is uncertainty of context, which is unavoidable due to the nature of sensed data which could be imperfect, incomplete, wrong or ambiguous. Uncertainty is a situation of inadequate information [6] which can be of three sorts: inexactness, unreliability, and border with ignorance. As itself has many forms and dimensions and may include concepts such as fuzziness or vagueness, disagreement and conflict, imprecision and non-specificity [10]. Many context modeling and retrieval architectures tend to over-simplify uncertainty by assuming a perfect knowledge in combination with perfect inference [1]. Many techniques could be used to handle the uncertainty aspect of context aware systems, one of the most used techniques is the BBN, which have been also used in fault detection and diagnosis of dynamic systems [11].

© Springer International Publishing Switzerland 2015
M. Benyoucef et al. (Eds.): MCETECH 2015, LNBIP 209, pp. 212–223, 2015.
DOI: 10.1007/978-3-319-17957-5_14

In this paper, we propose PHEN (Parkinson's Helper Engine using Network), a Bayesian based approach that aims to aid the Parkinson patients in their daily lives. Our system is designed to present relevant services for their users according to their needs. Specifically, during emergency situations.

This paper is organized as follows. Section 2 described briefly the related work, section 3 discuss our contribution. Section 4 illustrates the results and interpretation. Finally section 5 summarizes the paper and gives directions for future work.

2   Related Works

BBN is widely used in context aware systems. In [7] the authors proposed SOCAM (Service-Oriented Context-Aware Middleware), to reason about uncertainty by providing supports to construct a BBN. The work in [2] shows the different benefits of using BBN in context-aware systems. Moreover, BBN was found to support fault detection in context ubiquitous systems [1]. Ontology, was found to be the perfect match for BBN. Examples of merging ontology with BBN in context-aware systems is the work proposed [15] and [16] where the authors used ontologies and BBN to propose a unified context model to support representation and reasoning about uncertain context using both relational schema and probabilistic models.

Assisting PD (Parkinson Disease) patients have also had a noticeable care by the research community. In [4] the authors developed a wearable assistant for PD patients with the FOG (freezing of gait) symptom. This wearable system uses on-body acceleration sensors to measure the patients' movements. It automatically detects FOG by analyzing frequency components inherent in these movements. Also, [12] presented GaitAssist, a system which is also designed for FOG detection and support in unsupervised areas. It uses Bluetooth to stream data for processing and detecting FOG, after that an audio notification is sent to the patient.

It is also noteworthy that in a previous work [9] we proposed CARE (Context-Aware Reliable Engine) system, an AHP (Analytic Hierarchy Process) based context-aware system for health monitoring to support patients who could be subjected to serious emergencies.

3   Motivational Scenario

Sara is a 65 years old woman who lives with her grandson Peter. Recently, the symptoms of Parkinson disease started to appear on Sara.

Parkinson disease is a common neurological disorder caused by the progressive loss of dopaminergic and other subcortical neurons [3]. The loss of dopamine results in abnormal nerve-firing patterns within the brain that cause impaired movement [8]. The two most important problems the Parkinson disease (PD) patient may face are: Freezing of gait (FoG) and dysphagia. Freezing of gait is the state where the patients with Parkinson disease suffers from short periods during which they cannot continue walking and is associated to a fall risk and can be caused by a lot of triggers such as crowded places, turning corners, turning around in a circle. While the difficulty of swallowing which is called "dysphagia", it occurs while eating and can be fatal for patients with Parkinson disease. Sara was suffering from both symptoms.

To take care of Sara Peter bought PHEN, especially after hearing that PHEN can notify him when Sara has an emergency if she was alone at home. On a morning while Sara was walking at the backyard, wearing her wearable assistance, she started to feel something unusual happening to her legs. The PHEN system, using various sensors, directly detects FOG event by analyzing the frequency components of Sara's movements and sends an emergency notification to Peter and other neighbors that Peter entered their numbers to the system.

4   Context Modeling

4.1   System Architecture

PHEN system has four main functionalities:
- Detecting dysphagia
- Video tutorials for treatment
- Online physician consultant
- Health services

While eating, if the patient starts to cough, the PHEN server is able to detect dysphagia by analyzing the radio-frequency of the voice of the patient, and then it decide if it is a normal coughing or it is caused by the difficulty of swallowing. So the PHEN system sends a notification to the patient to give him some instructions to follow (e.g. Sit upright for at least 15 minutes after eating, drink frequent sips of water or suck on ice chips, reduce sugar intake, as sugar increases saliva, Take smaller bites of food, chew food thoroughly and eat slowly, take small sips of water or beverage when eating, drink tea with lemon or carbonated beverages to help thin phlegm, Sleep with head raised up to prevent choking). If the response is not achieved in few seconds, the system proposes that the patient is not able to react normally, so directly the system gives an emergency call to one of the patient's relatives.

In addition, PHEN system contains a set of video tutorials which consist of exercises to maintain strength and flexibility and treatments for difficulty swallowing (e.g. Take extra-small bites of food, chew thoroughly, and swallow carefully, take a breath before you start to speak, and pause between every few words or even between each word). Besides, the patient who has the PHEN application can consult his physician online before starting with exercises or following a healthy diet. Moreover, PHEN system contains healthy services to check the blood pressure, amount of glucose, and heartbeats. Also, a service for defining the food's contents percentages.

Figure-1 depicts the system architecture and its components. It is divided into three fundamental modules: Patient domain, PHEN application and PHEN server. This architecture is based on our exiting work [18, 19].

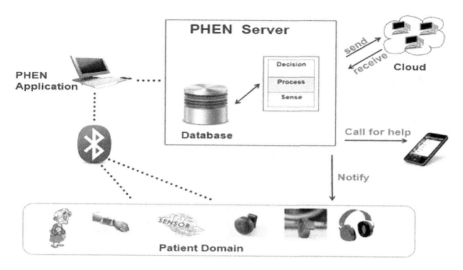

Fig. 1. PHEN system architecture

The PHEN system is made up of three components: The patient domain, PHEN application, and PHEN server.

Patient domain: The patient domain consists of a patient wearing a FOG detection and feedback device, wearable computer, earphones and three sensors. The first sensor is attached to the shank (just above the ankle), the second to the thigh (just above the Knee) using elasticized strap and Velcro, and the third sensor to the belt where also a wearable computer is attached to. On the other hand, the patient wears earphones to receive notifications.

PHEN application: The PHEN application is an application that listens for incoming connections via Bluetooth from the wearable devices and the wearable computer. Once connected, the application starts to track the patient situation and sends data to the PHEN server directly.

PHEN server: The PHEN server has three layers. The first layer is responsible for retrieving the sensed data, it sends it to the upper layer to process and then directed to the last layer to take the decision. At each level, the database is updated (send and receive data). Once the system took the decision, it stores the appropriate data in the cloud and at the same time it either notify the PD patient by the decision taken, or call someone for help in case something urgent happened and the patient can't behave by himself.

4.2   Ontology

Ontology is a formal, explicit description of concepts in a particular domain of discourse. It provides a vocabulary for representing domain knowledge and for describing specific situations in a domain [13] . In our work we use an ontology for modeling the profile of the user. The classes used in our ontology are: patient, location, state, situation, activity, wearable assistant, alarm and sensor.

4.3   Probabilistic Model

A probabilistic model is used as an extension to the ontology based model to represent uncertain context features. The probabilistic model has the form of Prob(Predicate(subject,value)) in which the probability measurement takes a value between 0 and 1 [7] . For example Prob(Activity(Patient,Eating)=0.96 means that the probability that the patient is eating is equal to 96%.

Figure 2 depicts the context ontology for relational and probabilistic Knowledge, it describes the relation chains and the conditional probability dependency.

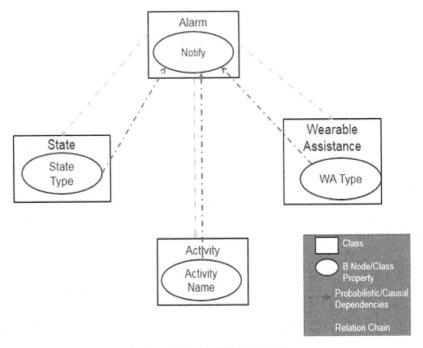

Fig. 2. PHEN Probabilistic Model

5   Bayesian Belief Network Modeling

The Bayesian belief network applied is a graphical, probabilistic model that represents cause and effect relationships [14]. It reflects the states of some part of a world that is being modeled and it describes how those states are related by probabilities.

The task of building the structure and assigning the probability distributions of a Bayesian Network is complex and knowledge-intensive [5]. During BBN construction nodes (variables of interest) and the relationships between these nodes must be identified. The transition from ontology to BBN is based on the approach presented in [15] where the authors developed a unified context ontology based on a given context model to which capture both structural and relational knowledge as well as the probabilistic knowledge of a domain. Then they derived in an autonomous and adaptive fashion which reflects most truthfully about the current state of the domain. Their BBN is constructed based on the OWL added concepts.

Fig. 3 depicts the updated context ontology after inference.

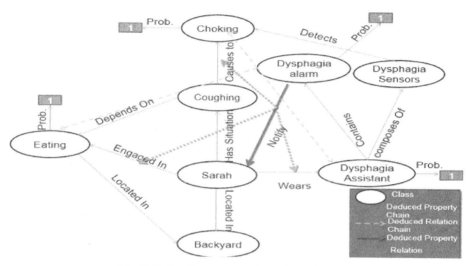

Fig. 3. Updated context ontology after inference

We take into consideration the case where Sarah (the PD patient described in the earlier scenario) starts to face difficulty of swallowing while eating. After inference the probabilities of the activity Eating and the wearing assistance dysphagia that is responsible for detecting the choking cases, and that the state of the patient is choking are equal to 1. So we can deduce a property to notify the patient or someone beside him that the patient is choking and that may lead to death. Based on the probabilistic model, and our domain specific ontology, we generate our Bayesian belief network as shown in figure. We conclude that the most three states that affect the alarm's notification are: the activity engaged in, the wearable assistant used, and the state of the patient noticed. Below is a simple Bayes net that illustrates these concepts. In this simple world, let us say the activity can have two binary states: eating or not, also that the wearable assistant can be dysphagia assist or no assist, furthermore the state of the patient can be choking or not and that the alarm notification can be yes or no.

Our BBN is constructed based on the OWL concepts. Where the nodes and the conditional probabilistic dependency depends on the individuals, deduced relation chain, deduced property chain, and deduced property. For example: To notify (deduced property), the conditional probabilistic dependency derived from the deduced property chain (ActivityName_Choking(Yes), WearableAssistant_DysphagiaAssist(Yes), and State-Name_Choking(Yes)).

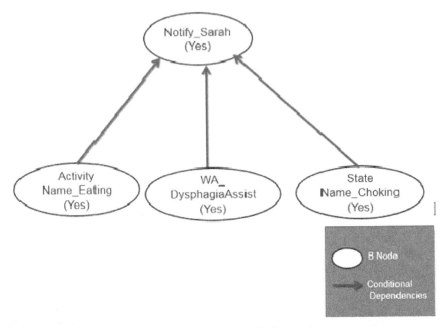

Fig. 4. PHEN Bayesian Belief Network

6   Results and Discussion

Netica [17] is used to implement the BBN. It is is a powerful, easy-to-use, complete program for working with belief networks and influence diagrams. The PHEN modeling process includes two stages. The first stage is building the model by determining the prior probabilities depending on the expert's knowledge. The second is interviewing experts to determine the posterior probabilities. Both stages will be discussed further in the upcoming sections.

6.1   BBN Learning

The BBN learning problem can be stated informally as follows:

1. Health services Given training data and prior information.
2. Estimate the BBN structure (graph topology).
3. Estimate the BBN parameters.

Training Data: Guided and supervised by an expert, our training data is gathered. The primary objective in the interview process with the expert is to determine from resource professionals, a cause and effect of the patient-related activities and test our approach by real examples (data) in our daily life and translate our scenario in a real action, especially the results of the inference part provided by BBN.

Table 1. Prior Probabilities

		Where:
P(Ea=T)	0.88	P(Ea)= P(Activity_Eating)
P(Ea=F)	0.12	
P(Dys=T)	0.9	P(Dys)= P(WA_DysphagiaAssist)
P(Dys=F)	0.1	
P(Ch=T)	0.92	P(Ch)= P(State_Choking)
P(Ch=F)	0.08	
P(N=T)	0.86	P(N)= P(Notify)
P(N=F)	0.14	

BBN Structure: The methodology of building BBN structure is intuitive, by using the domain-specific ontology and deriving the BBN structure as discussed in the previous sections.

BBN Parameters: After defining the BBN structure (Nodes and arcs between nodes) and the given training set with the prior probabilities. We can now import this training set to Netica depending on the BBN nodes as a learning data set to overcome by the conditional probability of each node.

Below is a table (table 2) showing the conditional probabilities calculated in Netica:

Table 2. Conditional Probability Table Generated by Netica

Node: NotiFy   ▼   Apply   OK

Chance   ▼   Probability ▼   Reset   Close

Activity_Eating	WearingAssist_DysphagiaAssist	StateName_Choking	False	True
False	False	False	.75	.25
False	False	True	.666667	.333333
False	True	False	.5	.5
False	True	True	.2	.8
True	False	False	.5	.5
True	False	True	.75	.25
True	True	False	.5	.5
True	True	True	.0465116	.953488

6.2   Results

The following information are monitored from a sample of PD patients to test PHEN dysphagia assist:

- Concentrating on the most important activity by a percentage of 86.8%
- 88.7% of the patients wear PHEN dysphagia assist
- 90.6% the dysphagia

Armed with these statistics we could set up the following Bayes net (Fig. 5):

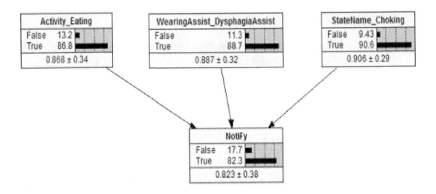

Fig. 5. Netica Software belief network example developed for PHEN model

6.3   Inference via BBN

Inferring over the net which gives information about the activity, wearable assistant, state, and alarm notification may answer many useful questions. For instance, "if the alarm gives a notification, what is the probability such that the patient is eating, choking and wearing his wearable assistant? ". Figure 6 shows a sample inference message that given by Netica.

```
Given a True Activity_Eating,

the probability of WearingAssist_DysphagiaAssist is 0.954

Given a True Notify,

the probability of Activity_Eating and
WearingAssist_DysphagiaAssist is 0.953

Given a True Activity_Eating,

the probability of State_Choking is 0.92
```

Fig. 6. Inference Message

Table 3- shows a list of inferences with their values that are computed by Netica and can be used as a base for decision making.

Table 3. List of inferences generated by Netica

P(Ea=T/N=T)	0.953
P(Ea=T/N=F)	0.046
P(Ea=T,Dys=T/N=T)	0.953
P(Ea=T,Dys=T/N=F)	0.046
P(Dys=T/Ea=T)	0.954
P(Dys=T/Ea=F)	0.04545
P(Ch=T,Dys=T,Ea=T/N=T)	0.7754
P(Ch=T,Dys=T,Ea=T/N=F)	0.224
P(Ch=T/Ea=T)	0.92
P(Ch=T/Ea=F)	0.08

For example if we want to calculate these probabilities manually:
P(Ch=T,Dys=T,Ea=T/N=T)=
P(N=T/Ch=T,Dys=T,Ea=T)*P(Ch=T,Dys=T,Ea=T)/P(N=T)=0.7754

Finally BBN are useful everywhere where modeling an uncertain reality is involved (and hence probabilities are present), and, in the case of decision nets, wherever it is helpful to make intelligent, justifiable, quantifiable decisions that will maximize the chances of a desirable outcome.

By interpreting our results. Inference is used to calculate the probability of any event conditioned by any another event, which helps in handling uncertain contexts by predicting the probability of the unknowns. We can compute the probability of the choking knowing that the patient is not eating (these two nodes are independent). So now our PHEN system can decide when the alarm must notify the patient knowing the state, activity and wearable assistant of the patient.

7   Results and Discussion

This paper proposed PHEN, a real-time system that supports the Parkinson patients in unsupervised environments. The framework is a personalized wearable assistant that0 detects the dysphagia events and it gives the patient an appropriate audio feedback.

PHEN is a multifunctional system that exceeds the role of being just a daily life assistant, to provide a set of services that varies between healthy, treatment, and exercising. The main point of strength of PHEN is that after a period of time of using the system as an assistive device or as a training device, the patients will experience an overall improvement of their swallowing difficulties.

We exploited the advantages of the ontology to the description of the general context of the patient's domain and captured as many concepts as possible to succeed a complete assistance personalized and fully adapted to the user needs. Indeed, as uncertainty can't be avoided, we used the probabilistic model to handle it by describing the relation chains and the conditional probability dependencies between the concepts. Moreover the Bayesian belief network is constructed and held to take the appropriate decision relative to the patient situation.

Moreover, a use case scenario was used to introduce our approach, which captures all the supported functionality and at the end we presented a demonstration to show a live application of the approach with real conditions and users. Moreover, PHEN system is applied and tested on real data using Netica software and detects dysphagia symptom by 82.3%.

Finally as a future work we would suggest to provide mechanisms at the level of activity recognition to handle and support parallel activities and to confirm the result of the activity recognition, and same for the raw data collected by the sensors. Moreover, we aim to develop our approach to be used in reality to help PD patients.

Acknowledgments. This work is supported by the Department of Computer Science at the University of Quebec at Chicoutimi, Quebec Canada; and by the Faculty of Science at the Lebanese University.

References

1. Ahmed, B., Lee, Y.-K., Lee, S., Zhung, Y.: Scenario Based Fault Detection in Context-Aware Ubiquitous Systems using Bayesian Networks. In: Proceedings of Computational Intelligence for Modelling, Control and Automation, 2005 and International Conference on Intelligent Agents, International Conference on Web Technologies and Internet Commerce, Vienna, vol(1), pp. 414, November 28–30 (2005)
2. Angermann, M., Robertson, P., Strang, T.: Issues and Requirements for Bayesian Approaches in Context Aware Systems. In: Strang, T., Linnhoff-Popien, C. (eds.) LoCA 2005. LNCS, vol. 3479, pp. 235–243. Springer, Heidelberg (2005)
3. Ben-Gal, I.: Bayesian Networks. In: Ruggeri, F., Faltin, F., Kenett R. (eds.) Encyclopedia of Statistics in Quality and Reliability. John Wiley & Sons (2007)
4. Bächlin, M., Plotnik, M., Roggen, D., Maidan, I., Hausdorff, J.M., Giladi, N, Tröster, G.: Wearable assistant for Parkinson's disease patients with the freezing of gait symptom. In: Proceedings of IEEE Transactions on Information Technology in Biomedicine: a Publication of the IEEE Engineering in Medicine and Biology Society (2010)
5. Druzdzel, M.J., Van Der Gaag, L.C.: Building bayesian networks: Where do the numbers come from? Proceedings of IEEE Transactions on Knowledge and Data Engineering **12**, 481–486 (2000)
6. Funtowicz, S.O., Ravetz, J.R.: Uncertainty and Quality in Science for Policy. Kluwer Academic Publishers, Dordrecht (1990)
7. Gu, T., Pung, H.K., Zhang, D.Q.: A Bayesian approach for dealing with uncertain contexts. In: Proceedings of Austrian Computer Society (2004)
8. National Institutes of Health ``What Causes Parkinson's Disease?'', Internet (2014). http://nihseniorhealth.gov/
9. Mcheick, H., Khreis, M., Al-Kalla, M., Sweidan, H.: CARE: Context-Aware Reliable Engine Health for Traffic Monitoring System. In: Proceedings of UKSim-AMSS 16th International Conference on Computer Modelling and Simulation, p. 410 (2014)

10. Klir, G., Wierman, M.: Uncertainty-Based Information: Elements of Generalized Information Theory, 2nd edn., October 19, 1999. http://www.amazon.com/Uncertainty-Based-Information-Generalized-FuzzinessComputing/dp/3790812420
11. Lerner, R., Parr, U.: Bayesian fault detection and diagnosis in dynamic systems. In: Seventeenth National Conference on Artificial Intelligence, pp. 531–537. AAAI (2000)
12. Mazilu, S., Hardegger, M., Blanke, U., Tröster, G., Gazit, E., Dorfman, M., Hausdorff, J.M.: GaitAssist: A Wearable Assistant for Gait Training and Rehabilitation in Parkinson's Disease. In: Proceedings of IEEE Percom (DEMO - technical details about the CHI system) (Best Demo Award) (2014)
13. Van Nguyen, T., Lim, W., Nguyen, H.A., Choi, D., Lee, C.: Context Ontology Implementation for Smart Home. In: Proceedings of CoRR abs/1007.1273 (2010)
14. Pearl, J.: Probabilistic Reasoning in Intelligent Systems: Networks of Plausible Inference. Morgan Kaufmann (1988)
15. Truong, B.A., Lee, Y.-K., Lee, S.-Y.: Modeling and Reasoning about Uncertainty in Context-Aware Systems. In: IEEE International Conference on Proceedings of e-Business Engineering, ICEBE 2005, October 12-18, p. 102 (2005)
16. Truong, B.A., Lee, Y.-K., Lee, S.-Y.: Modeling Uncertainty in Context-Aware Computing. In: Fourth Annual ACIS International Conference on Proceeding of Computer and Information Science, p. 676 (2005)
17. Norsys Software Corp. https://www.norsys.com/netica.html
18. Mcheick, H., Sbeity, H., Hazimeh, H., Naim, J., Alameh, M.: Context Aware Mobile Application Architecture (CAMAA) for Health Care Systems: Standardization and abstraction of context aware layers. In: 2014 IEEE International Humanitarian Technology Conference (IHTC-IEEE), Montreal, Canada, June 1-4 (2014)
19. Mcheick, H.: Modeling Context Aware Features for Pervasive Computing. In: The 5th International Conference on Emerging Ubiquitous Systems and Pervasive Networks (EUSPN-2014), Halifax, Canada, September 22-25. Elsevier; Procedia Computer Science, Procedia Computer Science, 135–142 (2014). 10.1016/j.procs.2014.08.022

Examining the Effects of Perceived Enjoyment and Habit on Smartphone Addiction: The Role of User Type

Chongyang Chen[1,2], Kem Z.K. Zhang[1,3(✉)], and Sesia J. Zhao[4]

[1] School of Management, University of Science and Technology of China, Hefei, China
chongy@mail.ustc.edu.cn, zzkkem@ustc.edu.cn
[2] Department of Information Systems, City University of Hong Kong, Hong Kong, China
[3] Telfer School of Management, University of Ottawa, Ottawa, Canada
[4] Management School, Anhui University, Hefei, China
sesia@ahu.edu.cn

Abstract. Existing studies have widely suggested that perceived enjoyment and habitual usage of information systems (IS) are favorable factors which lead to positive outcomes of IS adoption. In this study, we examine the dark sides of these factors with a sample of 384 respondents of smartphone users. Drawing upon previous research, we propose that perceived enjoyment can facilitate the formation of habit and smartphone addiction. However, habit shows no significant impact on smartphone addiction. Meanwhile, we argue that users who primarily use value-added functions of smartphone may experience higher enjoyment and easily form habitual usage behavior. Further, these users are more likely to become smartphone addicts. Theoretical and practical implications, limitations and future work directions are discussed.

Keywords: IT addiction · Smartphone addiction · Perceived enjoyment · Habit · User type

1 Introduction

The question "what will drive the initial and continued use of information technologies?" has been a prominent and fundamental subject in the information system (IS) area [1]. Following this line of studies, a majority of IS scholars have focused on identifying important driver behind the adoption of information technologies (IT). As an intrinsic motivation, perceived enjoyment, has been widely found to be an essential factor that drives the use of IS directly and indirectly [2]. Perceived enjoyment pertains to "the extent to which fun can be derived from using the system" [3 p. 697]. Prior research has shown that it can increase satisfaction while using a system [4] and promote IT use behavior [5]. The positive role of perceived enjoyment can also be found in the initial adoption and continued use of computer software, web-based information systems, and entertainment devices [6]. Prior studies further posit that perceived enjoyment in hedonic technology settings may have a stronger effect on IT usage than the salient factors like perceived ease of use and perceived usefulness [1, 3].

Meanwhile, the positive role of perceived enjoyment is questioned by some recent research. For instance, perceived enjoyment is found to reinforce substance abuse [7] and

© Springer International Publishing Switzerland 2015
M. Benyoucef et al. (Eds.): MCETECH 2015, LNBIP 209, pp. 224–235, 2015.
DOI: 10.1007/978-3-319-17957-5_15

behavioral addiction behaviors (e.g., pathological gambling) [8]. According to this perspective, it is possible that IT addiction may also be intrinsically rewarding. IT addiction is an emerging area in the IS literature. Prior research refers to IT addiction as users' maladaptive dependency on the use of IT and the obsessive-compulsive usage of IT [9, 10]. Thus, it is reasonable to explore whether perceived enjoyment will lead to negative outcomes like IT addiction. Given the potentially serious consequences of IT addiction, it is important for IS researchers to explore the largely uninvestigated research area about what facilitates the formation of this addiction behavior [11]. As one of the very few empirical studies, Turel and Serenko [12] explicitly pointed out the benefits and dangers of perceived enjoyment in social networking websites. They argued that perceived enjoyment could result in presumably positive outcomes (i.e., high engagement), as well as facilitating the formation of a strong habit and developing technology addiction. Enriching this emerging line of studies, this study attempts to revisit the roles of perceived enjoyment and habit in the context of smartphone addiction.

Smartphone is currently a popular information and communication technology that substantially affects people's everyday lives. With its multi-function nature, ranging from basic mobile phone functions (e.g., making calls and sending text messages) to many value-added functions (e.g., social networking, photo-taking, music, video, and game playing) [13–15], using a smartphone can be highly enjoyable [16, 17]. However, empirical research has shown that smartphone users may further develop into psychological dependency on smartphones, and then lose their control on the usage, which is also known as smartphone addiction [15]. Smartphone addiction is a form of IT addiction. Scholars begin to find that it may result in people's psychological and physiological disorders [18, 19], productivity impairment, and personal and social problems [15, 20]. To enrich the largely uninvestigated research on smartphone addiction, this study sheds light on the dark sides of perceived enjoyment and habit. Drawing upon previous theoretical insights, we propose that perceived enjoyment and habit may lead to the addiction of smartphones. Moreover, we consider the differences of two types of smartphone users, namely users who perform the basic mobile phone functions most often and users who primarily use the valued-added functions of smartphones. In this respect, the second type of users are more likely to have more demands, which cannot be fulfilled by traditional mobile phones. These users are more prone to using the "unique" and value-added functions provided by smartphones. We expect that the two types of users may show significant differences regarding their perceived enjoyment, habit, and smartphone addiction. In summary, we ask two research questions in this study:

(1) How do perceived enjoyment and habit affect smartphone addiction?
(2) Whether the two types of users differ in terms of their perceived enjoyment, habit, and smartphone addiction?

The rest of our article is structured as follows. First, we review the relevant theoretical background. Building on this knowledge, we then develop our research model and propose hypotheses. Next, we test the relationships in our model using an online survey, and report the results. Finally, we conclude the findings with discussions of implications and limitations.

2   Theoretical Background

2.1   Smartphone Addiction

The extant research posits that the inappropriately use of IT may result in a number of negative outcomes, and smartphone addiction is one of them. Building upon the definition of IT addiction, this study refers to smartphone addiction as users' maladaptive dependency on the usage of smartphones and the obsessive-compulsive use of the devices.

Similar to many instances of IT addiction, smartphone addiction can be understood with a few IT addiction symptoms, namely salience (i.e., usage dominates one's thought and behavior), withdrawal (i.e., negative emotions emerge when one cannot use smartphones), conflict (i.e., smartphone use conflicts with other important tasks) relapse and reinstatement (i.e., inability to reduce smartphone usage voluntarily), tolerance (i.e., a greater usage extent is needed to produce thrill), and mood modification (i.e., using smartphones to change moods) [1]. Nevertheless, since much still remains unknown for smartphone addiction, recent research has shown emerging interest in achieving a better understanding of this research area. For instance, a smartphone addiction scale (SAS) is developed as a self-diagnostic method to distinguish smartphone addicts [21]. Park et al. [22] examined the influence of individuals' psychological antecedents (e.g., innovativeness, behavioral activation system and locus of control) on smartphone use and dependency. Chiu [23] investigated the relationship between smartphone addiction and life stress.

2.2   Perceived Enjoyment

In the IS literature, perceived enjoyment often reflects the positive experience of using IT. This is especially significant in hedonic settings, where it has been regarded as the essence of leisure activities [24]. Initially, the salient role of perceived enjoyment was not identified in previous IS studies. Prior scholars often view IS as organizational tools to perform work-related tasks. Thus, some well-known research models like the technology acceptance model were employed extensively to investigate predictors of IS adoption. Prior research often favored the role of external motivations in organizational settings, while the role of intrinsic motivators was less emphasized. As time progresses, a number of emerging ITs are developed for individuals usage [25]. In this respect, the drivers behind IT adoption begin to shift to intrinsic factors [12]. Increasing research suggests that perceived enjoyment may be the dominant antecedent of IT usage as opposed to extrinsic factors. For instance, the findings from Heijden [3] posited that perceived usefulness is likely to lose the dominant predictive value due to the effect of perceived enjoyment. Many followers further indicate that perceived enjoyment plays an important role in driving continued IS usage [26]. Overall, a majority of these studies contend that perceived enjoyment is a desirable factor that can promote positive outcomes.

Meanwhile, several recent studies argue that perceived enjoyment may also lead to negative outcomes. For instance, research on substance abuse has shown that perceived enjoyment plays a significant role in the development of addiction [27]. Nevertheless, little research attention has been paid to the dark sides of perceived enjoyment. In the IS literature, more research efforts are therefore needed to understand how perceived enjoyment and other factors alike may influence people to become addicted to IT.

2.3   Habit

Prior research refers to habit as "learned sequences of acts that have become automatic responses to specific situations, which may be functional in obtaining certain goals or end states" [28 p. 540]. The concept of habit was originally introduced by Triandis [29] and Thorngate [30]. They indicated that, in contrast to the cognitive process, habit captures the automatic and non-deliberate response to related stimuli. Habit has been found to be an important factor that helps to explain behaviors [31]. Scholars posit that people are "cognitive misers" who intend to minimize the costs of cognitive efforts [12]. Therefore, after sufficient practice or repetition, behaviors are likely to be carried out automatically without devoting cognitive efforts [32].

Recent IS scholars have shown increasing interest in identifying the significance of habit on IT/IS usage. For instance, habit is found to influence the continuance behavior in the ecommerce context [33]. Based on the IS continuance model, research shows that online shopping habit positively affects people's repurchase intention [34]. Similarly, Shiau and Luo [35] suggested that habit increases trust and perceived website quality, and further strengthens ecommerce performance.

3   Research Model and Hypothesis Development

Drawing upon the work of Turel and Serenko [12] and the theoretical background, this study develops a theoretical model to articulate the effects of perceived enjoyment and habit on smartphone addiction. We also incorporate the role of smartphone user types in the model to produce more insights. Figure 1 describes the model of this research.

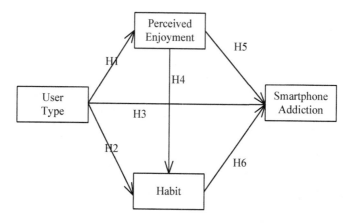

Fig. 1. Research model

3.1   User Type

As stated earlier, this study considers two types of smartphone users. We refer to the first type of users as *basic users*, who primarily adopt smartphones for basic mobile phone functions like making calls and sending text messages. In contrast, the second type of users, who are referred as *advanced users*, spend most of their time using smartphones for value-added functions such as connecting with friends with social networking mobile applications, or playing music, video, and games on the devices. Previous empirical research indicates that the level of user satisfaction is significantly different among various mobile phone features [36]. Scholars also point out that perceived enjoyment is closely related to whether one's intrinsic needs are satisfied [37], while habit is one of the outcomes of user satisfaction [38]. From these perspectives, we propose that different types of smartphone users may have different levels of perceived enjoyment, habit, and smartphone addiction in this study. More specifically, compared to basic users, advanced users are expected to be more likely to become enjoyable of using smartphones. They also tend to develop habitual usage of the devices due to having more fun. Finally, they may show a higher preference of becoming addicted to smartphones. This is consistent with a recent study, which points out that value-added functions like social networking may result in mobile phone addiction [15]. In summary, the following three hypotheses are provided in this study:

H1: Advanced users are likely to have a higher level of perceived enjoyment than basic users.
H2: Advanced users are likely to have a higher level of habit than basic users.
H3: Advanced users are likely to have a higher level of smartphone addiction than basic users.

3.2   Perceived Enjoyment

Smartphones have often been regarded as entertaining devices. People can gain play-fulness from smartphone usage [6]. In this study, we propose that perceived enjoyment of using smartphones may lead to the habit of using the devices. Prior research points out that enjoyable experience of using systems can enhance the habit of system use [12]. Scholars further contend that perceive enjoyment may also be related to cyber-game addiction [39] and substance abuse [7]. Thus, based on these studies, we develop the following two hypotheses:

H4: Perceived enjoyment is positively associated with habit.
H5: Perceived enjoyment is positively associated with smartphone addiction.

3.3   Habit

In this study, we expect that habit may be a potential prerequisite for the development of addiction. Familiar stimuli may trigger a user's repetitive behavior without mindfulness. When the repetition is beyond our control, the behavior may be at the risks of turning into addiction. Xu and Tan [40] posited that a strong habit may inevitably increase the strength of IT addiction. Based on these findings, we expect that habit positively affects smartphone addiction in this study. Thus, we propose that:

H6: Habit is positively associated with smartphone addiction.

4   Methodology

An online questionnaire survey was applied to collect data. Details about data collection and measurement are presented as follows.

4.1   Data Collection

We targeted at a convenient sample of students who used smartphones in two Chinese universities. We employed the snowball-sampling technique to increase the response rate. Since the respondents were Chinese, the translation and back-translation process was performed. That is, the original English questionnaire was translated into Chinese, and then translated back to identify and resolve any inconsistencies. Finally, we collected 384 responses. Table 1 describes the subjects' characteristics.

Table 1. Demographic characteristics

		Number	Percentage
Gender	Male	209	54.4%
	Female	175	45.6%
Age	Below 18	7	1.8%
	18-30	350	91.1%
	Above 30	27	7.1%
Usage duration per day	Below 1h	96	25.1%
	1h – 119min	73	19.0%
	2h – 179min	85	22.1%
	Above 3h	130	33.8%

4.2   Measures

Measurements were primarily adopted based on existing items from prior literature, with slight modifications to fit the context of this study. Seven-point Likert scales (1=strongly disagree to 7=strongly agree) were used for the measures. Table 2 lists the detailed measurements in this study.

Table 2. Constructs measurement

Construct	Items	Sources
Smartphone Addiction (SA)	SA1. My social life has sometimes suffered because of using my smartphone. SA2. Using my smartphone sometimes interfered with other (e.g., work or study). SA3. When I am not using my smartphone, I often feel agitated. SA4. I have made unsuccessful attempts to reduce the time using my smartphone. SA5. I find it difficult to control my smartphone use.	[12]
Perceived Enjoyment (PE)	PE1. Using my smartphone is enjoyable. PE2. Using my smartphone is fun. PE3. Using my smartphone is interesting.	[41]
Habit (HB)	HB1. Using my smartphone has become automatic to me. HB2. Using my smartphone is natural to me. HB3. When I want to interact with friends and relatives, using my smartphone is an obvious choice for me.	[38]
User Type (UT)	Which type of functions do you use most on your smartphone: UT1. Basic mobile phone functions include sending text messages and making phone calls. UT2. Value-added functions include social networking, browsing the Internet, playing music, video, and game, taking photos, and etc.	Self-developed

5   Data Analysis and Results

Partial Least Squares (PLS) was used for analysis with the measurement and structural model. PLS has no requirements for sample size and normal distribution [42], which is suitable for our study.

5.1   Measurement Model

To analyze the measurement model, this study examined the convergent and discriminant validity of the measures [43]. Sufficient convergent validity requires that the values of composite reliability (CR) should be greater than 0.7, while the values of average variance extracted (AVE) are more than 0.5. As shown in Table 3, the convergent validity was acceptable for this study. Meanwhile, discriminant validity shows the extent of differences between any two constructs. Table 3 also depicts the results of the AVE analysis, which ensured that the square root of AVE value in each construct was higher than the correlations with other constructs. In addition, the result of the confirmatory factor analysis with PLS was presented in Table 4, showing that items had higher loadings on their corresponding constructs than other constructs. In sum, these results indicated that this study had acceptable discriminate validity.

Table 3. Convergent and discriminant validity of the constructs

	CR	AVE	SA	PE	HB	UT
SA	0.92	0.69	**0.83**			
PE	0.95	0.87	0.50	**0.93**		
HB	0.91	0.78	0.20	0.41	**0.88**	
UT	1.00	1.00	0.21	0.13	0.14	1.00

Table 4. Confirmatory factory analysis with PLS

	SA	PE	HB	UT
SA1	**0.75**	0.35	0.22	0.12
SA2	**0.85**	0.49	0.27	0.25
SA3	**0.91**	0.43	0.14	0.16
SA4	**0.83**	0.39	0.11	0.18
SA5	**0.82**	0.38	0.07	0.15
PE1	0.46	**0.95**	0.37	0.09
PE2	0.46	**0.94**	0.34	0.11
PE3	0.47	**0.90**	0.42	0.15
HB1	0.14	0.34	**0.92**	0.13
HB2	0.17	0.39	**0.93**	0.15
HB3	0.21	0.34	**0.80**	0.10
UT	0.21	0.13	0.14	**1.00**

5.2 Structural Model

Before assessing the structural model, we incorporated usage duration per day, gender and age as control variables on smartphone addiction. Figure 2 shows the path coefficients, t-values, and explanatory power in the structural model. We found that

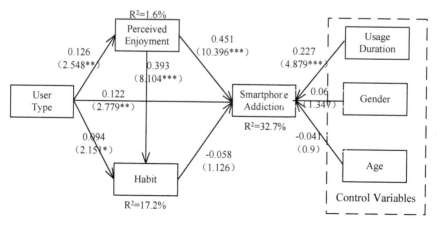

Fig. 2. Structural model (* denotes p<0.05, ** denotes p<0.01, *** denotes p<0.001)

user type positively affected perceived enjoyment (β=0.126, t=2.548), habit (β=0.094, t=2.151), and smartphone addiction (β=0.122, t=2.779). It implied that advanced users in the sample were more likely to have higher levels of perceived enjoyment, habit, and smartphone addiction than basic users. Thus, H1, H2, and H3 were supported. The results also showed that perceived enjoyment influenced habit (β=0.393, t=8.104) and smartphone addiction (β=0.451, t=10.396). Surprisingly, the effect of habit (β=-0.058, t=1.126) on smartphone addiction was not significant. Hence, H4, H5 were supported, but not for H6. Overall, 32.7% of variance was explained in smartphone addiction.

6   Discussion and Conclusions

Motivated by the needs to reveal the dangers of productive IS factors (e.g., perceived enjoyment and habit), we develop a research model and examine it with a survey of 384 smartphone users. Our findings support the idea that perceived enjoyment can lead to undesirable outcomes like smartphone addiction. The findings indicate that if smartphone users perceive enjoyment of using the devices, then they are more likely to develop a habit of usage and have a greater chance of becoming addicted to smartphones. In addition, we find that significant differences exist for basic and advanced users. That is, advanced users are more likely to find smartphone usage as enjoyable, habitual, and addictive.

6.1   Implications

First, the empirical evidence in this study supports the view about the dangers (i.e., smartphone addiction) of the productive factor, namely perceived enjoyment. It also highlights that increasing research attention may be paid to understand the dual roles of similar desirable factors in the extant IS literature.

Second, this study provides some new insights regarding the antecedents of IT addiction. More specifically, we revisit the effects of perceived enjoyment and habit in the context of smartphones by further incorporating the role of user type in the research model. Given that research on IT addiction, and certainly on smartphone addiction, is still scarce in the extant literature. The findings in this study can help to enrich our understandings of this research area.

Third, we find that habit does not directly affect smartphone addiction. On one hand, the result is different from Turel and Serenko's [12] work. It implies that direct effect of habit on addiction behavior may vary across different IT contexts. On the other hand, it also implies that more research effort may be needed to understand the complex role of habit in the formation of IT addiction.

Fourth, our findings also show that the process of smartphone addiction may differ for different users. Advanced users tend to have higher levels of perceived enjoyment, habit, and smartphone addiction. It indicates that user type plays a significant role in smartphone addiction. Since advanced users are those who emphasize the unique and value-added functions of smartphones, it implies that the influence of IT features may also be an important concern for the research on IT addiction.

Finally, this study also has practical implications. We point out that the significance of smartphone addiction and suggest that productive factors like perceived enjoyment of using smartphone may serve as its determinants. Thus, parents or practitioners should pay attention to this specific type of IT addiction. To monitor or reduce the likelihood of smartphone addiction, additional care may be needed to identify smartphone users who demonstrate high levels of enjoyment of using the devices. Similarly, users who mainly adopt smartphones for value-added functions instead of basic mobile phone functions may be reminded appropriately to regulate their usage behavior.

6.2   Limitations and Further Research

We have to point out that this study also has some limitations and opportunities for further research. The major limitation is related to the convenient sample that we use. In this study, we target at the students who use smartphones in two Chinese universities, and the sample size is relatively small. To increase the generalizability of this study, future research is thus suggested to collect a larger and more representative sample. Another limitation is related to the cross-sectional method that we use. Further study may consider adopting a longitudinal method to examine the causality among factors and provide more insights about the process of how smartphone addiction is developed. Finally, given the relatively small variances explained in smartphone addiction, some important factors may be missing in our research model. Future research may explore more key predictors to enrich the understandings of this new emerging research area.

Acknowledgements. The work described in this study was supported by a grant from National Natural Science Foundation of China (No. 71201149).

References

1. Turel, O., Serenko, A., Giles, P.: Integrating Technology Addiction and Use: An Empirical Investigation of Online Auction Users. MIS Q. **35**, 1043–1062 (2011)
2. Lee, M.K., Cheung, C.M., Chen, Z.: Acceptance of Internet-Based Learning Medium: the Role of Extrinsic and Intrinsic Motivation. Inf. Manage. **42**, 1095–1104 (2005)
3. van der Heijden, H.: User Acceptance of Hedonic Information Systems. MIS Q. **28**, 695–704 (2004)
4. Thong, J.Y.L., Hong, S.-J., Tam, K.Y.: The effects of post-adoption beliefs on the expectation-confirmation model for information technology continuance. Int. J. Hum.-Comput. Stud. **64**, 799–810 (2006)
5. Igbaria, M., Iivari, J., Maragahh, H.: Why do individuals use computer technology? A Finnish case study. Inf. Manage. **29**, 227–238 (1995)
6. Park, B.-W., Lee, K.C.: A Pilot Study to Analyze the Effects of User Experience and Device Characteristics on the Customer Satisfaction of Smartphone Users. In: Kim, T.-h., Adeli, H., Robles, R.J., Balitanas, M. (eds.) UCMA 2011, Part II. CCIS, vol. 151, pp. 421–427. Springer, Heidelberg (2011)
7. Wohl, M.J., Young, M.M., Hart, K.E.: Self-perceptions of dispositional luck: Relationship to DSM gambling symptoms, subjective enjoyment of gambling and treatment readiness. Subst. Use Misuse. **42**, 43–63 (2007)

8. McDaniel, S.R.: Investigating the roles of gambling interest and impulsive sensation seeking on consumer enjoyment of promotional games. Soc. Behav. Personal. Int. J. **30**, 53–64 (2002)
9. Cheung, C.M., Lee, Z.W., Lee, M.K.: Understanding Compulsive Use of Facebook Through the Reinforcement Processes. In: Proceedings of the 21st European Conference on Information Systems., Utrecht, Netherlands (2013)
10. Vaghefi, I., Lapointe, L.: Can IT Hurt Productivity? In: An Investigation of IT Addiction. 34th International Conference on Information Systems., Milan (2013)
11. Zhang, K.Z.K., Chen, C., Lee, M.K.O.: Understanding the Role of Motives in Smartphone Addiction. In: Proceedings of the 18th Pacific Asia Conference on Information Systems (2014)
12. Turel, O., Serenko, A.: The benefits and dangers of enjoyment with social networking websites. Eur. J. Inf. Syst. **21**, 512–528 (2012)
13. Hong, F.-Y., Chiu, S.-I., Huang, D.-H.: A Model of the Relationship Between Psychological Characteristics, Mobile Phone Addiction and Use of Mobile Phones by Taiwanese University Female Students. Comput. Hum. Behav. **28**, 2152–2159 (2012)
14. Khang, H., Kim, J.K., Kim, Y.: Self-Traits and Motivations as Antecedents of Digital Media Flow and Addiction: The Internet, Mobile Phones, and Video Games. Comput. Hum. Behav. **29**, 2416–2424 (2013)
15. Salehan, M., Negahban, A.: Social Networking on Smartphones: When Mobile Phones Become Addictive. Comput. Hum. Behav. **29**, 2632–2639 (2013)
16. Chun, H., Lee, H., Kim, D.: The Integrated Model of Smartphone Adoption: Hedonic and Utilitarian Value Perceptions of Smartphones Among Korean College Students. Cyberpsychology Behav. Soc. Netw. **15**, 473–479 (2012)
17. Lee, M.-B.: A Study of Factors Influencing the Intention to Use Smartphone. J. Korea Ind. Inf. Syst. Soc. **16**, 139–149 (2011)
18. Turel, O., Serenko, A.: Is Mobile Email Addiction Overlooked? Commun. ACM. **53**, 41–43 (2010)
19. Walsh, S.P., White, K.M., Hyde, M.K., Watson, B.: Dialling and Driving: Factors Influencing Intentions to Use a Mobile Phone While Driving. Accid. Anal. Prev. **40**, 1893–1900 (2008)
20. Turel, O., Serenko, A., Bontis, N.: Blackberry Addiction: Symptoms and Outcomes. In: Proceedings of the 14th Americas Conference on Information Systems., Milan (2008)
21. Kwon, M., Lee, J.-Y., Won, W.-Y., Park, J.-W., Min, J.-A., Hahn, C., Gu, X., Choi, J.-H., Kim, D.-J.: Development and Validation of a Smartphone Addiction Scale (SAS). PloS One **8**, e56936 (2013)
22. Park, N., Kim, Y.-C., Shon, H.Y., Shim, H.: Factors Influencing Smartphone Use and Dependency in South Korea. Comput. Hum. Behav. **29**, 1763–1770 (2013)
23. Chiu, S.-I.: The Relationship Between Life Stress and Smartphone Addiction on Taiwanese University Student: A Mediation Model of Learning Self-Efficacy and Social Self-Efficacy. Comput. Hum. Behav. **34**, 49–57 (2014)
24. Holbrook, M.B., Chestnut, R.W., Oliva, T.A., Greenleaf, E.A.: Play as a Consumption Experience: The Roles of Emotions, Performance, and Personality in the Enjoyment of Games. J. Consum. Res. **11**, 728–739 (1984)
25. Kim, H.-W., Chan, H.C., Gupta, S.: Value-based Adoption of Mobile Internet: An empirical investigation. Decis. Support Syst. **43**, 111–126 (2007)
26. Yeung, P., Jordan, E.: The continued usage of business e-learning courses in Hong Kong corporations. Educ. Inf. Technol. **12**, 175–188 (2007)

27. Fidler, J.A., West, R.: Enjoyment of smoking and urges to smoke as predictors of attempts and success of attempts to stop smoking: A longitudinal study. Drug Alcohol Depend. **115**, 30–34 (2011)

28. Verplanken, B., Aarts, H., Van Knippenberg, A.: Habit, information acquisition, and the process of making travel mode choices. Eur. J. Soc. Psychol. **27**, 539–560 (1997)

29. Triandis, H.C.: Values, attitudes, and interpersonal behavior. In: Nebraska Symposium on Motivtion: Beliefs, Attitude, and Values, pp. 195–259. University of Nebraska Press (1979)

30. Thorngate, W.: Must we always think before we act? Pers. Soc. Psychol. Bull. **2**, 31–35 (1976)

31. Limayem, M., Hirt, S.G.: Force of habit and information systems usage: Theory and initial validation. J. Assoc. Inf. Syst. **4**, 3 (2003)

32. Tiffany, S.T.: A cognitive model of drug urges and drug-use behavior: role of automatic and nonautomatic processes. Psychol. Rev. **97**, 147 (1990)

33. Liao, C., Palvia, P., Lin, H.-N.: The roles of habit and web site quality in e-commerce. Int. J. Inf. Manag. **26**, 469–483 (2006)

34. Khalifa, M., Liu, V.: Online consumer retention: contingent effects of online shopping habit and online shopping experience. Eur. J. Inf. Syst. **16**, 780–792 (2007)

35. Shiau, W.-L., Luo, M.M.: Continuance intention of blog users: the impact of perceived enjoyment, habit, user involvement and blogging time. Behav. Inf. Technol. **32**, 570–583 (2013)

36. Ling, C., Hwang, W., Salvendy, G.: Diversified users' satisfaction with advanced mobile phone features. Univers. Access Inf. Soc. **5**, 239–249 (2006)

37. Tamborini, R., Bowman, N.D., Eden, A., Grizzard, M., Organ, A.: Defining Media Enjoyment as the Satisfaction of Intrinsic Needs. J. Commun. **60**, 758–777 (2010)

38. Limayem, M., Hirt, S.G., Cheung, C.M.K.: How Habit Limits the Predictive Power of Intention: The Case of Information Systems Continuance. MIS Q. **31**, 705–737 (2007)

39. Chou, T.-J., Ting, C.-C.: The role of flow experience in cyber-game addiction. Cyberpsychol. Behav. **6**, 663–675 (2003)

40. Xu, H., Tan, B.C.: Why Do I Keep Checking Facebook: Effects of Message Characteristics On the Formation of Social Network Services Addiction. Presented at the Thirty Third International Conference on Information Systems, Orlando (2012)

41. Davis, F.D., Bagozzi, R.P., Warshaw, P.R.: Extrinsic and Intrinsic Motivation to Use Computers in the Workplace1. J. Appl. Soc. Psychol. **22**, 1111–1132 (1992)

42. Chin, W.W., Marcolin, B.L., Newsted, P.R.: A partial least squares latent variable modeling approach for measuring interaction effects: Results from a Monte Carlo simulation study and an electronic-mail emotion/adoption study. Inf. Syst. Res. **14**, 189–217 (2003)

43. Fornell, C., Larcker, D.F.: Structural Equation Models with Unobservable Variables and Measurement error: Algebra and Statistics. J. Mark. Res. 382–388 (1981)

eBusiness, eEducation and eLogistics

Teaching Enterprise Modeling Based on Multi-media Simulation: A Pragmatic Approach

Ilia Bider[1(✉)], Martin Henkel[1], Stewart Kowalski[1,2], and Erik Perjons[1]

[1] DSV Stockholm University, Stockholm, Sweden
{ilia,martinh,stewart,perjons}@dsv.su.se
[2] Gjøvik University College, Gjøvik, Norway

Abstract. The paper addresses the problem of how university students can acquire enterprise modeling skills so that they can build high quality models of organizational structure and behavior in practical settings after their graduation. The best way of learning such skills is apprenticeship where the students follow a modeling master in a real business case. However, in a university classroom setting this is difficult to arrange, if even possible. Therefore, the paper suggests the use of a computer-based simulation as a good approximation to apprenticeship. Moreover, it suggests a pragmatic, low-cost approach making the idea accessible even for courses with a low budget. A business case is simulated by providing the students with multi-media information sources that are usually used by system or business analysts when building models. The sources consist of recorded interviews with the stakeholders, a web-site of the enterprise under investigation, internal protocols from management meetings, results of twitter search on the company name, etc. The paper presents practical guidelines on how to build such simulation based on a trial successfully completed at the Department of Computer and System Sciences at Stockholm University.

Keywords: eEducation · Modeling skills · Information systems · Simulation · Multi-media · Apprenticeship

1 Motivation

This paper is devoted to the topic of teaching and learning how to model different aspects of organizational structure and behavior in order to provide proper IT solutions for businesses and public offices. This topic, which is often referred to as business or enterprise modeling, is of special importance for the university programs in Information System (IS), and other IT-related fields such as Computer Science and Software Engineering. Its importance for the IT professionals is well understood, and is discussed in the literature related to university teaching in IT-related fields, see, for example, [1], [2], [3].

The main problem with acquiring enterprise modeling skills, besides the formal knowledge on the syntax and semantics of enterprise modeling languages needed, is that enterprise modeling skills include knowledge on how to extract knowledge from the unstructured reality of business life. While the first kind of knowledge is quite

© Springer International Publishing Switzerland 2015
M. Benyoucef et al. (Eds.): MCETECH 2015, LNBIP 209, pp. 239–254, 2015.
DOI: 10.1007/978-3-319-17957-5_16

suitable for teaching in the classroom of a university, the second kind is not, as it belongs to the area of tacit knowledge [4] or Ways of Thinking and Practicing (WTP) [5]. The best known solution for acquiring WTP is apprenticeship where the students follow and help a modeling master in a real business case. However, in a university classroom setting this is difficult to arrange, if even possible.

Some approximation to a real business case could be achieved by simulating the enterprise in a computer. This type of simulation of real-life objects is already in use in some subject of university teaching, e.g. simulation of a patient in medical profession, where it showed good results [6], [7]. As far as IS and other IT related disciplined are concerned, we found only one example of using simulation of an enterprise for teaching systems analysis, HyperCase, which appeared as early as 1990. According to its designers, HyperCase showed to be more appreciated by the students than traditional methods [8]. Though HyperCase was introduced in 1990, it is still in use [9] as an accompanier for an IS course book [10].

The idea used in existing simulation of real objects for teaching is that the object itself is simulated, e.g. a patient, or an enterprise. With today's technology, it is certainly possible to create a virtual reality where a student can work through the enterprise, observe what employees are doing, ask them questions, etc. This is the main idea behind HyperCase. Though technically simulating a real enterprise is possible, it comes at a considerable cost. While it may be economically justifiable to simulate an enterprise as an accompanier to a course book that is sold in large volumes, building such a simulator for a single course would be hardly justifiable.

In the work reported in this paper, we tested another idea of using simulation in teaching enterprise modeling. Instead of simulating an enterprise, we simulate a situation of an apprenticeship where the students follow a modeling master and help him/her to do some part of the work on building models. More specifically, the analyst chooses the information sources to be used for building a model, and hands the work of building the model to the students. Such sources may include (but are not limited to): (a) interviews with stakeholders, e.g. CEO, CIO, (b) samples of relevant documents, e.g., meetings protocols, forms for managing orders, (c) web-based sources, e.g. a company web site, results of twitter search on company name. To simulate such sources, e.g. using video recorded interviews, is much easier than to build a virtual representation of an enterprise.

The goal of this paper is to present practical recommendations on how to build an apprenticeship simulator based on the trial completed at the department of Computer and System Sciences (DSV) at Stockholm University. The simulator has been built for an introductory course in IS for first year students. One of the main learning activities in the course is a project assignment that requires the students in groups to build different types of enterprise models of an imaginary company presented to them. In earlier occasions of the course, the company was presented in form of a text description. The simulator substituted the text description with a web site that contained multi-media sources of information as described above and a number of modeling assignments left to the students by the master. The site also contained some tips on what sources to use when completing particular assignments via links made from assignments to these sources. The simulator has been used in two course occasions and got positive feedback from both the students and teachers engaged.

Besides working with the simulator on their own, the students meet a teacher three times during the project, two of them for consultations, and one for presentation of the results to the teacher and peers. In the two first meetings, the teacher plays the role of modeling master, which makes the setting more close to the real apprenticeship.

In the paper, we use our simulator to illustrate the used design principles, and share our experience obtained when building and using the simulator. We believe that this experience may be of interest to other teachers in courses that have one of their learning objectives to acquire enterprise modeling skills.

The rest of the paper is structured in the following manner. Section 2 gives an overview of the trial course, and the project for which a simulator has been built. Section 3 describes the way the imaginary company was presented in the project before the simulator was introduced. Section 4 discusses the new way of presenting the imaginary company – using multi-media information sources – and our experience of developing these sources. Section 5 describes the structure of the project site that integrates all multi-media information sources with the assignments for the students related to building the models. Section 6 gives some results of the trial evaluation through surveying the students and the teachers. Section 7 contains our reflections on using the simulator at two course occasions, and Section 8 contains concluding remarks and plans for the future.

2   The Trial Course and the Project Business Case

The trial has been completed in the frame of the first year course called "IT in Organizations" (ITO). Below, we also will refer to this course as the "trial course". ITO is a first year course that is mandatory for approximately half of the students who enroll to bachelor programs at DSV. The number of enrolled students is approximately 250. The course is given each fall term, and it is the second course for the students. Before this course they have only completed one other course, "IT for personal use", which presents basic theories and concepts in IT and computer science. The trial course ITO can be classified as an introduction to IS. The overall goal of the course is to give the students basic knowledge and skills on the analysis, design and development of information systems, including theories, methods and techniques for this. Additionally, the course should create an understanding of how organizations - their goals, products and services, business processes and information - can be changed by using different forms of IS. The length of the course corresponds to five weeks of full-time work for the students. The course is 7.5 credits according to the European Credit and Transfer and accumulation Systems (ECTS). Being an introductory course, the course has a wide scope. It includes an overview of a number of modeling techniques, such as functional modeling (with the help of Icam DEFinition for Function Modeling 0, abbreviated IDEF0 [11]), process modeling (with Business Process Model and Notation, abbreviated BPMN [12]), goal modeling (with Business Motivation Model, abbreviated BMM [13]), and a number of others. The teaching and learning activities in the course include lectures, workshops, tutorials, labs and a project assignment. The project assignment is completed in groups of 4-5 students, and it is built around a fictitious company called "AFFE". The company is said to be engaged in development and sales of a business game.

3   Presenting the Project Case in a Textual Form

In previous years of the ITO course, the AFFE's business was presented to the students in a textual form. For example, a textual description of how the company handles invoices was available. Based on this textual description, the students needed to complete a number of tasks. For example, one task was to *"Build diagrams of business processes currently used in AFFE's practice using BPMN"*. Based on the textual description, the students were supposed to produce a process diagram. Table 1 gives examples of text fragment from the textual descriptions. As can be seen, the text contained several types of information to cover the company's current state of affairs, their products, working procedures, the IT system they use, and the organizational changes that the company is planning.

Table 1. Fragments of the text description of AFFE

Type of information	Example of text fragment
Company background information	"The company has a game development apartment with 14 game developers and a sales department with 20 salespersons. The sales department handles marketing, sales, order processing and delivery."
Current state of affairs	"The company needs to borrow money to fund further development of the game but the banks are unwilling to lend because of the insufficient profitability. Furthermore, the competition is hardening, as many game development companies start developing similar business games for the Swedish market. AFFE's game is still the best-known business game in Sweden, at least for manufacturing companies."
Facts on products	"The AFFE game can be played by one user which can take multiple roles in an enterprise governed in the game. The game can also be played by several users who then take different roles in the enterprise."
Working procedures	"Today, the development of the next game release is completed in the following way: After the previous version of the game has been released, the game developers are gathered to determine what requirements must be met in the next version."
Facts on systems used	"AFFE currently has the following support systems: a customer record system in the form of an excel sheet, an IT-based financial system for accounting, a version control system for the game's code, …"
Organizational change	"Management has discussed various solutions to increase the company's profitability. They have decided to implement the following five changes: • To offer clients customized variants of the business game. • To offer the game as a cloud service"

4   Presenting the Project Case as Multi-media Simulation

When designing a new way of presenting the project assignment to the student, we used the following guiding design principles:

1. *Give the student a more realistic understanding of the work of system and/or business analysts.* As the authors of this paper had experiences of consulting practice, we know that textual presentations like described in Section 3 are seldom handed to an analyst. Thus, using this kind of descriptions may create misconception in the student's mind of how an analyst works.
2. *Use several types of presentation media.* This is in-line with principle 1 above. An analyst, normally, does not rely on one type of information sources, but combine several, e.g., interviews with stakeholders, observations, facilitating workshops, documents analysis, etc.
3. *Apply a pragmatic, low cost approach.* Our goal was to develop an approach that could be used in any course that include modeling assignment without requiring a lot of expensive resources
4. *Keep the case already used intact.* We tested our approach on the same case as described in Section 3, partly to satisfy the principle 3 above, and partly to have a possibility to make a more adequate evaluation of the impact of the change in case presentation.

Based on the principles above we have chosen to use the following types of information sources and media for presenting the case to the students:

- *Video recording* – for simulating interviews with stakeholders. This media could also be used for simulating a facilitating workshop, or a management group meeting. However, we have not chosen to video recorded these latter types of information sources; it would have required much more resources to do (see principle 3 above).
- *Web-based* presentation – for simulating the company's website, or social media search on the company name. Based on our experience from being analysts, it is very important to use sources such as the web before the first visit to a company. For example, web-based presentations such as the company web page and other public information are important input for an analyst.
- *Document-based* presentation – for simulating internal and/or external document circulating in the company, e.g. protocol from steering committee meeting.

In Table 2 below we list all multi-media presentation fragments created for the business case outlined in Section 3. The listing is organized according to the media-type in the first column. The last column shows the approximate costs to produce each fragment in person-hours. The costs are divided in two sub-columns: *Design costs* (D), and *Execution costs* (E). The design costs are onetime costs that were required to find out the way to build a component. The execution costs represent the cost of producing the component. When developing a new project site, e.g. for another course, only the execution costs should be taken into consideration. The last row, which is separated by double line does not represent any presentation fragment, but is related to creating a site that integrates all fragments and project assignments. It is added to show the total cost for producing the new way of presenting the project assignment.

Table 2. Multi-media presentation fragments of AFFE

Media type	Presentation fragment	Costs[1]	
		D	**E**
Video recording	*Interview 1* with game development manager (simulated) *Interview 2* with sales manager (simulated) *Interview 3* with CEO (simulated)	3	2 2 2
Web-based sources	*Website* of the company (AFFE) (simulated) Twitter feed containing customer opinions (simulated) *Financial info* from http://www.proff.se/ (simulated) *IT systems in use* – links to real system vendors websites	1 1 1 0	3 1 1 1
Document-based sources	*Excel sheet 1-* sales leads management template (simulated) *Excel sheet 2* - customer management template (simulated) *Protocol* of internal management meeting (simulated)	1 1 0	1 1 1
Integration	Course project site	24	8

[1]All costs are in person-hours

Table 3 shows how various types of information from Table 1 have been incorporated in the presentation fragments listed in Table 2. For example, we choose to represent the need for organizational change with a protocol from a management group.

In the paragraphs that follow, we shortly describe each presentation fragment and the way it has been produced:

1. *Interviews 1-3* was created by letting three teachers play the role of CEO, development manager and sales manager respectively. A fourth teacher was acting as the analyst, asking questions to the interviewees. Fig. 1 shows an image from the resulting interview with the development manager. To save time (principle 3), and partially to make the interviews more authentic (principle 1), neither the analyst nor the interviewees had prepared any statements or questions. Instead of preparing by having a pre-defined script, the interviewees had read the textual description of the case and studied the intended outcome from the student work with assignments related to the interview. For example, the teacher playing the development manager studied the BPMN process diagram that would be the outcome of the student work with one of the assignments. The recording of the interview was done in the

university studio, with a professional backdrop and three cameras (left, full scene, and right). All cutting was done in real-time, so no post-processing was necessary. The "analyst" started the interview with a short presentation of the aim of the interview as well as involved persons. Since the teacher playing the role of analyst has extensive experience, he asked the development manager probing questions such as "How is this performed?", "If this happens, what do you do then?" etc. A central part of the interview was also that the analysts made brief summaries of what was being said, to get confirmations from the interviewee. Introducing these short summaries, besides being a practical technique applied by experienced analysts, also had the benefit of allowing the students to take notes without the need to rewind the video. Each interview lasted between five and seven minutes. The interviews had to be redone 2-3 times until a satisfactory final recording was done. *Each interview took about 40 minutes to record, which in total gives about 6 persons-hours for the three interviews, since three persons where engaged in the interview (interviewee, analyst, technician). Before starting the interview, 3 hours were spent on design, for example the number and type of interviews was decided.*

Table 3. Multi-media fragments usage to provide info needed for completing the project

Type of information	Presentation fragment
Company background information	Website
Current state of affairs	Twitter feed, Financial info, Protocol, Interview 3
Facts on products	Website
Working procedures	Interview 1, Interview 2
Facts on systems used	IT-systems in use, Excel sheet 1, Excel sheet 2
Organizational change	Meeting protocol

2. *Website of the company AFFE* was designed using the content management system WordPress. As any typical company website, the site included pages *About us, Customers, Contact us, Product,* etc. Most of the background information from the textual description was spread through these pages. The WordPress theme TwentyTen with a simple system of horizontal menus has been used for designing the site. *The design took about one hour, while the creation of pages and menus using WordPress took about 3 hours.* We used an existing WordPress installation provided by the university, and thus had no direct cost for installation.

Fig. 1. The Project site – interview with the game development manager (left)

3. *Twitter feed containing customer opinions* was created by getting a list of results from searching Twitter on an arbitrary search phrase. The search results were first converted into the PDF format and then edited, so that they represented customers' opinions and questions on AFFE and its product. Both negative and positive opinions were simulated in the feed, e.g. "the game is good by difficult to learn", "Oh, no it went down again". The PDF format was chosen as it took little time (principle 3) to edit the search results using Acrobat Adobe Pro and thus produce a realistic (principle 1) simulation. An alternative could be producing a HTML page. *In total the twitter feed took about 2 hours to create.*

4. *Financial info* simulation was created by experimenting with the on-line Swedish service http://www.proff.se/. This service provides basic financial information covering the last three years of any Swedish company. By testing the service on several real companies in the IT sector of the appropriate size, we found a company that corresponded roughly to the state in the affairs of AFFE. The information obtained was then converted to PDF and edited to produce simulated financial information for AFFE. Again, the PDF format was chosen as it took little time (principle 3) to edit the result and thus produce a simulation. *In total the financial info took about 2 hours to create.*

5. *IT systems in use* were not simulated; we have chosen three systems of the right type on the Swedish market and provided links to the vendors' sites where these systems were described: PVCS version management from www.serena.com, Visma accounting system and wages administration system from www.vismaspcs.se. *This step was straight-forward and required one hour.*

6. *Excel sheet 1, 2* were simulated by searching Internet for Excel based customer management and downloading available templates, see for example http://www.vertex42.com/ExcelTemplates/crm-template.html. Then, the templates where translated to Swedish and filled with simulated data. *To find an example of a sheet took about one hour for each sheet; another hour was spent for translation and adding data. In total this took 4 hours.*

7. *Protocol* containing meeting notes was simulated by reformatting the text already existing in the textual description of the project case from the previous year, see the last row of Table 1. Reformatting consisted of making the text look like a formal protocol; it was done based on the designer's experience of reading, and, sometimes, writing such protocols. *This activity took less than one hour.*

5   The Project Website

The multi-media presentation fragments and the project assignments were integrated in a project website [14]. The site lists all sources of information via having links to the fragments listed above, and it lists all assignments, and to each assignment it gives recommendations on what sources to use when completing the assignments, see, Fig. 2.

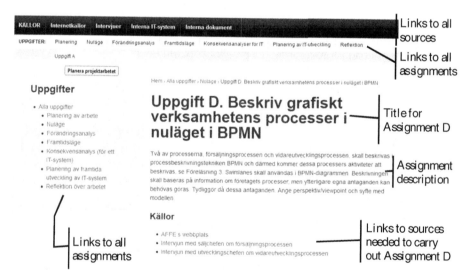

Fig. 2. The Project site – Description of a task that students need to carry out

Fig. 2 shows an example of an assignment – the assignment with the title: "Describe graphically the as-is business processes of the company in BPMN". The assignment page also provides links to sources needed to carry out the assignment.

The project website has been designed under the content management system WordPress using a theme called "Responsive" that allows several levels of menus, both in the top of the pages and on the sides. The menu system was used to connect presentation fragments to the assignments and arrange the fragments in groups. It took relatively long time to build the project site, 32 hours. However, most of this time (about 24 hours) went into designing the site structure. Now, when the structure is in place, it takes very little time to set up a website for a new project, provided that all presentation fragments are created, and the instructions for the project assignments are written.

6   Evaluation

The project website with multi-media presentation of a business case was used in two course occasions, fall 2013 and fall 2014. To understand how the change in case presentation impacts teaching/learning of modeling skills, a number of surveys have been completed. After the occasion of fall 2013 the following survey evaluations has been completed:

1. A project website evaluation by the students on the issue whether the multi-media presentation of the company had enough information to carry out the project tasks. Most of the students who participated agreed on that the information content of the site was satisfactory.
2. A project website evaluation by the teachers. The teachers agreed that the engagement of the students became higher and the quality of results in the project somewhat increased. They disagreed on other parameters that were related to their work, e.g. their workload for mentoring the project work did not decrease.
3. An evaluation by the students based on comparison with another course that used the textual presentation of the project. The majority of the students agreed that the multi-media presentation of project assignment was to be preferred in all courses that include business/enterprise modeling.
4. Comparative analysis of examination results for years 2012 (textual presentation) and 2013 (multi-media presentation). The result showed that the "tail" of the distribution of lower grades improved for 2013 compared to 2012. This means that the less performing students showed better results after the project site has been introduced (no change for the better performing students were detected).

After the occasion of fall 2014 a new evaluation has been conducted:

5. A project website evaluation by the students with the focus on comparative investigation of different media types used in the case presentation.

All first four evaluations pointed towards some improvement in learning environment and results. Due to the limited space, we do not present the results of the evaluations 1-4[1], but focus on the latest evaluation, evaluation 5 from the list above, as it is more relevant to the topic of this paper.

---

[1]   The results of evaluations 3,4 are to be published separately in [19]. Note that [19] is complementary to this paper, as it does not contain details on the simulation design.

When designing the survey for the latest evaluation, we used a combination of parameters from different frameworks, e.g. [15,16], as we failed to find a ready-made framework for our purpose; in addition to the used frameworks we also added a parameter to measure student engagement.. The design process resulted in selecting the following parameters:

1. *Usefulness* – the degree to which the project site helped to attain the goals set. This parameter corresponds to *Perceived Usefulness* (PU) of the TAM framework [15].
2. *Completeness* – the degree to which the information provided is sufficient for completing the assignments. This parameter corresponds to parameter *Completeness* from the data model quality framework [16].
3. *Effort* – the amount of time it takes for processing information in order to complete assignments. This parameter corresponds to *Perceived Ease Of Use* (PEOU) of the TAM framework [15]. However in our case measuring this parameter has another purpose than in TAM. Making it too easy to complete the assignments contradicts the learning goals of obtaining modeling skills nearing the level of acting practitioner. The time spent should be long enough but not too long so that the students lost their interest in completing assignments. The latter can be measured through parameter *Engagement*, see below.
4. *Engagement* – the degree to which working with the site was deemed interesting. This parameter interplays with the effort parameter, the idea is that if an assignment is interesting, increasing the student's motivation, the assignment could also be difficult and require an effort to be completed.

Based on the four parameters above, we created survey questions to measure them in relation to the whole project website (e.g. overall usefulness), and to the different types of media used for the case presentation (e.g. comparative usefulness). Out of the 210 students working with project assignments 49 responded to the survey. The response rate (23%) is to be considered normal for this type of survey in our department; the regular course evaluation surveys at DSV usually get about a 15-20% response rate.   The results are presented in Table 4.

The survey was designed to answer two questions:

1. Find out to what degree the project website was *suitable* as educational material
2. Find out the ways for *improvement*

As far as suitability is concerned, the answers show the following:

- *Usefulness.* The first two questions (Q1, Q2) about *overall usefulness* show that the students to a very large degree consider that the site helped them learn the subject matter, and understand how an analyst works. Note that in the second question (Q2) regarding the site's ability to aid the student understand the work analysts do, got a high degree (33%) of students who were undecided. This is quite natural since many students do not have work experience and thus cannot compare it with previous experiences. Several comments related to Q1 pointed out that what helped the student to learn to use models was the site in combination with lectures.
- *Completeness.* Based on Q5, the site was clearly deemed as containing enough information (86%).

Table 4. Results of Evaluation 5

Q1 - Overall usefulness (q3) The site helped me to learn to analyze existing organizations and their IT support with the aid of different kinds of models. 	**Q2 - Overall usefulness (q4)** The site helped me understand the work a business/systems analyst performs. 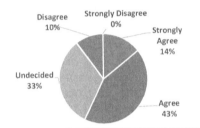
Q3 - Overall usefulness (q5) If the project site is to be re-designed, what should the purpose of the re-design be? 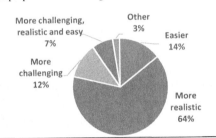	**Q4 - Comparative usefulness (q8)** If we change the project site, which information sources would you like to have more of? 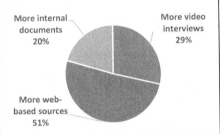
Q5 - Overall completeness (q1) Did the project web site contain enough information to complete the project tasks? 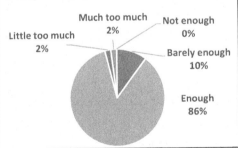	**Q6 - Overall effort (q2)** In general, was it easy to find information needed to complete the project tasks? 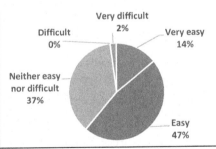
Q7 - Comparative effort (q6) Which information source required the MOST work to find information needed to complete the project tasks? 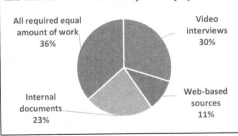	**Q8 - Comparative engagement (q7)** Which information source was most interesting to work with? 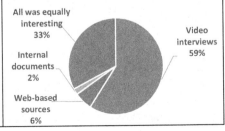

- *Effort.* Question Q6 and Q7 shows that 61% of the students thought it was easy or very easy to find the information on the site. As described before, it is not necessarily good that the information is too easy to find, since that would not reflect a realistic working situation. Thus, the site could probably be changed to actually increase the effort needed from the students. This is also reflected in a comment made in the survey, where a student pointed out that it was actually *too easy* to find relevant information in the video interviews. On the other hand when students needed to choose the information source that comparatively required the most work (Q7), the video interviews was pointed out by 30% of the students as requiring the most work.
- *Engagement.* From the responses on the question about which information source that was most interesting (Q8), 59 % of the students found the video interviews most interesting and 33 % found all sources equally interesting.

As far as *ways for improvement are concerned,* the answers show the following:

- From the answers of Q3 and Q4 it can be said that a future re-design targeting *usefulness* would be to make the site more realistic (64%) with a focus on the "AFFE" company's simulated web site (51%).
- The video interviews was considered the most interesting *information source* (Q8), at the same time they were considered the most challenging (Q7) - and 29% stated that they would like to have more video interviews in the future (Q4). This combination of challenging and engaging is something to tap into for future revisions of the site.

The survey gave us a clear indication of that the site design was successful. During the course the teachers also had the same subjective impression, as will be discussed in the next section.

7   Reflections

As stated in the beginning of the paper we set out to change a IS modeling course to make it more realistic, but we also aimed at doing it by using a low-cost pragmatic approach. Regarding the cost, we spent in total 32 person-hours on re-designing the course and 23 hours on executing/implementing the design. Thus, in total 55 hours were spent on remaking the course from using a text-only representation of the project assignment into a simulation using video, reports and a company website. Even though 55 hours is over a week of full-time work, it can still be said to be low-cost compared to the courses overall budget.

When doing the re-design of the course, and when teaching the course we also made several subjective observations about the effects of the re-designed course:

The first observation is that the students like the use of several media types, and are subjectively deemed as *more engaged* in the course. The survey showed that the student thought the usefulness of the project web site was high (see previous section on evaluation). This was also seen when observing the students present and discuss their work. For example, one teacher observed that several groups strongly objected when one group presented the idea that the fictitious "AFFE" company should buy an expensive ERP system. They simply felt that this would ruin the company's fragile economy without having any positive effect. This was one of several signs of an increased engagement in the project assignment.

An observation from the design work was that a part of adding a realistic touch to the information sources was to *add layers of information*. For example, the simulated protocol from the internal meeting was "decorated" with a formal introduction and signatures. Likewise, in the video interview with the development manager the manager expressed positive opinions on some parts of the development process. In both these examples, the added information was not used by the students in the assignment, but was added to give a feeling of authenticity.

It was furthermore observed that some *unintended information was conveyed in the video recordings*. While the main subject of the video interviews was the description of a business process or the company's current economic state, the students also interpreted how the interviewees behaved. For example, the sales manager was considered as being somewhat formal and "square" and some groups of students speculated that this could be the culprit of the issues the fictitious company had. The knowledge of different leadership styles and analysis thereof is not part of the current course, but observations like this may be of interest for future courses.

Another, *positive, unintended effect* that was observed during the survey was that one student had problems reading long text because of dyslexia. For this student, using mixed information sources made it easier to grasp the course content. This is one example of how mixing media types may be a way to appeal to a wider range of students.

8   Conclusion

The evaluations of the trial has indicated that pedagogical gains can be made in teaching modeling skills with relative simple and cost effective use of video technology paired with a straight-forward web site. The key to creating the web site has been to have a simulated apprenticeship approach, where the student examines an enterprise based on simulated material in form of information fragments, such as economic information and protocols. Furthermore the students, as "apprentices", were able to see a "master" analyst performing interviews.

Our approach to using simulation in teaching/learning modeling skills is via simulating apprenticeship. As such, it is complementary to other usages of simulation for the same purpose, e.g. simulation of an object to be modeled, as in case of HyperCase [9]. The latter approach can require considerable costs and can be justified only if the volume of usage of such a simulator is high, which is the case with HeperCase distributed as a book companion. Our approach based on simulation of apprenticeship is a low-cost approach and can be used in, more or less, any course.

The research presented in this paper is being conducted as Action Research (AR), i.e. in cycles. There are several ways of representing an AR cycle with the number of phases varying from 4 to 6, dependent on how detailed one wants to present the cycle. We use the version suggested by Kolb for experimental learning style theory [17], which can be represented as four stage learning cycle: Concrete experience → Reflective Observation → Abstract Conceptualization → Active Experimentation → Concrete Experience → .... We consider that Kolb's cycle is a good representation not only for student learning, but also for AR in a situation when researchers are also practitioners in the field where the given research project is conducted. In this case, learning is equal to obtaining new knowledge not only for the researchers involved, but also for the community of researchers and practitioners in the discipline.

We are currently on the second cycle, having applied the new course design for the second time, and now doing "Reflective Observation". In the next phase of our research (Abstract Conceptualization) we will investigate means to make the created information fragments reusable, so that several courses can share the same material. A start would be to see if the information fragments developed in the studied ITO course can be labeled in such a manner as to make them useful in another IS course where modeling skill are also developed. For this labeling different ontologies/taxonomies will be tested, including Bloom taxonomy [18], to map the formal intended learning objectives of the IS courses in the department to see which courses that may use the created information fragments. This would give economies of scale when reusing video and textual information fragments. Furthermore, video annotation could be used to make the video interviews more reusable by creating searchable libraries.

Acknowledgments. The project was sponsored by Stockholm University's program "Future Learn". The authors are grateful to our colleagues Jelena Zdravkovic and Anders Thelemyr who participated in interviews recording, and to the anonymous reviewers whose comments helped to improve the text. The first author is also grateful to Anthony Burden who encouraged him in writing texts related to teaching/learning.

References

1. Bezivin, J., France, R., Gogolla, M., Haugen, O., Taentzer, G., Varro, D.: Teaching Modeling: Why, When, What? In: Ghosh, S. (ed.) MODELS 2009. LNCS, vol. 6002, pp. 55–62. Springer, Heidelberg (2010)
2. Engels, G., Hausmann, J.H., Lohmann, M., Sauer, S.: Teaching UML Is Teaching Software Engineering Is Teaching Abstraction. In: Bruel, J.-M. (ed.) MoDELS 2005. LNCS, vol. 3844, pp. 306–319. Springer, Heidelberg (2006)
3. Fenstermacher, K.D.: If I had a Model, I'd Model in the Morning. In: Proceeding of OOPSLA 2004, pp. 88–89 (2004)
4. Polanyi, M.S.: Knowing and Being. University of Chicago, Chicago (1969)
5. McCune, V., Hounsell, D.: The development of students' ways of thinking and practising in three final-year biology courses. Higher Education 49(3), 255–289 (2005)
6. Bergin, R., Youngblood, Y., Ayers, M., Boberg, J., Bolander, K., Courteille, O., Dev, P., Hindbeck, H., Stringer, J., Thalme, A., Fors, U.: Interactive simulated patient: experiences with collaborative e-learning in medicine. J. Educ. Comput. Res 29(3), 387–400 (2003)
7. Bergin, R.A., Fors, U.: Interactive simulated patient—an advanced tool for student activated learning in medicine and healthcare. Computers & Education 40, 61–376 (2003)

8. Kendall, J., Kendal, K.E., Baskerville, R., Barnes, R.J.: An Empirical Comparison of a Hypertext-Based Systems Analysis Case with Conventional Cases and Role Playing. Data Base Advances **27**(1), 58–77 (1996)
9. Kendall, J., Kendall, K.E., Schmidt, A., Baskerville, R., Barnes, R.J.: HyperCase: A Hypertext-Based Case for Training Systems Analysts. http://www.pearsonhighered.com/hypercase/hypercase2.9 (accessed 2013)
10. Kendall, J., Kendall, E.: Systems Analysis and Design, 9th edn. Pearson (2013)
11. NIST: Integration definition for function modeling (IDEF0), Draft Federal Information Processing Standards, Publication 183 (1993). www.idef.com/downloads/pdf/idef0.pdf (accessed February 2015)
12. OMG: Business Process Model and Notation (BPMN), Version 2.0.2, Object Management Group (OMG), Document formal/2013-12-09 (December 2013). http://www.omg.org/spec/BPMN/2.0.2/PDF (accessed February 2015)
13. OMG: Business Motivation Model, Version 1.2, Object Management Group (OMG), Document formal/2014-05-01 (May 2014). http://www.omg.org/spec/BMM/1.2/PDF (accessed February 2015)
14. Bider, I., Perjons, E., Henkel, M., Kowalski, S.: Projektplatsen för ITO (2013). http://ito2013.blogs.dsv.su.se/ (accessed 2013)
15. Davis, F.: Perceived usefulness, perceived ease of use, and user acceptance of information technology. MIS Quarterly **13**(3), 319–340 (1989)
16. Moody, D.: Improving the quality of data models: empirical validation of a quality management framework. Information Systems **28**(6), 619–650 (2003)
17. Kolb, D.: Experiential learning: Experience as the source of learning and development 1. Prentice-Hall, Englewood Cliffs (1984)
18. Bloom, B.: Taxonomy of Educational Objectives, Handbook I: The Cognitive Domain. David McKay Co Inc., New York (1956)
19. Bider, I., Henkel, M., Kowalski, S., Perjons, E.: Technology Enhanced Learning of Modeling Skills in the Field of Information Systems. In: Nunes, M.P., Isaís, P., Powell, P. (eds.) Proceedings of 8th IADIS International Conference on Information systems, Maidera, Portugal, March 14-16, pp. 121–128. IADIS Press (2015)

Assessing the Potential of RFID Technologies on the Productivity of a Freight Forwarder

Ygal Bendavid[✉]

School of Management, University of Quebec at Montreal, Montreal, Canada
Bendavid.ygal@uqam.ca

Abstract. This research paper aims to identify the role of Radio frequency identification (RFID) technology in a logistic chain managed by an international freight forwarder providing multimodal logistic services. More specifically it aims to identify how RFID technology impacts both: the productivity of operations and the management of logistics processes. The focus of the research is on the processes within and between two Distribution Centers (DC), namely a DC in China (point of origin) and a DC in Canada (point of destination), with a specific emphasis on one critical process: the deconsolidation of a Less than Truck load (LTL) container.

Keywords: e-logistics · Supply chain management · Freight forwarder · RFID technologies

1   Introduction

During the past decade the profile of logistics has changed quite radically mainly because of the global market and e-commerce [1]. While companies keep focusing on their core business activities (and outsource non-core activities), this situation has provided opportunities for logistics and transportation companies, namely, third and fourth party logistics organizations (3PL, 4PL) [2]. This appears particularly true in the case of 3PLs *"where the rapid diffusion of IT has had significant impact on changing their traditional core competences and supply chain role"* [3, p.15]. In this context, Information Technology (IT) has played a pivotal role in disseminating shipment information to the parties in the logistics chain and has revolutionized the way supply chain and logistics activities are managed [4; 5] [1].

While the timely flow of data that informs the concerned parties about the state of the shipment at every step of the way is crucial, since the mid-1970s, supply chain organizations have leverage on the advent of various types of inter-organizational systems (IOS) to support e-commerce transactions [6;7]. During the same period, bar code technologies have developed further; and became widely deployed in all the industries [8]. Similarly, a decade ago, as Wal-Mart and the United States Department of Defense (US DoD) launched mandates to adopt Radio Frequency Identification (RFID) technologies, organizations around the world have started to explore the potential of these technologies in supporting their operations. Unfortunately, initial enthusiasm was hindered by numerous factors such as poor technology performance,

© Springer International Publishing Switzerland 2015
M. Benyoucef et al. (Eds.): MCETECH 2015, LNBIP 209, pp. 255–268, 2015.
DOI: 10.1007/978-3-319-17957-5_17

lack of standards, weak offer of software applications (RFID middleware), back end integration issues with existing Information Systems (IS), and data management challenges. Following early unsuccessful initiatives early adopters then entered in a period of "disillusionment" reaching its peak in 2008 when a global recession slowed many RFID initiatives and forced a market restructuring [9]. Since then, continuous improvements in technological performance, combined with maturing applications and decreasing prices have reversed the trend and contributed to the adoption of RFID technology in various domains making its diffusion global across industries. Today, the technology is mature and numerous foreseen applications are now implemented. The challenge is now to leverage on its potential for real time decision making and build innovative electronic business practice in logistics.

This research paper aims to evaluate the potential impacts of RFID technology in the logistics chain managed by an international freight forwarder providing multimodal logistic services. More specifically it aims to identify how RFID technology impacts both: the productivity of operations and the management of logistics processes. For this purpose we will look at a global supply chain that starts at a point of origin (manufacturer in China) and ends at the point of destination (importer or client in Canada) and will focus on the activities of the international freight Forwarder.

The rest of the paper is organized as follows. First, the field of logistics is introduced as a field of research that is greatly influenced by information technologies (IT) (Section 2). RFID technologies are then discussed in Section 3. In Section 4, the methodology of the research is presented in order to clarify how data was gathered and analyzed. In section 5 we present the analysis of the case study. Both processes and technology are reviewed to assess the potential impact on productivity. The paper concludes in section 6 with implications, limitations and future research avenues.

2   Logistics and Information Technology

Logistics has been in use for centuries [10] and many definitions coexist. Basically, it is the art of moving cargo from locations where goods are manufactured (point of origin) to locations where these same goods will be consumed (point of destination). According to the Council of supply chain Management Professionals [11] logistics is a process "of planning, implementing, and controlling procedures for the efficient and effective transportation and storage of goods including services, and related information from the point of origin to the point of consumption for the purpose of conforming to customer requirements. This definition includes inbound, outbound, internal, and external movements". This definition is interesting as it puts the emphasis on front end activities (the planning) as well as on the efficiency of the physical process (physical movements such as transporting and storing) while pointing to the importance of the information flow to support the processes in order to ultimately conform to the customer requirements. Accessing timely and accurate information and being able to share it with logistics stakeholders is a key aspect to support "intelligent" decisions and therefore constitutes the backbone of the logistic activities [12; 13], [4].

2.1   The Value of Global Trades and the Supply Chain Players Involved

Merchandise exports of World Trade Organisation members totalled US$ 17.3 trillion in 2012 [14]. The United States is the world's biggest trader in merchandise, with imports and exports totalling US$ 3,881 billion in 2012. China follows with merchandise trade totalling US$ 3,867 billion in 2012. More generally, Asia's exports of manufactured goods rose to US$ 4.4 trillion in 2012. Among leading exporters and importers in world merchandise trade, Canada ranks in the 12th position with a value of trades accounting for US$ 475 billion. In this context, numerous supply chain players are involved in global logistics processes (i.e., manufacturer, shipper, transporters, distribution centers, freight forwarder, customs authorities, international carriers, customs brokers, importer, etc.) [15] suggesting that a multitude of factors must be planned and managed between origin and destination to ensure that the cargo is transported safely and securely from origin, and that it arrives at the prescribed time-to-market parameters as requested by the customer, at an efficient cost. The role of the freight forwarder is to manage this complexity by orchestrating the flow of products and the flow of information.

At the freight forwarder there are several processes in the distribution center (DC) that are additional factors that will impact the time-to-market parameter. They are the receipt and de-stuffing of the container, the staging of cargo in a bonded area within the distribution center for inspection by the customs authorities, the pick, preparation and shipment of cargo to final destinations. Any problem that may occur during any of the above mentioned tasks may delay the delivery of the product and ultimately lengthen the time-to-market. Errors and inconsistencies in servicing the customers are prevalent and impacts negatively the productivity of employees because manual standard procedures are put in place to circumvent the shortcomings of the use of conventional systems. The use of RFID technology may streamline these processes and eliminate the manual procedures in place therefore, improving the overall productivity.

3   RFID Technologies in Logistics

Since RFID technologies are positioned to facilitate the implementation of best practices in logistics, thus rendering critical logistics operations more efficient throughout the supply chain, in this section, we propose to elaborate on this topic.

RFID is still considered an innovative technology and its adoption is the subject of considerable research, case studies and white papers globally. In fact, since 2002, when Wal-Mart and the US DoD initiated mandates that suppliers adopt the technology, there is a clear growing trend of overall RFID research as various literature reviews indicate an important increase in RFID related publications [e.g.,16;17, 18; 19; 20]. In a recent review [20] the authors note that interest in RFID in warehousing is rather stagnant and relatively small in comparison to other research domains (i.e., RFID, logistics + RFID, transport + RFID; supply chain + RFID). Additionally, among these reviews and research conducted by various authors, there is call for work to help bridge the gap between RFID theory and practice, and provide guidance to the practitioners in the adoption of RFID-enabled applications e.g., [9]; [19]; [21]. Furthermore, (i) most of the papers look at the impacts of RFID on intra-organizational processes vs. inter-organizational processes, (ii) while challenge to implementation are discussed in a closed loop context, very few papers are elaborating on relevant technological scenarios that support real-time information flows in supply chains, and (iii) most of the time the implementation model is discussed as if the adopters are the owners of the technology (the warehouse of a company) vs. an (international) freight forwarder providing logistic services and acting as an independent player in the chain. In fact, despite the importance of IT as a key element to support logistics activities, little study has been conducted on assessing the impact of technology on performance in 3PL research [3]. Finally, while RFID was expected to become a standard infrastructure component in the logistics industry, and despite the fact that the technology has been proven to optimize operations, the adoption is lagging, especially in the distribution centers of the logistic chain. In fact, according to the "2013 Third-Party Logistics Study", only 36% of 3PL organizations use RFID technology. In addition, according to the same study, 24% of shippers use RFID compared to 60% who use bar code technology [22].

3.1   RFID System – A Multi-layer System

Although an RFID system may appear simple at first glance, in reality, RFID systems are far more sophisticated and require a high level of expertise to integrate them into existing IT infrastructure. It is then important to describe in further details the technical aspects of RFID systems to better comprehend its potential and limitations.

RFID system is a multi-layer system of a hardware and software combination that integrates into an enterprise back end system and connects to the IOS (see figure 1). Each of the following layers is explained further. This first layer allows the automatic identification of tagged logistics' units (e.g., containers, cargo units, pallets, boxes) by automatically capturing RFID tags ID. For many applications bar code can also be used for item level tagging and linked to RFID tags on boxes in order to manage the parent/child relationships on a simple data base – and ensure traceability. Usually, passive (powered by the reader RF) Ultra High Frequency RFID tags are used in logistics due to their relative low cost and great performance (read range up to few meters, multi-tag reads, etc.). Semi passive tags equipped with embedded sensors (powered by a battery) can be used in applications such as cold chain logistic management. Active tags, on the other hand are used for Real Time Location Systems (RTLS) applications since they have a read range up to few hundred meters. For instance they are used for yard management application to track vehicle and container's movements.

Various types of RFID readers can be used to capture the data from RFID tags signal – such as RFID portals (fixed readers), portable gun (handheld) or vehicle mounted readers (i.e., on a forklift). In a logistics context within the DC, fixed RFID units and their associated antennas positioned at specific locations (e.g., receiving and shipping dock doors) use radio signals to communicate with the tags as the products enter or leave the DC. Handheld and forklift mounted RFID units could be used for inventory management and other DC functions as required by the application (e.g., picking). A communication network is then used to communicate the data captured by the RFID readers to the data management layer.

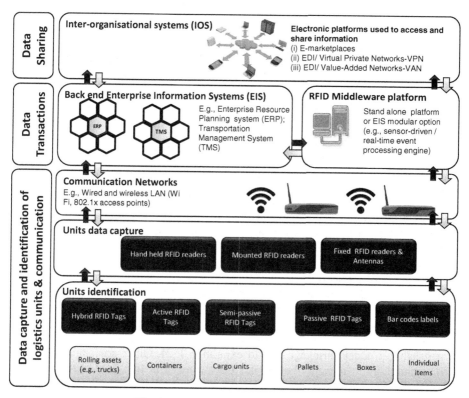

Fig. 1. RFID system - adapted from [23]

The second layer is the data management layer composed of (i) an RFID middleware used to process and distribute RFID based data into (ii) specific back end information systems (i.e., Enterprise Resource Planning systems-ERP, Transportation Management Systems-TMS) used to manage this information to improve the decision making process. The integration of business applications to different devices (i.e., RFID infrastructure) is then critical for an RFID system to be efficient [25; 26].

The third layer is the data sharing layer used to share the processed information among supply chain members. Existing IOS including Electronic Data Interchange(EDI) through Value Added Networks (VAN) and more recently the EPC Global Network (still in development) are used to ensure that RFID data is efficiently and accurately transmitted electronically to authorized supply chain members. Encouraging results from a series of pilots initiated initiated in 2009 and completed in 2012 by GS1 Italy and GS1 Hong Kong have demonstrated how RFID data could be exchanged using the EPC network and enable global real-time visibility of logistics units between global trading partners [27; 28; 29] – still, some standards are in development [5] but there is no more doubts on the feasibility to use RFID in order to provide greater visibility, and extend the service to importers and retailers as the technology enabled improved processes.

3.2   RFID in Logistics: Examples from the Industry

RFID solutions are found both in the context of closed loop solutions such as within the warehouse, or in an open loop implementation such as warehouse to warehouse context. For example, a supplier of IKEA that is based in Lithuania is using the technology to ensure that pallets of manufactured furniture are loaded into the correct trucks to ship to IKEA stores worldwide. The aim is to minimize costly shipping errors and improve efficiency [26]. Another company is using RFID to track and re-use plastic containers and has experience significant savings by switching from using corrugated, throw-away/cardboards containers [30]. Elsewhere, Panalpina Group, a global logistics company is using RFID to track the temperature of pharmaceutical products of its clients during the shipment. RFID tags are used to ensure that the environment in which the product is shipped or stored is within a specific range of temperatures to make sure it is compliant with government regulations. Southwest Airlines is gone one step further and is allowing its customers to place their own RFID enabled devices to track temperature of the shipping container in which their products is being transported [31].

While many applications are beginning to take advantage of RFID, this technology is still generally in the pilot stage for logistics application. For instance, the University of Parma's RFID Lab recently launched a third logistics pilot, to track perishable food from the manufacturer's warehouse to the retailer's point of sale. In this specific case, the aim is to assess the value of RFID-based data in reducing the incidence of perishable product shrinkage due to expiration [32]. Other companies are using RFID technology to manage their trailer fleet. Supervalu Inc. food chain uses Pinc Solutions RFID product to track the position of truck trailers in their yards and reduce labor cost by almost 80 hours per week [33]. A packaging company in the Denmark that ships its products in steel containers uses the technology to track these containers around the world. Because these containers must be returned for inspection, disinfection and re-use, RFID provides the company with the exact dates and locations for these containers and alerts the decision makers if the numbers of containers is running low at any of its facilities [34]. More recently, Inditex CEO Pablo Isla announced a major RFID deployment at *Zara*, where, by the end of 2016, more than 1,000 of the 2,000 stores will have the technology [35].

While several RFID projects are deployed in the context of a closed loop applications, such as within the warehouse, the examples above show that many RFID applications are mostly in the pilot stage in the context of open loop supply chain, such as warehouse-to-warehouse operations. Part of our research aims to complement the research related to this emerging type of projects and its potential impact on the productivity in the context of logistics' operations.

4   Research Methodology: Using a Case Study Approach

Since RFID-enabled applications in the logistic context is an emerging, complex and multidimensional phenomenon (i.e., multiple stakeholders involvement in logistics' transactions, numerous standards and various layers of technologies supporting logistics' systems, multiple products, numerous impacts along the logistic chain), the case study approach was selected as the preferred research strategy in order to facilitate the identification of the main concepts involved [36] and *investigate "a contemporary phenomenon within its real-life context"* [36, p. 16]. Bearing in mind that the case study research needs to be governed by scientific standards, in order to ensure the validity and the reliability of the results, we followed a formal procedure such as the ones proposed by [37] and used in the adoption of IT by SMEs. The main phases of the research process followed in order to conduct our study are presented in figure 2.

A case study was conducted at the freight forwarder, one of the largest logistics companies in Canada. We used the business process re-engineering approach in order to identify the impact of RFID technology on selected processes within the distribution center owned and managed by a freight forwarder at the point of origin and at the point of destination. The point of origin was a DC in China, and the point of destination was a DC facility in Canada. Strategically, the freight forwarder is the intermediary between demand and supply. The freight forwarder acts as single point of contact to arrange space and dispatch shipments via asset based carriers. As an international freight forwarder, the company provides multimodal logistic services including warehousing and distribution. It arranges cargo movement to and from international destinations, by preparing and processing the documentation (e.g., commercial invoice, export permits, compliance certifications, security certifications, etc. required by the authorities in the country of export and import) and related activities in order to perform international shipments.

Typical clients of the freight forwarder are the importers (buyers) and shippers (sellers) in the supply chain. The logistics processes at the freight forwarder are supported by an IT infrastructure composed of several modules that are interconnected. Specifically (i) an ERP system for internal operations such as shipment file creations and accounting functions (ii) a booking/purchase order (PO) module to manage orders that are received from the buyers (iii) a Warehouse Management System (WMS) to manage the operations at the DC which consists mainly in the receiving, storage and redistribution of products to the customers (iv) a web portal that allows the customers to login and get track and trace status updates on their shipments, and (v) finally an EDI platform that enables the exchange of data between the freight forwarders' systems and those of the other stakeholders in the supply chain (e.g., buyers, suppliers, customs authorities and international carriers).

4.1   Selecting and Analyzing Logistic Processes

With the objective to document the logistics processes, in order to evaluate the potential impacts of RFID technology on productivity in a logistics chain, data was collected through (i) semi-structured interviews (with 23 participants from three groups in Canada and China: business administrators, operations managers and members of the IT group) (ii) on-site observations (both in Canada DC and in China) (iii) and complementary documents (internal business and technical analysis such as productivity report for de-stuffing or IT infrastructure assessment) provided to support this phase of the research. For the China based interviews, a Chinese (Mandarin) questionnaire had to be made, especially when interviewing mid and low level employees. The emphasis of the research was on five main processes related to the management of a Less than a Container Load (LCL) shipment which is basically related to a container containing different shipments from different suppliers: (i) booking of a shipment (ii) consolidation of a shipment at the point of origin (iii) international transport (iv) deconsolidation of a shipment at the point of destination (v) delivery to the customers. Although numerous process mapping tools could be used to document the case, for the purpose of this research Excel based activity matrixes were used to collect and share the data with key respondents. This choice was made because (a) many respondents were not familiar with process mapping tools (b) all of them were familiar using Excel tools (c) all of them had access to Excel to share feed-back on the documents. In order to make sure the indicators accurately measure what we aim to measure, the SCOR model from the supply chain council [38] was used to identify specific Key performance indicators (KPIs), (e.g., order fulfillment cycle time, delivery time, etc.). Furthermore, targeted respondents are also asked to identify important KPIs they used in order to assess the performance of their logistics performance.

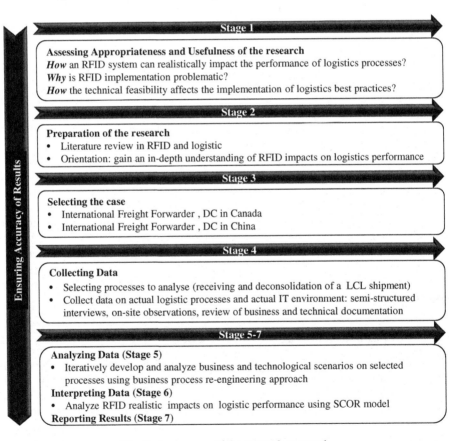

Fig. 2. A summary of the research approach

5   Analysis: Potential Use of RFID at the Freight Forwarder Level

In order to assess the impacts of RFID on logistic performance at the freight forwarder, each main process was decomposed into specific sub processes and activities. For each activity, we used the technological classification proposed in section 3, namely (i) data capture and identification technologies (e.g., bar codes, RFID) (ii) data management technologies (i.e., RFID Middleware, ERP, TMS) (iii) data sharing technologies (e.g., EDI)- and indentified which technologies are used – and where RFID could be used.

Table 1. Freight forwarder processes and supporting technologies

Freight Forwarder Process	Technologies used for:		
Shipping a LCL from a supplier overseas	Data capture	Data management	Data sharing
1- Booking Process			
All sub processes related to the receiving of an order to ship from the supplier at origin (basically exchange of e-document)	No RFID potential	ERP, Microsoft Tools (Excel)	B2B portal; EDI; emails
2- Consolidation of the shipments at the point of origin			
All sub processes related to combining a number of smaller shipments usually from different customers together and shipping it out in a larger single shipment, usually a container	Bar code; RFID (moderate potential)	ERP, Microsoft Tools (Excel)	B2B portal; EDI; proprietary systems, emails, fax, phone
3- international (intermodal) transport			
All sub processes which follow the shipment from point of origin (POO) to point of destination (POD) – i.e., destination distribution center	Bar code (scan paper work); RFID (low potential)	ERP, Microsoft Tools (Excel), pdf documents	Shipping lines systems; Rail B2B Portal, CBSA web site or EDI
4- Deconsolidation at the point of destination:			
All sub processes of separating the larger single shipment, into several smaller shipments and processing those shipments for delivery to the different customers?	Bar code; RFID (moderate potential)	ERP/WMS; Dispatch system (online)	EDI, email (e.g., container release number)
5- Delivery to the customers (final leg /last mile delivery),			
All sub processes which basically consist of bringing the shipment to final customers	RFID (low potential)	ERP, dispatch system (online)	Email to the buyer

Within this paper, for the purpose of simplifying the presentation of the results, in table 1 we will only present the macro processes in (i.e., each sub processes and activities won't be highlighted) related to the shipping of a LCL from a supplier overseas in China to the final customer in Canada.

In the *booking of the shipment process*, since it is purely an exchange of information to plan the transportation of the shipment, most of the transactions are performed using data management and data sharing technologies. Hence, for this process, there are no directs impacts of using RFID technologies. On the other hand all the documentation that will be generated during this process will be important to reconcile all the transactions occurring later in the process (e.g., PO number, product quantity, etc.).

Within the *process of consolidation of the shipments at the point of origin* logistics goods (i.e., boxes and pallets) are manipulated. During this process, the cargo is (i) received (ii) stored temporarily (iii) picked (iv) packed and (v) consolidated into a container. At this stage, generally, bar code technologies are used to identify cargo units and confirm the status of the processes. Once loaded, an ASN (Advanced Shipping Notice) document is then transferred using EDI to the freight forwarder-at the point of destination. In this case, RFID technologies can be used to support the consolidation of the shipment by the freight forwarder-at the point of origin and automate the production of a load plan (that will be sent to the freight forwarder-at the point of destination) when the LCL shipment will be loaded into the consolidation container. If logistics goods can be tagged by the local transporter (i.e., prior to receiving at the freight forwarder-at the point of origin), this could allow the automation of the receiving process (reducing process time and errors) – but it requires that RFID data is encoded following a specific standard and that data is shared between supply chain members. Today, it is not the case, especially for a freight forwarder that works with numerous independent suppliers and transporters.

The process of *international transport* is almost the same in every shipment: (i) container is received at the yard and (ii) loaded to the ship (iii) the ship departs at the POO and arrives at the POD where the container is (iv) discharged and (v) loaded to rail for discharge at the final destination. At this stage, the tracking and tracing is mostly done at the containers level using a unique container number. The use of automated identification technology can be useful to locate containers in yards or port's terminal – but the freight forwarder has no control in this portion of the process. Although RFID e-seals can be used to ensure container integrity and traceability of conditions, respondents did not seem to valorize enough their marginal contribution (vs. mechanical seals used today).

At the *deconsolidation at the point of destination,* the LCL container is received. Numerous warehouse processes are performed, starting from breaking the seal of the container and receiving the goods- i.e., separate, count and verify individual shipments. Presently, packing slips on the goods are scanned (using mobile or stationary bar code stations) and matched against the ASN to confirm the receiving and trigger the temporary put away (i.e., staging of cargo in a bonded area within the DC for inspection by the customs authorities). A WMS is often used to manage these processes and EDI transactions are performed to validate the information on the received shipments. At this stage, RFID potential and issues are similar to the *process of consolidation* previously presented.

Additionally, the deconsolidation is closely related to the next process which consists of *delivering the products to the customers*. These multiple boxes are then placed on a pallet and shrink wrapped. A bar code label is then generated (using the existing WMS system) and placed on the pallet. The bar code label contains the information about the shipment such as house bill of number, customer and number of boxes. The pallet is then placed either in the bonded area or in a staging area depending on whether a release notification has been received from the Canadian Border Services Agency (CBSA). We can observe that the physical movement of shipment is intensive at this stage. The manipulation of the shipment is recorded (storage, counting, separating…). Recording of the movement of the shipment within the warehouse triggers the billing module so that the customer is invoiced based on the work done. It is noticeable that the use of RFID is applicable in several aspects of this process especially when fetching the shipment from storage and loading into the truck for delivery.

5.1   RFID Potential Impacts on Logistic Performance at the Freight Forwarder Level

When analyzing RFID realistic impacts on *the consolidation at the point of origin,* RFID could clearly help in the picking process by confirming the transactions and automating the counting when cargos (pallet/boxes) are loaded on the container. In term of logistic process performance, when looking at the "supply chain responsiveness" metrics, some KPIs seem relevant to analyse the potential impact on the consolidation at the point of origin, namely: order fulfillment cycle time (and sub level metrics such as deliver cycle time, build loads cycle time, consolidate orders cycle time and pick product cycle time, ship product cycle time). Additionally, when looking at the "supply chain reliability" metrics, some KPIs seem relevant to analyse the potential impact on the consolidation at the point of origin, namely: perfect order fulfillment (and sub level metrics such as % of orders delivered in full, delivery item accuracy, delivery quantity accuracy). On the other hand, when asked about the usefulness of RFID technology in the warehouse in China, a senior manager commented that *"…we are customer driven, and will implement if the customer requires it. At this stage, it is too costly to implement without a clear ROI".* This citation identifies one issue in using technologies to improve the process: even though reliable RFID solutions are available to support logistic processes, managers don't always see their usefulness estimating that the marginal contribution is not yet relevant for some specific processes.

When analyzing RFID realistic impacts on the *international transport,* the main difficulty in related to the control (or the lack of control) by the freight forwarder of the RFID infrastructure in the supply chain - or at least the possibility to have access to RFID enabled data. Therefore, in order to realize realistic benefits, RFID technologies should be adopted collectively and data be shared among members. This seems particularly difficult since today, after more than four decades of EDI implementation, information sharing is still an issue with which freight forwarder have to deal on an everyday basis.

When looking at the RFID impacts on the *deconsolidation at the point of destination,* once the LCL container is received potential benefits are similar with one found at the Consolidation at the point of origin since these two processes shares numerous similarities in term of activities. While the container is de-stuffed and individual LCL shipments are separated before being temporally staged, numerous areas of improvements can be identified. These areas of improvements relates to all non-value added manual activities such as counting items/boxes and verifying information related to received products. Next, once the cargo is custom cleared, employees will perform the pick, *preparation and shipment of cargo to final destinations* (ultimate customer) where other verification activities will be performed. When asked about the usefulness of RFID technology at this step, a respondent suggested that *"...this may help reduce the risk of picking the wrong product. There could be situations where the fork lift driver may scan the product on the shelf but not pick it. Because the trucker may not notice either, the product may not be shipped on time. Currently, we alleviate this potential problem by having multiple checkpoints; this particular process may be improved by using RFID"*.

When analyzing RFID realistic impacts on the *delivery to customers* (i.e., bring the shipment from destination DC to customer site) a respondent suggested that *"...Once the shipment leaves our warehouse, we ensure its safe delivery to the customer. RFID benefits at this stage are not yet clear"*. It is important to note that RFID may be more useful to the customer, only if the product is RFID tagged by the supplier at origin. The customer will then be able to reconcile at the item level with the initial order to the supplier and leverage in the technology for the following processes in the DC and the retail stores. In fact, that's the main idea behind recent RFID deployment in proprietary chain such as the one owned by Zara [35]. This may have a secondary effect on the freight forwarder, because the faster the customer confirms receipt of the goods to the freight forwarder, the faster an invoice will be generated and send to the customer for payment.

6   Conclusion

Within the research, we have investigated the potential impact of RFID on five main processes in order to analyze the potential impacts on logistic performance. The overall consensus from the respondents at the senior management level is that RFID is not a "must have" for shipment execution. In fact at a freight forwarder level, a marginal positive impact is expected given that less than 20% of the shipments are LCL as opposed to FCL, according to our respondents in Canada. This is particularly important when considering that RFID may have a biggest impact on LCL shipments since (a) they require more steps than FCL to manage and (b) require more documentation since each container is related to numerous clients.

On the other hand, surprisingly, technical difficulties did not seem to be an obstacle to integrating RFID technology within the WMS, neither at the DC at origin nor at destination. Similarly, no specific difficulties was foreseen to integrate RFID data in the EDI platform and that customizing the EDI messages to allow for data fields to print RFID labels is possible. In fact, rather than technical difficulties, it appears that most of the difficulties may arise from a business process reengineering perspective where managers in charge of DCs and employees will need to adapt to this relatively new technology.

Some limits need be considered in this case study: (i) while the company studied is fairly representative of the freight forwarding industry, this study was conducted in one single entity. Further research into similar sized companies would have to be conducted to corroborate the existing findings (ii) Companies such as DHL and UPS may sway strong influence on their supply chain and dedicate more resources into the deployment of RFID solutions (iii) It is important to note that there is an increasing number of global RFID initiatives in supply chains and major government invest-ments in RFID technologies (including China) that might render the cost and deploy-ment of the technology more affordable for the SME in the supply chain.

Acknowledgment. The author would like to thank the personnel at the freight forwarder for providing access to the field of research and revising the paper.

References

1. Gunasekaran, A., Ngai, E.: The future of operations management: An outlook and analy-sis. Int. J. of Prod. Econ. **135**, 687–701 (2012)
2. Perego, A., Perotti, S., Mangiaracina, R.: ICT for logistics and freight transportation: a lite-rature review and research agenda. Int. J. Phy. Distrib. Log. Manag. **41**(5), 457–483 (2011)
3. Evangelista, P., Mogre, R., Perego, A., Raspagliesi, A., Sweeney, E.: A survey based anal-ysis of IT adoption and 3PLs' Performance. Supply Chain Manag. **17**(2), 172–186 (2012)
4. Melnyk, S., Lummus, R., Vokurka, R.J., Sandor J.: Supply Chain Management 2010 and Beyond, Mapping the future of the Strategic Supply Chain. APICS Educational and Re-search Foundation, Chicago (2007). http://www.thefairinstitute.org/downloads/SCM-2010FinalReportNov1rev2.pdf
5. GS1.: Standards in Transport and Logistics, GS1 AISBL (2012a). http://www.gs1.org/docs/transportlogistics/GS1_Standards_Transport_Logistics.pdf
6. Pramatari, K.: Collaborative supply chain practices and evolving technological approaches. Supply Chain Manag. **12**(3), 210–220 (2007)
7. Folinas, D., Manthou, V., Sigala, M., Vlachopoulou, M.: E-volution of a supply chain: cases and best Practices. Internet Res. **14**(4), 274–283 (2004)
8. GS1.: Bar Code Types, Global Standard One (2012b). http://www.gs1.org/barcodes/technical/bar_code_types
9. Bendavid, Y., Fosso Wamba, S., Barjis J.: RFID: towards Ubiquitous Computing & the Web of Things. J. Theor. Appl. Electron. Commer. Res. 8(2), III–XI (2013)
10. Islam, Z., Meier, J.F., Aditjandra, P.T., Zunder, T.H., Pace, G.: Logistics and supply chain management. Res. Trans. E. **41**(1), 3–16 (2012)
11. CSCMP-Council of supply chain Management Professionals. http://cscmp.org/default.asp
12. Lieb, R., Butner, K.: The North American Third-party Logistics Industry in 2006: The Provider CEO Perspective. Transport. J. **46**(3), 40–52 (2007)
13. Probert, A., O'Regan, D.: Supply Chain Intelligence, An Evolution From Process Automa-tion to Business Insight (2002). www.businessobjects.com/pdf/whitepapers/accenture_sci_wp.pdf
14. World Trade Organisation (WTO), International trade statistics (2013). http://www.wto.org/english/res_e/statis_e/its2013_e/its2013_e.pdf
15. Cassivi, L. et Bendavid, Y.: A study of emerging technological practices in logistics and transportation: A Canadian perspective. Technical report, Transport Canada strategic poli-cy and innovation directorate (2014)
16. Ngai, E.W.T., Moon, K.L., Riggins, F.J., Yi, C.Y.: RFID research: an academic literature review (1995–2005) and future research directions. Int. J. of Prod. Econ. **112**(2), 510–520 (2008)
17. Chao, C.C., Yan, J.M., Jen, W.Y.: Determining technology trends and forecasts of RFID by a historical review and bibliometric anal. from 1991 to 2005. Technovation 27, 268–279 (2007)

18. Liao, W.P., Lin, T.M.Y., Liao, S.H.: Contributions to RFID research: An assessment of SCI-, SSCI-indexed papers from 2004 to 2008. Decis. Support Syst. **50**(2), 548–556 (2011)
19. Sarac, A., Absi, N., Dauzère-Pérès, S.: A literature review on the impact of RFID technologies on supply chain management. Int. J. of Prod. Econ. **128**(1), 77–95 (2010)
20. Lim, M.K., Bahr, W., Leung, S.: RFID in the Warehouse: A Literature Analysis (1995–2010) of its Applications, Benefits, Challenges and Future Trends. Int. J. of Prod. Econ. **145**(1), 409–430 (2013)
21. Irani, Z., Gunasekaran, A., Dwivedi, Y.K.: RFID: research trends and framework. Int. J. of Prod. Res. **48**(9), 2485–2511 (2010)
22. Cap Gemini.: 2013 Third-Party Logistics Study, The State of Logistics Outsourcing-Results and Findings of the 17th Annual Study. www.capgemini.com/sites/default/files/resource/pdf/2013_Third-Party_Logistics_Study.pdf
23. Bendavid, Y.: Positioning RFID Technologies in the Enterprise Information Systems Portfolio: a Case in Supply Chain Management. Int. J. Autom. Id. Technol. **4**(11), 11–24 (2012)
24. Amaral, L.A., Hessel, F.P., Bezerra, E.A., Corrêa, J.C., Longhi, O.B., Dias, T.F.O.: ECloudRFID – A mobile software framework architecture for pervasive RFID-based applications. J. Netw. Comput. Appl. **34**(3), 972–979 (2011)
25. Al-Jaroodi, J., Mohamed, N.: Service-oriented middleware: A survey. J. Netw. Comput. Ap. **35**(1), 211–220 (2012)
26. Swedberg, C.: RFID Helps IKEA Furniture Maker Eliminate Shipping Errors. RFID J. (2012a). http://www.rfidjournal.com/article/view/10217
27. GS1 EPCglobal.: GS1 EPCglobal Transportation and Logistics Phase 3 Pilot Program Completion, Press release (2009). http://www.gs1.org/sites/default/files/docs/media_centre/gs1_pr_280409_epcglobal_tls_3.pdf
28. GS1.: An inebriant journey, global wine supply chain visibility via EPC IS network (2012c). http://www.gs1.org/docs/transportlogistics/2012_05_GS1HKItaly_WinetraceabilityCase.pdf
29. Swedberg, C.: GS1 Pilot Program Shows How RFID Can Track International Wine Shipments. RFID J. (2012e). http://www.rfidjournal.com/articles/view?9665/
30. Violino, B.: RFID made it economically feasible for the tortilla manufacturer to switch from disposable corrugated boxes to reusable plastic containers. RFID Journal (2011). http://www.rfidjournal.com/article/view/10217
31. Violino, B.: Global Logistics Company Monitors Shipments' Temperatures. RFID J. (2012). http://www.rfidjournal.com/article/purchase/10008
32. Swedberg, C.: Parma's RFID Lab Extends Logistics Pilot to the Manufacturer. RFID J. (2012b). http://www.rfidjournal.com/article/view/10166/1
33. Swedberg, C.: Supervalu Manages Trailer Yard Via RFID. RFID J. (2012c). http://www.rfidjournal.com/article/view/10032
34. Swedberg, C.: Packaging Company Tags Its Shipping Containers. RFID Journal (2012d). http://www.rfidjournal.com/article/print/9691
35. Bjork, C.: Zara Builds Its Business Around RFID. The Wall Street J. (2014). http://www.wsj.com/articles/at-zara-fast-fashion-meets-smarter-inventory-1410884519
36. Yin, R.K.: Case study research: Design and methods, 3rd edn. Sage, Thousand Oaks (2003)
37. Gagnon, Y.C.: The case study as a research method. A practical Handbook. Presses de l'université du Québec, Québec (2010)
38. SCC-supply chain council.: SCOR Framework /Supply chain operation reference model (2010). https://supply-chain.org/f/SCOR-Overview-Web.pdf

Towards Quality-Driven SOA Systems Refactoring Through Planning

Mathieu Nayrolles[1]([⊠]), Eric Beaudry[2], Naouel Moha[2],
Petko Valtchev[2], and Abdelwahab Hamou-Lhadj[1]

[1] SBA Research Lab, ECE Department, Concordia University, Montreal, Canada
m_nayrol@encs.concordia.ca, abdelw@concordia.ca
[2] Département d'informatique, Université du Québec Montréal, Montreal, Canada
{eric.beaudy,naouel.moha,petko.valtchev}@uqam.ca

Abstract. Service Based Systems (SBSs), like other software systems, evolve due to changes in both user requirements and execution contexts. Continuous evolution could easily deteriorate the design and reduce the Quality of Service (QoS) of SBSs and may result in poor design solutions, commonly known as SOA (Service Oriented Architecture) antipatterns. SOA antipatterns lead to a reduced maintainability and re-usability of SBSs. It is therefore critical to be able to detect and remove them to ensure the architectural quality of the software during its lifetime. In this paper, we present a novel approach named SOMAD-R (Service Oriented Mining for Antipattern Detection-Refactoring) which allows the refactoring of SOA antipatterns by building on a previously published tool named SOMAD (Service Oriented Mining for Antipattern Detection). SOMAD-R combines planning solving techniques and SOMAD detection algorithms to enable antipatterns driven refactoring of SBSs. As a first step towards refactoring antipatterns for SBSs, we successfully applied SOMAD-R to HomeAutomation, a SCA (Service Component Architecture) application and we removed three antipatterns (out of five) while improving application performance by 32%.

Keywords: SOA antipatterns · Quality-driven refactoring · SOA refactoring · Services orchestration · SOA planning

1 Introduction

Service Based Systems (SBSs) are composed of ready-made services that are accessed through the Internet [1]. Services are autonomous, interoperable, and reusable software units that can be implemented using a wide range of technologies like Web Services, REST (REpresentational State Transfer), or SCA (Service Component Architecture, on the top of SOA.). Most of the world largest computational platforms such as Amazon, Paypal, and eBay, for example, represent large-scale SBSs. Such systems are complex–they may generate massive

© Springer International Publishing Switzerland 2015
M. Benyoucef et al. (Eds.): MCETECH 2015, LNBIP 209, pp. 269–284, 2015.
DOI: 10.1007/978-3-319-17957-5_18

flows of communication between services–and highly dynamic: services appear, disappear, and can be modified over time.

The constant evolution of SBSs can easily deteriorate the overall architecture of the system, causing architectural defects, known as SOA antipatterns [2]. An antipattern is the opposite of a design pattern. While design patterns should be followed to create more maintainable and reusable systems [3], antipatterns should be avoided since they have a negative impact on the maintenance and reusability of SBSs.

Considering that SOA antipatterns reduce the capability to evolve, reuse, and understand these systems, it is thus important to detect and remove them. However, techniques to master the evolution of complex software systems are often based on historical change logs analyses rather than potentially harmful architectural impacts.

In this paper, we propose a new and innovative approach named SOMAD-R (Service Oriented Mining For Antipattern Detection and Refactoring). This approach is an evolution of another approach–we introduced in a previous contribution [4]–named SOMAD, which detects SOA antipatterns in execution traces produced by SBSs. Our approach goal is to leverage SOMADs detection to improve the overall software quality by means of refactoring.

Numerous approaches and tools have been proposed in the area of the detection and correction of antipatterns in object-oriented (OO) systems (for example, [5–9]). However, the dynamic nature of SBSs and the non-availability of the implementation of their interfaces do not allow to apply these approaches. Moreover, SOA focuses on services as first-class entities whereas OO focuses on object interactions, which are at the lower level of granularity.

To re-orchestrate the services communications while keeping the system working, we use automated planning techniques. Automated planning techniques will generate a plan to reach an objective by using a set of actions that have effects and preconditions. We use SOMAD reverse-engineering capacities to extract the set of actions that the system under study exposes and we generate plans that keep the system behaviour while proposing a better orchestration. The generated plans are then submitted to SOMAD in order to assess their quality in terms of SOA antipatterns. While there are time and memory available the iterative process of generating a plan and assess the amount of SOA antipattern detected by SOMAD continues.

In order to validate the effectiveness of our approach, we applied it to the HomeAutomation SCA (Service Component Architecture) system. HomeAutomation targets the domotic control of elderly citizens' houses to ease the work of doctors and nurses. On HomeAutomation, we performed the refactoring of the system and reduced the number of instances of antipatterns from five to two. Also, as a proof of the pertinence of our approach, the needed time to reach the same system state as in the initial services' orchestration has been reduced by 32%.

The main contribution of this paper is an approach that allows enhancing the overall quality of a SBS by refactoring its antipatterns.

The remainder of this paper is organized as follows. Section 2 presents related work in the area of SOA antipattern detection and quality-driven software refactoring, followed by related work on service oriented planning. In Section 3, we introduce background information on SOMAD and service orchestration to ease the reading of this paper. In Section 4, we showcase our approach in details while Section 5 presents our experimental. Finally, we provide some concluding remarks in Section 6.

2   Related Works

In this section, we present studies closely related to refactoring antipatterns in the object-oriented (OO) world , QoS based orchestration and services orchestration by planing in SBSs.

2.1   Quality Based Refactoring of Objects Systems

In the OO paradigm, two main trends arise for refactoring design deffects. In the first trend, researches first detect antipatterns and then remove them by applying refactoring technique. To date, they explore a wide-range of technology to do so such as FCA [10], RCA [11], model transformation [12], metric based [6–8] and rules based [9]. The second trend contains approaches that do not detect antipatterns per se but elements to modify in order to improve the overall quality of the system as in [13].

Although some of these approaches and tools could be re-used for SOA, especially the metric based by using SOA metrics [2,4,14,15], but it is difficult to define threshold values for metrics. Moreover, how to refactor SOA antipatterns, even manually, have only been explored based on strict use cases [16,17]. Finally, those approaches and techniques have been conceptualized and improved over the years to fit the OO paradigm and it will not be trivial to adapt them to the SOA paradigm.

2.2   QoS Based Service Composition

While not oriented towards antipatterns refactoring, a significant effort has been made to propose QoS-oriented approaches for service composition. These approaches can be separated into two distinct categories as proposed by [18]. Methods based on genetic algorithm [19,20] (and related [21,22]) and methods based on non-evolutionary algorithms such as dynamic programming [23]. All these approaches and techniques have in common that they try to maximize the availability and reliability while minimizing the cost and response time of the composed system. Although availability, reliability and response time are metrics to detect antipatterns, they did not have this level of abstraction and only target the Quality of Service. Quite the opposite, our approach deal with software quality as a vector to improve maintenance, re-usability and evolution of the system while keeping QoS in mind.

2.3 Service Composition by Planning

In service composition or orchestration by planning, several works have been proposed to compose stateless [24], statefull [25,26] and even coordinated asynchronous statefull services [27,28]. However, these works focus on how many goals, e.g. how many services, they are able to aggregate/orchestrate in a minimum amount of time using advanced planning techniques and algorithms. Moreover, most of these approaches will compose a super-service containing all composed services and expose the newly created service which is, by definition, a multi-service antipattern and/or even a sandpile [2].

3 Background

In this section, we provide some preliminaries to ease the reading of further sections. We first present SOMAD, the approach upon which we build SOMAD-R. Then, we present the planning domain and the SOA-planning or orchestration.

3.1 The SOMAD Approach

SOMAD relies on execution traces produced by SBSs in order to detect antipatterns. To achieve this, SOMAD uses data mining techniques. It discovers antipatterns by first extracting associations between services as expressed in the execution traces of an SBS. To that end, we apply a specific variant of the association rule mining task based on sequences and episodes [29]. In our case, the sequences represent services or, alternatively, method calls. Further, we filter these generated association rules by means of a suite of dedicated metrics. SOMAD includes the following three main steps.

Specification SOA Antipatterns: After a careful analysis of the SOA antipattern textual description, we create rule cards for six different antipatterns; Multi-Service, Tiny Service, Chatty Service, Knot Service, BottleNeck Service and Chain service. Rule cards are combinations of height different metrics dedicated to SOA antipattern detection. The definition of SOA antipatterns and metrics definition have been specified in [2] and [4], respectively. The rule card are combined to automatically create detection algorithms using java templates [14].

Mining Sequential Association Rules: In the data-mining field, Association Rule Mining (ARM) is a well-established method for discovering co-occurences between attributes in the objects of a large data set [30]. Plain association rules have the form $X \rightarrow Y$, where X and Y are sets of descriptors. While plain association rules could provide interesting information, we decide to use a variant named Sequential Association Rules to preserve the sequences of service/method calls. Applying this technique on execution traces files identify interesting relations between services like: *ServiceA, ServiceB* implies *ServiceC* meaning that if services A and B appear, there is a high probability for C to appear in the same sequence of service calls.

Detection of SOA Antipatterns: This step consists of applying the detection algorithms generated in Step 1 on the sequential association rules mined in Step 2. At the end of this step, services in the SBS suspected to be involved in an antipattern are identified.

Finally, the efficiency of SOMAD has been proved on two different systems named HomeAutomation and FraSCAti. The precision was 90.1% and 94.44% for HomeAutomation and FraSCAti respectively.

3.2   Automated Planning for SOA

Automated planning is a branch of Artificial Intelligence (AI) aiming to transform an environment on a given initial state to an environment that satisfies given goal(s) using a set of actions [31]. Each action have effect(s) on the environment and might require pre-condition(s) to be executed. A planning problem takes place in a state transition system defined by:

$$\sum = (S, A, E, \gamma) \tag{1}$$

Where S, A, E represent the states, actions and events, respectively and γ represents the state-transition function :

$$\gamma : S * (A \cup E) \tag{2}$$

The solution of the planning problem will decide what actions to use to achieve the set of goal(s). The required complexity to solve a planning problem can be much more than NP-Complete or even undecidable. A classical planning problem takes place in a finite, fully observable, deterministic, static system where goals can be reached with sequential plans and implicit time. This said, to solve a classical planning problem we have to find a sequence of actions $(a1, a2, ..., an)$ that produces a sequence of state transitions $(s1, s2, ..., sn)$ where sn satisfies our goals.

When applied to SOA, planning is often referred to as service orchestration. The complexity of manually orchestrating thousands of services participating in complex business logic led the community to use planning algorithms and techniques. However, techniques related to classical planning cannot be used as is. Indeed, in a SOA environment the system is not fully observable (inside logic of services are unknown), not always deterministic (services output can change overtime) and dynamic (services can be added or removed at any time). Despite these challenges, several works have been done and succeed to orchestrate services with conservative hypothesis. For example, they assume that the services outputs are deterministic and the environment static in a sense that every collaborating services and their actions are known beforehand.

In our study, we not only target the orchestration of services but a qualitative re-orchestration of services in terms of SOA antipatterns. Furthermore, we do not know what are the possible actions as we deduct them from SOMAD reverse engineering of a running SBS and not from the specification as previous studies.

Consequently, we try to construct qualitative plans with a sub-set of the actions provided by the system. Depending on how long SOMAD observed the targeted SBS and how complete the utilisation of SBS is, the sub-set size will vary.

4   The SOMAD-R Approach

SOMAD-R is a complete approach which supports the refactoring of SOA systems in order to improve their conceptual quality in terms of SOA antipatterns. SOMAD-R is composed of three main steps and is depicted in Figure 1. The first step uses SOMAD to reverse-engineer the targeted system and provide the services suspected to be involved in antipatterns. The second step builds and resolves a planning problem with the aim of reaching all the services previously consumed while re-orchestrating the order of calls in order to reduce the amount of antipatterns. Finally, the last step receives the solution proposed by the second step and send the plan to SOMAD for it to assess the quality of the solution. We iterate over these three steps until we cannot improve the solution anymore or total consumption of resources.

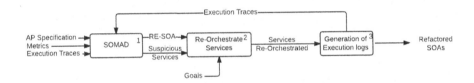

Fig. 1. The SOMAD-R approach

4.1   SOMAD Antipattern Detection

The first step consists in feeding SOMAD with the antipatterns specification, the metrics and the executions traces of a given SOAs as explained in section 3.1 and in [4].

Figure 2 presents the kind of execution traces that SOMAD requires to perform its detection. Every trace contains the IP address of a client, a timestamp, an in/out label and the service / method call. Note that the dots have been added to ease the reading and are not part of the SOMAD standard.

SOMAD extracts sequential association rules from these traces such as:

$$A \to B; A \to C; A \to D, C \tag{3}$$

Meaning that after executing A, there are good chances to see B, C or D then C in the trace. The conciseness of this example should not confuse the reader as in practical cases the sequences appearing in a rule can be of an arbitrary length. Finally, SOMAD performs the antipatterns detection on the mined sequential association rules and construct a call graph for the system as depicted in Figure 3.

```
192.168.1.1 1372366511048 in ServiceA.Ma
...192.168.1.1 1372366511148 in ServiceB.Ma
...192.168.1.1 1372366511156 out ServiceB.Ma
192.168.1.1 1372366511156 out ServiceA.Ma
192.168.1.1 1372366511156 in ServiceA.Ma
...192.168.1.1 1372366511356 in ServiceC.Ma
...192.168.1.1 1372366511386 out ServiceC.Ma
192.168.1.1 1372366511386 out ServiceA.Ma
192.168.1.1 1372366511386 in ServiceA.Ma
...192.168.1.1 1372366511436 in ServiceD.Ma
......192.168.1.1 1372366511536 in ServiceC.Ma
......192.168.1.1 1372366511566 out ServiceC.Ma
...192.168.1.1 1372366511586 out ServiceD.Ma
192.168.1.1 1372366511586 out ServiceA.Ma
```

Fig. 2. Imput execution traces for SOMAD

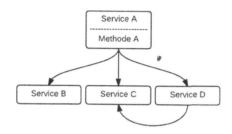

Fig. 3. SOMAD call graph

In this hypothetical example, SOMAD will likely detect Service A as a Tiny Service as it only has one method and its highly coupled with other services to complete its abstraction.

As a summary, the outcomes of this first step are reverse engineered SOAs given as a multi-oriented graph and a list of services suspected to be involved in antipatterns.

4.2   Re-orchestrate Services

In this step we aim to re-orchestrate the services calls in order to reduce the antipatterns detected by SOMAD in the previous step. To do so, we first select the goals we want to reach in the original targeted system and construct a multiple orienteering problem that will serve as heuristic for our planner. Next, we construct a planning problem using the outputs of the step 1 and we formalize it using the PDDL (Planning Domain Definition Language). Finally, we submit this problem to the LAMA [32] planer and forward the generated plan to SOMAD in order to assess its quality. In what follows, we will describe each process of this step in details.

Selecting Goals: Martin Fowler wrote in his best-seller [33] that refactoring refers to a change made to the internal structure of software to make it easier to understand and cheaper to modify without changing its observable behavior. Consequently, we want to be able to re-orchestrate the service without modifying the initial behavior of the targeted system. To achieve this, we want our plan to execute all of the methods executed by the SBSs before its re-orchestration. We can think of this as a SOA version of the traveling salesman problem where the city are services, districts of city correspond to methods of service and roads between cities and districts are the link found by SOMAD. The targeted system, before refactoring, visits all the city and required district but does it in a sub optimum way while after refactoring, it still visits all the cities but by walking the shortest path.

Planing Heuristic: In order to guide our planer towards the sequence of actions requiring the less time and providing the best quality, we use the solution of an orienteering problem where each node is a service and contains a set of sub-nodes accessible only by him and representing its methods. We construct this problem based on the actions pre-conditions and effects detected by SOMAD during the architecture reverse-engineering performed via the execution traces. The cost to travel from a service A to a service B corresponds to the initialization time of Service B and the cost to go from a service node to a method node corresponds to the execution time of the said method. The cost to travel back from the callee service to the caller is 0 and isn't modeled in the following figures for the sake of clarity. Figure 4 represents the orienteering graph constructed using the data provided by SOMAD in the first step. In addition, a reward of 100 has been attributed to $S_b.m_a, S_c.m_a, S_d.m_a$ and a reward of 80 for $S_a.m_a$. The reward of a method is reduced by 20 for each antipattern the service exposing this method is suspected to participate in.

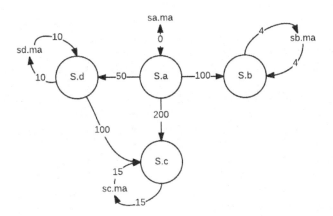

Fig. 4. Orienteering problem

While the solution of this generated orienteering problem could constitute a viable heuristic for our planner, it doesn't take advantage of one intrinsic characteristic of SBSs. To be able to consume a service, we need to build a reference to that service and our experiments showed that the first call to a service – where the reference is constructed – construct reference is twice as expensive as the following ones. In other words, if the Service A calls the Service B; the first time it will cost 100ms will and the second time only 50. To reflect this in our orienteering problem, we construct a multiple orienteering problem where the (simple) orienteering problem is cloned in as many dimension as ordering. We can travel through dimensions via costless edges connecting cloned nodes in each dimension as shown in Figure 5. where the cost to go from Sa to Sb has been divided by two, implying that A owns a reference to B in the lower dimension. The solution of the multiple orienteering problem will be an ordered list of node and sub-nodes to explore in order to visit them all while minimizing the time needed to do so and maximizing the rewards harvested.

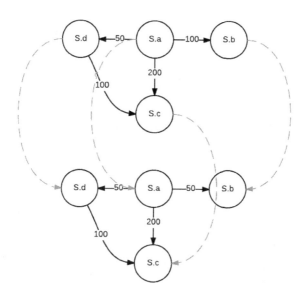

Fig. 5. Multiple Orienteering problem

Planning: In this step, we construct a planning problem using the PDDL and we forward it to the LAMA planner [32] which is an evolution of the Fast-Downward planner [34] and has won many prices on several IPC (International Planning Competition). The LAMA planner extends the planning process we discussed in Section III.B in three main ways.

Landmarks: The first improvement of LAMA over Fast-Downward is to replace its causal graph heuristic with fast forward based heuristic proposed in [35] and combine it with landmarks heuristics. Landmarks have been successfully used by Porteous et al. [36] and are propositional formulas that must be true in every generated plan for a given task. In order to speed-up the plan generation and find the shortest solution, LAMA directs its search towards states containing many true landmarks [37].

Action costs: In classical planning, actions don't have cost and execute themselves in discrete time. However, when solving real world problems, actions need to be considered with their costs and required time to be completed. LAMA adapts the heuristics so they use the time and the cost of actions. In our case, actions represent services methods calls and they take time; however they don't consume any finite resource. Consequently, we use the solution of the orienteering problem from the previous step as a baseline for the cost of actions. As an hypothetical example, if we have the following ordered list of actions $(a0, a1, ..., a10)$ as solution of the multiple orienteering problem, we will assign them the following cost $(0, 1, ..., 10)$ so the LAMA planner will execute the actions with the higher cost as a last resort to reach a valid plan.

Anytime Search: When LAMA reaches a solution to the planning problem, it continues to search for the best solution by using successive weighted A* graphs. Each iteration sees the weights of A* edges to be decrease and this process runs until resources or time become exhausted. In our case, finding optimal plan is not enough as this plan will be the best in terms of time and resources consumption but not in terms of antipatterns. Consequently, we allow LAMA only a few iterations and stop the anytime search as soon as the improvement starts to lower and forward the current plan to final step of SOMAD-R.

4.3   Generation of Mockup Traces

The output of the planning step is a set of executable actions; however, we still don't have assessed the quality of the newly generated solution. Indeed, only SOMAD knows how to compute the quality of the solution. Consequently, we need to generate a SOMAD understandable input that reflects the current solution. To do so, we generate mockup execution traces based on our current plan. For each action of the solution, a in and out traces are generated as same as a timestamp based on the real ones. For example, if the generated solution ordered calls such as Service A calls Service D, C and Service B, we will generate the traces presented by Figure 6.

The generated traces are sent back to SOMAD which will assess the quality of the solution in terms of antipatterns. The output of SOMAD will change as the orchestration of services is not the same in the generated solution and antipatterns might have been added / removed. Consequently, the solution to the orienteering problem will generate a different heuristic leading to a different solution. Each solution is saved and we return the most qualitative one when time or resources are exhausted.

192.168.1.1 1372366511048 in ServiceA.Ma
...192.168.1.1 1372366511436 in ServiceD.Ma
......192.168.1.1 1372366511536 in ServiceC.Ma
......192.168.1.1 1372366511566 out ServiceC.Ma
...192.168.1.1 1372366511586 out ServiceD.Ma
...192.168.1.1 1372366511686 in ServiceB.Ma
...192.168.1.1 1372366511694 out ServiceB.Ma
192.168.1.1 1372366511694 out ServiceA.Ma

Fig. 6. Generated execution traces

5   Experimentation

We perform our experiments on Home-Automation. Home-Automation has been developed independently for controlling remotely many basic household functions for elderly home care support. It includes 13 services with a set of 7 predefined uses-case scenarios. In our experiment, we try to remove as many antipatterns from Home-Automation by using the refactoring capacities of SOMAD-R while preserving the behaviour of the system. In this subsection, we discuss the process and results of the refactoring part of SOMAD-R.

5.1   Methodology

The creator of Home-Automation published their tool with a set of four test scenarios. In order to have near real-world execution traces we have instrumented Home-Automation as it does not produce qualitative execution traces by default. As Home-Automation is a Service Component Application (SCA, an architectural style on top of SOA) it supports aspect weaving and we leverage this feature to insert or tracing statement or probes. Aspects can be weaved by directly interacting with the running environment of an SCA, fraSCAti for Home-Automation and therefore, avoiding to weave directly the target system or to modify its source code. If neither the source code nor the running environments are accessible, alternatives consist in instrumenting the virtual machine if any, the web server, or the operating system. For example, LTTng [38] provides Linux instrumentation with a very low overhead.

5.2   Scenario

One of the four scenarios provided by the development team of Home-Automation consists in retrieving the personal information of a patient and send them to his doctor. The following figure presents the scenario with the services names, the purpose of the services, the instantiation time and the initial orchestration of services. The original orchestration requires 472 ms to complete and contains five different antipatterns.

- Multi-Service: IMediator
- Chatty-Service: PatientDAO and IMediator

- Knot: PatientDAO
- BottleNeck: PatientDAO, IMediator
- Chain Service : IMediator → Communicaton Service → PatientDAO → PatientDAO{1,2,4}

Home-Automation may appear to the reader as a poorly build system as all its services are involved in at least one antipattern. However, as explained in length in [2,4] Home-Automation has been built for the sole purpose of showing how to use the SCA functionalities of the fraSCAti environment. Consequently, many methods are duplicated or poorly encapsulated in order to showcase the different ways of using fraSCAti capabilities.

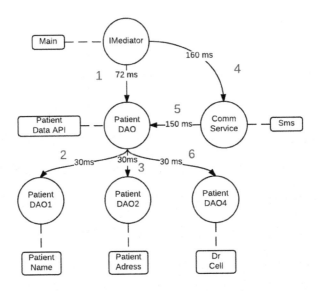

Fig. 7. HomeAutomation scenario: Send patient information to his doctor (original orchestration)

In order to test the efficiency of our heuristic based on the multiple orienteering problem, we ran the experiment with two different LAMA planners. The first planner uses the original greedy heuristics and the second one uses the heuristic presented in this paper.

5.3   Results

The figures 8 and 9 present the orchestration found by SOMAD-R under LAMA's original heuristic and under our orienteering heuristic, respectively. In figure 8, the generated plan requires the services to be consumed in the following order: *IMediator, PatientDAO, PatientDAO4, PatientDAO3, PatientDAO1* and *Communication Service* and is able to reach all the required goals in time

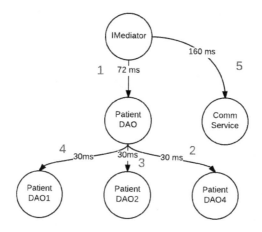

Fig. 8. HomeAutomation scenario: Send patient information to his doctor (greedy orchestration)

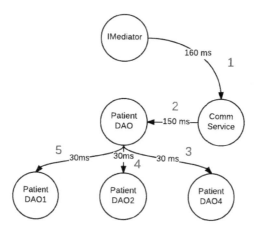

Fig. 9. HomeAutomation scenario: Send patient information to his doctor (orienteering orchestration)

t = 400 ms (-15%) while removing the Service chain antipattern which was present in the first orchestration according to SOMAD results.

In Figure 9, the generated plan requires the services to be consumed in the following order: *IMediator, Communication Service, PatientDAO, PatientDAO4, PatientDAO3, PatientDAO5* in a total of t = 322 ms (-32%). Furthermore, according to SOMAD's detection, the orienteering based orchestration remove three antipatterns: *The Knot, The BottleNeck* and the *MultiService.*

As a summary, SOMAD-R using the LAMA planner was able to improve the performance of this scenario by 15% while improving its quality through the removal of three antipatterns. We proved the efficiency of our orienteering heuristic and the relevance of our approach as SOMAD-R is able to improve the performance of the scenario by 32% while removing a total of three antipatterns when the LAMA planner uses it.

6 Conclusion and Future Work

The refactoring process is a critical life stage of every complex system if we are to ensure the architectural quality of these systems. Nevertheless, the service oriented architecture enables SOAs to be evolved quickly and easily and may allow poor design solution known as SOA antipattern to be inserted. In this paper, we present a novel approach named SOMAD-R which allows the refactoring of SBSs using the SOMAD detection approach and planning techniques. We perform experimentations on HomeAutomation aiming the formal validation of our approach: (i) We refactor the initial system using our approach and reduce the number of SOA Anitpatterns instances from 5 to 2 without loss any functionalities and (ii) we reduce the needed time for its execution by 32%.

As a future work, we shall investigate how to use SOMAD-R for steming the appearance of antipatterns during the development of SBSs. Also, antipatterns are not all dangerous in the same way; therefore, we would like to add, in a near future, a weight to SOA antipattern instead of counting their number and improve our heuristic.

References

1. Erl, T.: Service-Oriented Architecture. Prentice Hall (2006)
2. Palma, F., Nayrolles, M., Moha, N.: SOA Antipatterns: An Approach for their Specification and Detection. International Journal of Cooperative Information Systems **22**(04), 1–40 (2013)
3. Wolfgang, P.: Design patterns for object-oriented software development. Addison-Wesley, Reading (1994)
4. Nayrolles, M., Moha, N., Valtchev, P.: Improving SOA Antipatterns Detection in Service Based Systems by Mining Execution Traces. In: Working Conference on Reverse Engineering, Number i, pp. 321–330. IEEE (2013)
5. Kessentini, M., Kessentini, W., Sahraoui, H., Boukadoum, M., Ouni, A.: Design defects detection and correction by example. In: 2011 IEEE 19th International Conference on Program Comprehension (ICPC), pp. 81–90. IEEE (2011)
6. Erni, K., Lewerentz, C.: Applying design-metrics to object-oriented frameworks. In: Proceedings of the 3rd International Software Metrics Symposium, pp. 64–74. IEEE (1996)
7. Fenton, N.E., Pfleeger, S.L.: Software metrics: a rigorous and practical approach. PWS Publishing Co. (1998)
8. Moha, N., Gueheneuc, Y.G., Duchien, L., Le Meur, A.F.: DECOR: A Method for the Specification and Detection of Code and Design Smells. IEEE Transactions on Software Engineering **36**(1), 20–36 (2010)

 9. Opdyke, W.F.: Refactoring: A program restructuring aid in designing object-oriented application frameworks. PhD thesis, PhD thesis, University of Illinois at Urbana-Champaign (1992)
10. Moha, N., Rezgui, J., Guéhéneuc, Y.-G., Valtchev, P., El Boussaidi, G.: Using FCA to Suggest Refactorings to Correct Design Defects. In: Yahia, S.B., Nguifo, E.M., Belohlavek, R. (eds.) CLA 2006. LNCS (LNAI), vol. 4923, pp. 269–275. Springer, Heidelberg (2008)
11. Moha, N., Rouane Hacene, A.M., Valtchev, P., Guéhéneuc, Y.-G.: Refactorings of Design Defects Using Relational Concept Analysis. In: Medina, R., Obiedkov, S. (eds.) ICFCA 2008. LNCS (LNAI), vol. 4933, pp. 289–304. Springer, Heidelberg (2008)
12. Moha, N., Mahé, V., Barais, O., Jézéquel, J.-M.: Generic Model Refactorings. In: Schürr, A., Selic, B. (eds.) MODELS 2009. LNCS, vol. 5795, pp. 628–643. Springer, Heidelberg (2009)
13. O'Keeffe, M., Cinnéide, M.O.: Search-based refactoring: an empirical study. Journal of Software Maintenance and Evolution: Research and Practice 20(5), 345–364 (2008)
14. Palma, F.: Detection of SOA Antipatterns. In: Ghose, A., Zhu, H., Yu, Q., Delis, A., Sheng, Q.Z., Perrin, O., Wang, J., Wang, Y. (eds.) ICSOC 2012. LNCS, vol. 7759, pp. 412–418. Springer, Heidelberg (2013)
15. Demange, A., Moha, N., Tremblay, G.: Detection of SOA Patterns. In: Basu, S., Pautasso, C., Zhang, L., Fu, X. (eds.) ICSOC 2013. LNCS, vol. 8274, pp. 114–130. Springer, Heidelberg (2013)
16. Zhu, W., Melo, W.: Refactoring J2EE application for JBI-based ESB: a case study. In: IEEE International Enterprise Distributed Object Computing Conference, EDOC 2009, pp. 213–217. IEEE (2009)
17. Kim, Y., Doh, K.-G.: The Service Modeling Process Based on Use Case Refactoring. In: Abramowicz, W. (ed.) BIS 2007. LNCS, vol. 4439, pp. 108–120. Springer, Heidelberg (2007)
18. Pejman, E., Rastegari, Y., Esfahani, P.M., Salajegheh, A.: Web Service Composition Methods : A Survey. I (2012)
19. Canfora, G., Di Penta, M., Esposito, R., Villani, M.L.: An approach for QoS-aware service composition based on genetic algorithms. In: Proceedings of the 7th Annual Conference on Genetic and Evolutionary Computation, pp. 1069–1075. ACM (2005)
20. Zeng, L., Benatallah, B., Dumas, M., Kalagnanam, J., Sheng, Q.Z.: Quality driven web services composition. In: Proceedings of the 12th International Conference on World Wide Web, pp. 411–421. ACM (2003)
21. Xu, J., Reiff-Marganiec, S.: Towards heuristic web services composition using immune algorithm. In: IEEE International Conference on Web Services, ICWS 2008, pp. 238–245. IEEE (2008)
22. Ming, C., Zhen-wu, W.: An approach for web services composition based on QoS and discrete particle swarm optimization. In: Eighth ACIS International Conference on Software Engineering, Artificial Intelligence, Networking, and Parallel/Distributed Computing (SNPD 2007), vol. 2, pp. 37–41 (2007)
23. Yu, T., Lin, K.-J.: Service Selection Algorithms for Composing Complex Services with Multiple QoS Constraints. In: Benatallah, B., Casati, F., Traverso, P. (eds.) ICSOC 2005. LNCS, vol. 3826, pp. 130–143. Springer, Heidelberg (2005)
24. Narayanan, S., McIlraith, S.A.: Simulation, verification and automated composition of web services. In: Proceedings of the 11th International Conference on World Wide Web, pp. 77–88. ACM (2002)

25. Berardi, D., Calvanese, D., De Giacomo, G., Mecella, M.: Composition of Services with Nondeterministic Observable Behavior. In: Benatallah, B., Casati, F., Traverso, P. (eds.) ICSOC 2005. LNCS, vol. 3826, pp. 520–526. Springer, Heidelberg (2005)
26. Marconi, A., Pistore, M., Traverso, P.: Specifying data-flow requirements for the automated composition of web services. In: Fourth IEEE International Conference on Software Engineering and Formal Methods, SEFM 2006, pp. 147–156. IEEE (2006)
27. Pistore, M., Traverso, P., Bertoli, P.: Automated Composition of Web Services by Planning in Asynchronous Domains. ICAPS 5, 2–11 (2005)
28. Bertoli, P., Kazhamiakin, R., Paolucci, M., Pistore, M., Raik, H., Wagner, M.: Continuous Orchestration of Web Services via Planning. In: ICAPS (2009)
29. Mannila, H., Toivonen, H., Verkamo, A.I.: Discovery of Frequent Episodes in Event Sequences. Data Mining and Knowledge Discovery 1(3), 259–289 (1997)
30. G. Piatetsky-Shapiro: Discovery, analysis and presentation of strong rules. Knowledge Discovery in Databases, 229–249 (January 1991)
31. Ghallab, M., Nau, D., Traverso, P.: Automated planning: theory & practice. Elsevier (2004)
32. Richter, S., Westphal, M.: The LAMA planner: Guiding cost-based anytime planning with landmarks. Journal of Artificial Intelligence Research 39(1), 127–177 (2010)
33. Fowler, M., Beck, K., Brant, J., Opdyke, W.: Refactoring: Improving the Design of Existing Code. Addison Wesley (1999)
34. Helmert, M.: The Fast Downward Planning System. J. Artif. Intell. Res. (JAIR) 26, 191–246 (2006)
35. Hoffmann, J., Nebel, B.: The FF planning system: Fast plan generation through heuristic search. arXiv preprint arXiv:1106.0675 (2011)
36. Porteous, J., Sebastia, L., Hoffmann, J.: On the extraction, ordering, and usage of landmarks in planning. In: 6th European Conference on Planning (2001)
37. Richter, S., Helmert, M., Westphal, M.: Landmarks Revisited. In: AAAI, vol. 8, pp. 975–982 (2008)
38. Fournier, P.M., Dagenais, M.R.: Combined Tracing of the Kernel and Applications with LTTng. In: Linux Symposium, pp. 209–224 (2009)

Author Index